COMMERCIAL
AIRCRAFT
MARKINGS
& PROFILES

COMMERCIAL AIRCRAFT
MARKINGS & PROFILES

CHRISTY CAMPBELL

Clipper Juan T. Trippe

SMITHMARK

The publishers would like to thank Leo Marriott for his technical assistance in the preparation of this book

This edition first published in the United States in 1991 by SMITHMARK Publishers Inc., 112 Madison Avenue, New York, NY 10016.

SMITHMARK books are available for bulk purchase for sales promotion and premium use. For details write or telephone the Manager of Special Sales, SMITHMARK Publishers Inc., 112 Madison Avenue, New York, NY 10016. (212) 532-6600

ISBN 0-8317-1502-2

Produced by Mandarin Offset

Printed and bound in Hong Kong

Title: Pan Am, Boeing 747, Clipper ''Juan T.Trippe''. Above: KLM, McDonnell Douglas DC-9. Right: Qantas, Boeing 747-300. Page 192: SAA, Boeing 747.

Contents

Introduction

There must be a few people who can resist a skyward glance as an airliner passes overhead. Despite the advance of modern technology there is still a trace of romance in the thought of winging away, even though airports are busy and crowded, airline food is much the same anywhere, flights are often delayed, and air travel is no longer the preserve of a rich minority. Today the global airline industry has changed the nature of the world and made it seem a smaller place. Businessmen and employees of multi-national companies think nothing of commuting halfway around the world, while increased competition and modern fuel-efficient aircraft have led to reduced fares and a massive boom in the leisure travel market.

There can be no doubt that the introduction of jet airliners such as the Comet and the Boeing 707 on a large scale in the early 1960s changed the face of air transport for ever, and the coming of the first generation of wide-bodied aircraft a decade later, epitomized by the mighty Boeing 747, really opened up long-haul air travel to the mass market.

Externally, the latest generation of airliners seem little different from their immediate predecessors. The current Boeing 747-400 appears only slightly modified from the first example which flew in 1969 while, on a smaller scale, the Fokker 100 looks to be a slightly stretched version of the Fokker F28 which first took to the air as long ago as 1967. However, appearances are misleading. The intervening years have seen massive technological advances in aerodynamics, in engine performance and economy, and in navigation systems. Most significant has been the adaptation of digital computing techniques to aircraft management, navigation and control systems. With these refinements incorporated into proven airframes, performance, economy, reliability and safety have increased many times over.

This book provides a detailed survey of a selection of the world's most modern airliners, the history of the airlines that operate them, their present fleets and route networks. Ranging from the massive Boeing 747 to the 100-seater British Aerospace 146, the list also includes aircraft only just coming into service such as the McDonnell Douglas MD-11 and established favorites like the graceful Lockkheed TriStar. Not forgotten are the technically advanced Airbus products which now rival the giant American manufacturers, and also included are examples of aircraft from the Soviet aerospace industry, which is now racing to catch up with the technical superiority of western civil aircraft.

These aircraft, and numerous others, are flown by the many concerns which make up the world of civil air transport – the airlines. In this book will be found details of several hundred of the world's airlines, together with information about the colorful liveries applied to their aircraft. When the first airlines began to operate soon after the end of World War I there was little attempt at unified color schemes. In most cases the aircraft were finished in whatever color the manufacturer decided on and the airline name was added in simple lettering on the fuselage. Some airlines adopted symbols or logos which have survived in one form or another up to the present day such as Air France's famous winged horse or Lufthansa's stylized stork.

These icons have survived wars and political upheavals. Under these enduring symbols (like the British Airways "Speedbird", which goes back to Imperial Airways) there has been much commercial turbulence as airlines go out of business or new ones spring up in an industry which never stands still. The history of the many airlines recorded in this book is more often than not the story of pioneer operators coming together into a national carrier or a regional US giant. At the outset of the 1990s that process is accelerating as the US "mega-carriers" battle it out and national airliners look for trans-national partnerships. And, as air travel becomes more and more the same the world over, design and house style of everything – from tailfin logo to cocktail swizzle-sticks – assume greater importance as carriers compete to offer something "different" in what is, after all, now routine.

The period following World War II saw aircraft emerging from wartime drab once again into bright liveries, although most airlines left their aircraft in a natural metal finish with a colored roof. The livery normally consisted of colored stripes along the fuselage with the company name prominently displayed above and the airline symbol on the tail. In the US in the 1950s this was the heyday of the piston-engined airliner resplendent in unashamedly flamboyant liveries and a jumble of competing typefaces. The coming of jet aircraft with their cleaner lines, together with advances in paint technology and a cooler, Europeanized approach to graphic design, may have led to some toning down of the airborne exuberance of the past but still allows a kaleidoscope of colors and markings which form the main feature of this book.

One modern trend which is worth noting is the increasing use of aircraft leased from specialized companies such as GPS rather than outright purchase. This has led to many current liveries where the aircraft is painted white overall, the airline markings consisting of the name on the fuselage and a distinctive tail decoration. Thus, when a leased aircraft is transferred from one airline to another, the amount of repainting required is minimal.

The airline business must be one of the most unpredictable activities known to man. Even in normal times new companies are formed as others go to the wall, while the process of deregulation, begun in the US at the end of the 1970s, has led to takeovers, mergers and amalgamations. As this book goes to press the airline world is reeling from the dual effects of the Gulf War and a world trade recession. Even the largest and most profitable airlines such as British Airways are being forced to lay off staff, reduce flights and cancel or postpone orders for new aircraft. The effect on many less secure airlines may be more dramatic. Many of the major American carriers, including Pan Am, TWA and Continental, have already filed for protection from their creditors (the famous Chapter 11).

Nevertheless, this book is as up to date and as informative as it can be in this troubled world and it is hoped that it will be a source of interest, information and pleasure to the reader.

Airbus Industrie A310

1

LEADING AIRLINERS

Northwest Airlines, Boeing 747-400

EUROPE

Airbus A320

Airbus Industrie

An Airbus Industrie A320-300 in company colors

SPECIFICATION Model A320-200
Origin: European consortium
Type: wide-body short/medium-range jetliner
Accommodation: flight crew of 2; up to 179 passengers (in single class)
Powerplant: two 25,000-lb (11,340-kg) thrust CFM56-5A1 turbofans
Performance: maximum cruising speed 487kts (903km/h) at 28,000 ft (5830m); range with 150 passengers and standard fuel load 3160n.mls (5850km)
Weights: empty operating 87,800lb (39,800kg) maximum take-off 158,700lb (72,000kg)
Dimensions: span 111ft 3in (33.91m); length 123ft 3in (37.57m); height 38ft 7in (11.77m); wing area 1317.5 sq ft (122.4m^2)

Airbus Industrie was set up at the outset of the 1970s in a collaborative western European effort to be a counterweight to the growing US dominance of world airliner production. The first Airbus product was the A300, a large-capacity, short-to-medium range transport of which over 330 are in world airline service after the prototype first flew on 28 October 1972.

The 280+ seat A300-600, A300-600R (extended range) and A300-600 Convertible are the current production versions of this highly successful aircraft, offered to customers with a variety of engine options.

In 1984 Airbus launched another new aircraft program, the A320 single-aisle, short-medium range 180-seater, with many advanced technical features including fly-by-wire flight controls. First deliveries to Air France and British Airways began in March 1988.

Since it entered service in 1988, the A320 has carried more than 10 million passengers in over 100,000 revenue-earning flights. The highest operational usage is with Northwest Airlines, which flies its A320s for 9h 49min in an average four flights daily.

In December 1990 the Indian government formally cleared Indian Airlines to allow them to acquire 12 new Airbus A320s, the delivery of which had been postponed indefinitely after the crash of an A320 in February 1990 at Bangalore which temporarily grounded the entire fleet. The crash was later blamed on human error. Meanwhile, six of the 19 A320s in the airline's fleet were "reinducted" into service on the Delhi-Katmandu-Delhi sector. Eight of the aircraft were used to evacuate Indian nationals from the Middle East during the Gulf crisis. By the end of 1990 117 A320s were in airline service, with 657 on order, including 72 aircraft for America West and 92 for Northwest Airlines. The phenomenally successful A320 is claimed by Airbus to be the fastest-selling airliner of all time.

The Airbus A321 is a development program for a stretched version of the A320 available from 1994. It will have higher operating weights, a 7m-longer fuselage and will carry 186 passengers in a two-class layout – 36 more passengers than the earlier A320. By the end of 1990 11 customers had made commitments for 142 A321 aircraft.

Orders include: Alitalia (40), Ansett (10), Iberia (8), ILFC (12), Lufthansa (20) and Swissair (19). Airbus is also considering a "shrunk" version of the A320, possibly to be designated A319, which will carry 130 passengers and compete directly with the Boeing 737-500.

Final assembly of Airbus aircraft is carried out at Toulouse in southern France. Complete and often outsize airframe components are flown in from the places of manufacture all over Europe by a shuttle of Super Guppy transport aircraft.

CUTAWAY DRAWING OF AIRBUS INDUSTRIE A320-200

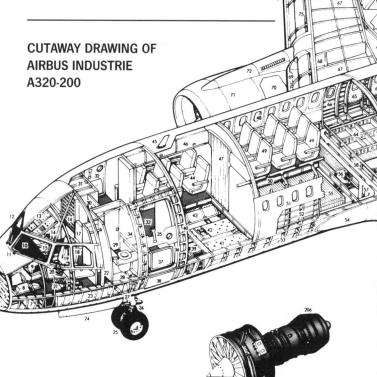

1 Radome
2 Weather radar scanner
3 Scanner mounting and tracking mechanism
4 VOR localizer aerial
5 Front pressure bulkhead
6 Windscreen panels
7 Windscreen wipers
8 Instrument panel shroud
9 Control column
10 Rudder pedals
11 Cockpit floor level
12 ILS aerial
13 Pitot heads
14 Access ladder on lower deck
15 Captain's seat
16 Center control pedestal
17 Direct vision opening side window
18 First Officer's seat
19 Overhead systems switch panel
20 Maintenance side panel
21 Observer's seat
22 Folding fourth seat
23 Cockpit bulkhead
24 Air conditioning ducting
25 Crew wardrobe/locker
26 Nose undercarriage wheel bay
27 Hydraulic retraction jack
28 Taxiing lamp
29 Twin nosewheels, forward retracting
30 Hydraulic steering jacks
31 Nosewheel leg doors
32 Nose undercarriage pivot fixing
33 Forward toilet compartment
34 Wash hand basin
35 Galley
36 Starboard entry/service door
37 Door-mounted escape chute
38 Cabin attendant's folding seat
39 Curtained cabin divider
40 Forward main entry door
41 Door latch

42 Door surround structure
43 Underfloor avionics equipment racks
44 Runway turn-off light
45 Fuselage lower lobe frame and stringer construction
46 Floor beam construction
47 Cabin window panels
48 Forward freight hold door
49 Cabin wall trim paneling
50 VHF communications aerial
51 Overhead stowage bins
52 Curtained cabin divider
53 First class passenger seating, 26 seats
54 Underfloor air system ducting
55 Door-mounted escape chute
56 Main cabin entry door
57 Overhead stowage bins
58 Central galley unit
59 Starboard General Electric CF680C2 engine nacelle
60 Pratt & Whitney JT9D-7R4H1 or PW4156 alternative engine installation
61 Common nacelle pylon beam
62 Pylon attachment links
63 Pylon tail fairing
64 Starboard wing engine pylon
65 Tourist class passenger cabin seating, 241 seats (267 seats total in mixed-class layout)
66 Air system distribution ducting
67 Conditioned air delivery ducting
68 LD3 baggage container, 12 in forward hold
69 Water tank
70 Slat drive shaft motor and gearbox
71 Wing spar center-section carry-through
72 Ventral air conditioning packs (two)
73 Wing center box fuel tank
74 Three-spar wing center section construction
75 Center-section floor beams
76 Front spar attachment mainframe
77 Fuselage center-section construction

78 Starboard wing inboard main fuel tank; standard fuel capacity 13,628 Imp gal (16,366 US gal/62,000 l)
79 Outer wing skin panel joint strap
80 Fuel system piping
81 Pressure refueling connections
82 Refueling valves
83 Fuel feed tank and pumps
84 Fuel tank dividing ribs
85 Leading-edge slat drive shaft
86 Three-segment leading edge slats, open
87 Wing fence
88 Slat screw jacks
89 Outer wing panel integral fuel tank
90 Fuel vent tank
91 Starboard navigation light (green)
92 Wing-tip fairing
93 Starboard wing-tip fence
94 Tail navigation and strobe lights (white)
95 Static dischargers
96 Fixed portion of trailing edge
97 One-piece single-slotted Fowler type flap, down position
98 Flap guide rails
99 Fuel jettison pipe
100 Outboard roll-control spoilers/lift dumpers (two)
101 Inboard airbrakes/lift dumpers (three)
102 Spoiler/airbrake hydraulic jacks
103 Flap screw jacks
104 Flap drive shaft
105 Starboard all-speed aileron
106 Aileron triplex hydraulic actuators
107 Wing root spoilers/lift dumpers (two)
108 Inboard flap segment
109 Cabin air system recirculation fan

110 Pressure floor above wheel bay
111 Rear spar attachment main frame
112 Starboard main undercarriage, retracted position
113 Undercarriage door jack
114 Equipment bay walkway
115 Undercarriage bay pressure bulkhead
116 Flap drive motor and gearbox
117 Hydraulic reservoir, triplex system
118 Eight-abreast tourist class passenger seating
119 Starboard Type 1 emergency exit door
120 Upper fuselage frame and stringer construction
121 Rear underfloor freight hold door
122 Freight/cargo compartment dividing bulkhead
123 Cabin wall insulating blanket
124 Cargo hold door
125 Cabin floor paneling
126 Seat mounting rails
127 Rear cabin air recirculation fan
128 AD F aerials
129 Fuselage skin paneling
130 Ceiling trim/lighting panels
131 Central overhead stowage bins
132 Rear galley
133 Fin root fairing
134 Fin spar attachment joints
135 Three-spar fin torsion box construction
136 Starboard trimming tailplane
137 Tailplane trim fuel tank additional capacity 1342 Imp gal(1611 US gal/6100 l)
138 Starboard elevator
139 Glass fiber-reinforced fin leading-edge
140 Fin rib construction
141 Fin tip fairing
142 Static dischargers
143 Carbon fiber rudder skin paneling
144 Honeycomb core construction
145 Rudder triplex hydraulic actuators
146 APU equipment bay
147 Garrett GTCP331-250 auxiliary power unit (APU)
148 Tailcone fairing
149 APU exhaust duct elevator construction
151 Elevator triplex hydraulic actuators
152 Static dischargers

153 Port tailplane rib construction
154 Leading-edge nose ribs
155 Port tailplane integral fuel tank
156 Tailplane pivot fixing
157 Moving tailplane sealing plate
158 Tailplane center-section carry-through
159 Tailplane trim screw jack
160 Fin support structure
161 Rear pressure bulkhead
162 Rear toilet compartments (four)
163 Cabin attendant's folding seat
164 Rear entry door
165 Rear cabin seven-abreast passenger seating
166 Cabin side-wall frames
167 Underfloor bulk cargo hold,610 cu ft (17.3 cu m)
168 Cabin window panels
169 LD3 baggage containers, 10 in rear hold
170 Port Type 1 emergency exit door
171 Lower fuselage skin paneling
172 Wing root trailing-edge fillet
173 Port inboard single-slotted flap
174 Wing root spoilers/lift dumpers
175 Flap guide rail
176 Spoiler hydraulic jacks
177 Auxiliary spar
178 Main undercarriage side struts
179 Retractable ventral landing lamp, port and starboard
180 Hydraulic retraction jack
181 Main undercarriage pivot fixing
182 Inboard flap track mechallism
183 Aileron triplex hydraulic actuators
184 Port all-speed aileron construction
185 Port airbrakes/lift durlpers
186 Flap down position
187 Flap guide rails
188 Fuel jettison pipe
189 Flap track fairings
190 Roll control spoilers/lift dumpers
191 Fixed portion of trailing edge
192 Trailing-edge composite construction
193 Static dischargers
194 Tail navigation and strobe lights (white)
195 Port wing-tip fence
196 Wing-tip fairing
197 Port navigation light (red)
198 Rear spar
199 Outer wing panel rib construction
200 Front spar
201 Port leading-edge slat segments
202 Slat screw jacks
203 Slat guide rails
204 Wing leading-edge de-icing air pipes
205 Telescopic de-icing air delivery ducts
206 Port wing integral fuel tank
207 Outer wing panel skin joint strap
208 Port main undercarriage four-wheel bogie
209 Main undercarriage leg strut
210 Nacelle pylon attachment joint
211 Engine pylon construction
212 Exhaust nozzle plug fairing
213 Core engine, hot stream, exhaust nozzle
214 Engine turbine section
215 Fan air, cold stream, exhaust duct
216 Reverser cascade, closed
217 Engine bleed air ducting
218 General Electric CF6-80C2A1 turbofan engine
219 Engine fan blades
220 Noise attenuating intake
221 Intake cowling nose ring
222 Detachable engine cowling panels
223 Bleed air system pre-cooler
224 Inboard leading-edge slat
225 Bleed air delivery ducting
226 Inner wing panel three spar construction
227 Inboard integral fuel tank
228 Inboard wing ribs
229 Wing root skin joint strap
230 Krüger flap actuator
231 Wing root Krüger flap extended

EUROPE

Airbus A340

Airbus Industrie

All Nippon Airways have placed orders for 10 A340-300 with delivery to start in 1995.

SPECIFICATION Model A340-300
Origin: European consortium
Type: wide-body medium/long-range jetliner
Accommodation: flight crew of 2; up to 401 passengers(in single class)
Powerplant: four 31,200-lb (14,152-kg) thrust CFM56-5C2 turbofans
Performance: maximum cruising speed 340kts (630km/h); range with maximum payload 5100 n.mls (9445km); take-off field length 9950ft (3030m)
Weights: empty operating 276,800lb (125,500kg) maximum take-off 553,400lb (251,000kg); fuel capacity 29,700 gal (35,668 US gal/135,000 l)
Dimensions: span 192ft 5in (58.64m); length 208ft 10in (63.65m); height 54ft 11in (16.73m); wing area 3894sq ft (361.79m^2)

The twin-engined A330 and four-engined A340 were launched as a joint program in 1987 and are intended to share the greatest possible commonality of parts, using the same fuselage cross-section, tail, systems and wing. The long-range 440-seat A340 is to fly first in 1991, with the A330 following a year later. First A340 deliveries are expected in the second half of 1992 and A330s in 1993.

A330 customers will have a choice of engines from three major manufacturers. Powerplants offered are the General Electric CF6-80E1, Pratt & Whitney PW4000 and Rolls-Royce Trent. Airbus is already planning A330 derivatives, starting with an increase in take-off weight and thrust, plus 1175 miles (1570km) of extra range and a typical 335-passenger load in a two-class layout. Passenger capacity may be increased by 50 seats, either by putting into effect a conventional fuselage stretch of 8.5m, or by providing a second passenger deck within the same fuselage cross-section. A longer-range version is also being considered, depending upon market requirements.

The four-engine A340 will have the longest unrefueled range of any airliner when it enters service in 1992. Flights lasting 14 hours mean extra attention to the comfort of both passengers and crews. The use of part of the lower deck as a lounge, dining area, gymnasium or for sleeping accommodation is under consideration.

The A340 will have an advanced in-flight entertainment systems using a sub-miniature coaxial cable with capacity for 24 mono or 12 stereo audio channels, plus liquid-crystal screen personal video systems fitted into the first and business classes.

Deutsche Airbus completed the first 14.9m-long front fuselage shell for the A340 at Hamburg in February 1990. This was flown by Super Guppy to Aérospatiale's St Nazaire factory for joining to the nose sections. The combined parts were then flown to Toulouse to be joined to the A340 wings brought in from British Aerospace's Chester factory.

Growth potential of the A340-200, currently designed for 262 passengers in a three-class layout, is seen as either a range increase to 9200 miles (14,800km) or an additional seven-tonne payload. Airbus is also studying a superstretch of the A340 to provide a 600- to 700-seat competitor to the Boeing 747-400 for earliest introduction into service in 2002.

At the beginning of 1991 Airbus had taken orders for 89 A340s and 138 A330s, TWA and Continental between them ordering 33 A330s and seven A340s.

CUTAWAY DRAWING OF AIRBUS INDUSTRIE A340-300

1 Radome
2 Weather radar scanner
3 Scanner mounting and tracking mechanism
4 Dual VOR localizer aerials
5 Dual glideslope aerials
6 Front pressure bulkhead
7 Radome hinges
8 Windscreen wipers

9 Windscreen panels
10 Instrument panel shroud
11 Thomson CSF Electronic Flight Instrument System
12 Rudder pedals
13 Cockpit floor level
14 Radar equipment racks
15 Access ladder from flightdeck
16 Pitot heads
17 Map/document/manual stowage
18 Sidestick controller
19 Captain's seat
20 Center control pedestal
21 First officer's seat
22 Overhead systems switch panel
23 Observer's swiveling seats (two, optional)
24 Video screen (crew recreation)
25 Flight crew rest compartment (two fold-down bunks)

26 Cockpit doorway
27 Crew wardrobe
28 Forward toilet compartment
29 Nose undercarriage wheel bay
30 Hydraulic retraction jack
31 Taxiing lamp
32 Twin nosewheels, forward retracting
33 Hydraulic steering jacks

34 Nosewheel leg doors
35 Nose undercarriage pivot fixing
36 Refrigeration packs, optional
37 Forward entry door
38 Door surround structure
39 Door latch
40 Door hinge arm
41 Cabin attendants' folding seats (two port and one starboard)
42 Starboard entry/service door
43 Forward galley compartment
44 Cabin-dividing bulkhead
45 VHF communications aerial
46 Overhead stowage bins
47 Cabin wall trim paneling
48 Cabin air distribution duct
49 Forward freight hold door
50 Forward underfloor freight hold; 2 808 cu ft (79.5 cu m) containerized volume
51 First-class passenger seating (18 seats six-abreast)
52 Reclining sleeper seats
53 Avionics equipment racks
54 Runway turn-off light
55 Fuselage lower lobe frame and stringer construction
56 Cabin window panels

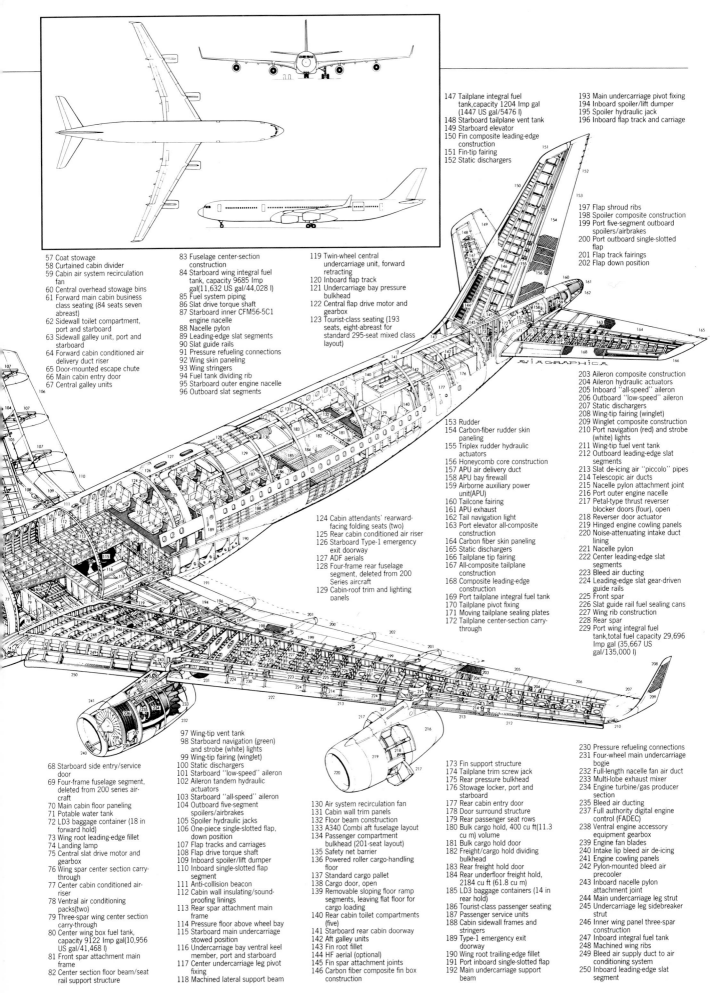

147 Tailplane integral fuel
    tank,capacity 1204 Imp gal
    (1447 US gal/5476 l)
148 Starboard tailplane vent tank
149 Starboard elevator
150 Fin composite leading-edge
    construction
151 Fin-tip fairing
152 Static dischargers

193 Main undercarriage pivot fixing
194 Inboard spoiler/lift dumper
195 Spoiler hydraulic jack
196 Inboard flap track and carriage

197 Flap shroud ribs
198 Spoiler composite construction
199 Port five-segment outboard
    spoilers/airbrakes
200 Port outboard single-slotted
    flap
201 Flap track fairings
202 Flap down position

57 Coat stowage
58 Curtained cabin divider
59 Cabin air system recirculation
   fan
60 Central overhead stowage bins
61 Forward main cabin business
   class seating (84 seats seven
   abreast)
62 Sidewall toilet compartment,
   port and starboard
63 Sidewall galley unit, port and
   starboard
64 Forward cabin conditioned air
   delivery duct riser
65 Door-mounted escape chute
66 Main cabin entry door
67 Central galley units

83 Fuselage center-section
   construction
84 Starboard wing integral fuel
   tank, capacity 9685 Imp
   gal(11,632 US gal/44,028 l)
85 Fuel system piping
86 Slat drive torque shaft
87 Starboard inner CFM56-5C1
   engine nacelle
88 Nacelle pylon
89 Leading-edge slat segments
90 Slat guide rails
91 Pressure refueling connections
92 Wing skin paneling
93 Wing stringers
94 Fuel tank dividing rib
95 Starboard outer engine nacelle
96 Outboard slat segments

119 Twin-wheel central
    undercarriage unit, forward
    retracting
120 Inboard flap track
121 Undercarriage bay pressure
    bulkhead
122 Central flap drive motor and
    gearbox
123 Tourist-class seating (193
    seats, eight-abreast for
    standard 295-seat mixed class
    layout)

124 Cabin attendants' rearward-
    facing folding seats (two)
125 Rear cabin conditioned air riser
126 Starboard Type-1 emergency
    exit doorway
127 ADF aerials
128 Four-frame rear fuselage
    segment, deleted from 200
    Series aircraft
129 Cabin-roof trim and lighting
    panels

153 Rudder
154 Carbon-fiber rudder skin
    paneling
155 Triplex rudder hydraulic
    actuators
156 Honeycomb core construction
157 APU air delivery duct
158 APU bay firewall
159 Airborne auxiliary power
    unit(APU)
160 Tailcone fairing
161 APU exhaust
162 Tail navigation light
163 Port elevator all-composite
    construction
164 Carbon fiber skin paneling
165 Static dischargers
166 Tailplane tip fairing
167 All-composite tailplane
    construction
168 Composite leading-edge
    construction
169 Port tailplane integral fuel tank
170 Tailplane pivot fixing
171 Moving tailplane sealing plates
172 Tailplane center-section carry-
    through

203 Aileron composite construction
204 Aileron hydraulic actuators
205 Inboard "all-speed" aileron
206 Outboard "low-speed" aileron
207 Static dischargers
208 Wing-tip fairing (winglet)
209 Winglet composite construction
210 Port navigation (red) and strobe
    (white) lights
211 Wing-tip fuel vent tank
212 Outboard leading-edge slat
    segments
213 Slat de-icing air "piccolo" pipes
214 Telescopic air ducts
215 Nacelle pylon attachment joint
216 Port outer engine nacelle
217 Petal-type thrust reverser
    blocker doors (four), open
218 Reverser door actuator
219 Hinged engine cowling panels
220 Noise-attenuating intake duct
    lining
221 Nacelle pylon
222 Center leading-edge slat
    segments
223 Bleed air ducting
224 Leading-edge slat gear-driven
    guide rails
225 Front spar
226 Slat guide rail fuel sealing cans
227 Wing rib construction
228 Rear spar
229 Port wing integral fuel
    tank,total fuel capacity 29,696
    Imp gal (35,667 US
    gal/135,000 l)

68 Starboard side entry/service
   door
69 Four-frame fuselage segment,
   deleted from 200 series aircraft
70 Main cabin floor paneling
71 Potable water tank
72 LD3 baggage container (18 in
   forward hold)
73 Wing root leading-edge fillet
74 Landing lamp
75 Central slat drive motor and
   gearbox
76 Wing spar center section carry-
   through
77 Center cabin conditioned air-
   riser
78 Ventral air conditioning
   packs(two)
79 Three-spar wing center section
   carry-through
80 Center wing box fuel tank,
   capacity 9122 Imp gal(10,956
   US gal/41,468 l)
81 Front spar attachment main
   frame
82 Center section floor beam/seat
   rail support structure

97 Wing-tip vent tank
98 Starboard navigation (green)
   and strobe (white) lights
99 Wing-tip fairing (winglet)
100 Static dischargers
101 Starboard "low-speed" aileron
102 Aileron tandem hydraulic
    actuators
103 Starboard "all-speed" aileron
104 Outboard five-segment
    spoilers/airbrakes
105 Spoiler hydraulic jacks
106 One-piece single-slotted flap,
    down position
107 Flap tracks and carriages
108 Flap drive torque shaft
109 Inboard spoiler/lift dumper
110 Inboard single-slotted flap
    segment
111 Anti-collision beacon
112 Cabin wall insulating/sound-
    proofing linings
113 Rear spar attachment main
    frame
114 Pressure floor above wheel bay
115 Starboard main undercarriage
    stowed position
116 Undercarriage bay ventral keel
    member, port and starboard
117 Center undercarriage leg pivot
    fixing
118 Machined lateral support beam

130 Air system recirculation fan
131 Cabin wall trim panels
132 Floor beam construction
133 A340 Combi aft fuselage layout
134 Passenger compartment
    bulkhead (201-seat layout)
135 Safety net barrier
136 Powered roller cargo-handling
    floor
137 Standard cargo pallet
138 Cargo door, open
139 Removable sloping floor ramp
    segments, leaving flat floor for
    cargo loading
140 Rear cabin toilet compartments
    (five)
141 Starboard rear cabin doorway
142 Aft galley units
143 Fin root fillet
144 HF aerial (optional)
145 Fin spar attachment joints
146 Carbon fiber composite fin box
    construction

173 Fin support structure
174 Tailplane trim screw jack
175 Rear pressure bulkhead
176 Stowage locker, port and
    starboard
177 Rear cabin entry door
178 Door surround structure
179 Rear passenger seat rows
180 Bulk cargo hold door, 400 cu ft(11.3
    cu m) volume
181 Bulk cargo hold door
182 Freight/cargo hold dividing
    bulkhead
183 Rear freight hold door
184 Rear underfloor freight hold,
    2184 cu ft (61.8 cu m)
185 LD3 baggage containers (14 in
    rear hold)
186 Tourist-class passenger seating
187 Passenger service units
188 Cabin sidewall frames and
    stringers
189 Type-1 emergency exit
    doorway
190 Wing root trailing-edge fillet
191 Port inboard single-slotted flap
192 Main undercarriage support
    beam

230 Pressure refueling connections
231 Four-wheel main undercarriage
    bogie
232 Full-length nacelle fan air duct
233 Multi-lobe exhaust mixer
234 Engine turbine/gas producer
    section
235 Bleed air ducting
236 Full authority digital engine
    control (FADEC)
237 Ventral engine accessory
    equipment gearbox
238 Engine fan blades
239 Intake lip bleed air de-icing
240 Engine cowling panels
241 Pylon-mounted bleed air
    precooler
242 Inboard nacelle pylon
    attachment joint
243 Main undercarriage leg strut
244 Undercarriage leg sidebreaker
    strut
245 Inner wing panel three-spar
    construction
246 Inboard integral fuel tank
247 Machined wing ribs
248 Bleed air supply duct to air
    conditioning system
249 Inboard leading-edge slat
    segment

USA

Boeing 737

Boeing Commercial Airplane Group

A Boeing 747-400 in pre-service company colors

SPECIFICATION Model 737-400

Origin: USA
Type: short/medium-range jetliner
Accommodation: flight crew of 2; up to 168 passengers (in single class)
Powerplant: two×1) 22,000lb (10,000kg)CFM56-3B-2, 2) 23,500lb (10,660kg) CFM56-3C-1, thrust turbofans
Performance: maximum cruising speed (M0.8); range with 146 passengers 2500n.mls (4633km)
Weights: empty operating 73,490lb (33,340kg) maximum take-off 138,500lb (62,822kg)
Dimensions: span 94ft 9in (28.88m); length 119ft 7in (36.45m); height 36ft 6in (11.13m); wing area 1135sq ft (105.4m^2)

Boeing's twin-jet short-range transport first went into production in 1965. It is the most ordered jet airliner in history and it is expected that production of further stretched and developed versions of this workhorse of the world's airlines will continue beyond the year 2000.

The initial model 737-100 flew for the first time in April 1967, but had only four customers. It was quickly followed into production by the slightly stretched 130-seat 737-200 in August the same year. A total of 1144 -100/200 series were produced before production ended in August 1988.

New noise legislation could impose non-structural limits on the 737-200's useful life, so several companies are working on noise reduction modifications for the large numbers of early Boeing 737s still in service, to enable them to comply with the new rules.

The new Boeing 737-300 model made its first flight in February 1984, from its program launch in March 1981. It is more than just a stretched 737-200; it has structural and aerodynamic improvements derived from technology developed for the 757 and 767 programs. Deliveries began in November 1984 with USAir as the launch customer. Stretched by 2.8m compared with the 737-200, this aircraft has as its most visible change the replacement of the Pratt & Whitney JT8D engines with CFM56-3s.

The Boeing 737-400 series, Boeing's main contender in the 150-seat market, made its maiden flight in February 1988. The 737-400 seats up to 18 more than the 737-300 with a fuselage stretched by 3m.

The latest in the line-up is the Boeing 737-500. Launch customers in early 1990 were Southwest Airlines and Braathens SAFE. The 737-500 is the smallest of the three new 737 variants powered by CFM56-series power plants and its 29.8m-long fuselage is just 25cm longer than the 737-200 it replaces. The 737-500 is powered by two CFM563B1-series engines with a choice of two thrust ratings, 82.3kN or 89.0kN. It carries 108 passengers in mixed-class configuration, 122 passengers in an all-economy layout, or seats 132 in high-density charter configuration.

Recent orders for the 737-500 include Aerolíneas Argentinas (6), Aer Lingus (5) Egyptair (10), Linjeflyg (4), Lufthansa (36) Maersk (5) and Southwest (42).

**CUTAWAY DRAWING OF
BOEING 737-400**

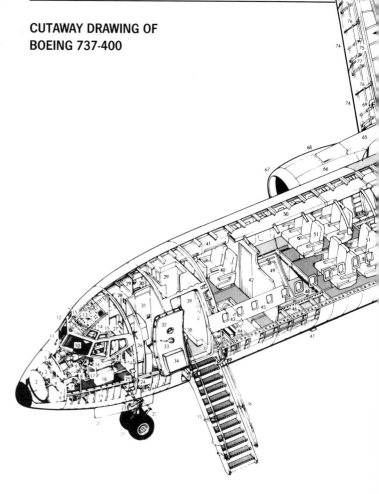

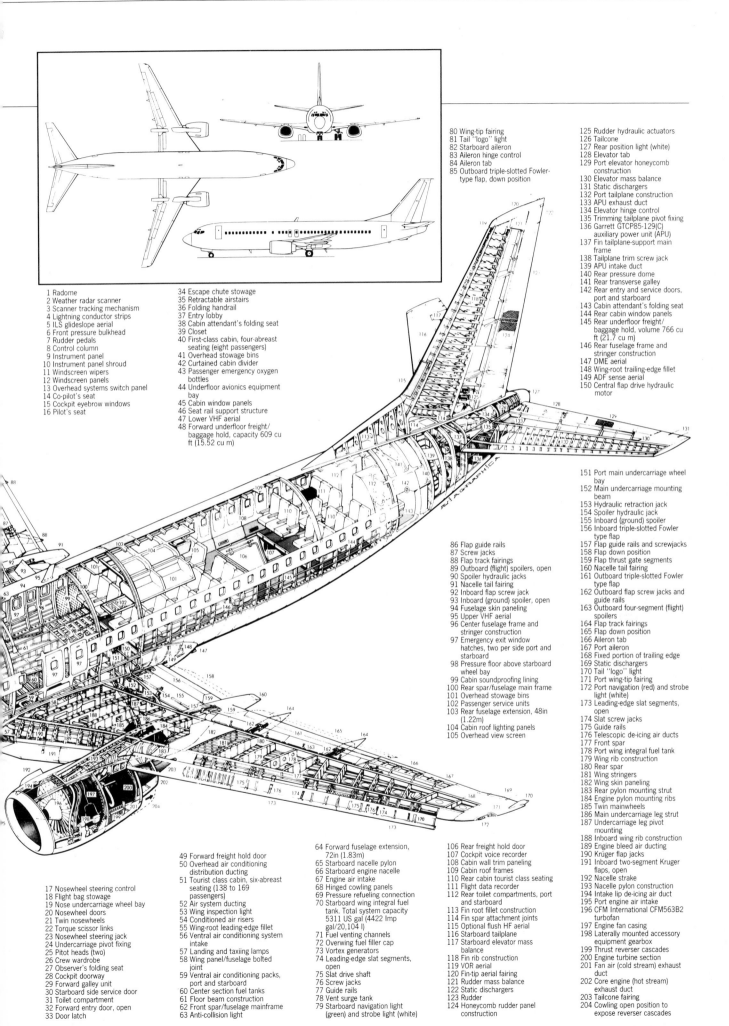

80 Wing-tip fairing
81 Tail "logo" light
82 Starboard aileron
83 Aileron hinge control
84 Aileron tab
85 Outboard triple-slotted Fowler-type flap, down position

1 Radome
2 Weather radar scanner
3 Scanner tracking mechanism
4 Lightning conductor strips
5 ILS glideslope aerial
6 Front pressure bulkhead
7 Rudder pedals
8 Control column
9 Instrument panel
10 Instrument panel shroud
11 Windscreen wipers
12 Windscreen panels
13 Overhead systems switch panel
14 Co-pilot's seat
15 Cockpit eyebrow windows
16 Pilot's seat

34 Escape chute stowage
35 Retractable airstairs
36 Folding handrail
37 Entry lobby
38 Cabin attendant's folding seat
39 Closet
40 First-class cabin, four-abreast seating (eight passengers)
41 Overhead stowage bins
42 Curtained cabin divider
43 Passenger emergency oxygen bottles
44 Underfloor avionics equipment bay
45 Cabin window panels
46 Seat rail support structure
47 Lower VHF aerial
48 Forward underfloor freight/baggage hold, capacity 609 cu ft (15.52 cu m)

86 Flap guide rails
87 Screw jacks
88 Flap track fairings
89 Outboard (flight) spoilers, open
90 Spoiler hydraulic jacks
91 Nacelle tail fairing
92 Inboard flap screw jack
93 Inboard (ground) spoiler, open
94 Fuselage skin paneling
95 Upper VHF aerial
96 Center fuselage frame and stringer construction
97 Emergency exit window hatches, two per side port and starboard
98 Pressure floor above starboard wheel bay
99 Cabin soundproofing lining
100 Rear spar/fuselage main frame
101 Overhead stowage bins
102 Passenger service units
103 Rear fuselage extension, 48in (1.22m)
104 Cabin roof lighting panels
105 Overhead view screen

125 Rudder hydraulic actuators
126 Tailcone
127 Rear position light (white)
128 Elevator tab
129 Port elevator honeycomb construction
130 Elevator mass balance
131 Static dischargers
132 Port tailplane construction
133 APU exhaust duct
134 Elevator hinge control
135 Trimming tailplane pivot fixing
136 Garrett GTCP85-129(C) auxiliary power unit (APU)
137 Fin tailplane-support main frame
138 Tailplane trim screw jack
139 APU intake duct
140 Rear pressure dome
141 Rear transverse galley
142 Rear entry and service doors, port and starboard
143 Cabin attendant's folding seat
144 Rear cabin window panels
145 Rear underfloor freight/baggage hold, volume 766 cu ft (21.7 cu m)
146 Rear fuselage frame and stringer construction
147 DME aerial
148 Wing-root trailing-edge fillet
149 ADF sense aerial
150 Central flap drive hydraulic motor

151 Port main undercarriage wheel bay
152 Main undercarriage mounting beam
153 Hydraulic retraction jack
154 Spoiler hydraulic jack
155 Inboard (ground) spoiler
156 Inboard triple-slotted Fowler type flap
157 Flap guide rails and screwjacks
158 Flap down position
159 Flap thrust gate segments
160 Nacelle tail fairing
161 Outboard triple-slotted Fowler type flap
162 Outboard flap screw jacks and guide rails
163 Outboard four-segment (flight) spoilers
164 Flap track fairings
165 Flap down position
166 Aileron tab
167 Port aileron
168 Fixed portion of trailing edge
169 Static dischargers
170 Tail "logo" light
171 Port wing-tip fairing
172 Port navigation (red) and strobe light (white)
173 Leading-edge slat segments, open
174 Slat screw jacks
175 Guide rails
176 Telescopic de-icing air ducts
177 Front spar
178 Port wing integral fuel tank
179 Wing rib construction
180 Rear spar
181 Wing stringers
182 Wing skin paneling
183 Rear pylon mounting strut
184 Engine pylon mounting ribs
185 Twin mainwheels
186 Main undercarriage leg strut
187 Undercarriage leg pivot mounting
188 Inboard wing rib construction
189 Engine bleed air ducting
190 Kruger flap jacks
191 Inboard two-segment Kruger flaps, open
192 Nacelle strake
193 Nacelle pylon construction
194 Intake lip de-icing air duct
195 Port engine air intake
196 CFM International CFM563B2 turbofan
197 Engine fan casing
198 Laterally mounted accessory equipment gearbox
199 Thrust reverser cascades
200 Engine turbine section
201 Fan air (cold stream) exhaust duct
202 Core engine (hot stream) exhaust duct
203 Tailcone fairing
204 Cowling open position to expose reverser cascades

17 Nosewheel steering control
18 Flight bag stowage
19 Nose undercarriage wheel bay
20 Nosewheel doors
21 Twin nosewheels
22 Torque scissor links
23 Nosewheel steering jack
24 Undercarriage pivot fixing
25 Pitot heads (two)
26 Crew wardrobe
27 Observer's folding seat
28 Cockpit doorway
29 Forward galley unit
30 Starboard side service door
31 Toilet compartment
32 Forward entry door, open
33 Door latch

49 Forward freight hold door
50 Overhead air conditioning distribution ducting
51 Tourist class cabin, six-abreast seating (138 to 169 passengers)
52 Air system ducting
53 Wing inspection light
54 Conditioned air risers
55 Wing-root leading-edge fillet
56 Ventral air conditioning system intake
57 Landing and taxiing lamps
58 Wing panel/fuselage bolted joint
59 Ventral air conditioning packs, port and starboard
60 Center section fuel tanks
61 Floor beam construction
62 Front spar/fuselage mainframe
63 Anti-collision light

64 Forward fuselage extension, 72in (1.83m)
65 Starboard nacelle pylon
66 Starboard engine nacelle
67 Engine air intake
68 Hinged cowling panels
69 Pressure refueling connection
70 Starboard wing integral fuel tank. Total system capacity 5311 US gal (4422 Imp gal/20,104 l)
71 Fuel venting channels
72 Overwing fuel filler cap
73 Vortex generators
74 Leading-edge slat segments, open
75 Slat drive shaft
76 Screw jacks
77 Guide rails
78 Vent surge tank
79 Starboard navigation light (green) and strobe light (white)

106 Rear freight hold door
107 Cockpit voice recorder
108 Cabin wall trim paneling
109 Cabin roof frames
110 Rear cabin tourist class seating
111 Flight data recorder
112 Rear toilet compartments, port and starboard
113 Fin root fillet construction
114 Fin spar attachment joints
115 Optional flush HF aerial
116 Starboard tailplane
117 Starboard elevator mass balance
118 Fin rib construction
119 VOR aerial
120 Fin-tip aerial fairing
121 Rudder mass balance
122 Static dischargers
123 Rudder
124 Honeycomb rudder panel construction

15

USA

Boeing 747

Boeing Commercial Airplane Group

A KLM Boeing 747-400 at Atlanta in Georgia

SPECIFICATION Model 747-400
Origin: USA
Type: wide-body long-range jetliner
Accommodation: flight crew of 2; up to 500 passengers (in single class)
Powerplant: four×1) 56,750lb (25,742kg) Pratt & Whitney PW4256, 2) 56,700lb (25,720kg) General Electric CF6-80C2B1F, 3) 58,000lb (26,310kg) Rolls-Royce RB.211-524G, thrust turbofans
Performance: maximum cruising speed 532kts (985km/h) at 30,000 ft (9145m); range with 412 passengers 8400n.mls (15,569km)
Weights: empty operating 393,880lb (178,661kg) maximum take-off 870,000lb (394,700kg)
Dimensions: span 211ft (64.3m); length 231ft 10in (70.66m); height 63ft 5in (19.33m); wing area 5650sq ft (524.9m^2)

The Boeing 747 is one of the most instantly recognizable of all aircraft – the mighty "Jumbo" which has become a familiar sight in the world's skies for over 20 years. When the outsize aircraft was conceived in the mid 1960s, it seemed a logical of way of bringing down seat-mile costs and of providing mass air travel by scaling up the airframe and capacity of proven aircraft like the 707, allied to new-generation powerful turbofan engines.

Pan American placed an order for 25 747s off the drawing board in 1966 and since then it seems that an airline cannot consider itself a world class contender without 747s in its fleet.

From the time of the first commercial flight from New York to London on 21 January 1970, 14 different versions of the 747 have entered service. The latest, the 747-400 Combi, became available early in 1989, and 29 of this model have been ordered by seven airlines, KLM being the first. A 15 variant, the 747-400 Freighter, is due for delivery to Air France in 1993.

The first of the latest model 747-400 series made its maiden flight, powered by Pratt & Whitney PW4000 engines, on 29 April 1988. Other engine options are General Electric's CF6-80C2 and the Rolls-Royce RB. 211-524G/H.

The 747-400, the only current production model, is a development of the 747-300, which featured structural changes to the aircraft's upper deck to increase passenger-carrying capacity. The first 747-300s went into service with Swissair and UTA in March 1983. The most significant external difference between the 747-400 and the 747-300 is an extension of about 1.8m to each wingtip, combined with vertical winglets of similar dimensions.

However the aircraft's flight systems have been substantially upgraded with a digital two-man crew flight deck, better fuel economy, increased range and more flexible interior configurations. The new model has more in common with the 757 and 767 than the 747-300. Although fuselage dimensions are the same, the 747-400 has a new interior layout, with sidewall stowage bins that can nearly double passenger carry-on baggage capacity. An in-flight entertainment system operates without wires, picking up audio and visual signals from floor-mounted transmitters.

The new 747-400 offers a 7-11% reduction in fuel-burn per seat compared with that of the 747-300 and up to a 25% reduction compared with older 747 models. It has increased fuel capacity, while maximum take-off weight has risen to 394,700kg. This increases the aircraft's range by 1100 miles (1930km) over that of the 747-300 to 8500 miles (13,600km) and allows 412 passengers to be flown on 8500-mile sectors nonstop.

By the end of 1990 93 747-400s had been delivered to 18 airlines, with 399 on order by 31 airlines in total. Major customers include British Airways (42), All Nippon (43), Japan Air Lines (40) and Air France (20).

CUTAWAY DRAWING OF BOEING 747-400

1 Radome
2 Weather radar scanner
3 Front pressure bulkhead
4 Scanner tracking mechanism
5 Wardrobe
6 First class cabin, 30 or 34 seats at 62-in (1.57-m) pitch
7 Nose undercarriage wheel bay
8 Nosewheel doors
9 Twin nosewheels
10 Hydraulic steering jacks
11 Nose undercarriage pivot fixing
12 Underfloor avionics equipment racks
13 Cabin window panels
14 First class bar unit
15 Flight deck floor level
16 Rudder pedals
17 Control column

18 Instrument panel, five-CRT electronic flight instrumentation system (EFIS)
19 Instrument panel shroud
20 Windscreen panels
21 Overhead systems switchpanel
22 First officer's seat
23 Captain's seat (two-crew cockpit)
24 Observer's folding seats (two)
25 Starboard side toilet compartments (two)
26 Cockpit bulkhead
27 Crew rest bunks (two)
28 Upper deck window panel
29 Conditioned air distribution ducting
30 Forward main deck galley unit
31 Plug-type forward cabin door, No 1 port and starboard
32 Business class passenger seating, 24 seats typical at 36-in(91-cm) pitch
33 Fuselage lower lobe skin paneling
34 Baggage/cargo pallet containers
35 Forward underfloor cargo hold, capacity 2768 cu ft (78.4 cu m)
36 Forward fuselage frame and stringer construction
37 Upper deck doorway, port and starboard
38 Cabin roof frames
39 Anti-collision light
40 No 1 UHF communications aerial

41 Upper deck passenger cabin, 52 business class seats or 69 economy class seats
42 Lower deck sidewall toilet compartment
43 No 2 passenger door, port and starboard
44 Air conditioning system heat exchanger intake ducting
45 Ventral flush air intakes

46 Faired wing root leading-edge fillet
47 Ventral air conditioning packs, port and starboard
48 Wing spar bulkhead
49 Economy class seating
50 Staircase to upper deck
51 Fresh water tanks
52 Wing center section fuel tankage, capacity 16,990 US gal(64,315 l)
53 Center section stringer construction
54 Floor beam construction
55 Front spar/fuselage mainframe
56 Upper deck lobby area
57 Curtained bulkhead
58 Galley units
59 Starboard wing inboard main fuel tank, capacity 12,546 US gal (47,492 l)
60 Fuel pumps
61 Engine bleed air supply ducting
62 Kruger flap-operating mechanism
63 Inboard Kruger flap segments
64 Starboard inner Pratt & Whitney PW4256 engine nacelle
65 Inboard nacelle pylon
66 Leading-edge Kruger flap segments
67 Pressure refueling connections, port and starboard
68 Kruger flap drive shaft
69 Kruger flap rotary actuators

70 Starboard wing outer main fuel tank, capacity 4482 US gal (16,966 l)
71 Starboard outer engine nacelle
72 Outer nacelle pylon
73 Starboard wing reserve tank provision, capacity 534 US gal (2021 l)

74 Outboard Kruger flap
75 Kruger flap drive mechanism
76 Outer wing panel dry bay
77 Vent surge tank
78 Wing-tip extension
79 Starboard navigation (green) and strobe (white) lights
80 Starboard winglet
81 Fixed portion of trailing edge

82 Fuel vent
83 Static dischargers
84 Outboard, low-speed, aileron
85 Outboard four-segment spoilers
86 Outboard triple-slotted Fowler type flap, down position
87 Flap screw jacks and segment linkages
88 Flap drive shaft
89 Inboard, high-speed aileron
90 Inboard triple-slotted flap, down position
91 Inboard two-segment spoilers/lift dumpers
92 Flap screw jack
93 Auxiliary trailing-edge wing spar
94 Cabin air distribution ducting
95 Extended upper deck rear bulkhead
96 Upper deck floor beam construction
97 Air system cross-feed ducting
98 Conditioned air risers
99 Machined wing spar attachment main frames
100 Central flap drive motors
101 Wing-mounted outboard main undercarriage wheel bay
102 Undercarriage mounting beam
103 Central keel section
104 Pressure floor above wheel bay

105 Center fuselage frame and stringer construction
106 Dual navigation aerials
107 Cabin wall trim paneling
108 Seal mounting rails
109 Main cabin floor paneling
110 Fuselage-mounted in board, main undercarriage wheel bay
111 Hydraulic retraction jack
112 Cabin window panel
113 Overhead conditioned air distribution ducting
114 Economy class seating, 302 to 410 passengers at 34-in(86-cm) pitch
115 Overhead stowage bins
116 Sidewall toilet compartments, port and starboard
117 Central cabin galley
118 No 4 passenger door, port and starboard
119 Rear cabin passenger seating
120 Rear cabin galley
121 Rear cabin air supply ducting
122 Fuselage sidewall stowage bins
123 Control cable runs
124 Central overhead stowage bins
125 Cabin roof panels
126 Ten-abreast economy class seating
127 Rear fuselage frame and stringer construction
128 Rear cabin seating
129 Access ladder to upper deck area
130 Overhead cabin-crew rest area, six bunks and four seats typical
131 Rear pressure bulkhead
132 Fin root fillet
133 Starboard trimming tailpane
134 Static dischargers
135 Starboard elevators
136 Fin leading-edge construction
137 Two-spar fin box construction
138 Fin-tip fairing
139 VOR localizer aerial
140 Static dischargers
141 Upper rudder segment
142 Lower rudder segment
143 Rudder hydraulic actuators
144 Tailcone frame construction
145 Pratt & Whitney Canada PW901A auxiliary power unit(APU)
146 Tail navigation and strobe lights (white)
147 APU exhaust
148 Port elevator inboard segment
149 Port elevator outboard segment
150 Static dischargers
151 Port trimming tailplane construction
152 Elevator hydraulic actuators
153 Long-range tailplane fuel tank, capacity 3300 US gal (12,492 l)
154 Tailplane sealing plate
155 Aft fuselage framing
156 Fin root attachment joint
157 Tailplane center section
158 Tailplane trim screw jack
159 Fin high-pressure air supply duct
160 Lower deck rear cabin toilet compartments
161 No 5 passenger door, port and starboard
162 Rear fuselage window panel
163 Underfloor bulk cargo hold, capacity 1 000 cu ft (28.3 cu m)

164 Rear fuselage baggage/cargo hold, capacity 2422 cu ft(68.6 cu m)
165 Baggage/cargo pallet
166 Fuselage lower lobe frame and stringer construction
167 Wing root trailing-edge fillet, composite construction
168 Fuselage-mounted main undercarriage pivot fixing
169 Trailing-edge auxiliary spar
170 Undercarriage leg breaker strut
171 Wing-mounted main undercarriage pivot fixing
172 Hydraulic retraction jack
173 Four-wheel inboard main undercarriage bogie
174 Flap drive shaft
175 Flap guide rails
176 Inboard spoilers/lift dumpers
177 Port inboard triple-slotted flap
178 Flap track fairings
179 Flap down position
180 Aileron hydraulic actuator
181 Inboard, high-speed aileron
182 Outboard triple-slotted flap
183 Outboard flap tracks
184 Outboard spoilers
185 Flap track fairings
186 Flap down position
187 Outboard, low-speed, aileron
188 Aileron hydraulic actuators
189 Static dischargers
190 Fuel vent
191 Port winglet
192 Winglet composite construction
193 Port navigation (red) and strobe (white) lights
194 Outboard leading-edge Kruger flap segments
195 Kruger flap drive mechanism
196 Outer wing panel rib construction
197 Wing bottom skin access panels
198 Rear spar
199 Outboard engine mounting rib
200 Port outer nacelle pylon
201 Thrust reverser cowling door,open
202 Reverser cascades
203 Outboard engine nacelle
204 Rolls-Royce RB.211-524G alternative engine installation
205 Full-length nacelle cowling
206 Internal exhaust stream mixer duct
207 Central leading-edge Kruger flap segments
208 Kruger flap drive mechanism
209 Leading-edge rib construction
210 Wing panel spar and rib construction
211 Flap track mounting beams
212 Inner engine pylon mounting rib
213 Inner engine pylon mounting rib
214 Wing stringers
215 Wing skin paneling
216 Wing-mounted main undercarriage leg strut
217 Pylon attachment strut
218 Four-wheel outer main undercarriage bogie
219 Nacelle pylon construction
220 Engine bleed air pre-cooler
221 Core engine, hot stream, exhaust duct
222 Fan air, cold stream, exhaust duct
223 Ventral engine accessory equipment package
224 Pratt and Whitney PW4256 turbo fan engine
225 Engine intake
226 Detachable engine cowling panels
227 Bleed air de-iced intake lip
228 Inboard Kruger flap segment
229 Kruger flap motor and drive shaft
230 Three-spar wing torsion box construction
231 Inboard wing ribs
232 Bolted wing root attachment joint strap
233 Front spar
234 Engine bleed air ducting
235 Leading-edge nose ribs
236 Twin landing lamps
237 General Electric CF6-80C2 alternative engine installation

USA

Boeing 767

Boeing Commercial Airplane Group

A British Airways Boeing 767-300

SPECIFICATION Model 767-300
Origin: USA
Type: medium-range jetliner
Accommodation: flight crew of 2; up to 325 passengers (in single class)
Powerplant: two 60,000-lb (27,488-kg) thrust Rolls-Royce RB.211-524H turbofans
Performance: maximum cruising speed 489kts (906km/h) at 39,000 ft (11,887m); range 4000n.mls (7410km)
Weights: empty operating 201,100lb (91,220kg) maximum take-off 407,000lb (184,615kg)
Dimensions: span 156ft 1in (47.57m); length 176ft 1in (53.67m); height 52ft (15.85m); wing area 3050sq ft (283.3m^2)

In 1978 the Boeing company decided to develop a new family of advanced-technology aircraft – the short-range 757 with a standard cross-section fuselage, and the medium-range 767 with a wide-body, twin-aisle fuselage and with a passenger capacity greater than that of a 707, but not so big as a 747's. The 767 has an advanced technology wing and a two-crew, digital flight deck.

It is offered in two models – the 767-200 series, and the stretched 767-300 series which uses a 6.43-m fuselage extension to increase passenger capacity to 250+ seats, 45 more than the 767-200.

The launch customer for the 767-200 was United Airlines which flew its first commercial service with the type between Chicago and Denver on 8 September 1982. Japan Airlines launched the 767-300 in 1986. Alternative engines from Pratt & Whitney and General Electric can be specified according to customer requirement and the Rolls-Royce RB.211-524G became an option in 1990. Both models are offered in standard and extended-range (ER) options with increased fuel capacity.

Customer preference continues to be for the extended-range versions, about evenly divided between 767-200ERs and 767-300ERs. Both can accommodate 747-type sleeper seats five abreast, medium-range six-abreast first class, seven-abreast economy class and two-four-two eight-abreast inclusive-tour layouts.

Boeing has developed a series of modifications for the 767-200ER and 767-300ER to gain licensing authority approval for ETOPS (extended-range twinjet operations) – flights over water along flight-paths by twin-engined aircraft, which now can pass up to three hours away from an emergency airfield flying at single-engine cruising speed. Initially, the aircraft were restricted to two hours' flying time from the nearest suitable diversion airfield.

The modifications comprise a fourth electric generator powered by a hydraulic motor, increased fire suppression for the lower-deck holds and additional devices to detect equipment overheating. El Al engineers have installed center-section fuel tanks in the airline's 767-200ERs to allow non-stop flights between Tel Aviv and Montreal with 195 passengers.

At the end of 1990, 292 767-200s were in airline service, and 83 767-300s, the majority of them ERs, had been delivered. By February 1991, 533 767s of all types were on order.

CUTAWAY DRAWING OF BOEING 767-300

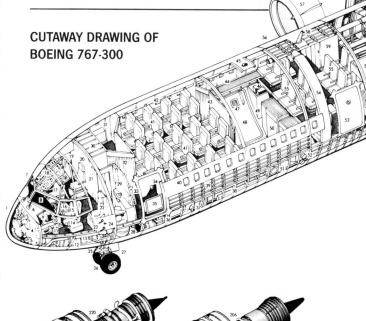

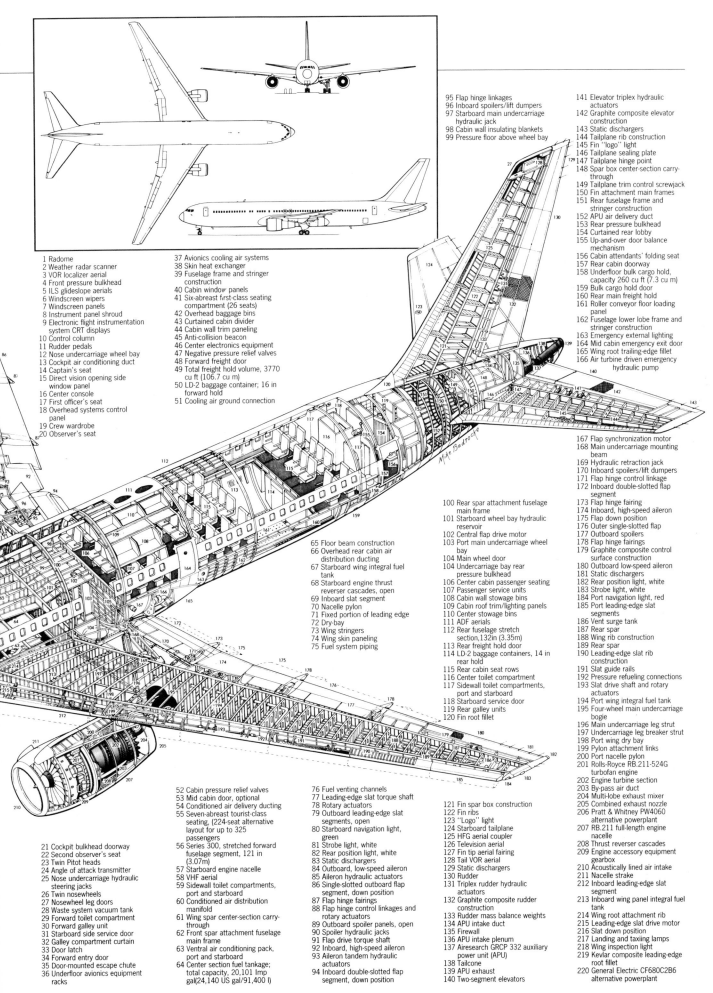

95 Flap hinge linkages
96 Inboard spoilers/lift dumpers
97 Starboard main undercarriage hydraulic jack
98 Cabin wall insulating blankets
99 Pressure floor above wheel bay

141 Elevator triplex hydraulic actuators
142 Graphite composite elevator construction
143 Static dischargers
144 Tailplane rib construction
145 Fin "logo" light
146 Tailplane sealing plate
147 Tailplane hinge point
148 Spar box center-section carry-through
149 Tailplane trim control screwjack
150 Fin attachment main frames
151 Rear fuselage frame and stringer construction
152 APU air delivery duct
153 Rear pressure bulkhead
154 Curtained rear lobby
155 Up-and-over door balance mechanism
156 Cabin attendants' folding seat
157 Rear cabin doorway
158 Underfloor bulk cargo hold, capacity 260 cu ft (7.3 cu m)
159 Bulk cargo hold door
160 Rear main freight hold
161 Roller conveyor floor loading panel
162 Fuselage lower lobe frame and stringer construction
163 Emergency external lighting
164 Mid cabin emergency exit door
165 Wing root trailing-edge fillet
166 Air turbine driven emergency hydraulic pump

1 Radome
2 Weather radar scanner
3 VOR localizer aerial
4 Front pressure bulkhead
5 ILS glideslope aerials
6 Windscreen wipers
7 Windscreen panels
8 Instrument panel shroud
9 Electronic flight instrumentation system CRT displays
10 Control column
11 Rudder pedals
12 Nose undercarriage wheel bay
13 Cockpit air conditioning duct
14 Captain's seat
15 Direct vision opening side window panel
16 Center console
17 First officer's seat
18 Overhead systems control panel
19 Crew wardrobe
20 Observer's seat

37 Avionics cooling air systems
38 Skin heat exchanger
39 Fuselage frame and stringer construction
40 Cabin window panels
41 Six-abreast first-class seating compartment (26 seats)
42 Overhead baggage bins
43 Curtained cabin divider
44 Cabin wall trim paneling
45 Anti-collision beacon
46 Center electronics equipment
47 Negative pressure relief valves
48 Forward freight door
49 Total freight hold volume, 3770 cu ft (106.7 cu m)
50 LD-2 baggage container; 16 in forward hold
51 Cooling air ground connection

65 Floor beam construction
66 Overhead rear cabin air distribution ducting
67 Starboard wing integral fuel tank
68 Starboard engine thrust reverser cascades, open
69 Inboard slat segment
70 Nacelle pylon
71 Fixed portion of leading edge
72 Dry-bay
73 Wing stringers
74 Wing skin paneling
75 Fuel system piping

100 Rear spar attachment fuselage main frame
101 Starboard wheel bay hydraulic reservoir
102 Central flap drive motor
103 Port main undercarriage wheel bay
104 Main wheel door
104 Undercarriage bay rear pressure bulkhead
106 Center cabin passenger seating
107 Passenger service units
108 Cabin wall stowage bins
109 Cabin roof trim/lighting panels
110 Center stowage bins
111 ADF aerials
112 Rear fuselage stretch section,132in (3.35m)
113 Rear freight hold door
114 LD-2 baggage containers, 14 in rear hold
115 Rear cabin seat rows
116 Center toilet compartment
117 Sidewall toilet compartments, port and starboard
118 Starboard service door
119 Rear galley units
120 Fin root fillet

167 Flap synchronization motor
168 Main undercarriage mounting beam
169 Hydraulic retraction jack
170 Inboard spoilers/lift dumpers
171 Flap hinge control linkage
172 Inboard double-slotted flap segment
173 Flap hinge fairing
174 Inboard, high-speed aileron
175 Flap down position
176 Outer single-slotted flap
177 Outboard spoilers
178 Flap hinge fairings
179 Graphite composite control surface construction
180 Outboard low-speed aileron
181 Static dischargers
182 Rear position light, white
183 Strobe light, white
184 Port navigation light, red
185 Port leading-edge slat segments
186 Vent surge tank
187 Rear spar
188 Wing rib construction
189 Rear spar
190 Leading-edge slat rib construction
191 Slat guide rails
192 Pressure refueling connections
193 Slat drive shaft and rotary actuators
194 Port wing integral fuel tank
195 Four-wheel main undercarriage bogie
196 Main undercarriage leg strut
197 Undercarriage leg breaker strut
198 Port wing dry bay
199 Pylon attachment links
200 Port nacelle pylon
201 Rolls-Royce RB.211-524G turbofan engine
202 Engine turbine section
203 By-pass air duct
204 Multi-lobe exhaust mixer
205 Combined exhaust nozzle
206 Pratt & Whitney PW4060 alternative powerplant
207 RB.211 full-length engine nacelle
208 Thrust reverser cascades
209 Engine accessory equipment gearbox
210 Acoustically lined air intake
211 Nacelle strake
212 Inboard leading-edge slat segment
213 Inboard wing panel integral fuel tank
214 Wing root attachment rib
215 Leading-edge slat drive motor
216 Slat down position
217 Landing and taxiing lamps
218 Wing inspection light
219 Kevlar composite leading-edge root fillet
220 General Electric CF680C2B6 alternative powerplant

21 Cockpit bulkhead doorway
22 Second observer's seat
23 Twin Pitot heads
24 Angle of attack transmitter
25 Nose undercarriage hydraulic steering jacks
26 Twin nosewheels
27 Nosewheel leg doors
28 Waste system vacuum tank
29 Forward toilet compartment
30 Forward galley unit
31 Starboard side service door
32 Galley compartment curtain
33 Door latch
34 Forward entry door
35 Door-mounted escape chute
36 Underfloor avionics equipment racks

52 Cabin pressure relief valves
53 Mid cabin door, optional
54 Conditioned air delivery ducting
55 Seven-abreast tourist-class seating, (224-seat alternative layout for up to 325 passengers
56 Series 300, stretched forward fuselage segment, 121 in (3.07m)
57 Forward engine nacelle
58 VHF aerial
59 Sidewall toilet compartments, port and starboard
60 Conditioned air distribution manifold
61 Wing spar center-section carry-through
62 Front spar attachment fuselage main frame
63 Ventral air conditioning pack, port and starboard
64 Center section fuel tankage; total capacity, 20,101 Imp gal(24,140 US gal/91,400 l)

76 Fuel venting channels
77 Leading-edge slat torque shaft
78 Rotary actuators
79 Outboard leading-edge slat segments, open
80 Starboard navigation light, green
81 Strobe light, white
82 Rear position light, white
83 Static dischargers
84 Outboard, low-speed aileron
85 Aileron hydraulic actuators
86 Triple-slotted outboard flap segment, down position
87 Flap hinge fairings
88 Flap hinge control linkages and rotary actuators
89 Outboard spoiler panels, open
90 Spoiler hydraulic jacks
91 Flap drive torque shaft
92 Inboard, high-speed aileron
93 Aileron tandem hydraulic actuators
94 Inboard double-slotted flap segment, down position

121 Fin spar box construction
122 Fin ribs
123 "Logo" light
124 Starboard tailplane
125 HFG aerial coupler
126 Television aerial
127 Fin tip aerial fairing
128 Tail VOR aerial
129 Static dischargers
130 Rudder
131 Triplex rudder hydraulic actuators
132 Graphite composite rudder construction
133 Rudder mass balance weights
134 APU intake duct
135 Firewall
136 APU intake plenum
137 Airesearch GRCP 332 auxiliary power unit (APU)
138 Tailcone
139 APU exhaust
140 Two-segment elevators

UK

BAe 146

British Aerospace Commercial Aircraft

SPECIFICATION Model 146-300
Origin: UK
Type: short-range jetliner
Accommodation: flight crew of 2; up to 112 passengers
Powerplant: four 6970-lb (3162-kg) thrust Avco Lycoming ALF502R-5 turbofans
Performance: typical cruising speed 425kts (787km/h) at 30,000 ft (9145m); range with 100 passengers 1100n.mls (2038km)
Weights: empty operating 54,000lb (24,495kg); maximum take-off 95,000lb (43,092kg)
Dimensions: span 86ft 5in (26.34m); length 101ft 8in (30.99m); height 28ft 3in (8.61m)

This British Aerospace 146-300, painted in company colors, prepares for landing

Britain's last home-designed airliner has found itself a worldwide market niche in the ten years since the prototype first flew. Eleven carriers operate the type in the Americas, 18 in Europe, eleven in Asia and Australia and two in Africa. Over 160 of this four-engined regional transport were in service at the outset of 1991, with over 210 on order. In March 1990 a BAe-146-200 operated by LAN-Chile became the first commercial jet transport to operate in Antarctica, when it opened a route from Punta Arenas to an air force base on King George Island.

At the end of 1990 British Aerospace announced plans to develop the current BAe 146-300 series into a stretched 130-seater, the so-called New Regional Aircraft (NRA), to be powered by twin engines (CFM56 or IAE V2500), each in the 98kN thrust class.

The BAe 146-100 series prototype first flew on 3 September 1981. The first scheduled operation of the 88-seat aircraft was made by Dan-Air on 21 May 1983. The stretched series 200 can accommodate up to 112 passengers. The first production aircraft was delivered to the launch customer, Air Wisconsin, in June 1983.

The latest major production model is the BAe 146-300. It made its maiden flight from Hatfield, north of London, in May 1987, using the original prototype, which was extensively modified by the addition of two new fuselage sections fore and aft of the wing. The fuselage is lengthened to 31m and the aircraft carries 103 passengers five-abreast or 122 passengers in a high-density arrangement. Again Air Wisconsin was the launch customer, in May 1987. Other models are the 146 QT (Quiet Trader), the freighter version of any series, for which the TNT transport operation has been a major customer. BAe also make a "QC" version of the -200 and -300 series – standing for quick-change convertible between passenger and freight configuration.

The aircraft are fabricated at Woodford, near Manchester, and at Hatfield from structures manufactured at several sites in the UK. Wing components are made in the US by Textron Aerostructures and the tailplane assembly by Saab in Sweden.

The aircraft range is the subject of constant development. Major improvements and additions to the 146 range were announced in mid-1991. These included Textron Lycoming 31.5kN LF507 engines,

providing 7.5% more thrust at temperatures above 23C, compared with the earlier ALF502R5, giving the aircraft better performance in high-temperature conditions. The first delivery of the upgraded aircraft will be to the Swiss operator, Crossair, in 1992.

Flight deck avionics have been improved with a digital flight guidance inertial reference system. A revised Honeywell EFIS is incorporated and a new integrated windshear warning system, a digital radio altimeter and radio/navigation systems.

Wing, fuselage and undercarriage strengthening will allow increased design weights on all three 146 versions. Maximum take-off, maximum landing and maximum zero-fuel weights will be increased by 2720kg for the 146-100 and 1814kg for the 146-200 and 146-300. The company claims that the increased engine thrust and higher design weights improve airfield performance and give up to double the range from limited runways. Payload is also increased by 28% for the 146-100, 13% for the 146-200 and 12% for the 146-300.

CUTAWAY DRAWING OF BAe 146

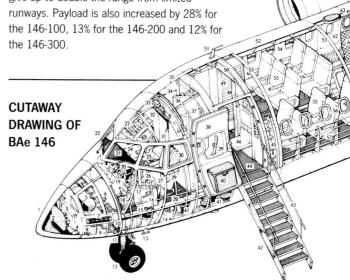

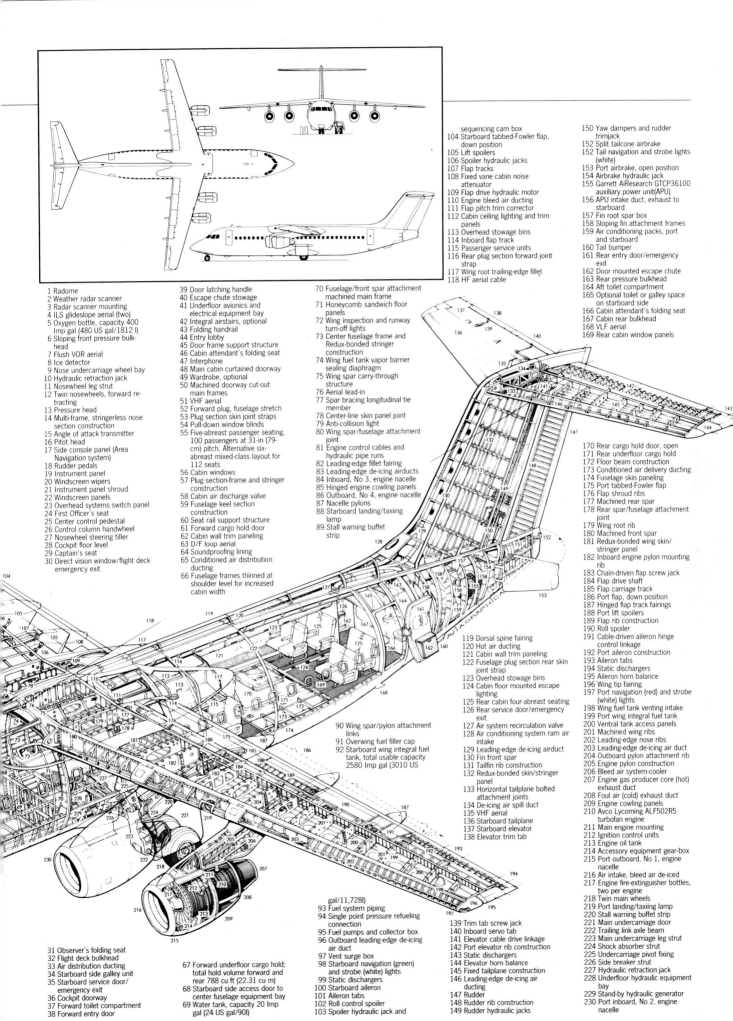

sequencing cam box
104 Starboard tabbed-Fowler flap, down position
105 Lift spoilers
106 Spoiler hydraulic jacks
107 Flap tracks
108 Fixed vane cabin noise attenuator
109 Flap drive hydraulic motor
110 Engine bleed air ducting
111 Flap pitch trim corrector
112 Cabin ceiling lighting and trim panels
113 Overhead stowage bins
114 Inboard flap track
115 Passenger service units
116 Rear plug section forward joint strap
117 Wing root trailing-edge fillet
118 HF aerial cable

150 Yaw dampers and rudder trimjack
152 Split tailcone airbrake
152 Tail navigation and strobe lights (white)
153 Port airbrake, open position
154 Airbrake hydraulic jack
155 Garrett AiResearch GTCP36100 auxiliary power unit(APU)
156 APU intake duct, exhaust to starboard
157 Fin root spar box
158 Sloping fin attachment frames
159 Air conditioning packs, port and starboard
160 Tail bumper
161 Rear entry door/emergency exit
162 Door mounted escape chute
163 Rear pressure bulkhead
164 Aft toilet compartment
165 Optional toilet or galley space on starboard side
166 Cabin attendant's folding seat
167 Cabin rear bulkhead
168 VLF aerial
169 Rear cabin window panels

1 Radome
2 Weather radar scanner
3 Radar scanner mounting
4 ILS glideslope aerial (two)
5 Oxygen bottle, capacity 400 Imp gal (480 US gal/1812 l)
6 Sloping front pressure bulkhead
7 Flush VOR aerial
8 Ice detector
9 Nose undercarriage wheel bay
10 Hydraulic retraction jack
11 Nosewheel leg strut
12 Twin nosewheels, forward retracting
13 Pressure head
14 Multi-frame, stringerless nose section construction
15 Angle of attack transmitter
16 Pitot head
17 Side console panel (Area Navigation system)
18 Rudder pedals
19 Instrument panel
20 Windscreen wipers
21 Instrument panel shroud
22 Windscreen panels
23 Overhead systems switch panel
24 First Officer's seat
25 Center control pedestal
26 Control column handwheel
27 Nosewheel steering tiller
28 Cockpit floor level
29 Captain's seat
30 Direct vision window/flight deck emergency exit

31 Observer's folding seat
32 Flight deck bulkhead
33 Air distribution ducting
34 Starboard side galley unit
35 Starboard service door/emergency exit
36 Cockpit doorway
37 Forward toilet compartment
38 Forward entry door

39 Door latching handle
40 Escape chute stowage
41 Underfloor avionics and electrical equipment bay
42 Integral airstairs, optional
43 Folding handrail
44 Entry lobby
45 Door frame support structure
46 Cabin attendant's folding seat
47 Interphone
48 Main cabin curtained doorway
49 Wardrobe, optional
50 Machined doorway cut-out main frames
51 VHF aerial
52 Forward plug, fuselage stretch
53 Plug section skin joint straps
54 Pull-down window blinds
55 Five-abreast passenger seating, 100 passengers at 31-in (79-cm) pitch. Alternative six-abreast mixed-class layout for 112 seats
56 Cabin windows
57 Plug section-frame and stringer construction
58 Cabin air discharge valve
59 Fuselage keel section construction
60 Seat rail support structure
61 Forward cargo hold door
62 Cabin wall trim paneling
63 D/F loop aerial
64 Soundproofing lining
65 Conditioned air distribution ducting
66 Fuselage frames thinned at shoulder level for increased cabin width

67 Forward underfloor cargo hold; total hold volume forward and rear 788 cu ft (22.31 cu m)
68 Starboard side access door to center fuselage equipment bay
69 Water tank, capacity 20 Imp gal (24 US gal/90l)

70 Fuselage/front spar attachment machined main frame
71 Honeycomb sandwich floor panels
72 Wing inspection and runway turn-off lights
73 Center fuselage frame and Redux-bonded stringer construction
74 Wing fuel tank vapor barrier sealing diaphragm
75 Wing spar carry-through structure
76 Aerial lead-in
77 Spar bracing longitudinal tie member
78 Center-line skin panel joint
79 Anti-collision light
80 Wing spar/fuselage attachment joint
81 Engine control cables and hydraulic pipe runs
82 Leading-edge fillet fairing
83 Leading-edge de-icing airducts
84 Inboard, No 3, engine nacelle
85 Hinged engine cowling panels
86 Outboard, No 4, engine nacelle
87 Nacelle pylons
88 Starboard landing/taxiing lamp
89 Stall warning buffet strip

90 Wing spar/pylon attachment links
91 Overwing fuel filler cap
92 Starboard wing integral fuel tank, total usable capacity 2580 Imp gal (3010 US gal/11,728l)
93 Fuel system piping
94 Single point pressure refueling connection
95 Fuel pumps and collector box
96 Outboard leading-edge de-icing air duct
97 Vent surge box
98 Starboard navigation (green) and strobe (white) lights
99 Static dischargers
100 Starboard aileron
101 Aileron tabs
102 Roll control spoiler
103 Spoiler hydraulic jack and

119 Dorsal spine fairing
120 Hot air ducting
121 Cabin wall trim paneling
122 Fuselage plug section rear skin joint strap
123 Overhead stowage bins
124 Cabin floor mounted escape lighting
125 Rear cabin four-abreast seating
126 Rear service door/emergency exit
127 Air system recirculation valve
128 Air conditioning system ram air intake
129 Leading-edge de-icing airduct
130 Fin front spar
131 Tailfin rib construction
132 Redux-bonded skin/stringer panel
133 Horizontal tailplane bolted attachment joints
134 De-icing air spill duct
135 VHF aerial
136 Starboard tailplane
137 Starboard elevator
138 Elevator trim tab

139 Trim tab screw jack
140 Inboard servo tab
141 Elevator cable drive linkage
142 Port elevator rib construction
143 Static dischargers
144 Elevator horn balance
145 Fixed tailplane construction
146 Leading-edge de-icing air ducting
147 Rudder
148 Rudder rib construction
149 Rudder hydraulic jacks

170 Rear cargo hold door, open
171 Rear underfloor cargo hold
172 Floor beam construction
173 Conditioned air delivery ducting
174 Fuselage skin paneling
175 Port tabbed-Fowler flap
176 Flap shroud ribs
177 Machined rear spar
178 Rear spar/fuselage attachment joint
179 Wing root rib
180 Machined front spar
181 Redux-bonded wing skin/stringer panel
182 Inboard engine pylon mounting rib
183 Chain-driven flap screw jack
184 Flap drive shaft
185 Flap carriage track
186 Port flap, down position
187 Hinged flap track fairings
188 Port lift spoilers
189 Flap rib construction
190 Roll spoiler
191 Cable-driven aileron hinge control linkage
192 Port aileron construction
193 Aileron tabs
194 Static dischargers
195 Aileron horn balance
196 Wing tip fairing
197 Port navigation (red) and strobe (white) lights
198 Wing fuel tank venting intake
199 Port wing integral fuel tank
200 Ventral tank access panels
201 Machined wing ribs
202 Leading-edge nose ribs
203 Leading-edge de-icing air duct
204 Outboard pylon attachment rib
205 Engine pylon construction
206 Bleed air system-cooler
207 Engine gas producer core (hot) exhaust duct
208 Foul air (cold) exhaust duct
209 Engine cowling panels
210 Avco Lycoming ALF502R5 turbofan engine
211 Main engine mounting
212 Ignition control units
213 Engine oil tank
214 Accessory equipment gear-box
215 Port outboard, No 1, engine nacelle
216 Air intake, bleed air de-iced
217 Engine fire-extinguisher bottles, two per engine
218 Twin main wheels
219 Port landing/taxiing lamp
220 Stall warning buffet strip
221 Main undercarriage door
222 Trailing link axle beam
223 Main undercarriage leg strut
224 Shock absorber strut
225 Undercarriage pivot fixing
226 Side breaker strut
227 Hydraulic retraction jack
228 Underfloor hydraulic equipment bay
229 Stand-by hydraulic generator
230 Port inboard, No 2, engine nacelle

NETHERLANDS

Fokker 100

SPECIFICATION Model 100
Origin: Netherlands
Type: short/medium-range jetliner
Accommodation: flight crew of 2; up to 107 passengers
Powerplant: two 15,100-lb (6850-kg) thrust Rolls Royce Tay (Mk 650-15) turbofans
Performance: maximum cruising speed 465kts (861km/h) at 24,200 ft (7375m); range with 107 passengers 1340n.mls (2483km)
Weights: empty operating 54,100lb (24,540kg) maximum take-off 98,000lb (44,450kg)
Dimensions: span 92ft 1½in (28.08m); length 116ft 6¾in (35.53m); height 27ft 10½in (8.5m); wing area 1006sq ft (93.5m²)

An Air Europe Fokker 100 lands at London, Gatwick

The Dutch Fokker company, with its important niche in the regional aircraft market, launched the Fokker 100 in November 1983, along with the Fokker 50, the successor to the twin-turboprop F27 Friendship. The Fokker 100 itself followed on from the Fokker F28-4000 twin-jet transport. It has a stretched fuselage, Rolls Royce Tay turbofans and modernized flight deck (allowing Category IIIB autolandings) and passenger cabin interior. Since the first production model was delivered in February 1988 world airlines have more than 55 of the type in service.

Fokker claim the 100 to be the world's quietest airliner, meeting the most stringent international noise regulations. In 1989 the aircraft was accepted for operations at John Wayne Airport in California, which imposes one of the strictest noise limitations in the world.

The Fokker 100 Convertible being developed by the company is designed for quick transfer between cargo and palletized seating, allowing the same aircraft to be used for passengers during the day and freight at night. The changeover would take a three-man ground crew just 20 minutes. In January 1991 total orders stood at 246 aircraft, with another 128 options. From 1993 the basic Fokker 100 will be offered with an increased take-off weight of 45,900kg. Increased fuel capacity will extend the maximum range by up to 280 nautical miles. Fokker is currently considering the launch of a derivative aircraft, the Fokker 130. Featuring a six-metre fuselage stretch and powered by higher-thrust engines, this aircraft will carry 130 passengers and may enter service in 1996.

Orders include: Air Europe (15), American Airlines (75), Garuda Indonesia (12), GPA Fokker 100 (40), ILFC (7), Ivory Coast (1), KLM (6), Pelita (1), Swissair (10), Taiwan Airlines (2), TAT (8), USAir (40).

CUTAWAY DRAWING OF FOKKER 100

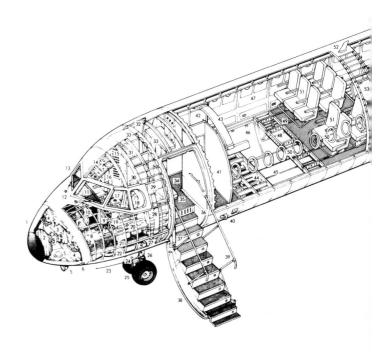

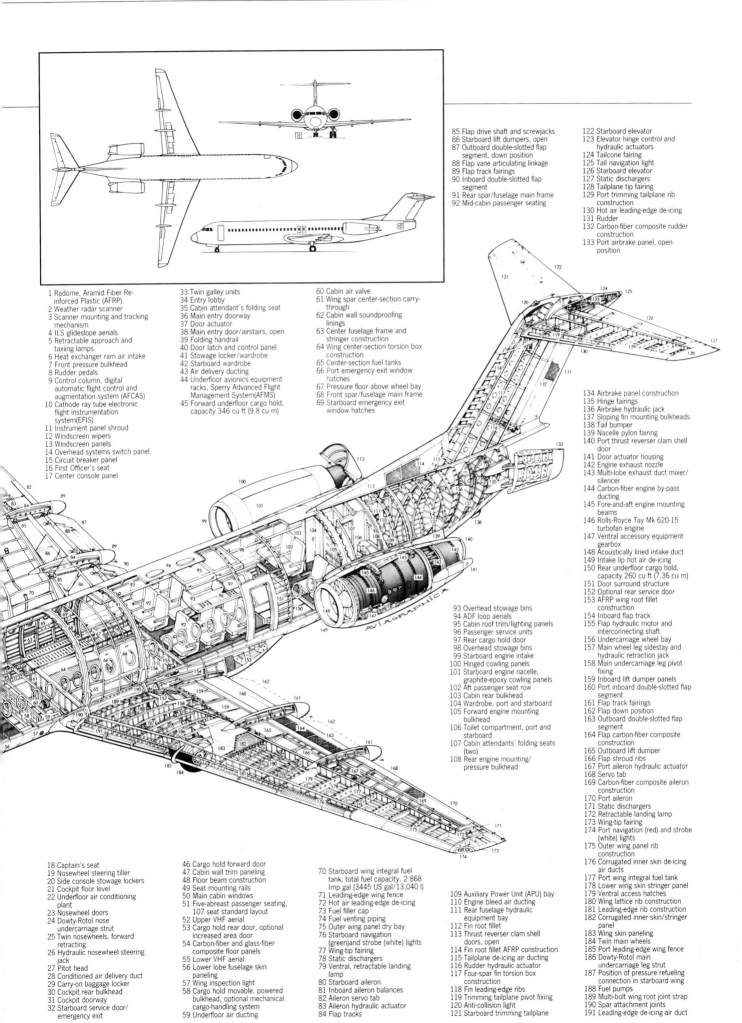

85 Flap drive shaft and screwjacks
86 Starboard lift dumpers, open
87 Outboard double-slotted flap segment, down position
88 Flap vane articulating linkage
89 Flap track fairings
90 Inboard double-slotted flap segment
91 Rear spar/fuselage main frame
92 Mid-cabin passenger seating

122 Starboard elevator
123 Elevator hinge control and hydraulic actuators
124 Tailcone fairing
125 Tail navigation light
126 Starboard elevator
127 Static dischargers
128 Tailplane tip fairing
129 Port trimming tailplane rib construction
130 Hot air leading-edge de-icing
131 Rudder
132 Carbon-fiber composite rudder construction
133 Port airbrake panel, open position

1 Radome, Aramid Fiber Reinforced Plastic (AFRP)
2 Weather radar scanner
3 Scanner mounting and tracking mechanism
4 ILS glideslope aerials
5 Retractable approach and taxiing lamps
6 Heat exchanger ram air intake
7 Front pressure bulkhead
8 Rudder pedals
9 Control column, digital automatic flight control and augmentation system (AFCAS)
10 Cathode ray tube electronic flight instrumentation system(EFIS)
11 Instrument panel shroud
12 Windscreen wipers
13 Windscreen panels
14 Overhead systems switch panel
15 Circuit breaker panel
16 First Officer's seat
17 Center console panel

33 Twin galley units
34 Entry lobby
35 Cabin attendant's folding seat
36 Main entry doorway
37 Door actuator
38 Main entry door/airstairs, open
39 Folding handrail
40 Door latch and control panel
41 Stowage locker/wardrobe
42 Starboard wardrobe
43 Air delivery ducting
44 Underfloor avionics equipment racks, Sperry Advanced Flight Management System(AFMS)
45 Forward underfloor cargo hold, capacity 346 cu ft (9.8 cu m)

60 Cabin air valve
61 Wing spar center-section carry-through
62 Cabin wall soundproofing linings
63 Center fuselage frame and stringer construction
64 Wing center-section torsion box construction
65 Center-section fuel tanks
66 Port emergency exit window hatches
67 Pressure floor above wheel bay
68 Front spar/fuselage main frame
69 Starboard emergency exit window hatches

134 Airbrake panel construction
135 Hinge fairings
136 Airbrake hydraulic jack
137 Sloping fin mounting bulkheads
138 Tail bumper
139 Nacelle pylon fairing
140 Port thrust reverser clam shell door
141 Door actuator housing
142 Engine exhaust nozzle
143 Multi-lobe exhaust duct mixer/silencer
144 Carbon-fiber engine by-pass ducting
145 Fore-and-aft engine mounting beams
146 Rolls-Royce Tay Mk 620-15 turbofan engine
147 Ventral accessory equipment gearbox
148 Acoustically lined intake duct
149 Intake lip hot air de-icing
150 Rear underfloor cargo hold, capacity 260 cu ft (7.36 cu m)
151 Door surround structure
152 Optional rear service door
153 AFRP wing root fillet construction
154 Inboard flap track
155 Flap hydraulic motor and interconnecting shaft
156 Undercarriage wheel bay
157 Main wheel leg sidestay and hydraulic retraction jack
158 Main undercarriage leg pivot fixing
159 Inboard lift dumper panels
160 Port inboard double-slotted flap segment
161 Flap track fairings
162 Flap down position
163 Outboard double-slotted flap segment
164 Flap carbon-fiber composite construction
165 Outboard lift dumper
166 Flap shroud ribs
167 Port aileron hydraulic actuator
168 Servo tab
169 Carbon-fiber composite aileron construction
170 Port aileron
171 Static dischargers
172 Retractable landing lamp
173 Wing-tip fairing
174 Port navigation (red) and strobe (white) lights
175 Outer wing panel rib construction
176 Corrugated inner skin de-icing air ducts
177 Port wing integral fuel tank
178 Lower wing skin stringer panel
179 Ventral access hatches
180 Wing lattice rib construction
181 Leading-edge rib construction
182 Corrugated inner skin/stringer panel
183 Wing skin paneling
184 Twin main wheels
185 Port leading-edge wing fence
186 Dowty-Rotol main undercarriage leg strut
187 Position of pressure refueling connection in starboard wing
188 Fuel pumps
189 Multi-bolt wing root joint strap
190 Spar attachment joints
191 Leading-edge de-icing air duct

93 Overhead stowage bins
94 ADF loop aerials
95 Cabin roof trim/lighting panels
96 Passenger service units
97 Rear cargo hold door
98 Overhead stowage bins
99 Starboard engine intake
100 Hinged cowling panels
101 Starboard engine nacelle, graphite-epoxy cowling panels
102 Aft passenger seat row
103 Cabin rear bulkhead
104 Wardrobe, port and starboard
105 Forward engine mounting bulkhead
106 Toilet compartment, port and starboard
107 Cabin attendants' folding seats (two)
108 Rear engine mounting/pressure bulkhead

109 Auxiliary Power Unit (APU) bay
110 Engine bleed air ducting
111 Rear fuselage hydraulic equipment bay
112 Fin root fillet
113 Thrust reverser clam shell doors, open
114 Fin root fillet AFRP construction
115 Tailplane de-icing air ducting
116 Rudder hydraulic actuator
117 Four-spar fin torsion box construction
118 Fin leading-edge ribs
119 Trimming tailplane pivot fixing
120 Anti-collision light
121 Starboard trimming tailplane

18 Captain's seat
19 Nosewheel steering tiller
20 Side console stowage lockers
21 Cockpit floor level
22 Underfloor air conditioning plant
23 Nosewheel doors
24 Dowty-Rotol nose undercarriage strut
25 Twin nosewheels, forward retracting
26 Hydraulic nosewheel steering jack
27 Pitot head
28 Conditioned air delivery duct
29 Carry-on baggage locker
30 Cockpit rear bulkhead
31 Cockpit doorway
32 Starboard service door/emergency exit

46 Cargo hold forward door
47 Cabin wall trim paneling
48 Floor beam construction
49 Seat mounting rails
50 Main cabin windows
51 Five-abreast passenger seating, 107 seat standard layout
52 Upper VHF aerial
53 Cargo hold rear door, optional increased area door
54 Carbon-fiber and glass-fiber composite floor panels
55 Lower VHF aerial
56 Lower lobe fuselage skin paneling
57 Wing inspection light
58 Cargo hold movable, powered bulkhead, optional mechanical cargo-handling system
59 Underfloor air ducting

70 Starboard wing integral fuel tank, total fuel capacity, 2 868 Imp gal (3445 US gal/13,040 l)
71 Leading-edge wing fence
72 Hot air leading-edge de-icing
73 Fuel filler cap
74 Fuel venting piping
75 Outer wing panel dry bay
76 Starboard navigation (green)and strobe (white) lights
77 Wing-tip fairing
78 Static dischargers
79 Ventral, retractable landing lamp
80 Starboard aileron
81 Inboard aileron balances
82 Aileron servo tab
83 Aileron hydraulic actuator
84 Flap tracks

23

USSR

Ilyushin Il-96

Aviaexport

This Ilyushin Il-96-300, in Aeroflot colors, demonstrates its manoeuverability in flight

SPECIFICATION Model Il-96-300

Origin: USSR
Type: wide-body long-range jetliner
Accommodation: flight crew of 3; up to 300 passengers
Powerplant: four 35,275-lb (16,000-kg) thrust Soloviev PS-90A high bypass ratio turbofans
Performance: maximum cruising speed 486kts (900km/h) at 39,400 ft (12,000m); range with full passenger payload 4860n.mls (9000km)
Weights: empty operating 258,000lb (117,000kg) maximum take-off 476,200lb (216,000kg)
Dimensions: span 189ft 2in (57.66m); length 181ft 7in (55.34m); height 57ft 7in (17.55m) wing area 4215sq ft (391.6m^2)

The Soviet Union's first attempt to build a practical wide-body airliner, the Il-86, was not a success. It was hampered by range problems (with its thirsty engines) and by the fact that passenger comfort fell below western standards. A completely new aircraft, the Ilyushin Il-96, seems set to supplant the less than fully successful Il-86. The first prototype flew on 28 September 1988. A "stretched" 375-seat version, intended for high-capacity medium-range operations, the Il-96-M, is also under development. It is hoped that this version will benefit from the use of advanced western avionics. The US engine manufacturer, Pratt & Whitney, had discussions with the US government in order to obtain approval for the possible installation of its PW2037 engines on the Il-96-M.

The Il-96 is a four-jet wide-body, seemingly derived from the earlier aircraft, but is in fact a virtually new design. The use of four Soloviev PS-90A, high-bypass turbofans is intended to solve the range problems experienced with the Il-86. The aircraft can carry 300 passengers over 5600 miles (9000km) compared with the Il-86's 2200 miles (3500km) range.

The Il-96 is the Soviet Union's first "fly-by-wire" airliner. Although it is superficially similar to the earlier aircraft, only the tailplanes and the fuselage's six-meter diameter are identical. At 216 tonnes, the Il-96-300 is eight tonnes heavier than the fully loaded Il-86. It has an increased wingspan (57.6m compared to the Il-86's 48.1m), shorter fuselage (55.4m against 59.5m) and a thrust-to-weight ratio of 0.3 (Il-86: 0.25). The range of the Il-96-300 is almost double that of the Il-86, because of more efficient engines and a lighter structure of new alloys and composites, combined with aerodynamic improvements, including the use of winglets.

Two other studies for future developments have been reported – a heavy-weight version, with a range of 9300 miles (15,000km) carrying 235 to 300 passengers, and a twin-engined version using turbofans similar to the outsize, heavy-lift Antonov An-124 transport's Lotarev D-18Ts.

CUTAWAY DRAWING OF ILYUSHIN IL-96-300

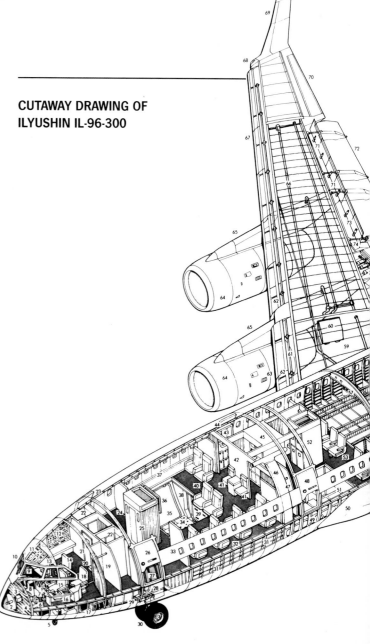

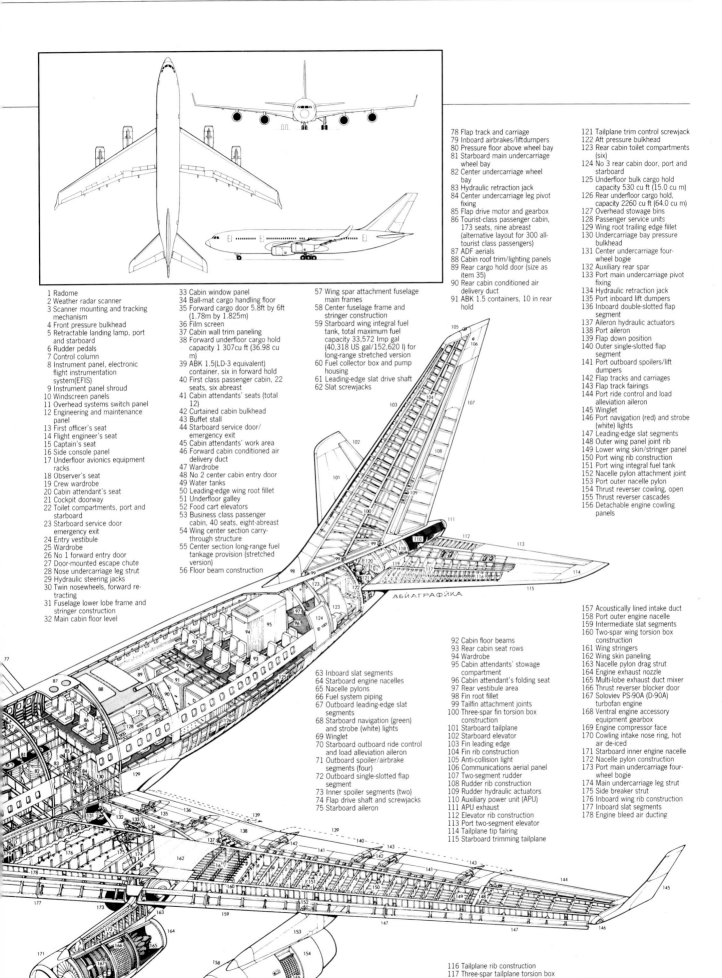

78 Flap track and carriage
79 Inboard airbrakes/liftdumpers
80 Pressure floor above wheel bay
81 Starboard main undercarriage wheel bay
82 Center undercarriage wheel bay
83 Hydraulic retraction jack
84 Center undercarriage leg pivot fixing
85 Flap drive motor and gearbox
86 Tourist-class passenger cabin, 173 seats, nine abreast (alternative layout for 300 all-tourist class passengers)
87 ADF aerials
88 Cabin roof trim/lighting panels
89 Rear cargo hold door (size as item 35)
90 Rear cabin conditioned air delivery duct
91 ABK 1.5 containers, 10 in rear hold

121 Tailplane trim control screwjack
122 Aft pressure bulkhead
123 Rear cabin toilet compartments (six)
124 No 3 rear cabin door, port and starboard
125 Underfloor bulk cargo hold capacity 530 cu ft (15.0 cu m)
126 Rear underfloor cargo hold, capacity 2260 cu ft (64.0 cu m)
127 Overhead stowage bins
128 Passenger service units
129 Wing root trailing edge fillet
130 Undercarriage bay pressure bulkhead
131 Center undercarriage four-wheel bogie
132 Auxiliary rear spar
133 Port main undercarriage pivot fixing
134 Hydraulic retraction jack
135 Port inboard lift dumpers
136 Inboard double-slotted flap segment
137 Aileron hydraulic actuators
138 Port aileron
139 Flap down position
140 Outer single-slotted flap segment
141 Port outboard spoilers/lift dumpers
142 Flap tracks and carriages
143 Flap track fairings
144 Port ride control and load alleviation aileron
145 Winglet
146 Port navigation (red) and strobe (white) lights
147 Leading-edge slat segments
148 Outer wing panel joint rib
149 Lower wing skin/stringer panel
150 Port wing rib construction
151 Port wing integral fuel tank
152 Nacelle pylon attachment joint
153 Port outer nacelle pylon
154 Thrust reverser cowling, open
155 Thrust reverser cascades
156 Detachable engine cowling panels

1 Radome
2 Weather radar scanner
3 Scanner mounting and tracking mechanism
4 Front pressure bulkhead
5 Retractable landing lamp, port and starboard
6 Rudder pedals
7 Control column
8 Instrument panel, electronic flight instrumentation system(EFIS)
9 Instrument panel shroud
10 Windscreen panels
11 Overhead systems switch panel
12 Engineering and maintenance panel
13 First officer's seat
14 Flight engineer's seat
15 Captain's seat
16 Side console panel
17 Underfloor avionics equipment racks
18 Observer's seat
19 Crew wardrobe
20 Cabin attendant's seat
21 Cockpit doorway
22 Toilet compartments, port and starboard
23 Starboard service door emergency exit
24 Entry vestibule
25 Wardrobe
26 No 1 forward entry door
27 Door-mounted escape chute
28 Nose undercarriage leg strut
29 Hydraulic steering jacks
30 Twin nosewheels, forward re-tracting
31 Fuselage lower lobe frame and stringer construction
32 Main cabin floor level

33 Cabin window panel
34 Ball-mat cargo handling floor
35 Forward cargo door 5.8ft by 6ft (1.78m by 1.825m)
36 Film screen
37 Cabin wall trim paneling
38 Forward underfloor cargo hold capacity 1 307cu ft (36.98 cu m)
39 ABK 1.5(LD-3 equivalent) container, six in forward hold
40 First class passenger cabin, 22 seats, six abreast
41 Cabin attendants' seats (total 12)
42 Curtained cabin bulkhead
43 Buffet stall
44 Starboard service door/emergency exit
45 Cabin attendants' work area
46 Forward cabin conditioned air delivery duct
47 Wardrobe
48 No 2 center cabin entry door
49 Water tanks
50 Leading-edge wing root fillet
51 Underfloor galley
52 Food cart elevators
53 Business class passenger cabin, 40 seats, eight-abreast
54 Wing center section carry-through structure
55 Center section long-range fuel tankage provision (stretched version)
56 Floor beam construction

57 Wing spar attachment fuselage main frames
58 Center fuselage frame and stringer construction
59 Starboard wing integral fuel tank, total maximum fuel capacity 33,572 Imp gal (40,318 US gal/152,620 l) for long-range stretched version
60 Fuel collector box and pump housing
61 Leading-edge slat drive shaft
62 Slat screwjacks

63 Inboard slat segments
64 Starboard engine nacelles
65 Nacelle pylons
66 Fuel system piping
67 Outboard leading-edge slat segments
68 Starboard navigation (green) and strobe (white) lights
69 Winglet
70 Starboard outboard ride control and load alleviation aileron
71 Outboard spoiler/airbrake segments (four)
72 Outboard single-slotted flap segment
73 Inner spoiler segments (two)
74 Flap drive shaft and screwjacks
75 Starboard aileron

92 Cabin floor beams
93 Rear cabin seat rows
94 Wardrobe
95 Cabin attendants' stowage compartment
96 Cabin attendant's folding seat
97 Rear vestibule area
98 Fin root fillet
99 Tailfin attachment joints
100 Three-spar fin torsion box construction
101 Starboard tailplane
102 Starboard elevator
103 Fin leading edge
104 Fin rib construction
105 Anti-collision light
106 Communications aerial panel
107 Two-segment rudder
108 Rudder rib construction
109 Rudder hydraulic actuators
110 Auxiliary power unit (APU)
111 APU exhaust
112 Elevator rib construction
113 Port two-segment elevator
114 Tailplane tip fairing
115 Starboard trimming tailplane

157 Acoustically lined intake duct
158 Port outer engine nacelle
159 Intermediate slat segments
160 Two-spar wing torsion box construction
161 Wing stringers
162 Wing skin paneling
163 Nacelle pylon drag strut
164 Engine exhaust nozzle
165 Multi-lobe exhaust duct mixer
166 Thrust reverser blocker door
167 Soloviev PS-90A (D-90A) turbofan engine
168 Ventral engine accessory equipment gearbox
169 Engine compressor face
170 Cowling intake nose ring, hot air de-iced
171 Starboard inner engine nacelle
172 Nacelle pylon construction
173 Port main undercarriage four-wheel bogie
174 Main undercarriage leg strut
175 Side breaker strut
176 Inboard wing rib construction
177 Inboard slat segments
178 Engine bleed air ducting

116 Tailplane rib construction
117 Three-spar tailplane torsion box construction
118 Tailplane pivot fixing
119 Sealing plate
120 Tailplane center-section carry-through structure

76 Triplex hydraulic actuators
77 Inboard double-slotted flap segment

179 Ventral air conditioning pack, port and starboard
180 Wing root rib attachment joint
181 Air conditioning system heat exchanger ram air intake

USA

Lockheed TriStar

Lockheed Aeronautical Systems

This Lockheed L-1011-500 of German airline, LTU, lands at Miami, Florida

SPECIFICATION Model L-1011-500
Origin: USA
Type: wide-body long-range jetliner
Accommodation: flight crew of 3; up to 330 passengers
Powerplant: three 50,000-lb (22,680-kg) thrust Rolls Royce RB.211-524B turbofans
Performance: maximum cruising speed 518kts(959 km/h) at 30,000 ft (9145m); range (at M0.83) with 246 passengers and fuel reserves 5098n.mls miles (9442km)
Weights: empty operating 242,967lb (110,208kg) maximum take-off 496,000 lb (224,992 kg)
Dimensions: span 164ft 4in (50.08m); length 164ft 4in (50.05m); height 55ft 9in (17.01m)

During the late 1960s America's three major civil air transport builders were trying to find the right technical and marketing formula for the coming wide-body era of mass air travel. Boeing chose to scale up the 707 into the huge four jet 747.

Lockheed, like their rivals McDonnell Douglas with the DC-10, chose a tri-jet layout after intensive market research showed the excellent prospects for a short to medium range, mass people-mover. American Airlines effectively provided the impetus for the project with a requirement, stated in 1966, for a 250-seater to operate the Chicago-Los Angeles route.

After discussions with other potential clients, Lockheed moved from an original twin-jet to a tri-jet configuration and selected the as yet unproven Rolls-Royce RB.211 turbofan as the powerplant because of its promised fuel economy. Early difficulties with the RB.211 led to intervention by the British government to rescue the British engine maker in 1971 and brought huge problems for Lockheed, beaten to the punch by their rivals in getting wide-bodies to their airline customers.

Frustrated by the delay, American Airlines eventually bought the DC-10 instead. This went into revenue-earning service on the Chicago-Los Angeles route on 5 August 1971.

The prototype TriStar flew on 16 November 1971. The first revenue-earning flights were made by Eastern in April 1972 and by TWA a few days later, both flying the first production model, the L-1011-1. The L-1011-100, which entered service in 1975, is an extended-range model with extra fuel carried in center-section tanks. The L-11011-200 model, which followed, was powered by RB.211-524 engines. These delivered improved take-off and climb performance from hot-and-high airfields and longer range.

The L-1011-500 model introduced a substantial improvement in range. In contrast to the normal stretch process of developing aircraft, the -500's airframe was shortened with a 4.11-m reduction in length of a fuselage now accommodating 246 standard and 300 high-density passengers. Maximum range with a full load was, however, increased to over 6000 miles (9600km) on the power of three RB.211-524Bs. The first L-1001-500 entered service in May 1979 with British Airways. The last TriStar was delivered in 1983.

Of the total of 250 TriStars built, 237 remain in airline service. The biggest single fleet operator is Delta with 22 -1 series, one -200, six -250s and ten -500s. British Airways operates nine -1 series and eight -500s.

**CUTAWAY DRAWING OF
LOCKHEED
L-1011-500 TRISTAR**

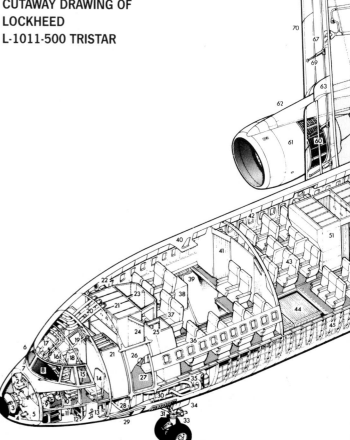

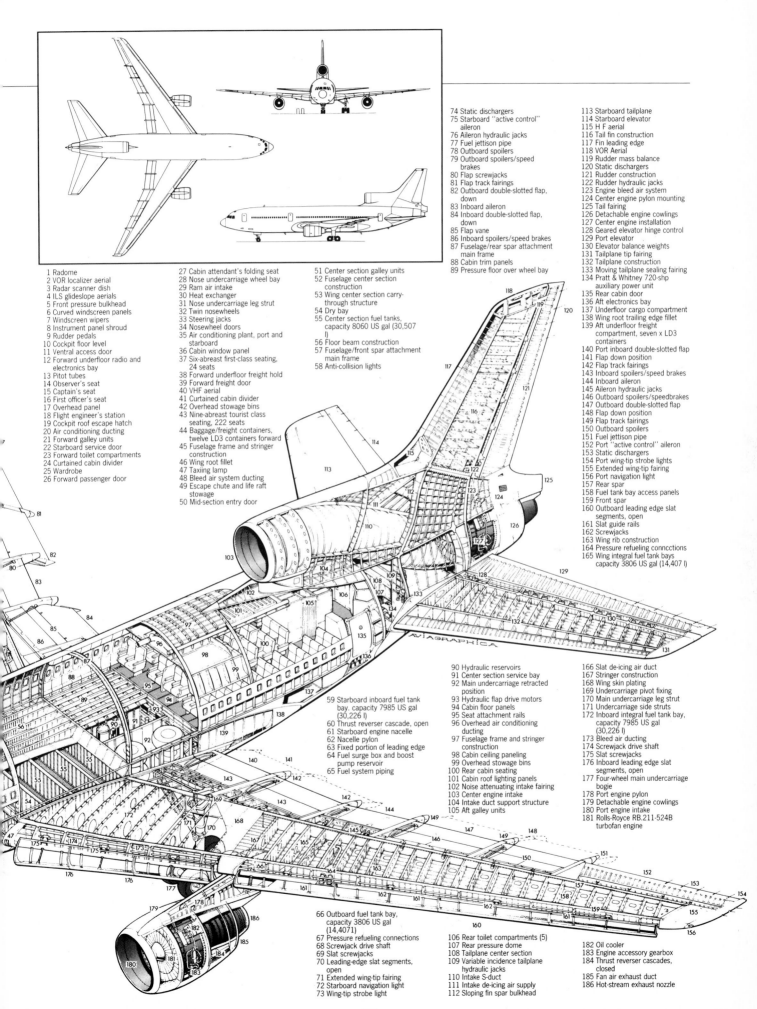

74 Static dischargers
75 Starboard "active control" aileron
76 Aileron hydraulic jacks
77 Fuel jettison pipe
78 Outboard spoilers
79 Outboard spoilers/speed brakes
80 Flap screwjacks
81 Flap track fairings
82 Outboard double-slotted flap, down
83 Inboard aileron
84 Inboard double-slotted flap, down
85 Flap vane
86 Inboard spoilers/speed brakes
87 Fuselage/rear spar attachment main frame
88 Cabin trim panels
89 Pressure floor over wheel bay

113 Starboard tailplane
114 Starboard elevator
115 H F aerial
116 Tail fin construction
117 Fin leading edge
118 VOR Aerial
119 Rudder mass balance
120 Static dischargers
121 Rudder construction
122 Rudder hydraulic jacks
123 Engine bleed air system
124 Center engine pylon mounting
125 Tail fairing
126 Detachable engine cowlings
127 Center engine installation
128 Geared elevator hinge control
129 Port elevator
130 Elevator balance weights
131 Tailplane tip fairing
132 Tailplane construction
133 Moving tailplane sealing fairing
134 Pratt & Whitney 720-shp auxiliary power unit
135 Rear cabin door
136 Aft electronics bay
137 Underfloor cargo compartment
138 Wing root trailing edge fillet
139 Aft underfloor freight compartment, seven x LD3 containers
140 Port inboard double-slotted flap
141 Flap down position
142 Flap track fairings
143 Inboard spoilers/speed brakes
144 Inboard aileron
145 Aileron hydraulic jacks
146 Outboard spoilers/speedbrakes
147 Outboard double-slotted flap
148 Flap down position
149 Flap track fairings
150 Outboard spoilers
151 Fuel jettison pipe
152 Port "active control" aileron
153 Static dischargers
154 Port wing-tip strobe lights
155 Extended wing-tip fairing
156 Port navigation light
157 Rear spar
158 Fuel tank bay access panels
159 Front spar
160 Outboard leading edge slat segments, open
161 Slat guide rails
162 Screwjacks
163 Wing rib construction
164 Pressure refueling connections
165 Wing integral fuel tank bays capacity 3806 US gal (14,407 l)

1 Radome
2 VOR localizer aerial
3 Radar scanner dish
4 ILS glideslope aerials
5 Front pressure bulkhead
6 Curved windscreen panels
7 Windscreen wipers
8 Instrument panel shroud
9 Rudder pedals
10 Cockpit floor level
11 Ventral access door
12 Forward underfloor radio and electronics bay
13 Pitot tubes
14 Observer's seat
15 Captain's seat
16 First officer's seat
17 Overhead panel
18 Flight engineer's station
19 Cockpit roof escape hatch
20 Air conditioning ducting
21 Forward galley units
22 Starboard service door
23 Forward toilet compartments
24 Curtained cabin divider
25 Wardrobe
26 Forward passenger door

27 Cabin attendant's folding seat
28 Nose undercarriage wheel bay
29 Ram air intake
30 Heat exchanger
31 Nose undercarriage leg strut
32 Twin nosewheels
33 Steering jacks
34 Nosewheel doors
35 Air conditioning plant, port and starboard
36 Cabin window panel
37 Six-abreast first-class seating, 24 seats
38 Forward underfloor freight hold
39 Forward freight door
40 VHF aerial
41 Curtained cabin divider
42 Overhead stowage bins
43 Nine-abreast tourist class seating, 222 seats
44 Baggage/freight containers, twelve LD3 containers forward
45 Fuselage frame and stringer construction
46 Wing root fillet
47 Taxiing lamp
48 Bleed air system ducting
49 Escape chute and life raft stowage
50 Mid-section entry door

51 Center section galley units
52 Fuselage center section construction
53 Wing center section carry-through structure
54 Dry bay
55 Center section fuel tanks, capacity 8060 US gal (30,507 l)
56 Floor beam construction
57 Fuselage/front spar attachment main frame
58 Anti-collision lights

59 Starboard inboard fuel tank bay. capacity 7985 US gal (30,226 l)
60 Thrust reverser cascade, open
61 Starboard engine nacelle
62 Nacelle pylon
63 Fixed portion of leading edge
64 Fuel surge box and boost pump reservoir
65 Fuel system piping

66 Outboard fuel tank bay, capacity 3806 US gal (14,4071)
67 Pressure refueling connections
68 Screwjack drive shaft
69 Slat screwjacks
70 Leading-edge slat segments, open
71 Extended wing-tip fairing
72 Starboard navigation light
73 Wing-tip strobe light

90 Hydraulic reservoirs
91 Center section service bay
92 Main undercarriage retracted position
93 Hydraulic flap drive motors
94 Cabin floor panels
95 Seat attachment rails
96 Overhead air conditioning ducting
97 Fuselage frame and stringer construction
98 Cabin ceiling paneling
99 Overhead stowage bins
100 Rear cabin seating
101 Cabin roof lighting panels
102 Noise attenuating intake fairing
103 Center engine intake
104 Intake duct support structure
105 Aft galley units

106 Rear toilet compartments (5)
107 Rear pressure dome
108 Tailplane center section
109 Variable incidence tailplane hydraulic jacks
110 Intake S-duct
111 Intake de-icing air supply
112 Sloping fin spar bulkhead

166 Slat de-icing air duct
167 Stringer construction
168 Wing skin plating
169 Undercarriage pivot fixing
170 Main undercarriage leg strut
171 Undercarriage side struts
172 Inboard integral fuel tank bay, capacity 7985 US gal (30,226 l)
173 Bleed air ducting
174 Screwjack drive shaft
175 Slat screwjacks
176 Inboard leading edge slat segments, open
177 Four-wheel main undercarriage bogie
178 Port engine pylon
179 Detachable engine cowlings
180 Port engine intake
181 Rolls-Royce RB.211-524B turbofan engine

182 Oil cooler
183 Engine accessory gearbox
184 Thrust reverser cascades, closed
185 Fan air exhaust duct
186 Hot-stream exhaust nozzle

USA

MD-11

McDonnell Douglas

A Delta Airlines McDonnell Douglas MD-11 lands at London, Gatwick

SPECIFICATION Model MD-11

Origin: USA

Type: long-range jetliner

Accommodation: flight crew of 2; up to 405 passengers

Powerplant: three (1) 61,500lb (27,900kg) General Electric CF-680C2-DIF, (2) 60,000lb (27,215kg) Pratt & Whitney PW4460, (3) 65,000lb (29,494kg) Rolls Royce Trent 50, thrust turbofans

Performance: maximum cruising speed 473kts (876km/h) at 35,000 ft (10,670m); range with 323 passengers and fuel reserves 6988n.mls (12,941km)

Weights: empty operating 245,600lb (76,895kg) maximum take-off 602,500lb (273,289kg)

Dimensions: span 169ft 6in (51.7m); length 200ft 10in (61.2m); height 57ft 9in (17.6m)

Development of the MD-11 began in 1985 as a redesigned and renamed follow-on to the DC-10. The aircraft has a fuselage 5.7m longer than the DC-10-30, an advanced wing featuring tip winglets, an advanced two-crew flight deck, revamped interior, an internal fuel "trim-tank" and a smaller horizontal tail with integral fuel tanks The program was launched in December 1986 with orders from launch customers including Federal Express, British Caledonian and Finnair. Construction of the first aircraft began in March 1988.

The prototype MD-11's first flight took place on 10 January 1990 from Long Beach, California. McDonnell Douglas is offering three versions of the aircraft: the 320-passenger MD-11 with a range of 8500 miles (13,700km); a freighter with a payload of 91 tonnes; and a Combi which carries both passengers and freight, capable of taking ten pallets on the main deck, with additional freight below the main deck. Seating capacities on the standard aircraft range from 250 passengers in a three-class arrangement to more than 400 in an all-economy layout. Three power plants are being offered – General Electric's CF6-80C2, the Pratt & Whitney PW4460 and Rolls-Royce's Trent 650.

Stretched versions of the MD-11 are planned as the MD-12X, with a 10.4-m fuselage extension and modified wing. The first will be a shorter-range, 303,500-kg, higher-payload variant. The second MD-12 stretched version will have a completely new wing and regain the range of the original aircraft, with the increased payload.

As at the end of 1990 174 MD-11s had been ordered by 27 airlines. The first to be handed over was to Finnair in December of that year. American, Delta, Varig, KLM, Swissair, CAAC, Garuda and JAL have all placed significant orders.

CUTAWAY DRAWING OF McDONNELL DOUGLAS MD-11

1 Radome
2 Weather radar scanner
3 ILS glidescope aerials
4 Pitot heads
5 Front pressure bulkhead
6 Radome hinge points
7 Windscreen wipers
8 Electrically heated windscreen panels
9 Overhead systems switch panel
10 Maintenance engineering panel
11 Observer's seat
12 First Officer's seat
13 Instrument panel shroud
14 Captain's seat
15 Electronic flight instrumentation system (EFIS), six-colour CRT displays
16 Underfloor avionics equipment bay

24 Forward cabin doorway, port and starboard
25 Cabin attendant's folding seat
26 Nose undercarriage wheel bay
27 Air conditioning system intake ducts
28 Nosewheel steering jacks
29 Twin nosewheels, forward retracting
30 Torque scissor links
31 Nosewheel leg doors
32 Air conditioning packs (two port and one starboard)
33 Sidewall toilet compartment, port and starboard
34 Central galley unit
35 Conditioned air distribution ducting
36 Overhead lockers
37 First-class passenger cabin,

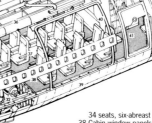

17 Floor hatch access to avionics bay
18 Optional second observer's seat
19 Crew wardrobe
20 Cockpit bulkhead doorway
21 Conditioned air delivery ducting
22 Sidewall galley units, port and starboard
23 Curtained entry lobby

34 seats, six-abreast
38 Cabin window panels
39 Fuselage lower lobe skin paneling
40 Outline of cargo door on windowless all-freight version
41 Mid-cabin entry door, port and starboard
42 Mid-cabin galley unit
43 ATC aerial
44 Sidewall toilet compartments port and starboard
45 Forward freight hold door
46 Door actuating motor
47 Forward underfloor freight hold, capacity 2844cu ft (80.5 cu m)
48 LD3 baggage containers, 18 in forward hold

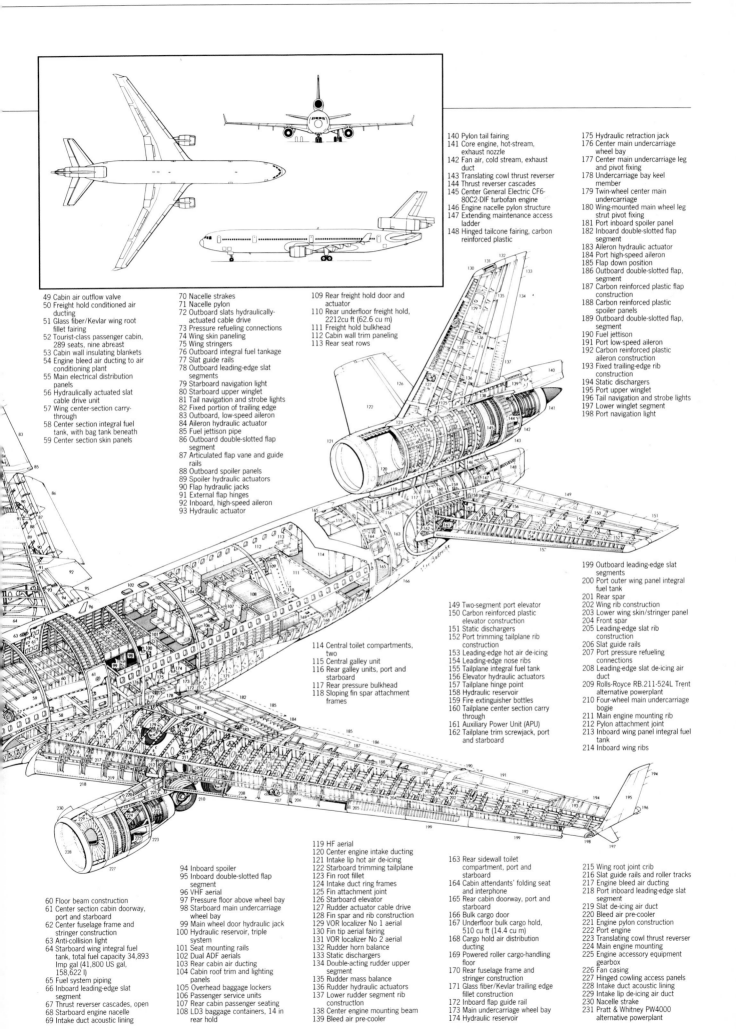

49 Cabin air outflow valve
50 Freight hold conditioned air ducting
51 Glass fiber/Kevlar wing root fillet fairing
52 Tourist-class passenger cabin, 289 seats, nine abreast
53 Cabin wall insulating blankets
54 Engine bleed air ducting to air conditioning plant
55 Main electrical distribution panels
56 Hydraulically actuated slat cable drive unit
57 Wing center-section carry-through
58 Center section integral fuel tank, with bag tank beneath
59 Center section skin panels

70 Nacelle strakes
71 Nacelle pylon
72 Outboard slats hydraulically-actuated cable drive
73 Pressure refueling connections
74 Wing skin paneling
75 Wing stringers
76 Outboard integral fuel tankage
77 Slat guide rails
78 Outboard leading-edge slat segments
79 Starboard navigation light
80 Starboard upper winglet
81 Tail navigation and strobe lights
82 Fixed portion of trailing edge
83 Outboard, low-speed aileron
84 Aileron hydraulic actuator
85 Fuel jettison pipe
86 Outboard double-slotted flap segment
87 Articulated flap vane and guide rails
88 Outboard spoiler panels
89 Spoiler hydraulic actuators
90 Flap hydraulic jacks
91 External flap hinges
92 Inboard, high-speed aileron
93 Hydraulic actuator

109 Rear freight hold door and actuator
110 Rear underfloor freight hold, 2212cu ft (62.6 cu m)
111 Freight hold bulkhead
112 Cabin wall trim paneling
113 Rear seat rows

140 Pylon tail fairing
141 Core engine, hot-stream, exhaust nozzle
142 Fan air, cold stream, exhaust duct
143 Translating cowl thrust reverser
144 Thrust reverser cascades
145 Center General Electric CF6-80C2-DIF turbofan engine
146 Engine nacelle pylon structure
147 Extending maintenance access ladder
148 Hinged tailcone fairing, carbon reinforced plastic

175 Hydraulic retraction jack
176 Center main undercarriage wheel bay
177 Center main undercarriage leg and pivot fixing
178 Undercarriage bay keel member
179 Twin-wheel center main undercarriage
180 Wing-mounted main wheel leg strut pivot fixing
181 Port inboard spoiler panel
182 Inboard double-slotted flap segment
183 Aileron hydraulic actuator
184 Port high-speed aileron
185 Flap down position
186 Outboard double-slotted flap, segment
187 Carbon reinforced plastic flap construction
188 Carbon reinforced plastic spoiler panels
189 Outboard double-slotted flap, segment
190 Fuel jettison
191 Port low-speed aileron
192 Carbon reinforced plastic aileron construction
193 Fixed trailing-edge rib construction
194 Static dischargers
195 Port upper winglet
196 Tail navigation and strobe lights
197 Lower winglet segment
198 Port navigation light

114 Central toilet compartments, two
115 Central galley unit
116 Rear galley units, port and starboard
117 Rear pressure bulkhead
118 Sloping fin spar attachment frames

149 Two-segment port elevator
150 Carbon reinforced plastic elevator construction
151 Static dischargers
152 Port trimming tailplane rib construction
153 Leading-edge hot air de-icing
154 Leading-edge nose ribs
155 Tailplane integral fuel tank
156 Elevator hydraulic actuators
157 Tailplane hinge point
158 Hydraulic reservoir
159 Fire extinguisher bottles
160 Tailplane center section carry through
161 Auxiliary Power Unit (APU)
162 Tailplane trim screwjack, port and starboard

199 Outboard leading-edge slat segments
200 Port outer wing panel integral fuel tank
201 Rear spar
202 Wing rib construction
203 Lower wing skin/stringer panel
204 Front spar
205 Leading-edge slat rib construction
206 Slat guide rails
207 Port pressure refueling connections
208 Leading-edge slat de-icing air duct
209 Rolls-Royce RB.211-524L Trent alternative powerplant
210 Four-wheel main undercarriage bogie
211 Main engine mounting rib
212 Pylon attachment joint
213 Inboard wing panel integral fuel tank
214 Inboard wing ribs

119 HF aerial
120 Center engine intake ducting
121 Intake lip hot air de-icing
122 Starboard trimming tailplane
123 Fin root fillet
124 Intake duct ring frames
125 Fin attachment joint
126 Starboard elevator
127 Rudder actuator cable drive
128 Fin spar and rib construction
129 VOR localizer No 1 aerial
130 Fin tip aerial fairing
131 VOR localizer No 2 aerial
132 Rudder horn balance
133 Static dischargers
134 Double-acting rudder upper segment
135 Rudder mass balance
136 Rudder hydraulic actuators
137 Lower rudder segment rib construction
138 Center engine mounting beam
139 Bleed air pre-cooler

163 Rear sidewall toilet compartment, port and starboard
164 Cabin attendants' folding seat and interphone
165 Rear cabin doorway, port and starboard
166 Bulk cargo door
167 Underfloor bulk cargo hold, 510 cu ft (14.4 cu m)
168 Cargo hold air distribution ducting
169 Powered roller cargo-handling floor
170 Rear fuselage frame and stringer construction
171 Glass fiber/Kevlar trailing edge fillet construction
172 Inboard flap guide rail
173 Main undercarriage wheel bay
174 Hydraulic reservoir

60 Floor beam construction
61 Center section cabin doorway, port and starboard
62 Center fuselage frame and stringer construction
63 Anti-collision light
64 Starboard wing integral fuel tank, total fuel capacity 34,893 Imp gal (41,800 US gal, 158,622 l)
65 Fuel system piping
66 Inboard leading-edge slat segment
67 Thrust reverser cascades, open
68 Starboard engine nacelle
69 Intake duct acoustic lining

94 Inboard spoiler
95 Inboard double-slotted flap segment
96 VHF aerial
97 Pressure floor above wheel bay
98 Starboard main undercarriage wheel bay
99 Main wheel door hydraulic jack
100 Hydraulic reservoir, triple system
101 Seat mounting rails
102 Dual ADF aerials
103 Rear cabin air ducting
104 Cabin roof trim and lighting panels
105 Overhead baggage lockers
106 Passenger service units
107 Rear cabin passenger seating
108 LD3 baggage containers, 14 in rear hold

215 Wing root joint crib
216 Slat guide rails and roller tracks
217 Engine bleed air ducting
218 Port inboard leading-edge slat segment
219 Slat de-icing air duct
220 Bleed air pre-cooler
221 Engine pylon construction
222 Port engine
223 Translating cowl thrust reverser
224 Main engine mounting
225 Engine accessory equipment gearbox
226 Fan casing
227 Hinged cowling access panels
228 Intake duct acoustic lining
229 Intake lip de-icing air duct
230 Nacelle strake
231 Pratt & Whitney PW4000 alternative powerplant

2

THE WORLD'S MAJOR AIRLINES

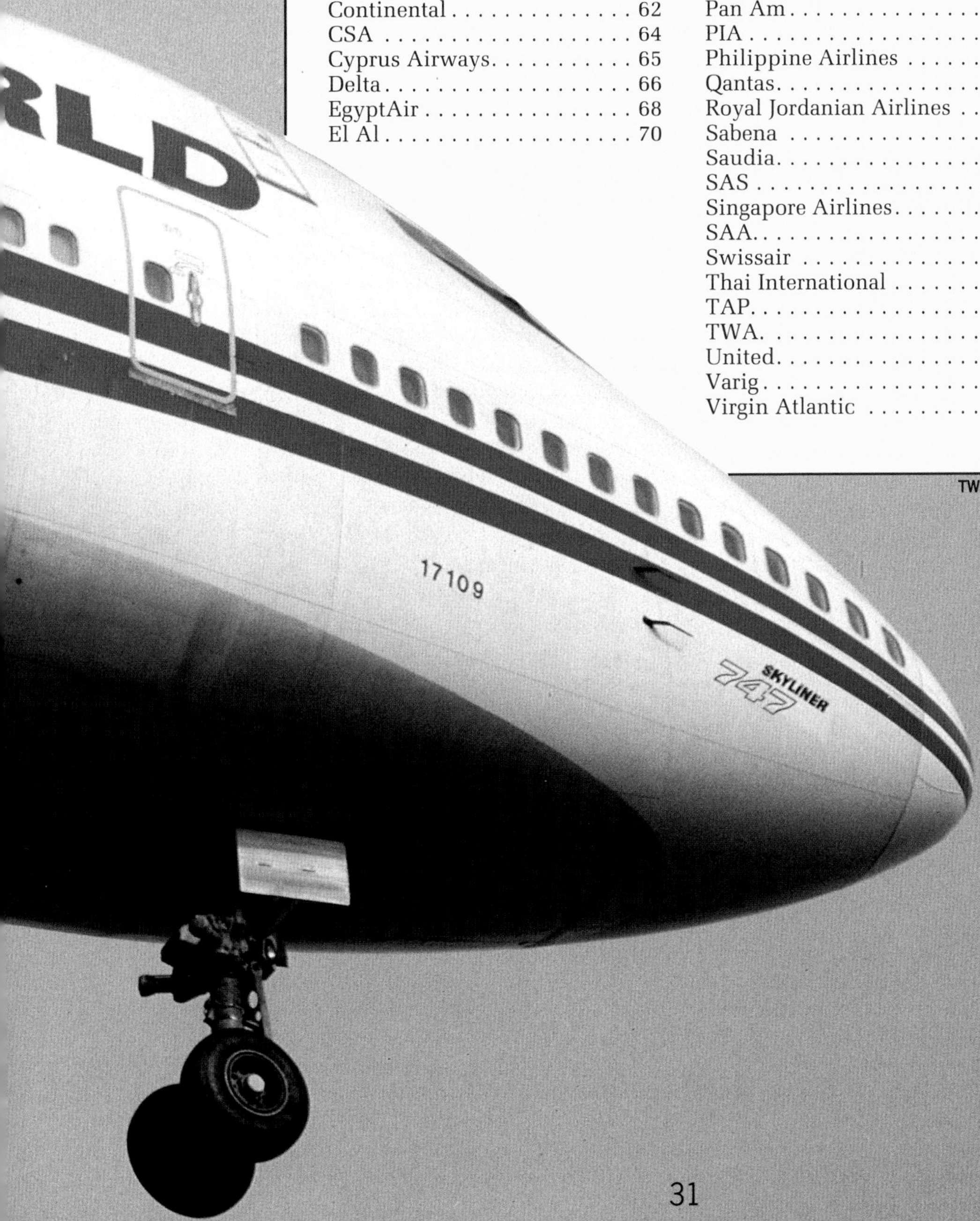

TWA, Boeing 747

REPUBLIC OF IRELAND

Aer Lingus

A Boeing 737 prepares for take-off

The flag carrier of The Republic of Ireland began operations in April 1936, opening the first scheduled passenger service between Eire and Great Britain. It was flown from Dublin to Bristol by a DH 84 Dragon. Later that year the service was extended to London and Aer Lingus established a monopoly of air routes between the United Kingdom and Ireland. Throughout the war years an air link across the Irish Sea was maintained by Aer Lingus between Dublin and either Liverpool or Manchester.

The acquisition of DC-3s in 1948 allowed routes to be opened up linking Dublin directly with the continnent of Europe, with services to Paris and Amsterdam. Aer Lingus was one of the first airlines to operate an all turbine-powered fleet, swapping its DC-3s in 1959 for Fokker F27s, which joined eight Viscount 808s. The airline was subsequently an early customer for the BAC.111 and the Boeing 737.

In 1958 a second airline, called Aerlinte Eireann (Irish International Airlines), also owned by the state holding company, Air Rianta, was put into operation. It provided a transatlantic service using L-1049H Lockheed Constellations (leased from Seaboard and Western) flying to New York and Boston with their large ethnic Irish populations. In 1960 the Constellations were replaced by Boeing 720-048s. The activities of Aerlinte Eireann were later merged with those of Aer Lingus. Current long-haul equipment consists of three Boeing 747s. Two leased Boeing 767-300ER were to be introduced in 1991.

Today, after a policy decision taken in the late 1970s to diversify business activities, the company has several important subsidiaries operating in hotels, leisure and contract air transport and airport services. Associated firms include Irish Helicopters, Guinness Peat Aviation (the biggest aircraft leasing company in the world), Air Tara and Air Taras Teo – a cargo airline with three DC-8s. Team Aer Lingus is a recently formed company which will handle all the airline's major engineering as well as providing services for other operations. A $60 million investment includes a massive new hangar at Dublin, capable of holding two Boeing 747-400 and four narrow bodies. This was due for completion in 1991.

Scheduled passenger and freight services are operated from Dublin to London (Heathrow and Gatwick), Birmingham, Bristol, East Midlands,

Vickers Viscount 808s were operated by Aer Lingus in the late 1950s

The Shorts 360, 36-seat commuter airliner, first entered service in 1984

Edinburgh, Glasgow, Leeds/Bradford, Manchester, Jersey, Paris, Brussels, Amsterdam, Copenhagen, Düsseldorf, Frankfurt, Zurich, Rome, Madrid, Milan, New York, Boston and Chicago. Domestic links are flown to Cork, Connaught Regional airport, Derry, Kerry County, Shannon and Waterford. From Cork airport services are flown to London, Jersey, Amsterdam, Dublin, Paris, Bristol and Rennes.

And from Shannon on the west coast scheduled passenger services are operated to London, Amsterdam, Dublin, Paris, New York, Boston and Chicago. The airline also offers services from Manchester to Amsterdam, Copenhagen, Hamburg and Zurich in a fifth freedom operation made possible by EC deregulation.

The fully owned subsidiary, Aer Lingus Commuter, was established in 1984 and operates a fleet of twin-prop Fokker 50s and Shorts 360s on domestic routes and to Bristol, East Midlands, Edinburgh, Leeds/Bradford, Newcastle, Bristol and Manchester in the UK and Rennes in Brittany.

Fleet: three Boeing 747-100, 14 Boeing 737-200, two Boeing 737-300, four 737-400, three Boeing 737-500; four BAe One-Eleven 200 (for sale); one Lockheed L-1011 (on lease). On order two Boeing 737-500, two Boeing 767-300ER.
Fleet (Air Lingus Commuter): four Fokker 50; five Shorts 360

Aer Lingus first flew the Fokker F27 Friendship, on the Dublin-Glasgow route in 1959

USSR

Aeroflot

Grazhdensky Vozdushny Flot

Tupolev Tu-154M (1985)

Much of the history of the biggest civil aircraft operator in the world remain wreathed in mystery because of its close integration with the Soviet armed forces and the strategic interests of the state. The exact composition of its fleet still remains secret. With a huge internal market – Aeroflot carries 10% of the world's air travelers – backed by a massive and technologically competitive civil aircraft industry, the airline should be a global supercarrier. Yet today Aeroflot reflects the economic turmoil and quest for new commercial mechanisms in the Soviet Union as a whole.

The reformist plan, agreed in 1988, to break the giant up into divisional profit centers – involving joint marketing deals with world airlines in a bid to compete internationally with western standards of service and technical efficiency, appeared to come to a halt at the outset of 1991.

The airline was founded soon after the birth of the Soviet state. In 1923 the Civil Aviation Council was formed to operate the new state airline, Dobrolet. Two years later Dobrolet swallowed fledgling operations in the Caucasus and the Ukraine. Dobrolet was renamed Dobroflot in1930 and dubbed Aeroflot two years later. In the 1930s Antonov and Tupolev aircraft began to open up air routes across Russia's vast land mass.

The makers of Aeroflot's equipment have striven to mirror the pace of technical development in the west. After the ravages of World War II, the airline restarted operations with the Soviet-built DC-3 clone, the Lisunov Li-2. Later the twin piston-engined Iluyshin Il-14 took up the burden of air operations in the massive country with its developing Siberian region and harsh climatic conditions.

The need to operate from rugged airstrips, sometimes in sub-zero temperatures with minimal support equipment, and the close integration with the military have shaped the rugged style of Aeroflot operations. In the late 1950s Aeroflot stayed in step with the West, introducing the Il-18 and Tu-114 turboprops and the Tu 104 jet airliner. Indeed, when the Tu 104 entered service in September 1956, it was for a few years the world's only jet airliner in service until the later Comets and the Boeing 707 were introduced. The Iluyshin Il-62, still very much in active service, mirrored Britain's VC-10. But the attempt to emulate the Anglo-French Concorde with the Tu-144 SST ended in disaster.

The wide-body revolution inaugurated by the Boeing 747 passed the Soviets by. The four-jet Ilyushin-86 with its twin deck "walk-on" baggage hold, again designed for operations from primitive airfields, fell behind western standards of comfort and efficency.

Aeroflot has struggled hard to catch up, as the internal demand for air travel within the USSR has steadily increased but, as a source of hard currency competing on the world market, the airline was failing to deliver. It was decided therefore to split the giant up into seven new carriers – with a new international operation called ASDA operating western aircraft, including Boeing 747s and 757s, and six regional carriers.

In 1989 the new International Aviation Directorate (IAD) submitted a proposal to the Ministry of Civil Aviation to the effect that it should transform itself into an independent company called Soviet Airlines. A crop of joint venture deals were signed, meanwhile, with western operators such as Lufthansa, Aer Lingus, Marriott and TNT to operate new Airbus A310s, redevelop Moscow's grossly congested Sheremtyevo airport and upgrade customer services and air traffic control.

Early in 1990 Aeroflot signed an agreement to lease five Airbus A310s on its Moscow-London-New York service, beginning in late 1991. Aeroflot executives were also exploring deals to lease or buy Boeing 747-400s, Airbus A330/A340 and McDonnell Douglas MD-11s.

Fleet: 200 international aircraft; 4500 helicopters, domestic and utility types. Passenger aircraft include 194 Antonov An-12, 400 An-24/

26/30, eight An-28, three An-72, one An-74; 147 Ilyushin Il-14, 50+ Il-18, 154 Il-62, 72 Il-76, 65+ Il-86; 80+ Let L410/610; 389 Tupolev Tu-134, 369 Tu 154; 750+ Yakovlev Yak 40, 70+ Yak-42-200M. On order 100+ Ilyushin Il-96-300, Il-114, Tu 204, Tu 334, Let L610; five Airbus A310-300. Note: Figures for the Aeroflot fleet are approximate only, because of the difficulty in distinguishing aircraft used for commercial and military purposes.

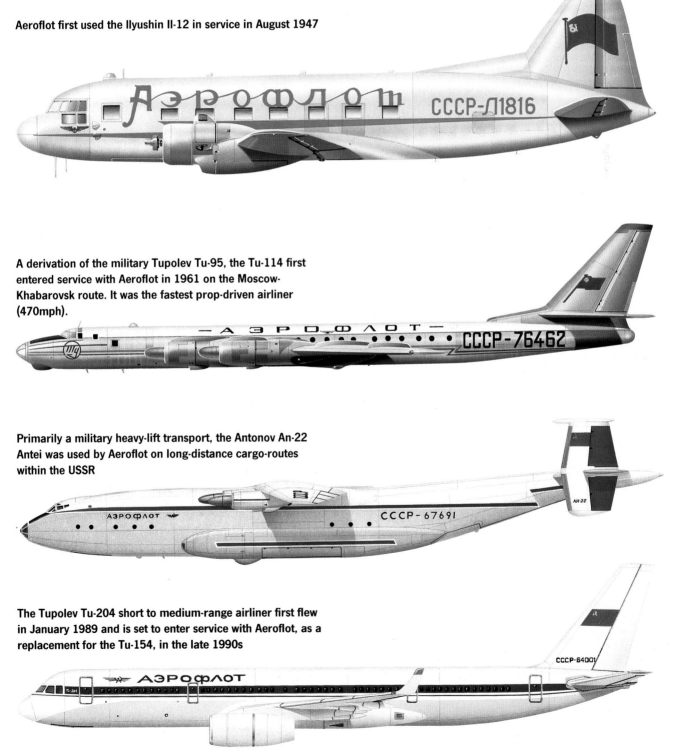

Aeroflot first used the Ilyushin Il-12 in service in August 1947

A derivation of the military Tupolev Tu-95, the Tu-114 first entered service with Aeroflot in 1961 on the Moscow-Khabarovsk route. It was the fastest prop-driven airliner (470mph).

Primarily a military heavy-lift transport, the Antonov An-22 Antei was used by Aeroflot on long-distance cargo-routes within the USSR

The Tupolev Tu-204 short to medium-range airliner first flew in January 1989 and is set to enter service with Aeroflot, as a replacement for the Tu-154, in the late 1990s

ARGENTINA

Aerolíneas Argentinas

A Boeing 747 lands at Los Angeles

The national carrier of Argentina was created in 1949 when several independent operators, FAMA, ALFA, Aeroposta and ZONDA, were shunted together under the Peronist umbrella of a state corporation – in effect a department of the Ministry of Transport. In the 1950s the new airline operated a fleet of DC-3s, DC-4s and DC-6s, several Convair CV 240s and six Sandringham flying boats – operating to points in the US, Europe and the Caribbean.

The first jets, Comet 4Cs, were ordered in 1958 in a move designed to keep the airline competitive with BOAC, who were introducing jets on their South American routes. The airline was thus the first in South America to operate jets. Caravelles arrived in 1960 and turboprop HS 748s in 1962. Boeing 707s replaced the Comets in 1966, Boeing 737s appeared in the fleet in 1969 and Boeing 747-200Bs were introduced on intercontinental routes in 1976.

Situated at the southern end of the South American subcontinent, the airline has always been involved in long-range flying. For example, in 11967 it introduced a non-stop service from Buenos Aires to Madrid using Boeing 707s. A distant of 6275 miles made this the world's longest non-stop scheduled service at the time. Today the Boeing 747 is the workhorse of the long-haul fleet which includes one of the short-fuselage, long-range 747SP models. The Falklands war in 1982 led to the suspension of services to London, although the airline maintained links to other European countries. With the normalization of diplomatic relations the London link was reinstituted as an extension of the Paris service in 1990. This means that Aerolíneas Argentinas is the only air-line to fly a scheduled service from London to Paris (Orly), since all other airlines use the newer Charles de Gaulle airport.

Since 1982 Argentine has experienced severe economic problems and the airline has not been able to raise the necessary funds to renew its aging fleet, despite being the third largest South American carrier in terms of passenger-miles flown. The government saw privatization as the only way to raise capital and this was carried out in late 1990 after protracted discussions with many interested parties. Subject to the negotiation of the financial arrangements, the airline is now owned by a consortium including Iberia (30% holding), Cielos del Sur/Austral (35%), and other investors (20%). The government retains 15%, some of which will eventually be transferred to airline employees.

The airline's route network covers the whole of the Americas and stretches across the Pacific and South Pole to New Zealand, Australia and the Far East, and across the Atlantic to Europe and South Africa. From the capital, Buenos Aires, scheduled passenger services are flown to Cape Town, Madrid, Rome, Zurich, Frankfurt, Paris, Los Angeles, Miami, New York, Montreal, Rio de Janeiro, São Paulo, Asunción, Montevideo, La Paz, Lima, Caracas, Santiago, Guayaquil, Bogotá, Pôrto Alegre, Mexico City, Hong Kong, Auckland, Sydney, and London.

Fleet: six Boeing 747-200B, one 747SP, one Boeing 707-320B, eight Boeing 727-200, nine Boeing 737-200, two 737-200C; three Fokker F28-100, one Fokker F28-4000

AFRICA

Air Afrique

Société Aérienne Africaine Multinationale

A McDonnell Douglas DC-10

This airline was set up in 1961 as a joint venture by 11 newly independent former French African colonies, each with a 6% interest: Cameroon, the Central African Republic, Congo, Ivory Coast, Dahomey, Gabon, Upper-Volta, Mauritania, Niger, Senegal and Chad. Air France and UAT each held a 17% interest through a controlling body called Sodetraf (Société pour le Développement du Transport Aérien en Afrique). The initial equipment consisted of 11 DC-4s and one DC06A formerly operated by Air France in the region. International services began late in 1961, using three Lockheed Super Constellations.

Ownership has been somewhat redistributed with the withdrawal of Cameroon and Gabon and the entry of Benin and Togo into the consortium. Each member owns 7%, the remainder belonging still to Sodetraf. The company's administrative headquarters are at Abidjan, capital of the Ivory Coast.

An extensive route network is flown within Francophone Africa and from the relevant national capitals to Paris, London and Frankfurt, New York and Jeddah.

Fleet: three Airbus A300B4; one McDonnell Douglas DC-8-63F, three McDonnell Douglas DC-10-30 (plus other aircraft on short term lease)

CANADA

Air Canada

Livery changes have been restrained over the years. A Boeing 767 showing the latest version

The major Canadian airline, state-owned since it was founded in 1937, was privatized in 1989. It carries over 12 million passengers a year and ranks as the world's 17th biggest airline.

Canada's international flag carrier was founded as Trans-Canada Airlines, with its shares held by the state-owned Canadian National Railways. Two Lockheed L10As flew the airline's first international route between Vancouver and Seattle, opened in 1938. By the following year transcontinental connections between the eastern and western seaboards had been established. In such a vast country many of its domestic routes were commercially unviable, but were deemed politically and socially necessary. During 1943-47 TCA pilots operated a transatlantic air bridge for mail and key supplies for Canadian armed forces in Europe.

After the war the airline acquired a fleet of war surplus C-47/DC-3s to replace its Lockheeds. The first Canadair-built North Stars (a pressurized, Merlin-powered version of the DC-4) entered service on the North Atlantic in 1947, the airline's growing long-distance services reaching out to the Caribbean and Florida a year later.

In the mid-1950s the fleet consisted of DC-3s and North Stars with Super Constellations now flying the long-haul routes and allowing a Vancouver-Winnipeg- Gander-London service to be introduced. The first turboprops were Vickers Viscounts, introduced in April 1955, and in 1960 the first pure jets, DC-8-50s, went into service between Montreal and Vancouver.

Vickers Vanguard turboprops were introduced in 1961 on the intra-Canadian routes and on services to the cities of the northern US. By 1963 the last DC-3 had been retired and TCA was all turbine-equipped.

The name was formally changed from TCA to Air Canada in 1965, reflecting the airline's international activities. DC-9s replaced the Viscounts and there was even a short-lived scheme to get aboard the Concorde program. Boeing 747s were introduced on the Toronto-London route in 1971 and Lockheed TriStars on the trans-Canadian routes in 1973.

Today the airline operates an extensive network of scheduled passenger flights within the country, serving Calgary, Charlottestown, Edmonton, Fredericton, Halifax, Moncton, Montreal, Ottawa, Quebec, Regina and Saint John's.

International services are flown to San Francisco, Los Angeles, Chicago, Tampa, Miami, New York, Boston, Freeport, Nassau, Havana, Montego Bay, Kingston, Bermuda, Antigua, St Lucia, Guadeloupe, Martinique, Barbados, Haiti and Puerto Plata, London, Birmingham, Manchester, Paris, Geneva, Zurich, Düsseldorf, Frankfurt, Lisbon, Nice, Vienna and Zagreb.

A group of regional and commuter airlines provide hub and spoke feeder services under the marketing banner Air Canada Connector, and in early 1991 the airline acquired a 100% holding in the Halifax-based Air Nova. In November 1990 the airline had announced the layoff of 2900 personnel and the sale of three Boeing 747-400 on order.

Fleet: seven Airbus A320; three Boeing 747-200B Combi, three 747-100, nine Boeing 767-200ER, ten Boeing 767-200, 33 Boeing 727-200; four Lockheed L-1011-1, four Lockheed L-1011-100, six Lockheed L-10011-500; six McDonnell Douglas DC-8-73F, 36 McDonnell Douglas DC-9-32. On order 28 Airbus A320; three Boeing 747-400 Combi

A Lockheed L-1011 preparing for take-off at London, Heathrow

Vickers Vanguard (1961)

The series 100 version of the Boeing 747 first flew in 1970
with Air Canada as an early operator

FRANCE

Air France

Air France was the first airline to put the Airbus A300B2 into service, in May 1974

The French national airline, the second biggest in Europe, can trace its origin back to 1933 when the Société Centrale pour l'Exploitation de Lignes Aériennes merged with the smaller Compagnie Générale Aéropostale, under the operating title Air France, and adopted the famous Pegasus badge.

Shortly before the merger the Sociéte had been encouraged by the French government to take over the assets and operations of several smaller airlines which had proliferated in the 1920s, one of which traced its origin back as far as 1919.

In the years before the outbreak of World War II Air France expanded rapidly, with a fleet of over 200 aircraft and flying boats reaching out to

Africa, across the Atlantic and to the French colonies in Indo-China. Some routes to North Africa were maintained under Vichy government control during the war, but in 1942 the airline was re-formed in North Africa and operated services based on Algiers, Dakar and Damascus.

Operations were revived in 1946 under the nationalized Société Nationale Air France. In 1948 the operation was merged with Air Bleu (flying airmail) and Air France Transatlantique. Air France's first prestige international route was Paris-New York operated by DC-4s.

The airline once again grew rapidly, building up in the 1950s the world's longest route network and interests in many semi-independent airline operations in France's colonies – interests it kept after their independence. In this period the backbone of the fleet remained DC-3s and DC-4s, with Constellations, Super Constellations and Starliners flying the long-haul routes.

Portly Bréguet Deux Ponts were operated over the Mediterranean until the arrival of the first turboprops, Vickers Viscounts, in 1958 and pure-jet Caravelles and Boeing 707s in 1960. Supersonic services with Air France's fleet of seven Concorde SSTs were inaugurated in 1976 from Paris to New York and to South America.

In November 1990 the European Commission cleared Air France's takeover of Air Inter and UTA (Union de Transports Aériens), giving the state-owned flag carrier its own near monopoly on the domestic route network – and access to many more French international routes – in return for giving up eight domestic and 50 international routes to independent and foreign carriers. In 1991 the operations were in the process of merging. The airline was compelled to sell its share of TAT.

Fokker F.VIIb/3m's were flown on part of Air France's Far East
routes before World War II

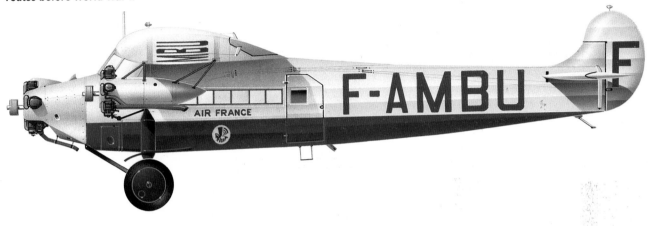

Air France took delivery of 12 Bréguet 763 Provence's in early
1953. The twin-deck airliner was known as "Deux-Ponts".

Transall C-130Ps were operated by Air France – starting in
1973 – for night mail deliveries.

Air France

UTA itself had been formed in 1963 by the merger of Union Aéromaritime de Transport (UAT) and Compagnie de Transports Aériens Intercontinentaux. UTA had considerable shareholdings in Air Inter, The French domestic operator, and Sodetraf, the holding company for Air Afrique. It has other interests in airport services, hotels and holiday villages in Polynesia and New Caledonia.

UTA operates flights from Paris (Charles de Gaulle), Nice, Marseilles, Lyon and Toulouse to 23 points in Africa, to Bahrain and Muscat, Los Angeles, San Francisco, Honolulu and Tokyo, and to eight other destinations in the Pacific area.

Fleet (Air France): seven Aérospatiale/BAe Concorde; 20 Boeing 727-200, 16 Boeing 737-200, 16 Boeing 747-100, two 747-200B, 11 Boeing 747-200M Combi, eight 747-200F; 15 Airbus A300B2/B4, seven Airbus A310-200, two A310-300, 13 Airbus A320. On order 15 Boeing 747-400, five 747-400F, two 747-200F; two Airbus A310-300, 13 Airbus A320, seven Airbus A340-300. NOTE: Figures do not include Air Inter aircraft

Fleet (UTA): one Boeing 747-400, four 747-300 Combi, one 747-200; six McDonnell Douglas DC-10-30. On order one Boeing 747-400; six Airbus A340-300

A Douglas DC-8-50 in UTA colors. Air France acquired a controlling interest in 1989

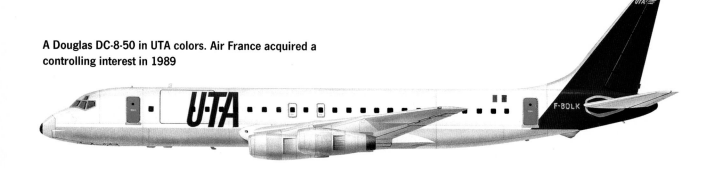

A McDonnell Douglas DC-9 comes in to land at London, Heathrow

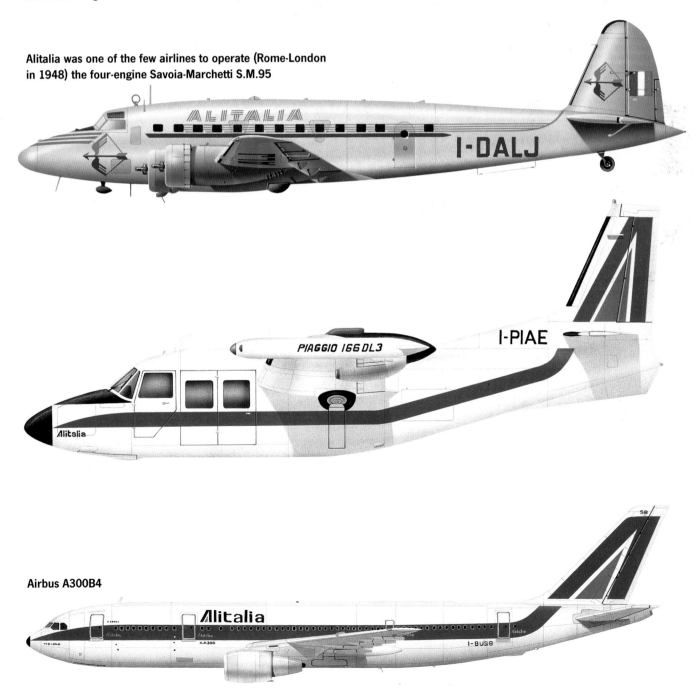

Alitalia was one of the few airlines to operate (Rome-London in 1948) the four-engine Savoia-Marchetti S.M.95

I-DALJ

PIAGGIO 166 DL3

I-PIAE

Airbus A300B4

I-BUSB

USA

American Airlines

An Airbus A300-600, at Miami

Texas-based American Airlines has grown into one of the world's most significant air transport operations. It was founded in 1934 as the successor to American Airways. This had been formed four years earlier to fly the southern transcontinental air mail route generously awarded by the US postmaster general, having already in 1929 taken over several smaller airlines under its previous name, Aviation Corporation. Soon passengers were being carried bu American Airlines and the big biplane, Curtiss Condor, was introduced, with sleeping berths and an in-flight stewardess to tend travelers as they fitfully slumbered between multiple stops.

The first DC-3 went into service in June 1936, flying Chicago-New York. In its flamboyant livery, the modernity of the new airliner, plus its comfort and efficiency, were the focus of an aggressive marketing effort. In common with other US airlines, much of American's fleet was called up for war service during 1942-5. In 1945 American merged with American Export Airlines to form American Overseas Airlines, flying a marginally profitable service from New York to London with DC-4s. In 1950 the operation was sold to Pan American.

American got its first postwar-built equipment, the Douglas DC-6s, into service in 1947 and began a major program that would eclipse its competitors. The DC-4s were retired by 1948, the DC-3s a year later, to be replaced by Convair CV240 twinprops. The turboprop Lockheed Electra went into service in January 1959, followed a few days later by the first Boeing 707 – flying non-stop from New York to Los Angeles.

British Aerospace 146

A 1933 Curtiss T-32 Condor, which could carry up to 12 passengers in overnight sleeper berths

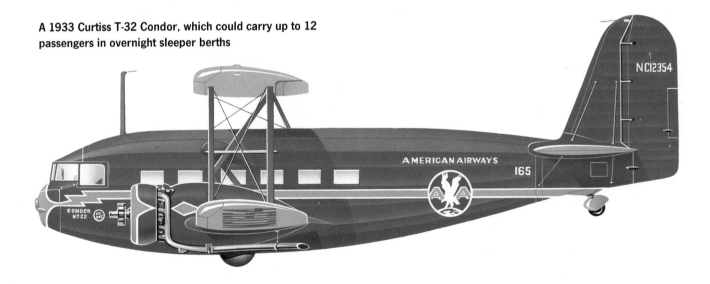

Simmons Airlines flies this ATR (Avions de Transport Régional) 42 under the "American Eagle" banner, feeding into the American Airlines commuter network

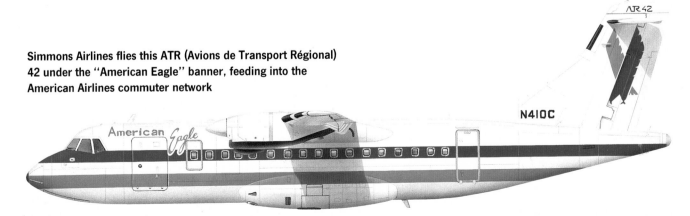

American Airlines

Above: Boeing Stratocruisers flew the North Atlantic route in the late 1940s. Left: Boeing 767. Below left: A British Aerospace Jetstream 31, operating under the "American Eagle" commuter network banner. Below: McDonnell Douglas MD-80

The new jet gave American a tremendous edge over its rival United, still waiting for delivery of its first DC-8s and meanwhile having to plug away with piston power over its transcontinental routes. American put turbo-fan-powered Boeing 720Bs into service in 1961 and the flamboyant but commercially unsuccessful Convair CV990 Coronado in 1962.

Boeing 727s began to replace the DC-6s and DC-7s now flying American's regional feeder routes, until the airline's last piston-powered flight was made on 17 December 1966. As the wide-body era loomed, American ordered the Boeing 747 off the drawing board in 1967 and was an important launch customer for the Douglas DC-10 in 1969.

In 1986 American took over the California-based Air Cal, giving the carrier an extensive route network along the US west coast. Today American's US-wide domestic network operates from five main hubs at Chicago, Dallas, Nashville, Raleigh/Durham and San Juan. A sixth hub, at San José, was due to come on stream in 1991. American's parent organization, AMR, also controls a number of regional and commuter airlines which feed passengers into the AA hubs under the marketing banner "American Eagle", operating a combined fleet of 211 twin turboprops. Those companies include Air Midwest, AVAir, Command Airways, Simmons Airlines and Wings West. Other independents in the network are Chaparral Airlines, Executive Air Charter and Metroflight. A national feeder network is being developed called AMR Eagle.

Transatlantic scheduled passenger services are flown to London (Gatwick), Brussels, Düsseldorf, Frankfurt, Geneva, Hamburg, Lyon, Madrid, Manchester, Munich, Paris, Stockholm and Zurich. Operations across the Pacific from Dallas to Tokyo commenced in 1987. Other points are served in the Caribbean, Canada and Mexico. In early 1991 American was negotiating to take over TWA's Heathrow services. McDonnell Douglas MD-11 services to Tokyo began in March 1991.

Fleet: 25 Airbus A300-600R; two Boeing 747SP, 20 Boeing 757-200, 15 Boeing 767-300ER, 17 767-200ER, 13 767-200, eight Boeing 737-300, ten 737-200, 125 Boeing 727-200, 39 727-100; six BAe 146-200; 10 McDonnell Douglas DC-10-30, 49 DC-10-10, 202 McDonnell Douglas MD-80. On order ten Airbus A300-600R; 55 Boeing 757-200, ten 767-300ER; 75 Fokker 100; 15 McDonnell Douglas MD-11, 58 McDonnell Douglas MD-80

UK

British Airways

Above: Lockheed L-1011-200 Below: BEA started operations with Vickers-Armstrong Vikings in 1946

T he biggest airline in Europe is also one of its oldest. Through a multiplicity of precursor companies, BA has an exotic and complex pedigree. In August 1919 the Air Transport and Travel Company flew the world's first scheduled civil airline international flight – from London to Paris. A DH4A bomber, with its rear fuselage converted into a primitive cabin, carried a single passenger and a crate of letters and cargo from capital to capital in two and a half hours. A month later a rival sprang up, the Handley Page company, famous for its World War I bomber designs, flying one of its 0/400 bombers from Cricklewood, north London, also to Paris. A third operator on the London-Paris route, Instone Airlines, began operations in 1920.

The pioneers found great difficulties in making their operations profitable, in spite of British government subsidies introduced in 1921 as part of a plan to nurture civil aviation. Government and commercial pressure shunted the three airlines together, along with a fourth, British Marine Air Navigation. In April 1924 Imperial Airways, as the new carrier was dubbed, made its first flight from London to Paris. With the vast span of the British empire as its market and a government-granted monopoly of international operations, Imperial Airways began to reach out to India, the Far East and Australia, using both landplanes and increasingly sophisticated and luxurious flying boats. A through route to India was opened in 1929 and by 1933 it had reached Singapore where Qantas Empire Airways picked up the connection to Brisbane. In July 1937 flying boats began a transatlantic service from Southampton to New York. The Empire Air Mail scheme of 1938, which underwrote a flat fee air mail price throughout the British colonies, boosted the airline's revenue.

In spite of Imperial's international monopoly granted in the original agreement of 1924, in 1936 a challenger sprang up on the European routes. British Airways flew from Heston airfield in west London to Paris and other European capitals, with a fleet of DH86s, Fokkers, Junkers and Lockheed L.10s. On 1 April 1940, with Britain at war on the eve of the German offensive in the west, the British Overseas Airways Corporation (BOAC) was created, under state sopnsorship. It had a fleet of 82 aircraft.

In the face of enemy action throughout the war BOAC maintained services to the outposts of Empire and across the Atlantic (using

A British Aerospace (originally Hawker Siddeley) Trident 3B in the livery used when BEA and BOAC were finally merged as one airline in 1976

The Bristol Britannia 312 first entered service with BOAC in July 1957 as part of a round-the-world service

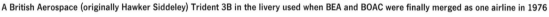

Boeing 314 flying boats). The airline emerged into the postwar world with a huge route network and a rag-bag of worn-out aircraft. There were only converted bombers like the Avro Lancastrian and Handley-Page Halton to take up the burden. The new Labour government set about reorganizing Britain's nationalized air transport industry. British South American Airways (BSAA) was established to operate services across the South Atlantic, but much more significant was the creation of British European Airways (BEA) in 1946 to fly the flag in Europe.

Soon new aircraft rather than converted bombers began to join BOAC's fleet – Constellations to fly London-New York in 1946 and Canadair built DC-4s (known by BOAC as Argonauts), plus Boeing Stratocruisers in 1949. That year BSAA was merged with BOAC after a series of crashes had grounded its fleet of Avro Tudors. BEA swallowed up a number of smaller operators after the war, flying its growing fleet of DC-3s, Vikings and DH89s to an increasing number of destinations in and around the British Isles and to an equally expanding number of European capitals. BEA played an important role during the 1948 Berlin airlift.

On 2 May 1952 the revolutionary de Havilland Comet jet airliner went into service on BOAC's London-Johannesburg route, heralding what should have been a tremendous technical and commercial break-through for the loss-making airline – the first to offer civil jet transport. However, two tragic Comet crashes over the Mediterranean in 1954 grounded the fleet and dashed BOAC's and the British aircraft industry's hopes of seizing the lead from the Americans. urboprop Bristol Britannias went into service on the African routes in 1955. The longer-

Civil conversions of Short Seaford flying boats were used by BOAC in the late 1940s, under the designation, Solent 3

range Britannia 312 began to span the Atlantic in 1957, supplanting Constellations and Douglas DC-7Cs. The redesigned Comet 4C began the first pure-jet transatlantic service in October 1958 (narrowly beating Pan Am who started services with the Boeing 707 a few days later), but the Corporation's management had already placed orders for the aircraft that was truly to be the harbinger of mass jet air travel – the Boeing 707. Powered by Rolls-Royce Conway turbofan engines, the 707s entered service on BOAC's North Atlantic routes in 1960, as the Comets were switched to the Far East and Australia.

BEA's postwar fleet, still largely made up of DC-3s (dubbed "Pionairs" by the airline) was augmented in 1952 by the introduction of the Air-speed Ambassador (named Elizabethan Class by the airline) and the first turboprop Viscount in 1953. Medium-range Comet 4Bs furnished

British Airways

the airline's first pure-jets in 1958. Vanguard turboprops and Trident tri-jets (the first aircraft certificated for fully automated landings) followed in the early 1960s together with a fleet of BAe One-Elevens mostly committed to the airline's intra-West German route network. This was a hangover from the war, but it proved an important commercial operation for BEA and its successor, British Airways, until Germany regained the right to operate internal air services in 1990.

In the early 1960s Vickers VC-10s and Super VC-10s joined the BOAC fleet at the same time, during a period when the airline was struggling to make a profit as it contemplated a leap into a new era of air travel with the development of the Anglo-French Concorde SST (supersonic transport). This technological marvel was on the margins of commercial practicality, and meanwhile US industry had stolen a march on Britain and Europe with the development of the wide-body generation of airliners. In 1968 BOAC ordered its first Boeing 747s, while BEA opted for the Lockheed TriStar.

In 1969 a British government inquiry recommended the merger of the two operations. The new British Airways was formed in 1972 and began formally integrated operations on 1 April 1974. The airline made history in 1976 when, along with Air France, it began regular supersonic scheduled passenger services with Concorde. In April 1977 the airline was further rationalized into a single unified operating structure, with an aggressive marketing strategy looking for worldwide business.

In February 1987 the state-owned airline was privatized and within ten months had swallowed up British Caledonian, the major independent British carrier, overturning policy that it should be a "second source" competitor. BA's charter operation, British Airtours, was re-

Above: A line-up of Boeing 747s. Below: The British Aerospace ATP regional turboprop is replacing the BAe 748.

Above: A Rolls-Royce powered version of the latest 400 series Boeing 747

named Caledonian Airways in 1989. In 1990 BA conceived an ambitious plan to develop a new European hub at Brussels, with a shareholding in a new operation called Sabena World Airways (SWA), in partnership with the Belgian flag carrier and KLM. Fuel price rises and the airline recession caused the scheme to collapse early in 1991.

British Airways flies scheduled passenger services to over 170 destinations in 77 countries in Europe, the Near, Middle and Far East, the Caribbean and the Americas. The airline's domestic operations link 15 points in the UK and include the high-frequency "super shuttle" service between London, (Heathrow) and Glasgow, Edinburgh, Manchester

and Belfast. All routes to Ireland were abandoned in 1991 as part of a rationalization program to combat recession in the industry.

Fleet: seven Aérospatiale/BAe Concorde; ten Airbus A320; 15 Boeing 747-400, 18 747-200B, six 747-200 Combi, 16 747-100, nine Boeing 767-300, 36 Boeing 757-200, 44 Boeing 737-200, four 737-300; 30 BAe One-Eleven-500; eight BAe ATP; nine BAe 748; nine Lockheed L-1011-1, eight L-1011-200; eight McDonnell Douglas DC-10-30. On order 27 Boeing 747-400, eight Boeing 767-300, eight Boeing 757-200, 24 Boeing 737-300. NOTE: BAe ATPs and 748s are operated by BA's Glasgow-based Highland Division

British Airways and Air France are the sole operators of the Mach 2 Concorde. BA has seven in its fleet

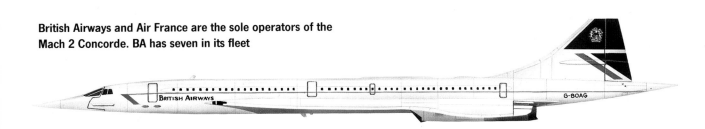

TRINIDAD

BWIA

Trinidad and Tobago Airways

A McDonnell Douglas MD-80, at Miami

Trinidad and Tobago Airways was formed on 1 January 1980, through the merger of British West Indian Airways International and Trinidad and Tobago Air Services (TTAS). BWIA was originally founded in 1940 as one of the TACA group of Central American airlines by the New Zealand-born entrepreneur Lovell Yerex. During World War II the operation was run down and in 1947 control passed to British South American Airways, which was merged with BOAC in 1947 after a series of disastrous crashes with the Avro Tudor. The title British West Indian Airways was adopted in 1948 and the airline became a Caribbean regional operator under BOAC's control, provifding services all over the West Indies and to Miami , New York and London. By the late 1950s the local fleet consisted of Viscount 702s and 772 Series, plus three DC-3s. The long-haul fleet was made up of Britannias and crews leased from BOAC. In November 1961 the Trinidad government acquired a 90% holding, acquiring the remainder in 1967.

BWIA operated international services to North and South America and Europe. TTAS, formed in June 1974 by the government, operated high-frequency shuttle flights linking the islands of Trinidad and Tobago.

In 1990 there were moves, led by the management of Trinidad and Tobago, to merge the airlines of several Caribbean islands including BWIA, Antigua-based LIAT, Guyana Airways and Air Jamaica, into a single airline The air committee of the regional interest group Caricom recommended that a joint Caribbean airline be established, after considering a multinational airline study carried out by Aer Lingus.

The airline operates scheduled passenger and cargo services from Piarco Airport, Port of Spain, to Tobago, Georgetown, Paramaribo, Caracas, Barbados, St Lucia, Grenada, St Kitts, Antigua, San Juan (Puerto Rico), Kingston, St Maarten, Curaçao, Miami, New York, Toronto, Frankfurt and London (Heathrow).

Fleet: four Lockheed L-1011-500; four McDonnell Douglas DC-9-50, six McDonnell Douglas MD-83.

The extended-range Lockheed L-1011-500

YUGOSLAVIA

JAT

Jugoslovenski Aerotransport

Above and below: Port and starboard views of a Boeing 737-300

The government-owned JAT was formed in 1947 to take control of all Yugoslav civil air transport activities. First-generation equipment included DC-3s, Junkers Ju 52/3Ms and Ilyushin Il-14s, reflecting the nation's political stance between east and west. In the mid-1950s, JAT purchased three Convair CV340 and six Ilyushin Il-14P. An attempt in the early 1950s to form a Balkan confederation of airlines with neighboring countries, on the lines of SAS, came to nothing.

The airline operates an extensive domestic route network serving 16 destinations. Internationally flights are operated to 48 cities in Scandinavia, western and eastern Europe, the Middle and Far East, North America and Australia.

Fleet: eight Boeing 727-200, nine Boeing 737-300; eight McDonnell Douglas DC-9-30, four McDonnell Douglas DC-10-3, one DC-10-30CF; three ATR 42. On order three ATR 72; four McDonnell Douglas MD-11

NETHERLANDS

KLM

Koninklijke Luchvaart Maatschappij NV

Airbus A310

T he national flag-carrier of the Netherlands is the oldest operating airline in the world. Founded in 1919, it began operations in 1920 with a service from Amsterdam to London using four-passenger DH16s. During the 1920s the operation spread across Europe and in 1929 an air route was opened to the Dutch East Indies. The eight-point route, flown by Fokker FVIIIs from Amsterdam to Batavia on the island of Java (later Djakarta), was at the time the longest regular air service in the world.

The advanced DC-2 airliner went into service with KLM (the first European airline to operate this aircraft) in 1934, the year the airline forged its first transatlantic link with a route to Curaçao using a Fokker FXVIII. In 1936 KLM was the first European airline to order the DC-3. In 1935 intra-Caribbean services were started from the Netherlands Antilles. These continued unbroken during World War II allowing KLM to claim over 65 years of continuous operations. Some aircraft escaped the German invasion, to fly a wartime route from Bristol to Gibraltar via Lisbon under charter to BOAC. The new Lockheed Lodestars ordered by the company were diverted to the Caribbean where they opened a service to Miami in 1943.

With a fleet of refurbished DC-3s and DC-4s the airline struggled to start up again after the ravages of war. The link to Batavia was renewed in November 1945, New York joined the route network in 1946, and Rio and Buenos Aires were on KLM's map by 1948 as long-range Constellations and DC-6s joined the fleet. Turboprop Vickers Viscounts began to operate the European routes in 1957, to be joined by Lockheed Electras ten years later. The first pure-jets, Douglas DC-8-30s, went into service in 1960. DC-9s progressively began to replace the Viscounts and Electras from 1966 onwards. These in turn have been re-

Douglas DC-4s went into airline service with KLM in early 1946

placed with Boeing 737s. In 1966 KLM established a domestic subsidiary called NLM which linked Amsterdam with Gronigen, Enschede, Eindhoven and Maastricht with a fleet of twin prop Fokker F27 Friendships.

KLM has a 14.9% shareholding in Air UK which provides feeder services into Amsterdam from nine UK regional airports. It also operates Netherlines as part of NLM, its fully owned domestic subsidiary and all aircraft are flown in the NLM Cityhopper livery. The airline also has a 40% stake in the charter operator, Transavia. Plans to join Sabena and BA in a new European venture called Sabena World Airways were aborted at the end of 1990.

KLM

A Boeing 747

KLM today operates a network of scheduled passenger and cargo services from its Schipol headquarters to 142 cities in 77 countries worldwide.

Fleet: ten Airbus A310-200; nine Boeing 747-400, 13 747-300, two 747-200B, five Boeing 737-400, 13 737-300; five McDonnell Douglas DC-10-30. On order six Boeing 747-400, two 747-400F, five Boeing 737-400; ten McDonnell Douglas MD-11.
Fleet (Netherlines): 12 Saab 340 (by 1992). Fleet (NLM): ten Fokker 50 (by 1992)

KLM flew this Douglas DC-2 in 1934

The extended range Lockheed L.1049G Super Constellation served with KLM from 1956 to 1962

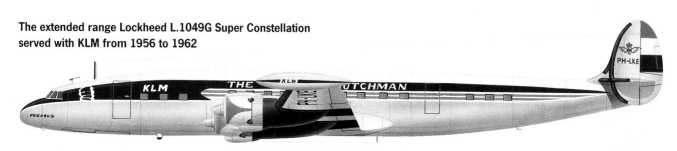

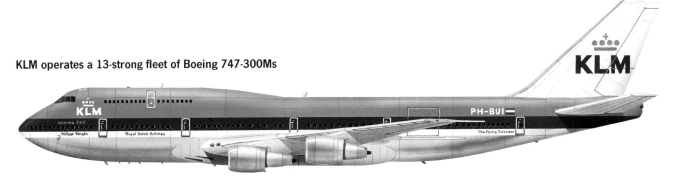

KLM operates a 13-strong fleet of Boeing 747-300Ms

SOUTH KOREA

Korean Air

An Airbus A300 arrives at Hong Kong

Right: A Boeing 747-200F, windowless cargo version, at Los Angeles

The flag carrier of South Korea was formed in 1962 and today is one of the fastest-growing airlines in the world with significant numbers of aircraft on order. It is the successor to Korean National Airlines, which had been founded in 1947 by the Ministry of Transport. The Korean War ended operations, which began again in 1952. The airline started to fly a domestic network within South Korea and to Hong Kong, with a small fleet of DC-3s, DC-4s and a single Lockheed Constellation. Later two Super Constellations were acquired in the 1960s and remained in service until the first jets (DC-9s) were delivered in 1967.

The airline was sold to private commercial interests (the Han-Jin Transportation Group) in 1969 and began a period of rapid and still accelerating expansion, acquiring a large fleet of Boeing 707s, 727s and 747s and later Airbus A300s and MD-82s. In 1983 a KAL Boeing 747 was tragically shot down when its strayed over Soviet air defenses northwest of Japan.

Domestic scheduled passenger services are operated from Seoul to Cheju and Pusan with international services to Frankfurt, London, Paris, Vienna, Zurich, Los Angeles, New York, Toronto, Vancouver, Bahrain, Jeddah, Riyadh, Bangkok, Fukuoka, Hong Kong, Kuala Lumpur, Manila, Nagasaki, Nagoya, Nigata, Osaka, Sapporo, Singapore, Taipei and Tokyo.

Fleet: eight Airbus A300B4, ten A300-600; three Boeing 747-400, two 747-300, one 747-300 Combi, six 747-200B, one 747-200 Combi, five 747-200F, two 747SP, eight Boeing 727-200; three McDonnell Douglas DC-10-30, eight McDonnell Douglas MD-82; four Fokker F28-4000, one F27-500. On order ten Airbus A300-600R, two A300C4; 29 Boeing 747-400; five McDonnell Douglas MD-11

KUWAIT

Kuwait Airways

Kuwait Airways Corporation

A Boeing 767. Despite the problems caused by the dispersal of the fleet during the 1991 Gulf conflict, Kuwait Airways still managed to maintain some flights

The Iraqi invasion of August 1990 caught much of Kuwait's national airline on the ground. The Iraqis seized most of the aircraft, leaving four Boeing 747s, three 727s and one 767 dispersed around the Middle East. Kuwait Airways was soon re-established after the invasion, with its headquarters in Cairo. In October 1990 the airline started twice weekly services from Cairo to Dubai, Jeddah and Bahrain, and at the end of the year, free Kuwait Airways began flying to European capitals, and to New York and Bombay.

The carrier had been formed as Kuwait National Airways Company in 1954 with two DC-3s, Viscounts later being acquired (1958). National was dropped from the title in 1957 and the following year BOAC took over technical management under a five-year contract. British International Airlines was taken over in 1959 and Trans Arabia Airways, flying DC-4s and -6s from Kuwait to Beirut, was taken over in 1964.

Fleet: (pre-2 August 1990) three Airbus A300C4-600, five Airbus A310-200; four Boeing 747-200 Combi, three Boeing 767-200ER, four Boeing 727-200; two Gulfstream III

The Hermes 4 was leased from BOAC for the last six months of 1965.

Fleet: nine Airbus A300-600, nine Airbus A310-200, seven Airbus A310-300, 11 Airbus A320; six Boeing 747-400, 12 747-200B Combi, five 747-200B, five 747-200F, four 747-400M, 18 Boeing 727-200, 23 Boeing 737-300, 38 737-200, two 737-200C; 11 McDonnell Douglas DC-10-30. On order two Airbus A300-600, three Airbus A310-300, 20 Airbus A320, 20 Airbus A321, 15 Airbus A340; two Boeing 747-400, three 747-400M, six Boeing 737-300, 39 737-500

Boeing 727-200

93

MALAYSIA

Malaysia Airlines

Boeing 737-200

The forerunner to Malaysia Airlines, Malayan Airways was originally founded in 1947 using Airspeed Consuls flying from Singapore via Kuala Lumpur to Penang. In the immediate post-colonial period of the late 1950s Malayan Airways Ltd (formed in 1958), with its headquarters in Singapore, was jointly owned by BOAC, Qantas and by the newly independent governments of Singapore, Malaya, Sarawak, Brunei and North Borneo. The airline flew DC-3s locally and (from 1960) Constellations and Britannias on international routes. Jet services began with Comets leased from BOAC in 1962.

During 1963-67 the carrier operated as Malaysian Airlines, and from 1967 to 1971 as Malaysia-Singapore airlines. During this period the Comets were replaced with Boeing 737s and 707s. In 1971 Malaysia Airlines was formed out of the old consortium.

Operations began the following year under the banner Malaysian Airlines System. The name changed to its present form in 1987. At the end of 1990 the airline announced plans to develop the northern Malaysian city of Johore Bahru as a domestic and international air travel base, following government plans to upgrade the airport at nearby Senai.

In the same year several South East Asian carriers, including Malaysia, Thai, Garuda, Singapore and Royal Brunei, set up a working group to examine commercial co-operation between them. In January 1991 Malaysia ordered 10 Boeing 737-400s and took options on ten more. The carrier also firmed up two of its eight options for Airbus A330s and ordered another Fokker 50.

The airline operates from its Kuala Lumpur base to 38 domestic destinations and to Singapore, Djakarta, Beijing, Medan, Manila, Phuket, Hong Kong, Taipei, Tokyo, Dubai, Amman, Colombo, Bangkok, Melbourne, Perth, Sydney, Delhi, Zurich, Madras, Seoul, Honolulu, Los Angeles, Amsterdam, Jeddah, London, Frankfurt, Paris and Mauritius. The airline is the parent of Pelangi Air, a new internal operator.

Fleet: four Airbus A300B4; two Boeing 747-400 Combi, one 747-400, one Boeing 747-300 Combi, two 747-200B, two Boeing 737-400, 11 737-200, one 737-200C; three McDonnell Douglas DC-10-30; ten Fokker 50, 11 Fokker F27-500; four DHC Twin Otter. On order ten Airbus A330-300; three Boeing 747-400, 20 Boeing 737-400, six 737-500; one Fokker 50

NIGERIA

Nigeria Airways

Nigeria Airways operate four of the 200 series Airbus Industrie A310

The flag carrier of Nigeria traces its origin to West African Airways Corporation formed in 1946 to operate within the British colonies of Nigeria and the Gold Coast with a small fleet of DC-3s and DH Doves. Argonauts and Boeing Stratoliners chartered from BOAC operated over the international routes from 1957, being later replaced by Comets and VC-10s.

When Ghana became independent in 1958 the new nation withdrew from WAAC in order to set up its own national airline. It was re-formed as Nigeria Airways in which BOAC held a 17% interest. Operations began with DC-3s flying domestic routes, while Britannias chartered from BOAC flew the Lagos-London route.

The airline, which was adversely affected by the 1968-69 civil war and by continuing political turbulence, has had many commercial ups and downs, buoyed up by the country's basic oil wealth. In the the late 1980s it began a program of cut-backs and suspension of unprofitable services. Today the airline offers scheduled passenger services over a comprehensive domestic route network within Nigeria, and regional services to destinations in West and East Africa.

It flies international services from Lagos and Kano to London, Amsterdam, Rome, New York and Jeddah, and from Port Harcourt to London. Fleet: four Airbus A310-200; three Boeing 707, eight Boeing 737-200; two McDonnell Douglas DC-10-30. On order six ATR 42-300

USA

Northwest

A McDonnell Douglas DC-9 Series 30 showing the new 1989 livery, at Miami

Northwest is a major US carrier, with its traffic hubs at Detroit, Minneapolis/St Paul and Memphis.

It was founded in 1926 as an air mail carrier and operated between Detroit and Minneapolis/St Paul using a Curtiss CX-5. Passenger services began in July 1927 with a fleet of three Stinsons. Locked out of the 1930 agreement to give US Mail contracts to a handful of operators, Northwest struggled to keep airborne until the mail routes were reallocated in 1934. Slowly the airline, now called Northwest Orient, began to build a spreading route network using a wide collection of aircraft, including Hamilton monoplanes, Ford trimotors, Lockeed Orions, Beech Travelairs, Lockheed Electras and Lockheed L14s. DC-3s were introduced in 1939. In 1942 the bulk of Northwest's fleet was committed to support of military operations in Alaska and the northern Pacific. In the postwar period the acquisition of a fleet of DC-4s and DC-6Bs allowed Northwest to build a transcontinental route network within the US, flying from New York and Washington to Portland and Seattle and out across the Pacific to Alaska, Hawaii, Japan and Korea. In 1947 the airline changed its name to Northwest Orient, reflecting its commitment to the transpacific routes. Boeing Stratocruisers were acquired in 1949 for the long-haul routes, DC-7Cs and

Super Constellations following in the mid-1950s.

The company ordered Martin 2-0-2s as replacements for the DC-3s on its domestic routes but a series of accidents caused the fleet to be grounded. The first turboprops were Lockheed Electras (introduced in 1959) and the first pure-jets, Douglas DC-8-30s, went into operation in 1960 followed two years later by Boeing 720Bs. Wide-body 747-100s joined the Northwest Orient fleet in 1972 followed by DC-10-10s. After deregulation of the US airline industry in the late 1970s Northwest moved vigorously to build up its route network, opening a service from Chicago to Tokyo and all-cargo flights across the North Atlantic. Northwest almost doubled in size when it took over Republic Airlines with a fleet of 170 aircraft in 1986.

The airline was the launch customer for the Boeing 747-400 in 1989 when the first of these new-generation, fuel-efficient 630-seaters went into service on the transpacific routes. Northwest also has large numbers of Airbus aircraft on order. In 1985 the operation was commercially restructured and retitled simply Northwest Airlines. It has marketing agreements with four commuter airlines – Big Sky, Express, Mesaba and Precision – which feed passengers to the hubs under the banner "Northwest Airlink." Northwest has recently taken a 25% stake

The regional US airline, Fischer Brothers Aviation, operated this Dornier 228-201 for the Northwest "Airlink" commuter network

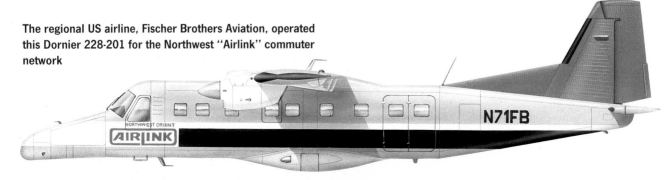

A Boeing 747-400, the latest version of the giant carrier, at Phoenix, Arizona

in Hawaiian Airlines.

Northwest flies a large domestic network within the US and in Canada. The airline flies internationally to Hawaii, Tokyo, Osaka, Seoul, Okinawa, Taipei, Manila, Hong Kong, Shanghai, Guam, Singapore, Saipan and Bangkok, London, Glasgow, Frankfurt, Paris, Amsterdam, Cancun, Montego Bay and the Cayman Islands.

Fleet: eight Airbus A320-200; ten Boeing 747-100, 19 747-200, eight 747-200F, nine 747-400, 33 Boeing 757-200, nine Boeing 727-100, 62 727-200; eight McDonnell Douglas MD-82, 20 McDonnell Douglas DC-10-40, 34 McDonnell Douglas DC-9-10, 72 DC-9-30, 28 DC-9-50. On order 92 Airbus A320-200, 16 Airbus A330, 20 Airbus A340; seven Boeing 747-400, 40 Boeing 757-200

GREECE

Olympic

A Boeing 747 at London, Heathrow

The national airline of Greece has a troubled commercial history. Now wholly government-owned, Olympic was founded in 1957 by the shipping tycoon, Aristotle Onassis, took who over the routes operated by Greek National Airlines (TAE) and Hellenic Airlines. TAE itself had been created in 1951 through a merger with Hellas and Aero Metafoa Ellados and TAE itself. The resulting airline was nationalized three years later.

Onassis was granted a 50-year concession with a monopoly on domestic routes and authority to operate the national flag carrier internationally. Operations began to points in Europe and the Near East with a fleet of DC-3, DC-4s and, from 1957, the first DC-6Bs flying a route from Athens to London via Rome and Paris. Comet 4Bs went into service in 1960. Boeing 707s inaugurated a non-stop Athens-New York service in July 1966.

The 1960s were prosperous for Olympic. Boeing 727s were brought in on European routes, Japanese-built NAMC YS-11As replaced the DC-3s on local networks and five 720Bs supplanted the DC-6Bs on the long-haul flights. But the level of commercial cosseting afforded by the state could not guarantee profitability. With a fanfare Boeing 747-200Bs inaugurated both Athens-New York and Athens-Sydney services in June 1973 but by now, hit by the steep rise in fuel costs, the airline was losing a lot of money.

After heavy losses Onassis withdrew in 1974. The airline virtually ceased to operate until it was reorganized, and resumed flying under state ownership in 1976. In 1979 the airline embarked on a new aircraft acquisition program, basing its intra-Europe operations on Airbuses, its domestic short haul on the Boeing 737 and its intercontinental services on the 747.

Today Olympic operates scheduled passenger services to 31 cities and island destinations in Greece and to 39 destinations in Europe, Africa, Asia and North America. An Athens-Bangkok-Tokyo service was inaugurated in 1990.

Fleet: eight Airbus A300B4; four Boeing 747-200B, three Boeing 707-320C, two 707-320B, six Boeing 727-200, 11 Boeing 737-200. On order two Airbus A300-600R

Airbus A300

USA

Pan Am

Pan American World Airways

An Airbus A310-300 lands at London, Heathrow

A dominant force in world aviation for over 60 years, at the outset of the 1990s Pan Am flew into the financial turbulence facing many airlines, hampered by a crippling legacy of losses made during the preceding decade. In late 1990 most of its routes ex-Heathrow were sold to United in a $400 million deal.

Pan American World Airways was founded on 28 October 1927 with the ambitious aim of opening up international services to South America and the Caribbean. The first service was flown from Key West to Cuba using a Fairchild FC-2 seaplane carrying mail. Very soon its was replaced by a Fokker FVII trimotor landplane. The first passengers were carried in January 1928 but already the airline's founder, the dynamic Juan Trippe, was peering further south anxious to compete with growing German influence in the potentially vast market of Central and South America. A contract from the US Mail gave Pan Am a monopoly of international air mail operations and within 18 months PAA was operating a route network of 12,000 miles. The flying boats dubbed "Clippers" by a management which wrote much of the airline marketing book in that heady period, dominated the PAA fleet as it grew during the 1930s. Sikorsky S42s and S43s, Martin M130s and, later, giant Boeing 314s, began to span to Atlantic and Pacific oceans.

In South America the expansion of PAA proceeded by way of buy-up deals and a series of mergers. Pan American Grace Airways, or Panagra, was formed in conjunction with the Grace shipping line to operate in Peru, Chile and Bolivia. PAA-owned Avianca had a near monopoly in Colombia. When the Brazilian government demanded local ownership of airlines, PAA bought a stake in Panair do Brasil.

America's war in Europe and the Pacific made great calls on PAA's transport fleet. After the war PAA ended its great flying boat tradition,

When Pan Am acquired the east-coast carrier NYRBA do Brasil in 1930, it changed the name to Panair do Brasil

switching first to the DC-4 and then rushing to get into service the new aircraft on offer by US manufacturers. PAA was first in the air with the great propliners of the period – the Constellation, the DC-6 and the Boeing Stratocruiser. In 1956 the Douglas DC-7C was introduced, which could fly the Atlantic from New York to western European capitals with only one intermediate refueling stop.

Pan Am ordered the Boeing 707 in 1955 just a year after the first flight of the revolutionary Boeing Jet Transport and flew the first revenue-earning flight, from New York to Paris on 26 October 1958. PAA was to operate 707s until October 1983. The Pan Am order started the rush for the aircraft which, although preceded into scheduled passenger

The 14-seater Fokker F.Xa, a version built in the US, was used
by Pan Am in the late 1920s

The Consolidated Commodore seaplane was used by Pan Am
after being proven in flight by the New York, Rio and Buenos
Aires Line in 1930

With seating for up to 32 passengers, three Martin M-130
seaplanes were notable additions to the Pan Am long-distance
fleet in 1935-37

Pan Am

Top: Boeing 737-200. Above: Boeing 727

service by the DH Comet, was the true begetter of the jet age in civil air transport. Pan Am was first, too, into the wide-body age, placing an order for 25 Boeing 7474s, off the drawing board in 1966. The first 747-121 started commercial service with a non-stop flights from New York to London on 21 January 1970.

PAA was denied a domestic network – it could not even operate transcontinental-US connecting flights, but deregulation at the end of the 1970s allowed it to build a domestic service. A short cut to this objective was provided when Pan Am took control of Miami-based National Airlines with a large route network around the eastern seaboard and Gulf coast, plus ready-made trans-US services. In 1986, under severe cash constraints, the airline sold its entire Pacific division to United Airlines. Continuing financial problems, not helped by loss of passenger confidence in the wake of the Lockerbie disaster in 1988,

have left the carrier in a precarious position, with its long-term future in doubt.

The airline acquired Ransome Airlines in 1986, turning it into a feeder operation called Pan Am Express to service its New York hubs and West Berlin's Tegel airport where the carrier retained rights to operate domestic services to West Germany.

Pan Am operates an extensive international network of scheduled passenger services to the Caribbean, South America, Europe, the Middle East, Africa and the Far East.

Fleet: 12 Airbus A300B4, four A310-200, 14 Airbus A310-300; seven Boeing 747-200B, 28 747-100, 21 Boeing 727-100, 59 727-200, five Boeing 737-200. On order two Airbus A310-300. NOTE five Boeing 747s were to be disposed of in 1991

A British Aerospace Jetstream 31, used on commuter and feeder flights

Intense competition with TWA at the end of World War II
prompted Pan Am to introduce the luxurious Boeing
Stratocruiser onto its transatlantic routes

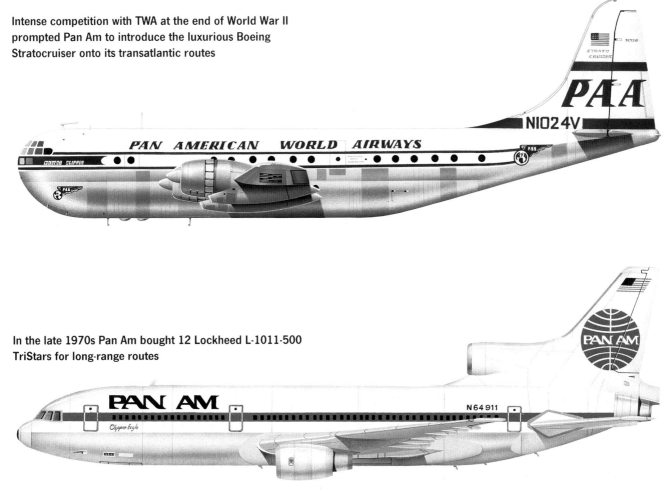

In the late 1970s Pan Am bought 12 Lockheed L-1011-500
TriStars for long-range routes

PAKISTAN

PIA

Pakistan International Airways

McDonnell Douglas DC-10

F ounded in 1954, it became a corporation a year later when it was merged with the smaller Orient Airways (founded in 1946). First-generation equipment included DC-3s operating services within West Pakistan and between West and East Pakistan (now Bangladesh). Lockheed Super Constellations flew long-haul routes and a Boeing 707 was acquired in 1960. Vickers Viscounts and Fokker F27 turboprops were operated from the late 1950s.

Today PIA flies to 32 domestic destinations, and offers scheduled passenger services to 40 points in 37 countries including Abu Dhabi, Bahrain, Dhaka, Beijing, Copenhagen, Dubai, Cairo, Frankfurt, Paris, Athens, Delhi, Bombay, Tehran, Rome, Tokyo, Amman, Nairobi, Tripoli, Kuala Lumpur, Katmandu, Amsterdam, Muscat, Manila, Doha, Jeddah, Dharan, Riyadh, Singapore, Colombo, Damascus, Bangkok, Istanbul, Moscow, London, New York, Malé, Toronto, and Sana'a.

Fleet: eight Airbus A300B4; six Boeing 747-200B, two 747-200 Combi, six Boeing 737-300, three Boeing 707-320C, one 707-320B; 13 Fokker F27; two DHC Twin Otter. On order three Airbus A310-300

A Boeing 747

PHILIPPINES

Philippine Airlines

Above: A Boeing 747 at London, Gatwick, showing the current airline trend towards simplified but striking colors (1989).
Below: An Airbus A300 at Singapore (1986)

The national carrier of the Philippines was formed in 1941 by the entrepreneur Andre Sorianao, just before the outbreak of the Pacific War, to operate domestic services only. Operations were resumed in 1946 with one route between Manila and Legaspi, but soon spread out among the myriad islands that make up the sprawling country with its teeming population. International flights started a year later, with a route from Manila to California via Guam, Wake Island and Honolulu using DC-4s and DC-6s, but these were suspended in 1954. A service was maintained with Hong Kong with DC-6s and later with Viscounts.

Domestic network equipment included DC-3s, DHC Otters and Scottish Aviation Twin Pioneers hopping between 72 points on the islands, many of them just strips in the jungle. Viscounts and Fokker F27s arrived in the late 1950s and DC-8s in 1962 to begin international operations once more. The airline was nationalized in 1977.

The airline today flies a 42-point domestic network and international scheduled passenger services to Singapore, Kuala Lumpur, Taipei, Hong Kong, Honolulu, San Francisco, Los Angeles, Tokyo, Melbourne, Sydney, Brisbane, Ho Chi Minh City, Jakarta, Bangkok, Karachi, Rome, Frankfurt, Amsterdam, Paris, Beijing, Xiamen, Dharan, Dubai, Bahrain, Riyadh and London.

Fleet: seven Airbus A300B4; seven Boeing 747-200B, ten Boeing 737-300; two McDonnell Douglas DC-10-30; ten British Aerospace One-Eleven 500; six Shorts 360-300; seven Fokker 50. On order four Boeing 737-300; three Fokker 50. (Two Boeing 747-200 to be leased from February 1991)

AUSTRALIA

Qantas

Qantas Airways

Boeing 747-300

Australia's national long-haul airline can trace its roots back to 1920 when the company was founded as Queensland and Northern Territory Aerial Services. With just an Avro 504K and a Royal Aircraft Factory BE2e the fledgling airline began flying mail services between dusty wool towns. In 1928 Q.A.N.T.A.S. began the first scheduled air service in Australia – the 80 miles from Brisbane to Toowoomba. The same year the Flying Doctor service was inaugurated.

In 1934 the airline started operating the Singapore-Brisbane sector of the new Imperial Airways mail route between Britain and Australia. De Havilland DH86s in the livery of Qantas Empire Airways began the service and, after some initial technical snags, the service settled down – flying a long overwater hop from Timor to Singapore. The journey from Brisbane to London's Croydon airport took between 12 and 14 days. In

1938 Qantas was re-equipped with 'C' class Empire flying boats and moved its headquarters to Sydney. The journey time for the Southampton-Sydney flying boat service was cut to nine and a half days. Eventually there were six 'C' class in service.

The airline made a major contribution to the Australian war effort in the Pacific. Qantas flying boats ferried men and equipment into New Guinea where Australian troops held the southern flank of the Japanese advance. The airline also managed to operate Catalinas across the Pacific and to Ceylon (Sri Lanka) on a journey that took 28 hours in the air. The building of an airstrip on the Cocos Islands permitted landplanes take over the London-Sydney journey, allowing a break between Perth and Ceylon. At the end of the war Qantas flew a motley collection of aircraft, including DC-3s, Liberators, Lancastrians and DH Dragons, as well as various flying boats.

A British Aerospace 125-3B, used in flight-crew training

Qantas

In October 1947 Lockheed Constellations took over on the so-called 'Kangaroo Route' flying London-Sydney in four days, with stops at Cairo and Singapore. That year the government of the Commonwealth of Australia bought out first BOAC's 50% shareholding, then the rest of the airline.

In the 1950s the airline introduced Super Constellations and opened new routes to the Philippines and Japan. A service was opened to Johannesburg via Mauritius in 1952. Five years later the airline was granted route authority to fly a round-the-world service from Sydney to San Francisco, New York and London. The first jets, long-range short-fuselage Boeing 707-138s, went into service in 1959 and had supplanted the Super Constellations by 1964. The company bought Lockheed Electra turboprops in 1960 to fly its regional and Asian routes and services across the Tasman Sea to New Zealand. The airline's first 747-200Bs entered service in 1973, and they still provide the backbone of the all-Boeing fleet. Two short-fuselage 747SPs were acquired to fly the less frequented routes to the smaller Australian and New Zealand cities.

In November 1990 Qantas decided to sell its older 747s (nine Pratt & Whitney-powered 747-200s) in a bid to raise cash in the build-up to the airline's proposed privatization and the deregulation of the Australian airline industry. Subsequently seven were sold in early 1991 to leasing companies for use by United Airlines.

The airline operates scheduled passenger services from Sydney,

The McDonnell Douglas MD-81 – originally the DC-9 Super 80 – first entered airline service in late 1980

SAS put ex-military DC-4s into airline service in the late 1940s

The McDonnell Douglas DC-9-20 first entered service with SAS in 1968

SAS flies an extensive intra-Scandinavian route network of scheduled passenger services to the major cities of Europe, Africa, the Near, Middle and Far East, and the Americas.

Fleet: two Boeing 767-200ER, seven 767-300ER; ten McDonnell Douglas DC-10-30, 15 McDonnell Douglas MD-81, 11 McDonnell Douglas MD-82, two McDonnell Douglas MD-83, seven McDonnell Douglas MD-87, 48 McDonnell Douglas DC-9-40, three DC-9-50, nine DC-9-20; eight Fokker F27-600, one F27-200. On order four Boeing 767-300ER; one McDonnell Douglas MD-81, seven MD-82, five MD-83, 11 MD-87; 13 Fokker 50

SINGAPORE

Singapore Airlines

Above: An unmistakable Airbus A310

Right: Boeing 737-300

The flag carrier of Singapore was formed in 1972 when Malaysia-Singapore Airlines was broken up. The joint airline had a short but complex history. In the immediate post-colonial period of the late 1950s Malayan Airways Ltd, with its headquarters in Singapore, was jointly owned by BOAC, Qantas and the newly independent governments of Singapore, Malaya, Sarawak, Brunei and North Borneo. During 1963-66 the carrier operated as Malaysian Airlines; from 1966 to 1971 as Malaysia-Singapore airlines, the consortium was split. Singapore Airlines prospered with the country's newly acquired independence and grew at a phenomenal rate – purchasing Boeing 747-200Bs, Douglas DC-10-30s, Boeing 727-200s and Airbus A300B4s for a growing network of regional routes and long-haul operations across the Pacific and to Europe. During 1977-79 it operated Concorde on the London – Singapore route via Bahrain in a joint venture with British Airways. As the airline has expanded, the government has adopted a policy of gradually selling its shareholding to local investors and currently retains just over 50%.

Singapore Airlines operates scheduled passenger services to 58 cities in 37 countries linking Singapore with Auckland, Christchurch, Adelaide, Brisbane, Darwin, Melbourne, Sydney, Perth, Port Moresby, Denpasar, Jakarta, Medan, Kuala Lumpur, Kuantan, Penang, Langawi, Bangkok, Hong Kong, Taipei, Nagoya, Fukuoka, Osaka, Tokyo, Seoul, Beijing, Shanghai, Manila, Bandar Seri, Begawan, Katmandu, Dhaka, Calcutta, Colombo, Madras, Bombay, New Delhi, Karachi, Malé, Mauritius, Cairo, Dubai, Dharan, Bahrain, Istanbul, Athens, Rome, Vienna, Zurich, Frankfurt, Amsterdam, Paris, Brussels, Copenhagen, London, Manchester, Honolulu, San Francisco, Los Angeles, and Vancouver. Fleet: six Airbus A310-300, six A310-200; seven Boeing 747-400, 11 747-300, three 747-300 Combi, six 747-200, one 747-200F. On order 22 Boeing 747-400; four Airbus A310-300

Singapore Airlines operate the Pratt & Whitney powered version of the Boeing 757-200 rather than the Rolls-Royce variant that launched the series in 1983

REPUBLIC OF SOUTH AFRICA

SAA

South African Airways

Above: A Boeing 747.   Right: A Pratt & Whitney powered Boeing 747-300. The type originally entered service in 1983.

The flag carrier of South Africa was founded in 1934 as a state-owned enterprise controlled by the SA Railways Administration. The new airline took over the assets and liabilities of the financially struggling Union Airways, which since 1929 had been operating an airmail service between the country's population centers.

South African Airways also took possession of Union's small fleet of Junkers F13s and W34s, with three Ju52/3ms on order. These 14-seaters inaugurated a Johannesberg – Kimberley – Cape Town route on 1 November 1934. New routes were opened as the decade progressed, reaching ever further out across Africa. In 1936 18 ten-seat Junkers Ju 86s went into service. In 1939 28 Lockheed Lodestars were ordered. In 1935 SAA swallowed up the Windhoek-based South West African Airways, which was also flying a small fleet of Junkers aircraft on mail services around the former German colony.

The war saw SAA's airliners being called up by the government as military transports. In 1944 some of the Lodestars were returned to civil service, to be joined by several DC-4s, DC-3s and Avro Yorks in late 1945.

SAA expanded rapidly after the war. A Johannesburg-London service with three intermediary stops was opened in 1946, while a mixed fleet of DC-3s, Vikings, DH Doves and Lodestars flew a growing internal and regional network. Lockheed Constellations entered service on the airline's long-haul routes in 1950.

When BOAC introduced the DH Comet on the route from London to Johannesburg in a bid to stay competitive, SAA did a leasing deal to fly the Comets, still in BOAC colors but with SAA crews. After the Comet was grounded following a series of crashes, the Constellations were put back into service. Long-range DC-7Bs supplanted the Lockheed aircraft in 1956, flying the route to London, now with just one inter-mediary stop at Kano in Nigeria. Technically SAA had already entered the jet age with the Comet 1, but the turbine revolution came in longer lasting form with a fleet of seven Viscount 813s, introduced on the main internal routes in November 1958. Three long-range Boeing 707-344s, special models with full-span leading edge flaps for operations from hot and high-altitude airports, went into service in 1960.

The national government's apartheid policy, meanwhile, made South Africa a pariah in decolonizing black Africa. Overflying rights were progressively denied, but aircraft manufacturers did not hold back from supplying the airline with new equipment. Boeing 727-100s began to replace the Viscounts on the internal routes in 1965. In 1976 the Boeing 747-200 took the airline into the wide-body era, flying from Johannesburg to London following the line of the west African coast in 12 hours. SAA was also a customer for the 747SP or "Special Performace", the very long range version of the airliner which has allowed the airline to beat overflying bans. On a delivery flight a 747SP was flown from Boeing's Everett plant 10,290 miles non-stop to Cape Town, a record for civil aircraft at the time (1976).

Today SAA flies scheduled passenger and freight services to African destinations including Harare, Gaberone, Moroni, Bulawayo, Windhoek, Maputo, Mauritius, Réunion, Victoria Falls, Lusaka, Lubumbashi and Lilongwe. Long-haul international flights link Johannesburg, Durban and Cape Town with Rio de Janeiro, Hong Kong, Ilha do Sal, Lisbon, Taipei, Rome, Abidjan, Vienna, Zurich, Frankfurt, Paris, Amsterdam, Tel Aviv and London.

Fleet: four Airbus A300B2, four A300B4, one A300C4; two Boeing 747-300, five 747-200B, one 747-200B Combi, four 747SP, 17 Boeing 737-200. On order seven Airbus A320; two Boeing 747-400

Above: The Boeing 747-300 entered service with Swissair in March 1983
Left: Airbus A310

THAILAND

Thai International

Thai Airways International

An Airbus A300 taking on passengers

T he International flag-carrier of Thailand began operations in 1959 with three ex-SAS Douglas DC-6Bs. The Scandinavian airline provided technical and managerial assistance while building up its own hub for Asian services at Bangkok. Flights to Burma, India, Hong Kong and Singapore were begun in 1960.

The Thai government bought out the 15% holding of SAS in 1977. In 1988 the domestic operator, Thai Airways, was merged with the airline. Intercontinental services were launched in 1971 with flights to Australia, followed a year later by services to Europe as Thailand grew in importance as a business and leisure destination. That growth has been reflected in Thai International's modern fleet — with Airbus, Boeing and

McDonnell Douglas MD-11 aircraft on order.

Today an extensive network of scheduled passenger services connects Bangkok to 43 destinations in 31 countries throughout the southeast Asia region, the Middle East, Australia, Europe and the US. Thai Airways flies an extensive internal network of domestic services.
Fleet: 11 Airbus A300B4, one A300C4 Combi, eight A300-600, two Airbus A310-200; two Boeing 747-400, two 747-300, six 747-200, one Boeing 737-400, three 737-200; three McDonnell Douglas DC-10-30ER; one BAe 748; four Shorts 330, two Shorts 360. On order one Airbus A300-600, eight Airbus A330; five BAe 146-300; six Boeing 747-400, six Boeing 737-400; four McDonnell Douglas MD-11

Boeing 747-300

PORTUGAL

TAP

Air Portugal

Boeing 707

Overleaf, above: A Boeing 737-200 at London, Heathrow
Overleaf, below: Boeing 727-200

Transportes Aeroes Portugueses was founded in 1944 as a department of the ministry of transport and began operations flying from Lisbon to Casablanca with a Lockheed L18 Lodestar. Scheduled services began with a DC-3 in 1946. In 1953 the operation was acquired by private business and merged with Aero Portuguesa, founded in 1934. It was built up to serve Portugal's African and Asian colonies and points in Europe with a fleet of Constellations and DC-6Bs. A route to London was flown jointly with BEA using the latter's Viscounts and Comet 4Bs. In 1962 TAP took delivery of its first jet, a Caravelle. TAP was nationalized following the revolution of 1975, the

first Boeing 727s being delivered in that year.

Scheduled international passenger and freight services are flown to Montreal, Toronto, Boston, Newark, New York, Los Angeles, Caracas, Curaçao, Recife, Rio de Janeiro, São Paulo, Kinshasa, Brazzaville, Casablanca, São Tomé, Harare, Abidjan, Dakar, Johannesburg, Luanda, Sal, Bissau and Maputo. There are also flights to the Portuguese Atlantic islands of Madeira and the Azores.
Fleet: five Airbus A310-300; two Boeing 727-200, eight Boeing 737-200, one 737-200C, five 737-300; seven Lockheed L-1011-500. On order two Airbus A340; two Boeing 737-300

Lockheed L-1011-500 Tristar

TAP

USA

TWA

Lockheed L-1011 TriStar

rans World Airlines, one of the most famous names in airline history, was at the end of 1990 struggling for commercial survival as losses mounted once again in a period of worldwide recession in the aircraft industry. In January 1991 American Airlines agreed to buy TWA's routes from the US to London, Gatwick, in a cash-raising bid, a move which precipitated a bitter Anglo-US battle over rights to fly from Heathrow.

The airline was formed on 1 October 1930 as Transcontinental and Western Air, the result of a merger between Transcontinental Air Transport, a part of Western Air Express (the other part became Western Airlines) and Pittsburgh Aviation Industries Corporation. The new com-

pany had a key contract – to fly air mail on a central multi-stop trans-America route from New York to Los Angeles, which effectively subsidized the passenger operation. Locked out of the production run for rival United Airline's Boeing 247, the airline commissioned a new transport aircraft from Douglas which emerged in July 1933 as the single prototype Douglas DC-1 in TWA markings. The first of 20 follow-on DC-2s was delivered in mid-1934. The DC-2s were able to make the transcontinental mail flights in 18 hours.

The larger DC-3 joined the TWA fleet in 1936, followed by the first of five Boeing Model 307 Stratoliners in 1940. In 1939 Howard Hughes bought a large block of the company's stock. The mercurial millionaire

TWA first flew the Northrop Alpha mailplane in 1931. A fast single-engined monoplane, it could also carry six passengers

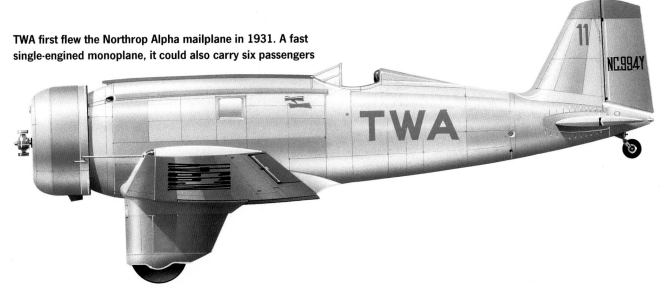

TWA

pressed for a long-range luxurious aircraft that would eventually emerge as the Constellation (it entered service in 1944) and provoked some heated boardroom dramas. The war meant that TWA's operations were largely militarized – including a transatlantic air bridge flown by the Stratoliners.

During the postwar air travel boom TWA opened intercontinental routes via Gander and Shannon to London and Paris and to North Africa. A Constellation-flown route onwards from western Europe to China was opened in 1948 via Athens, Cairo, Dharan, Bombay and Colombo to Hanoi, Canton and Shanghai. Financial and industrial problems at the end of the 1940s, including a prolonged pilot's strike in 1946, slowed down the company's growth. But in 1950 the carrier officially retitled itself Trans World Airways and began a new period of confident expansion. It ordered a fleet of Martin 4-0-4s for its internal routes and Super Constellations for the long-haul routes.The last DC-3 was retired by 1953. However, boardroom battles with the increasingly eccentric Howard Hughes began to dominate the management's attention from the mid-1950s onwards. Hughes was forced to surrender his voting power to a committee of trustees. In 1961 a damages suit was

filed against him for breaches of anti-trust laws in the monopolizing supply of equipment and finance. This legal battle did not end until 1968 when the court found in the airline's favor. Hughes by this time had become a complete recluse.

TWA had mananged meanwhile to get into the jet age early. Its first Boeing 707-131 entered service on 20 March 1959, flying non-stop from San Francisco to New York. In 1961 the Convair 880 was introduced on domestic routes – this aircraft was built to Howard Hughes' own specification.

In 1964 Boeing 727s began operations on domestic services, followed by DC-9s. The last TWA Constellation scheduled passenger service was flown in 1967, into Kansas City. TWA's management toyed with the ideas of ordering either a US-built supersonic transport or the Anglo-French Concorde but recoiled from trying to make SST operations a commercial reality without massive government subsidies. In 1971 TWA entered the wide-body era with its first Boeing 747-100s, Lockheed L-1011 TriStars following in 1972.

On 26 September 1985 TWA was taken over by the Wall Street entrepreneur Carl Icahn, who acquired 52% of the company's shares. The

UK

Virgin Atlantic

Exuberant nose-art forms part of the livery of Virgin, as seen on this Boeing 747

Formed in 1984 as a subsidiary of the Virgin entertainment group run by the entrepreneur Richard Branson, Virgin Atlantic Airways is now a separate, privately owned company which still holds to the founding principles of offering cut-price, long-haul air travel with some attendant stylishness. The airline began with a single Boeing 747 in a blaze of publicity when it took over the Gatwick-Newark route abandoned three years earlier by Freddie Laker's defunct Skytrain.

In 1988 the airline began a considerable expansion, opening new routes to Tokyo and to New York (John F Kennedy), adding two more 747-200s to the fleet and opening a new maintenance facility at its London/Gatwick base. As Virgin's passenger figures have grown and as the airline has matured, its image has slowly evolved from that of a cheap-ticket transatlantic carrier to one that offers solid competition for the business traveler with its upper class service providing the bulk of its operating profit.

After a legal battle at the beginning of 1991 Virgin Atlantic was allotted four British Airways landing slots at Tokyo's congested Narita Airport, which would allow it to operate two additional round trips a week to Japan. Virgin launched a London-Los Angeles route in May 1990.

The airline operates from London, Gatwick, to Miami, New York (JFK), Newark, Los Angeles, Singapore and Tokyo.It is seeking government approval to operate out of London (Heathrow).

Fleet: six Boeing 747-200

Virgin still use the venerable and reliable Vickers Viscount 802
to connect with their Gatwick base

3

A-Z GUIDE TO AIRLINES

A directory of the world's smaller carriers, regional and domestic airlines

Dan Air, Boeing 727

AeroMexico

This airline, originally known as Aeronaves de Mexico, began flights between Mexico City and Acapulco in September 1934. In the 1950s several smaller operations were swallowed up including Aerovías Reforma, Lamsa, Aerovías Guest and Aerolíneas Mexicanas. In 1959 the airline was nationalized and the stake held by Pan Am was bought by the government. The airline, although state-owned, was declared bankrupt in 1988. After restructuring a 65% stake was sold to a banking consortium, the rest going to the Mexican pilots' union. The airline was renamed Aerovías de Mexico but still is marketed as AeroMexico. Privatization was commercially successful and the airline was back in profit in 1990. From Mexico City 35 domestic destinations are served, plus five US cities.

Fleet: three McDonnell Douglas DC-10-30, two DC-10-15, eight MD-82, 16 DC-9-30, five MD-88. On order five McDonnell Douglas MD-88

McDonnell Douglas DC-10-30

AeroPeru

Empresa de Transporte Aéreo del Peru

The national carrier of Peru is a small airline with a complex pedigree. The first Peruvian airline, Líneas Aéreas Nacionales, was formed in 1931. It was subsequently taken over by the air force and in 1960 split into a regional and trunk network. In 1973 the latter operation, known as Satco, was transmuted into a national airline. The operation was denationalized in 1981. From the capital, Lima, AeroPeru serves domestic destinations across the length of the mountainous country. International operations to major Latin American capitals and to Miami

began in October 1973. There are plans to update the fleet by the acquisition of four Boeing 767-200ER and up to eight Boeing 737-300 over the next five years.

Fleet: two Boeing 727-100, one 727-100C; two Fokker F28-1000; five McDonnell Douglas DC-8-62

Fokker F28

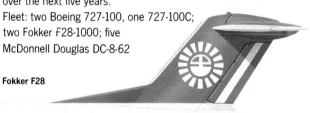

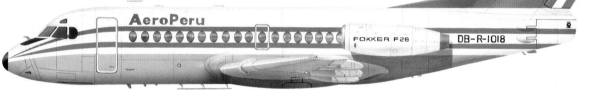

Avianca

Aerovías Nacionales de Colombia

The national carrier of Colombia has its roots in the oldest airline in the Americas, SCADTA, founded in 1919 by German investors. In 1940 this operation merged with Servicio Aéreo Colombiano, founded in 1931, and with 80% backing from Pan American to form Avianca. The last shares owned by Pan Am in the company were acquired in 1978. Bogotá is the hub of an extensive domestic network. International services are flown to major South American cities, to the Caribbean, Miami, New York and Los Angeles, and to Madrid, Paris and Frankfurt.

Fleet: one Boeing 747-200 Combi, four Boeing 707-320B, eight Boeing 727-200, ten 727-100, three 727-100C, two Boeing 767-200ER

Boeing 747-124

Aero California

This Mexican regional carrier is based at La Paz close to the tip of the long spur of Baja (Lower) California, from where scheduled passenger, cargo and charter operations are flown. The company began operations in 1960 with DC-3s. From the La Paz hub scheduled passenger services are flown today to Mexico City and other major Mexican towns including Guadalajara, Tijuana, Ciudad Obregón and Hermosillo.
Fleet: three Douglas DC-3, three Douglas DC-9-15; one Convair 340; one Cessna 402C; one Beech C45

Air Algérie
Société Nationale des Transports Aériens

The original Air Algérie was founded in the former French colony in 1949. In 1953 it merged with the Compagnie Air Transport to form the present operation, which became the national carrier in 1962 after independence. Initial equipment included Constellations, DC-4s and Caravelles. The airline was nationalized in 1972. As well as providing a comprehensive domestic network, Air Algérie flies scheduled passenger and cargo services to 34 international destinations in North and West Africa, Europe and the Middle East.
Fleet: two Airbus A310-200; two Boeing 767-300, 11 Boeing 727-200, 16 Boeing 737-200C (including three cargo variants); eight Fokker F27-400; three Lockheed L-100-30

Boeing 737-200

Air Atlantic

This carrier based at St John's, Newfoundland, was founded in 1986. It is largely a commuter operation with a fleet of Dash 8s and BAe 146s flying a network of scheduled passenger services to destinations in eastern and central Canada – and to Bangor, Portland and Boston in the US. These flights feed Canadian Airlines International's hubs at St John's, Halifax and Montreal.
Fleet: 15 Boeing Canada Dash 8-100; three BAe 146-200

Air BC

This British Columbia-based airline was founded in 1980 through the merger of a number of small regional operators. Today it flies a fleet of BAe 146s and twin-props on regional and commuter services in western Canada and to Portland in the US, with its main operating hub at Vancouver where it operates as an "Air Canada Connector". The international airline acquired a 75% holding in Air BC in 1987.
Fleet: five BAe 146, six BAe Jetstream 31; four Boeing Canada Dash 7, 16 Dash 8; eight DHC Twin Otter

British Aerospace 146

Airborne Express

This Ohio-based overnight air parcel operator was founded in 1980. It is a subsidiary of the Seattle-based Airborne Freight Corporation and from its operating hub at Wilmington, Ohio, its fleet of DC-8 and DC-9 cargo aircraft fly all over the US with express freight and parcels.
Fleet: nine McDonnell Douglas DC-8-61F, six DC-8-62F, two McDonnell Douglas DC-9-15, six DC-9-30, ten DC-9-30F, one DC-9-40; 12 NAMC YS-11A. On order four McDonnell Douglas DC-8-61, three DC-8-63, nine McDonnell-Douglas DC-9-30, 13 DC-9-40

Air Charter International

This major French charter operator was founded in 1966 as a subsidiary of Air France. In 1978 Air Inter was granted a 20% shareholding in return for a route-swap. The airline operates inclusive tours and charters from 35 points of departure within France to holiday and leisure destinations world wide.
Fleet: two Airbus A300B4; three Boeing 737-200, seven Boeing 727-100; four Aérospatiale Caravelle 10B

Airbus Industrie A300

America West Airlines

This company, which began operations in 1981, became the tenth largest airline in the United States less than a decade later, with its annual revenues topping $1 billion. With its headquarters at Sky Harbor International airport, outside Phoenix, Arizona, in the heart of the US "sunbelt", the airline operates from two major hubs, Phoenix and Las Vegas, with scheduled services to destinations all over the mid- and south-west, Texas and California. Passenger services are also flown to Minneapolis, Newark, Ontario, Washington DC and Honolulu.
Fleet: 16 Airbus A320; 32 Boeing 737-200, 22 737-300, 11 Boeing 757-200; 9 Boeing Canada Dash 8-100. On order 58 Airbus A320; 15 Boeing 737-300, two Boeing 747-400, three Boeing 757-200; 12 Boeing Canada Dash 8-100

Boeing 757-200

American Trans Air

This Indianapolis-based US charter operator was founded in 1973 as a travel club management service. It now operates domestic and international charters, plus an Indiana-Fort Myers link and a service from San Francisco to Hawaii.
Fleet: five Boeing 727-100, four Boeing 757 (leased); ten Lockheed L-1011-1. On order six Boeing 757

Ansett Australia

This Melbourne-based major Australian domestic carrier traces its roots to Ansett Airways founded in 1936 by Reginald M.Ansett with a single Fokker Universal. In 1957 it took over Australian National Airways (ANA) in a heavily regulated political deal, allowing the airline to stay profitable while bringing in new equipment such as Viscounts and Electras. Ansett grew quickly by swallowing more companies including, in 1963, the Perth-based MacRobertson Miller, one of the oldest Australian airlines. The first jets came in 1964 – Boeing 727s, followed by DC-9s in 1967. Rapid growth continued through the 1970s. In 1980 the holding company, Ansett Transport Industries (ATI), was bought out by a consortium led by the TNT transport group and Rupert Murdoch's News Corporation. ATI has a number of subsidiaries of which Ansett Australia is just one. Scheduled services are flown on a network covering the whole of Australia.
Fleet: eight Airbus A320; five Boeing 767-200, five Boeing 727-200, one 727-200F, 16 Boeing 737-300; two Fokker F27, ten Fokker 50. On order, four Airbus A320

Boeing 737-300

Ariana Afghan Airlines

The national carrier of Afghanistan was founded in 1955, initially with a shareholding and technical support from Pan Am. Its first equipment was four DC-3s and two DC-4s. Today the airline operates as best it can (the airport at Kabul often coming under rocket attack) to a range of domestic destinations and to Amritsar, Delhi, Dubai, Moscow, Tashkent and Prague.

Fleet: two Boeing 727-100C; two Antonov An-24, three Antonov An-26; two Tupolev Tu-154M; two Yakovlev Yak-40

Boeing 727

Australian Airlines

The state-owned domestic airline was founded in 1946 as Trans-Australia Airlines. The present name was adopted in 1986. In 1988 it changed its status from a statutory corporation to a public limited company in preparation for privatization and the de-regulation of the Australian airline industry.

Fleet: five Airbus A300B4; 16 Boeing 737-300, five 737-400, nine Boeing 727-200, one 727-100C; four Boeing Canada Dash 8; two Fokker F27-600. On order 12 Boeing 737-400

Boeing 737

Austrian Airlines

Formed in 1957 with the help of SAS and a consortium of Austrian banks, this airline began operating with four chartered Viscounts. Today the airline operates major international routes to 56 cities in 36 countries in Europe, North Africa, the Middle East and Japan. A Vienna-Moscow-Tokyo service is jointly operated with Aeroflot and All Nippon Airways. Austrian also flies an extensive network of charters through its 80%-owned subsidiary, Austrian Air Transport. Internal and commuter flights are flown by the wholly-owned subsidiary, Austrian Air Services, using a fleet of Fokker 50s. Austrian Airlines is 61% owned by the state government, 8% by Swissair, 3.5% by All Nippon and 1.5% by Air France.

Fleet: two Airbus A310-324; five Fokker 50; eight McDonnell Douglas MD-81, five MD-82, five MD-87. On order two Airbus A310-324, six Airbus A320, seven Airbus A321; two McDonnell Douglas MD-83; one Fokker 50

McDonnell Douglas MD-81

148

Aviaco

Aviación y Comercio

Founded in 1948 in Bilbao as a cargo airline with a fleet of three Bristol Freighters, this Spanish domestic carrier began to offer scheduled passenger services in the 1950s – across Spain and to the Balearics – with a fleet of DC-3s, DH Herons and prewar Sud-Est Languedocs. Holiday charters also brought important business. Today the airline is Spain's major domestic carrier and a subsidiary of Iberia. From the Madrid hub services are flown to Valencia, Murcia, Málaga, Jérez, Badajoz, Vigo, Valladolid, La Coruña, Santander, Granada, Almería, Bilbao, San Sebastian, Pamplona, Reus, Zaragoza, Ibiza, Palma and Mahon.
Fleet: eight Fokker F27-600; two McDonnell Douglas MD-83, 21 McDonnell Douglas DC-9-30. On order 13 McDonnell Douglas MD-88 (deliveries began in 1990)

McDonnell Douglas DC-9

Aviogenex

This state-owned Yugoslav air charter company operates holiday and leisure flights in conjunction with Yugotours. It was founded as Genex Airlines in 1968.
Fleet: five Boeing 727-200, five Boeing 737-200; two Tupolev Tu-134A-3

Boeing 737-200

Bahamasair

The national carrier of the Bahamas is wholly government-owned and was formed in 1973. It succeeded Bahamas Airways Ltd, set up after World War II as a subsidiary of BOAC, which operated DC-3s and Grumman Goose amphibians between the islands and to Florida. Today twin-props provide links between the islands and services to the Turks and Caicos. From the base at Nassau airport, international services are operated to Newark, Philadelphia, Washington, Miami, Orlando and Tampa.
Fleet: four Boeing 737-200, two Boeing 727-200; four BAe 748. On order five Boeing Canada Dash 8-300

Balair

This Swiss company, with its headquarters in Basle, operates passenger and cargo charters to world-wide destinations. The company was incorporated in 1953 and Swissair holds a substantial stake.
Fleet: one Airbus A310-300; three McDonnell Douglas DC-10-30, three MD-82, one MD-83. On order one Fokker F27-400

McDonnell Douglas DC-10   Airbus Industrie A310-300

Balkan Bulgarian Airlines

The Bulgarian state airline TABSO was formed in 1949 with Soviet help and a small fleet of Ilyushin Il-14s and Lisunov Li-2s, Soviet-built DC-3 clones. The operation came under full national control in 1954 and the name was changed to its present form in 1968. With an all Soviet-built fleet, the airline flies to seven domestic destinations and to 52 further points in Europe, Asia and Africa.
Fleet: three Boeing 737-500 (leased); four Antonov An-12V, 16 An-24; seven Ilyushin Il-18; 21 Tupolev Tu-154, 16 Tu-134; 11 Yakovlev Yak 40

Yakovlev Yak-40

Bangladesh Biman

A national airline was formed in 1972 soon after the creation of the new state of Bangladesh from what had been East Pakistan. Domestic services link the capital Dhaka with Chittagong, Cox's Bazar, Sylhet, Jessore, Ishurdi and Saidpur. International services are flown to London, Amsterdam, Rome, Athens, Singapore, Kuala Lumpur, Bangkok, Rangoon, Katmandu, Calcutta, Bombay, Karachi, Dubai, Abu Dhabi, Muscat, Doha, Dharan, Jeddah and Tripoli.
Fleet: four DC-10-30; two Fokker F28-4000; two BAe ATP. On order 1 BAe ATP

McDonnell Douglas DC-10-30

Birmingham European Airways

This small business-orientated airline was founded in 1983 as Birmingham Executive Airways. It was acquired by the Plimsoll Line shipping group in 1988 when the name was changed to its present form. Scheduled passenger services are flown from its operating hub at Birmingham International Airport to Amsterdam, Belfast, Copenhagen, Frankfurt, Milan, Oslo, Newcastle, Stuttgart and Cork. Closely allied to British Airways, BEA flies several services for the flag carrier.
Fleet: three BAe Jetstream 31, five BAe One-Eleven 400; one Shorts 360

British Aerospace One-Eleven 400

Braathens SAFE

This independent Norwegian airline was founded after World War II as a subsidiary of Braathens shipping line. Early equipment included DC-3s and DC-4s, and a service was operated to Hong Kong during 1949-54 – hence the initials, which stood for South American and Far East air transport. Today a small, modern fleet operates a network of scheduled domestic services within Norway and, in addition, a service to the island of Spitsbergen above the Arctic Circle from Bergen and Tromsö. The airline is the launch customer for the Boeing 737-500. Holiday charters provide important business in the summer. The Busy Bee charter operation, a wholly owned subsidiary, is,together with Braathen Helicopter, active in the North Sea oilfields. In 1991 Braathens began international scheduled services from Norway to Newcastle in the UK and Billund in Denmark. Further expansion was planned.
Fleet: 16 Boeing 737-200, three 737-400, two 737-500. On order three Boeing 737-4, 23 737-500

Boeing 737-200

Britannia Airways

The Luton-based Britannia has, through a series of mergers and changes of ownership, become the largest charter company in the world. Originally founded in 1962 as Euravia, operating inclusive tours, it successfully rode the 1960s boom in package holidays. In 1964 it began operating the big turboprop Bristol Britannia and changed its name. A year later it was acquired by the Canadian-based Thomson Organization. In 1988 Thomson bought the Horizon Travel business and merged its airline, Orion, with Britannia. Although hit by a profits slump in 1990, Britannia announced its intention of replacing its aging 737-200 fleet, with up to 20 150-seaters expected in 1992. Britannia operates charter flights from the UK to Mediterranean holiday destinations and long-haul services to Australia, the Caribbean and the US. Scheduled flights are also operated to European resorts and from Luton to Belfast.
Fleet: three Boeing 767-200, six Boeing 676-200ER, four Boeing 757 (leased), 25 Boeing 737-200, two 737-200C, seven 737-300. On order six Boeing 767-200ER, six Boeing 757

Boeing 767-200

British Midland

Derbyshire-based British Midland traces its parentage to Derby Aviation founded in 1938. In 1953 Derby Airways began flying domestic services in the UK with a fleet of six DC-3s. In 1964 the name British Midland was adopted and a series of changes of ownership followed. In 1978 came a management buy-out and the airline has successfully expanded its activities and revenues since then, through internal growth and through takeovers. Manx Airlines is a subsidiary, as is Loganair Airways through the holding company, Airlines of Britain Holdings plc,

formed in 1987. SAS acquired 24.9% of the company at the end of 1988. British Midland currently operates a comprehensive scheduled services network.
Fleet: two Boeing 737-400, four 737-300; six McDonnell Douglas DC-9-32, six DC-9-15; two Boeing Canada Dash 7; three BAe ATP. On order two Boeing 737-300

Short 360

G-BMHX

Brymon

This British regional airline began life as an independent in 1972, with a route linking London and Plymouth. The airline was an early enthusiast for the DHC Dash 7 short take-off and landing twin-prop. Today Brymon is owned by the shipping group Plimsoll, itself owned in part by British Airways and by Maersk. Brymon's services link Heathrow with Plymouth and Newquay, Gatwick with Plymouth, Exeter and Birmingham, and Plymouth with the Channel Islands. There are also services from Plymouth, Exeter and Bristol to the Scilly Isles. International flights are

made from London City Airport to Paris and from Plymouth to Cork and Dublin. In 1990 a new route using Dash 8s was set up, with Bristol as a hub.
Fleet: six Boeing Canada Dash 7, two Dash 8. On order two Boeing Canada Dash 8; five Canadair RJ

Boeing Canada Dash 8

BRYMON

Cameroon Airlines

Formed in 1971 when the Cameroon government pulled out of Air Afrique, this national airline is still owned in part (25%) by Air France. The rest is owned by the government of this former French West African territory. From the capital, Douala, the airline operates an extensive domestic network and international services to African capitals and to London, Paris, Rome, Zurich, Geneva and Frankfurt.
Fleet: one Boeing 747-200B Combi (leased), one Boeing 737-200, two 737-200C; two BAe 748

British Aerospace 748

China Airlines

The airline of the Republic of China, or Taiwan, was founded in 1949, as China Air Transport, with leftover US military transports. It became the national carrier in 1965. The carrier's rapid growth has mirrored that of the Pacific rim region. In late 1990 the carrier ordered three Boeing 747-400s to operate the transpacific route to Los Angeles. From Taipei international passenger services are flown to Hong Kong, Bangkok, Manila, Nagoya Singapore, Kuala Lumpur, Dharan, Dubai, Jakarta, Tokyo, Okinawa, Seoul, Honolulu, Los Angeles, New York, San Fran-cisco, Dallas, Anchorage, Luxembourg and Amsterdam. In 1991 the airline's subsidiary, Hua Hsin, was to begin flights to Canada and Australia, using some of the new 747-400s. Fleet: six Airbus A300B4, three A300-600R; two Boeing 747-400, three 747-200B, one 747-200B Combi, three 747-200F, four 747SP, four Boeing 737-200. On order three 747-400; three A300-600; five MD-11

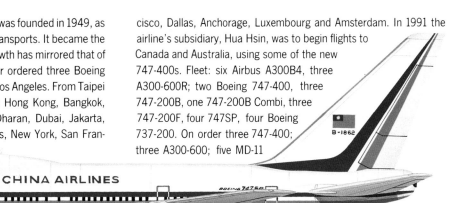

Boeing 747SP

Chosonminhang Korean Airlines

The state airline of the Democratic People's Republic of Korea was established in 1954 as UKAMPS, a department of the Ministry of Communications. It succeeded a joint North Korean-Soviet operation called SOKAO which had operated a Lisunov Li-2 between Pyongyang and Chita. Today the airline flies an internal network of scheduled passenger services, plus international routes, from the capital, Pyongyang, to Beijing, Berlin, Khabarovsk, Sofia and Moscow.
Fleet: eight+ Antonov An-24; four Ilyushin Il-18, five+ Il-14, four Il-62M, one Il-62; four Tupolev Tu-154, two Tu-134

CrossAir

This Swiss regional airline was founded in 1975, but scheduled passenger services did not begin until 2 July 1979, using Saab 340 regional twin-props. Today the airline, 38% of which is owned by Swissair, operates an extensive passenger network throughout western Europe. It has recently acquired a 35% share in the Czechoslovakia-based Tatra Air, which will fly a Saab 340 between Bratislava, Zurich and Munich. Fleet: three BAe 146-200; 24 Saab 340A. On order four BAe 146-200; 11 Saab 340B

British Aerospace 146-200

Cruzeiro

One of the pioneering airlines of South America, the Rio de Janeiro-based Cruzeiro was founded in 1927 by German entrepreneurs as the Condor Syndikat. It became Serviços Aéreos Condor in 1941, backed by Brazilian private capital. In January 1943 it was nationalized as Serviços Aéreos Cruzeiro do Sul. After World War II a large fleet of DC-3s, Convair 440s and Fairchild C-82 freighters was operated on domestic services and to regional capitals. In 1975 control was bought by the owners of the rival airline, Varig, and flight schedules were integrated. The airline operates a large network of scheduled passenger services within Brazil and to the capitals of Bolivia, Uruguay and Argentina.
Fleet: two Airbus A300B4; six Boeing 727-100, six Boeing 737-200

Boeing 737-200

Cubana

The Compañía Cubana de Aviación began domestic services in 1930 with a small fleet of Ford Trimotors. International services were started in 1946. The present name was adopted after the 1959 revolution when the airline was nationalized. Starved of western spares, Cubana became all-Soviet equipped and reorientated its routing to the eastern bloc. Today passenger services are operated from Havana to Lima, Buenos Aires, Mexico City, Montreal, Panama City, Kingston, Georgetown, Barbados and Managua, and, in addition, to Madrid, Brussels, Moscow, Basle, Paris, Prague and Berlin.
Fleet: 26 Antonov An-26, 12 An-24RV; four Ilyushin Il-18, 10 Il-62M, two Il-76TD; five Tupolev Tu-154B2, three Tu-154M; 11 Yakovlev Yak-40, one Yak-42. On order two Yakovlev Yak-42

Dan Air

Dan-Air is still better known as a holiday charter company than as a scheduled airline – although by 1990 it had become the UK's second largest scheduled carrier to international destinations. The airline's engineering division was put up for sale at the end of 1990 to raise cash. Dan Air was formed in 1953 as a subsidiary of the shipping brokers, Davies and Newman Holdings, from where the name is derived. In its early years local services were flown to France and the Channel Islands using Airspeed Elizabethans, DC-3s and Doves, while Avro Yorks flew freighting contracts. Today scheduled passenger flights depart from Heathrow, Gatwick, Manchester, Bristol, Leeds-Bradford and Newcastle airports to holiday and business destinations all over western Europe.
Fleet: one Airbus A300B4; ten Boeing 727-200, two 727-100 (for disposal), three 737-400, two 737-300, four 737-200; 11 BAe One-Eleven 500, three One-Eleven 300, two One-Eleven 200, two BAe 146-300, three BAe 146-100

British Aerospace 146

DHL Air

With a fleet of three veteran cargo-carrying Vickers Merchantmen (converted Vanguards), DHL Air is the British-based air component of the DHL International overnight express delivery service. Operations began in 1983 as Elan Air and today, from its hub at East Midlands Airport, flying operations are conducted by Air Bridge Carriers Ltd, on DHL's behalf, to Cologne, Belfast, Shannon, Dublin and Brussels.
Fleet: three Vickers V.953C Merchantman

Boeing 727

DLT

Deutsche Luftverkehrgesellschaft or DLT is a major German domestic operator, 52% owned by the national carrier, Lufthansa. It was founded in 1958 as Ostfriesische Lufttaxi, adopting its present name in 1974. The airline operates joint ticketing and scheduling arrangements with Lufthansa, serving destinations across the newly united country and using its twin-prop fleet as feeders. DLT also makes its own international flights to European centers from Cologne, Munich, Hamburg and Frankfurt.
Fleet: 12 Embraer EMB-120 Brasilia; ten Fokker 50

Embraer EMB-120 Brasilia

Dominicana

The airline of the Dominican Republic, Compañia Dominicana de Aviación, C por A, was founded in 1944 by a cartel of local businessmen with a 40% holding by Pan Am. Early equipment included DC-3s, DC-4s and Curtiss C-46s flying to Haiti and Miami. Today it is wholly state-owned and scheduled passenger services are flown to Curaçao, Caracas, Port-au-Prince, Aruba, Miami, San Juan, and New York. The Spanish airline, Iberia, was approached, with a view to taking a 40% shareholding in order to overcome financial problems.
Fleet: one Boeing 707-320C, one Boeing 727-200, one 727-100, one 727-100C

Boeing 727

Dragonair

A dynamic, semi-independent regional airline, Hong Kong Dragon Airlines, or Dragonair, was founded by Macau- and Hong Kong-based business interests in 1985, with a network of routes into southern and eastern China. In early 1990 sizeable shareholdings were sold to the Swire Group (owners of Cathay Pacific) and to the International Trust and Investment Corporation of China. The airline flies direct to eight regional cities of the People's Republic and to Beijing and Shanghai. Services to Beijing are flown in Cathay-liveried TriStars. Scheduled passenger services are also flown to the Thai resorts of Phuket and Pattaya, Kagishima, Dhaka and Katmandu.

Fleet: five Boeing 737-200; one Lockheed Tristar (leased)

Boeing 737-200

Eastern Air Lines

The Miami-based Eastern was a casualty of the US airline shakeout, strikes and corporate raiding. Eastern shrank in 1989-90, with the sale of a large number of aircraft (to American Airlines). The airline originally began in 1926 as Pitcairn Aviation; three years later it became Eastern Air Transport. Expansion came rapidly through the acquisition of smaller airlines. In 1967 it swallowed Miami-based Mackey and in 1974 it absorbed Caribair. In 1986 the airline was acquired by Texas Air Corporation. In the 1960s Eastern flew more passengers than any other US airline, more than a million a month. Over the years it was launch customer for important new

aircraft such as the Lockheed Electra and the Boeing 757. By the end of the decade Eastern's shrunken network covered 90 destinations in the US and Canada. Operating under US Chapter 11 bankruptcy status since 1989, the airline ceased operations in January 1991.

Fleet: 34 Airbus A300B4; 60 Boeing 727-200, 25 Boeing 757-200; 20 Lockheed L-1011-1; 40 Douglas DC-10-30, 25 DC-10-51

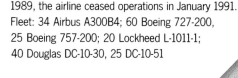
Boeing 757

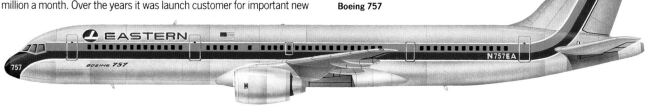

East West Airlines

This Australian domestic carrier was founded in 1947, with four DC-3s flying between Brisbane and Sydney and points in New South Wales and southern Queensland. The company was taken over by Rupert Murdoch's News Corporation and the TNT transport group in 1987. Today East West operates scheduled passenger services to major cities and to leisure and holiday destinations, including Mount Isa, Ayers Rock, Canberra, Brisbane, Melbourne, Sydney, Ayers Rock, Hobart and Norfolk Island. The current F28 fleet is being replaced by the BAe 146.

Fleet: seven Fokker F28; two BAe 146. On order six BAe 146

British Aerospace 146

Ecuatoriana

An airline was formed in Ecuador in 1947, the Compañía Ecuatoriana de Aviación (CEA) SA, flying two war-weary C-46s on a route between Miami and Santiago, Chile, stopping at Panama, the capital, Quito, Guayaquil and Lima along the way. The present company took over the operating rights and assets of CEA in 1974. A small fleet links Quito and Guayaquil to New York, Los Angeles, Chicago, Mexico City and other capitals in Latin America. An all-cargo service is flown to New York, Panama City and Miami. Contract technical support is provided by Israeli Aircraft Industries.
Fleet: three Boeing 707-320B, one 707-320C; one McDonnell Douglas DC-10-30. On order two Airbus A310-300

McDonnell Douglas DC-10-30

Emery Worldwide

This US air parcel service was founded in 1946 as Emery Air Freight. For many years the venture functioned using aircraft chartered from other operators. However, in 1981, when the airline began to acquire its own operational fleet, it changed its name and moved its hub to Dayton, Ohio. The airline was acquired by Consolidated Freightways in 1989 and was merged with CF Airfreight. Today its almost 100-strong fleet moves overnight parcels around the US, the actual flying operations being the responsibility of subcontractors including Ryan International Airlines, Jet East, Orion Air and Rosenbalm Aviation. There is a European hub at Maastricht.
Fleet: two Boeing 707, 38 Boeing 727-100C; 34 McDonnell Douglas DC-8-54/-62/-63/-73, eight McDonnell Douglas DC-9-15

Emirates

Formed as the national airline of the United Arab Emirates (UAE) in 1985, on the initiative of the government of Dubai, Emirates has quickly won an international reputation for service and efficiency with a modern Airbus-based fleet. Scheduled passenger services are flown from Dubai to Amman, Bandar Abbas, Bombay, Cairo, Colombo, Damascus, Delhi, Dhaka, Frankfurt, Istanbul, Jeddah, Karachi, Kuwait (until the invasion of August 1990), London and the Maldives.
Fleet: two Airbus A300-600R, two Airbus A310-300; three Boeing 727-200; one Boeing Canada Dash 7. On order two Airbus A300-600R, three Airbus A310-300

Airbus Industrie A300-600R

Ethiopian Airlines

When this was founded in 1946, initial support came from TWA, with aircraft drawn largely from the TWA fleet, including DC-6Bs and DC-3s serving a largely domestic route network. Today the airline of this troubled country manages to operate scheduled passenger services to 40 domestic destinations. Intra-African services are operated from the capital, Addis Ababa, to Abijdan, Abu Dhabi, Accra, Aden, Bamako, Brazzaville, Conakry, Dakar, Djibouti, Harare, Niamey, Sana'a, Nairobi, Entebbe, Dar-es-Salaam, Kilimanjiro, Lomé, Kinshasa, Douala, Lagos, Monrovia, Luanda, Khartoum, Jeddah and Cairo. There are also international services to Athens, Berlin, Bombay, Beijing, Rome, Frankfurt, Berlin and Moscow.

Fleet: three Boeing 767-200ER, two Boeing 707-320C, three Boeing 727-200, two Boeing 737-200; seven Douglas DC-3; two DHC-5A, six DHC Twin Otter; two ATR42

Boeing 767-200ER

Euralair International

This privately owned charter company, based at Le Bourget airport in Paris, was formed in 1964 as an air-taxi service. Today the airline is a fast-growing operator of charter passenger, cargo and parcel freight to destinations all over Europe and the southern Mediterranean.

Fleet: one Boeing 747-100, three Boeing 737-500, six 737-200; two BAe 146-200QT; seven Cessna Citation I/II/III/V; two Dassault Falcon 10, two Falcon 20. On order two Airbus A321, three Airbus A330

Europe Aero Service

This French charter company, with its headquarters at Perpignan on the French Mediterranean coast, was formed in 1965 and is still a significant operator of the graceful, early-1960s vintage Caravelle airliner. The airline flies charters and inclusive tours to European holiday destinations and to Africa and the Middle East, together with a scheduled service from Paris to Valence, south of Lyons. In 1988 an international scheduled passenger service was opened between Paris and the West African country of Guinée-Bissau.

Fleet: 11 Aérospatiale Caravelle 10B; two Boeing 727-200, three Boeing 737-200; one Saab 340

Express Airlines

This US regional and commuter airline services 40 cities in 15 states, operating its twin-props as part of the Northwest Airlink feeder network into Northwest Airline's trunk route system. Its main operating center is at Memphis and there other hubs with radiating spokes at Milwaukee, Minneapolis and Columbus, Georgia.
Fleet: 25 BAe Jetstream 31; 17 Saab 340

FAT

Far Eastern Air Transport Corporation

This Taiwan domestic airline began charter operations in 1957, starting scheduled passenger services in 1965. Today routes are flown from the capital, Taipei, to Kaoisung, Hualien, Tainan and Makung. International charters are also flown.
Fleet: six Boeing 737-200, two 737-100. On order two ATR72

Boeing 737-200

Federal Express

This is the largest air freight carrier in the world, which has enjoyed spectacularly rapid growth throughout the 1980s. Fedex is a public corporation, founded in 1971. It specializes in door-to-door collection and delivery of parcels and packages and offers a range of ranked-priority services. The operational center is at Memphis International Airport, Tennessee, from where loads are despatched every night all over the US. Operations began in 1973 with a small fleet of Falcon 20 biz-jets. Deregulation of the US air cargo industry in 1977 allowed long-range services to be opened up. A British subsidiary was acquired in 1986 and London and Brussels sorting centers were opened. In 1989 the California-based Flying Tiger Line was acquired with its fleet of Boeing 747 freighters and extensive air cargo operations in the Pacific rim, Asia and Latin America. An all-cargo service between New York and Moscow was scheduled to begin in June 1991.
Fleet: 93 Boeing 727-100C, 51 727-200, 22 727-200C, seven Boeing 747-100F, 13 747-200F; 24 McDonnell Douglas DC-10, two DC-8-73F; 26 Fokker F27-500; 192 Cessna 208 Caravans. On order eight McDonnell Douglas MD-11F (plus 11 options)

Flanders Air

A new airline formed at the beginning of 1990 from the merger of local Belgian airlines, Servisair of Wevelgem and Antwerp-based Frevag airlines. Flanders Air flies passenger charters and cargo and parcel traffic under contract.
Fleet: three Embraer EMB-100 Bandeirante; two Fairchild Metro; one Fokker F27

Florida West Airlines

An all-freight carrier with a fleet of ten Boeing 707-320Cs – operating from Miami to destinations in the Caribbean and to Colombia, Costa Rica, Guatemala and Panama.
Fleet: ten Boeing 707-320C

Boeing 707-320C

Formosa Airlines

This domestic Taiwanese operator was founded in 1966 and flies an internal network of scheduled passenger and freight services from the capital, Taipei, to Kaohsiung, Taitung, Taichung, Makung, Huailien, Orchid Island and Green Island.
Fleet: three BN Islander; five Dornier Do 228-200; three Saab 340; one Short 360

Dornier Do 228-200

160

Ghana Airways

Formed as a national airline in July 1958, following Ghana's independence, the flag carrier took over the local operations of the former West African Airways Corporation with a small fleet of DC-3s and DH Herons. A famously ambitious expansion program in the early 1960s saw the airline operating Viscounts and Ilyushin Il-18s on local networks and Britannias, 707s and VC-10s on international routes. Today a small fleet of Fokker F28s operates domestic and regional services from the capital, Accra, to Kumasi, Sunyani and Tamale, and to the West African capitals, Abijdan, Conakry, Dakar, Lomé, and Monrovia. Longer-haul services are flown to Las Palmas, Düsseldorf, London and Rome.

Fleet: one McDonnell Douglas DC-10-30, one McDonnell Douglas DC-9-50; one Fokker F28-4000, one F28-2000

McDonnell Douglas DC-9-50

Great American Airways

This tiny charter operator has a grandiose name but operates only two DC-9s from its Reno, Nevada, base on charter flights around the western US, bringing vacationers to Reno's casinos.
Fleet: two DC-9-15

McDonnell Douglas DC-9-15

Guyana Airways Corporation

The flag carrier of Guyana can trace its roots back to British Guiana Airways (BGA), founded in 1939. In 1955 the government bought out the private shareholders, and management for BGA (Government) Ltd was initially supplied by British West Indies Airlines. In those days the airline flew to local destinations and to West Indian islands with a fleet of three DC-3s and three Grumman Goose amphibians. The present corporation was founded in 1963 and today Aer Lingus provides contract management and technical support. Guyana's small fleet of aging aircraft operates a network of scheduled passenger services from the capital, Georgetown, with 24 domestic destinations within Guyana itself, and also services to Miami, New York and Barbados.
Fleet: one Boeing 707-320B; two BAe 748; two DHC Twin Otter; one Tupolev Tu-154M

Hapag-Lloyd Flug

This major German charter operator is a subsidiary of the Hapag Lloyd shipping line and was founded in 1972. In 1979 it absorbed Bavaria-German Air. The Hanover-based company flies holiday tours and charters to the Mediterranean, the Canaries, eastern Europe and West Africa.

Fleet: four Airbus A310-200, two A310-300; one Boeing 737-500, seven Boeing 737-400, four Boeing 737-200, two Boeing 727-100. On order one Airbus A310-300; five Boeing 737-500

Airbus Industrie A310-200

Hawaiian Airlines

This airline was founded as Inter-Island Airways in 1929, operating Sikorsky amphibians between the islands. The present name was adopted in 1941. Today Hawaiian operates scheduled passenger services between the islands of Lanai, Maui, Molokai, Oahu, Kauai, Hilo and Kona. International services are flown to the South Pacific islands of American Samoa, Western Samoa, Tonga, Tahiti and Rarotonga, and also to Sydney. Flights are made to the continental US cities of Los Angeles, Las Vegas, San Francisco, Portland, Seattle and Anchorage. In early 1991 Northwest Airlines paid $20 million for a 25% holding in Hawaiian.

Fleet: five Lockheed L-1011-50; two McDonnell Douglas DC-8-72, three DC-8-62, two McDonnell Douglas DC-9-15F, nine DC-9-50, two McDonnell Douglas MD-81; eight Boeing Canada Dash 7

McDonnell Douglas DC-8-62

Horizon Air

This Seattle-based airline was founded in 1981. In 1982 it swallowed Air Oregon and two years later Transwestern Airlines, making it the major regional airline for the northwest US. Scheduled passenger services are operated to 34 cities in the states of Washington, Oregon, Idaho, Montana and Utah.

Fleet: two Fokker F28-100; 16 Boeing Canada Dash 8-100; 32 Fairchild Metro III

Boeing Canada Dash 8-100

Indian Airlines

With over 20,000 employees and carrying more than ten million passengers a year, Indian Airlines is one of the world's largest domestic carriers. It was formed in 1953, taking over the regional services of eight private operators. In the 1950s and 1960s, a fleet of DC-3s and Vickers Vikings, latterly supplemented by F27s and Viscounts, flew a huge network within the sub-continent itself and to Afghanistan, Burma, Nepal and Pakistan. Re-equipment with Airbuses began in 1986 but the airline suffered and services were disrupted by the crash of an A320 at Bangalore in early 1990. The airline's operations are divided into four regions, offering scheduled passenger services to 73 cities including regional links to India's neighboring countries. As many as five A320s were used to assist in the evacuation of Indian nationals from the Persian Gulf area during 1990/91.

Fleet: 11 Airbus A300B4/B2, 19 Airbus A320; 23 Boeing 737-200, one 737-200C. On order three Airbus A300, 12 Airbus A320

Airbus Industrie A320

Intair

This major Canadian regional airline was formed in 1987 when Quebec Aviation, Quebecair and Nordair Metro merged. With operations centered on Montreal, Intair operates a network of scheduled passenger services across central and eastern Canada, with connections to Prince Edward Island and Newfoundland.

Fleet: six ATR 42; eight Fairchild Metro (to be sold in 1991); seven Fokker F100

Fokker 100

Interflug

The national airline of the former German Democratic Republic had shrunk rapidly from 38 to 18 aircraft in the year when the East German state was wound down and attracted offers for its routes and assets from both Lufthansa and British Airways. The airline was formed in 1954 under the prewar name of Deutsche Lufthansa. It adopted its new name in 1963, using a small fleet of Ilyushin Il-18s and Il-14s to fly to capitals in eastern Europe. In the 1960s new routes to Cuba and Viet Nam were opened, using Ilyushin Il-62s. In mid-1990 Interflug was operating to over 50 international destinations including Moscow, Hanoi, Havana, Beijing, and Luanda. New Airbus A310s had replaced Il-62Ms on the main long-haul routes in 1989. Only 17 of the Soviet-built aircraft were in use in February 1991 when it was announced that the airline was to shut down.

Fleet: three Airbus A310-300; 12 Ilyushin Il-62/62M, eight Ilyushin Il-18, 18 Tupolev Tu-134A, eight Let 410UVP; plus approximately 300 small aircraft for agricultural aviation.

Ilyushin Il-18

Iraqi Airlines

The flag carrier of Iraq was founded in 1946 as a subsidiary of Iraqi State Railways. In the 1950s and 1960s the airline operated domestic and regional services in the Middle East with a small fleet of Viscounts and DH Doves. Re-equipment followed, with new aircraft supplied by US and Soviet manufacturers. After the invasion of Kuwait in August 1990 15 Kuwaiti airliners were captured on the ground and subsequently repainted in Iraqi colors. The subsequent international air blockade led to transit and landing rights being withdrawn worldwide. Fleet: three Boeing 747-200C, one 747SP, two Boeing 707-320C, six Boeing 727-200, one Boeing 737-200; six Lockheed JetStar II; four Dassault Falcon 50, two Falcon 20F; four Piaggio P166.30; five Antonov An-12, three An-24; Ilyushin Il76T/M.
N.B. Figures relate to fleet strength prior to Gulf War.

YI-AKC

Istanbul Airlines

Istanbul Hava Yollari, IHY

This Turkish charter operator was formed in 1985 and operates from Turkey to western European countries and to northern Cyprus. Scheduled services to Munich, Hamburg and Cologne began in 1989-90.
Fleet: two Boeing 737-400; four Super Caravelle 10R. On order two Boeing 737-300

Super Caravelle 10R

Jamahiriya

Libyan Arab Airlines

The Kingdom of Libya airlines was formed in 1964; five years later it was renamed Libyan Arab Airlines. Jamahiriya Air Transport was a charter operation formed in 1982, now absorbed into the main organization. An extensive domestic network is operated, with international scheduled passenger services flown from Tripoli to destinations in North Africa, Europe and the Middle East.
Fleet: two Airbus A310-200; five Boeing 707-320C, ten Boeing 727-200; three Fokker F28-4000, 13 Fokker F27-600, two F27-500, one F27-400; five Lockheed L-100-20/30; five DHC Twin Otter; 21+ Ilyushin Il-76

Boeing 727-200

Japan Air System

This large Japanese domestic airline was formed in 1971 with the merger of Toa Airways and Japan Domestic Airlines. It operates a modern fleet along 66 routes to 38 cities throughout Japan.
Fleet: five Airbus A300B2, five Airbus A300B4; two McDonnell Douglas DC-10-30ER, 17 McDonnell Douglas MD-81, two McDonnell Douglas MD-87, 14 McDonnell Douglas DC-9-40; 33 NAMC YS-11. On order seven Airbus A300-600; 21 McDonnell Douglas MD-81, six McDonnell Douglas MD-87

Airbus Industrie A300

Japan Asia Airways

Formed in 1975 to operate services between Japan and Taiwan, this airline is a subsidiary of Japan Air Lines and operates scheduled passenger and cargo services from Tokyo and Osaka to Taipei and Hong Kong, and from the island of Okinawa to Taipei.
Fleet: two Boeing 747-100, one 747-300; four McDonnell Douglas DC-10-40

Boeing 747-300

Jersey European Airways

Formed in 1979, this small British independent has its headquarters at Exeter. Scheduled passenger services are flown to Belfast, Birmingham, Bournemouth, Exeter, the Isle of Man, London, Teeside and Southampton, and to Dinard and Paris. A major expansion was prepared for 1991, using six Fokker F27s leased from the Australian airline East West.
Fleet: nine Fokker F27-500; four Shorts 360; four Embraer Bandeirante; four DHC-6 Twin Otter

Fokker F27-500

Karair

This small Finnish airline began life in 1950 as Karhumaki Airways, flying scheduled domestic passenger services with a couple of DC-3s and a Lockheed Lodestar. In 1957 it became Kar-Air O/Y and is now a subsidiary of Finnair. A scheduled service is flown from Helsinki to Lappeenranta near the Soviet border with aircraft leased from the parent company. The airline was the launch customer for the ATR 72 and took delivery of the first aircraft in 1989.
Fleet: two Airbus A300B4; three ATR 72. On order two ATR 72

Airbus Industrie A300B4

Kenya Airways

The national carrier of Kenya was established in 1977 after the collapse of the East African Airways Corporation. Today the airline flies scheduled international passenger services to London, Paris, Rome, Athens, Frankfurt and Zurich, within Africa to Cairo, Khartoum, Addis Ababa, Mogadishu, Entebbe, Harare, Dar-es-Salaam, Lusaka, Kigali, Bujumbura, Ligongwe, Gaborone and Zanzibar, and also to Dubai and Jeddah. Domestic services are flown from Nairobi to Mombasa, Malindi and Kisumu.
Fleet: two Airbus A310-300; three Boeing 707-320B, one Boeing 720B, two Boeing 757; one McDonnell Douglas DC-8-73CF, one McDonnell Douglas DC-9-30; two Fokker F50, one Fokker F27-200. On order one Fokker F50

Airbus Industrie A310-300

Ladeco

This Chilean domestic airline was formed in 1958 as Línea Aérea del Cobre Ltda, with two DC-3s flying from Santiago to copper-mining centers in northern Chile. Today the airline, in which Ansett Transport Industries had a substantial holding, flies an extensive route network linking the capital with 16 destinations in this long, mountainous country. Regional services are flown to Mendoza in Argentina, Asunción, Guayaquil, Bogota, São Paulo and Rio de Janeiro. Flights are also made to Miami and New York and Washington.
Fleet: two Boeing 737-200, two 737-300, four Boeing 727-100, two 727-100C, two Boeing 707-320C; two Fokker F27-500. On order two Boeing 757

Boeing 707-320C

LTU

This major German charter operator was founded in 1955 as Lufttransport Union. Today it operates holiday and inclusive tour operations from major German cities to worldwide leisure resort destinations. Its primary operating base is Düsseldorf.

Fleet: six Lockheed L-1011-1, one L-1011-200, three L-1011-500. On order three Airbus A330-300; three McDonnell Douglas MD-11

Lockheed L-1011-200

Luxair

Société Luxembourgeoise de Navigation Aérienne

The national airline of the Duchy of Luxembourg was formed in 1961 as Luxembourg Airlines. It is 20%-owned by the government, the rest by banks and industrial holding companies. Scheduled passenger services are flown to Amsterdam, Copenhagen, Geneva, Athens, Faro, Frankfurt, Hamburg, Málaga, Palma, Paris, Rome, Nice and Munich. There are commuter and air taxi subsidiary companies.

Fleet: one Boeing 747SP, three Boeing 737-200; six Fokker 50; two Fairchild Metro II. On order two Boeing 737-400; three Fokker 50

Boeing 737-200

Maersk Air

This commercially ambitious Danish airline was formed in 1969 as a subsidiary of the A P Moller (Maersk Line) shipping group. It has a 40% shareholding in TPL which owns in turn, Brymon and Birmingham Executive Airways. It owns 38% of Danair Air Services, together with Maersk Air Cargo, plus air taxi, North Sea helicopter support and aircraft leasing operations. It formally abolished the operation of its subsidiary, Maersk Commuter, in 1990. Maersk operates a network of scheduled passenger services within Denmark and to Southend in Britain and Stavanger in Norway.

Fleet: two Boeing 737-200, seven 737-300, one 737-500; eight Fokker 50; two Shorts 360; plus several helicopters. On order three Boeing 737-300, four 737-500

Boeing Canada Dash 7

Malev

The Hungarian state airline was formed in March 1946 as a joint Hungarian-Soviet venture (called Magyar-Szovjet Polgari Légiforgalani Tarsasag), using Lisunov Li-2s and Ilyushin Il-14s. In 1954 the Hungarian state acquired the Soviet 50% holding. Malev was one of the first eastern bloc countries to acquire western airliners. A BAe-146 QT was operated with TNT on an express parcels network which branched out to Budapest in 1990 in an venture which proved to be commercially unsuccessful. The airline flies scheduled passenger services to the capitals of Europe and to points in the Middle East and North Africa.
Fleet: three Boeing 737-200; one BAe 146-200QT; 14 Tupolev Tu-154B2, ten Tupolev Tu134/134A; one Yakovlev Yak 40

Boeing 737-200

Manx Airlines

The aircraft of this comparatively new airline, bearing the three legged badge of Man on their tails, have developed a comprehensive route network linking the Isle of Man in the Irish Sea with points in Britain and Ireland. Founded in 1982, Manx became a wholly owned subsidiary of the Airlines of Britain Group in 1988. Scheduled passenger services link the island with Belfast, Birmingham, Blackpool, Dublin, Edinburgh, Glasgow, Liverpool, London, Manchester, Luton, Leeds/Bradford and Newcastle.

Fleet: one BAe 146-100, three BAe ATP; three Shorts 360

Vickers Viscount

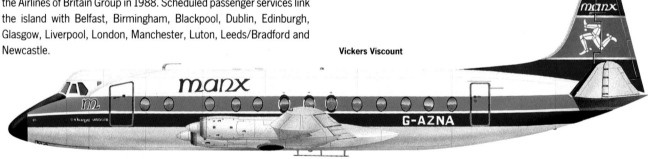

MarkAir

This important regional operator in Alaska traces its origins from Interior Airways founded in 1946. It operated as Alaska International from 1972 until 1984 when the present name was adopted. Based at Anchorage, MarkAir flies scheduled passenger services to 13 points within the state, while the subsidiary MarkAir Express provides lightplane services to 80 more destinations scattered across the huge Alaskan land mass and the Aleutian island chain.
Fleet: five Boeing 737-200C; three Lockheed L-100-30; one Boeing Canada Dash 7. On order two Boeing Canada Dash 8-300

Martinair

Founded in 1958 by J Martin Schröder as Martin's Air Charter, this diversified company has as the major part of its business, worldwide passenger and freight charters. The present name was adopted in 1974 and the company has branched into inclusive tours and air taxi operations, with, in addition, an important in-flight service and catering subsidiary supplying other operators. Martinair maintains and operates under contract the Dutch government's VIP Fokker F28. Scheduled passenger and freight services are flown from Amsterdam to Baltimore, Detroit, Los Angeles, Miami, San Francisco, Minneapolis, New York, Seattle and Toronto.

Fleet: one Airbus A310-203, one A310-203C; two Boeing 747-200C, two Boeing 767-300ER; three McDonnell Douglas DC-10-30CF, one McDonnell Douglas MD-82; two Cessna Citation II. On order four Boeing 767-300ER

McDonnell Douglas DC-10-30F

Metro Airlines

This major US regional airline, with its operations base at Dallas-Fort Worth, Texas, operates all over the southeast and southwest of the US, serving 23 airports in 13 states and in the Caribbean. The airline is divided into five operating companies, which reflect the company's growth by takeover since its was founded in 1966. They are Metro, Metro Express, Chaparral Airlines and Metro Air Northeast. Metroflight and Chaparral participate in the American Eagle marketing link which feeds the American Airlines trunk network. The Virgin Islands operator, Sunaire, was acquired in 1985 and now operates as Aviation Associates. An all-freight subsidiary is known as Starlite Express.

Fleet: 36 BAe Jetstream 31; eight Boeing Canada Dash 8-100; three CASA/IPTN CN-235; 11 DHC Twin Otters; 18 Saab 340; five Gulfstream G-IC. On order eight Saab 340 (Metroflight)

Mexicana

Compañía Mexicana de Aviación de CV

This was founded in 1921, making it the second oldest airline in the Americas. At one time it was wholly owned by Pan American who reduced their stake in the 1950s when the fleet was nearly all Douglas DC types: -3s, -4s and -6s. The first jets were three DH Comet 4Cs, ordered in 1960. In 1989 the Mexican government sold its remaining 54% shareholding to private investors. In 1990 the airline ordered a large number of Airbus A320s, with a strategy of competing head-on with the US mega-carriers. The first four were to be delivered during 1991. Today the airline operates from its Mexico City base to 30 points within the country. Connections are offered to all the major cities of the US, plus Havana, San Juan, Guatemala City, and San José in Costa Rica.

Fleet: 44 Boeing 727-200; one McDonnell Douglas DC-10-10, five DC-10-15. On order 22 Airbus A320

McDonnell Douglas DC-10-15

MGM Grand Air

Reviving a tradition of prewar luxury air travel, this airline, owned by a Hollywood studio, began operations in 1987 between Los Angeles and New York with three renovated Boeing 727s. The airliners' interiors have been reworked to provide super luxury travel with business facilities en suite for 33 passengers only. In 1990 the airline acquired three DC-8-62s with the intention of refurbishing them with 39 first- and 40 business-class seats for an equivalent New York-London-Paris service, although in early 1991 the airline had not yet been able to obtain a license for this route.

Fleet: three Boeing 727-100; three McDonnell Douglas DC-8-62. On order two Boeing 757-200

McDonnell Douglas DC-8-62

Middle East Airlines

Throughout the travails of the civil war, Lebanon's Middle East Airlines has managed to keep flying, although services have been severely curtailed. MEA was formed by private business interests in 1945. It was assisted by Pan American from 1949 to 1955 when it became an associate of BOAC which took a 49% stake. In 1965 the company took over Air Liban which had grown with the help of Air France. In 1969 MEA also took over the Sabena protégé, Lebanese International Airways, which had operated from Beirut to points in the Middle East and to European capitals. Today the airline, conditions permitting, operates a network of scheduled passenger services in Europe, the Middle East and northwest Africa.

Fleet: three Boeing 747-200M, six Boeing 707-320C, five Boeing 720B

Boeing 707

Midway Airlines

This major US domestic regional operator began revenue-earning services in 1979. Air Florida was taken over in 1984. With hubs at Chicago and Philadelphia (opened in 1989), the airline flies scheduled passenger services to 54 destinations in the eastern and southeastern US. There are two commuter subsidiaries, Iowa Airways and Midway Commuter, jointly marketed under the banner of the Midway Connection. Midway sold its Philadelphia hub operation to USAir at the end of 1990 in a $65 million deal.

Fleet: 11 Boeing 737-200; nine McDonnell Douglas DC-9-15, 19 DC-9-30, four McDonnell Douglas MD-82, eight McDonnell Douglas MD-87; 21 Dornier Do 228. On order 33 Dornier Do 328 (Midway Connection); 40 McDonnell Douglas MD-82

Boeing 737-200

Midwest Express

This Milwaukee-based US regional airline was founded in 1984. From the hub it operates its 13-strong fleet to major US cities including Boston, Denver, Detroit, New York, Dallas/Fort Worth, Atlanta, Philadelphia, Kansas City, Los Angeles, San Francisco, San Diego, Washington DC, Fort Lauderdale and Tampa.
Fleet: eight McDonnell Douglas DC-9-10, three DC-9-30, two MD-88

McDonnell Douglas DC-9-10

Monarch

A major British holiday and charter airline carrying almost 3 million passengers a year, Monarch began operations in 1968 with Bristol Britannias. Today the airline has a fleet of Boeings and Airbuses, offering inclusive tour and seat-only flights to many Mediterranean resort destinations. The airline began operations to Miami in 1988, and to New York and Boston in 1990. Scheduled passenger services are flown to Mahon, Málaga and Tenerife.
Fleet: two Airbus A300-600R; nine Boeing 737-200; nine Boeing 757-200. On order two Airbus A300-600R

Airbus Industrie A300-600R

Nationair

This Montreal-based Canadian charter airline began operations in 1984. Two years later it bought Quebecair's charter operations and its fleet of McDonnell Douglas DC-8s. Passenger and cargo charters are flown to Europe and South America and a scheduled passenger service from Montreal to Brussels. Following the bankruptcy of Soundair in 1990, Nationair acquired Odyssey to become Canada's third largest carrier.
Fleet: four Boeing 747, four Boeing 757; Four McDonnell Douglas DC-8-61, two DC-8-62, two DC-8-63

Boeing 747-100

Ontario Express

In mid-1987 Ontario Express began operations from Toronto to destinations in Canada and the US. As a member of the 'Canadian Partner'' domestic airline alliance, it is partly owned by the PWA Corporation, the owners of Canadian Airlines International. A subsidiary, Frontier Air, operates from Timmins, in Ontario, across the state. Ontario Express was due to be the first Canadian airline to operate the ATR 72.
Fleet: three ATR 42; 14 British Aerospace Jetstream 31. On order five ATR 42, eight ATR; eight Embraer EMB-120-Brasilia

British Aerospace Jetstream 31

PLUNA

Primeras Líneas Uruguayas de Navegación Aérea

The national airline of Uruguay was founded in 1936 and nationalized in 1951. Postwar equipment consisted largely of DC-3s; the first turboprops were Viscounts in 1960. Domestic flights have been operated by TAMU, the transport command of the air force, since 1963. From Montevideo the small fleet flies scheduled passenger and cargo services to Pôrto Alegre, São Paulo, Rio de Janeiro, Asunción, Santiago, Buenos Aires, Punta del Este and Madrid.
Fleet: two Boeing 707-320B, two Boeing 737-200

Reeve Aleutian

This was founded in 1931 as a charter operator, scheduled operations beginning in 1948 from Anchorage, Alaska, to points in the Aleutian and Pribilof Islands with a small fleet of DC-3s and Grumman Goose amphibians. Today the same network is served and charter work is also undertaken.
Fleet: two Boeing 727-100C; two Lockheed L-188 Electra; three NAMC YS-11A

Rich International Airways

This US charter airline was founded in 1971. Passenger charters are flown from points in the northeastern US to Europe, the Middle East, Africa, Mexico and the Caribbean. A scheduled route is flown from New York to Guyana. The airline also operates extensive troop charters for the US government.
Fleet: two McDonnell Douglas DC-8-62

McDonnell Douglas DC-8-62

Royal Air Maroc

This national airline was formed as Compagnie Nationale de Transports Aériens in 1957, shortly after Moroccan independence, to take over the operations of the former private airline, CTA. A fleet of DC-3s and Beech 18s originally operated the airline's domestic sevices while four L-749 Constellations served the international routes. The airline's first jets were Caravelles, supplied in 1961. Today the airline is almost wholly state-owned, with a hotel and catering business subsidiary and a domestic airline, Royal Air Inter, also wholly state-owned. An all-Boeing fleet flies from Casablanca to destinations in Morocco itself, and to major cities in North and West Africa, the Middle East and Europe. Transatlantic flights are operated to New York, Montreal and Rio de Janeiro.
Fleet: two Boeing 707-320C, eight Boeing 727-200, five Boeing 737-200, two 737-200C, one 737-400, one Boeing 747-200 Combi, one 747SP, two Boeing 757-200. On order nine Boeing 737-400; three ATR 42

Boeing 727-200

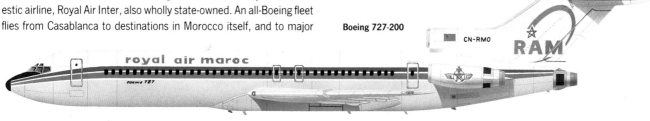

Royal Brunei Airlines

The national carrier of the Sultanate of Brunei was established in 1974 with some technical assistance provided by British Airways. The airline flies regular passenger and cargo services from the capital, Bandar Seri Begawan, to Singapore, Hong Kong, Kuala Lumpur, Manila, Bangkok, Taipei, Darwin, Jakarta and Dubai.
Fleet: five Boeing 757-200 (two leased)

Boeing 757-200

177

Royal Nepal Airlines

The Katmandu-based national airline of Nepal was founded in 1958 as a state-run enterprise to serve domestic routes in the mountain kingdom and fly the route to Calcutta previously operated by Indian Airlines. The first equipment was three DC-3s. Today this small but modern airline flies passenger and cargo services from Katmandu to 37 domestic destinations and also to Delhi, Calcutta, Karachi, Singapore, Dhaka, Dubai, Rangoon, Hong Kong, Bangkok and Frankfurt.
Fleet: one Boeing 727-100C, one 727-100, one Boeing 757-200, one 757-200 Combi; three BAe 748; 12 DHC Twin Otter

British Aerospace 748

Ryanair

A pioneer of cut-price scheduled air travel, this privately owned Irish airline has had several commercial ups and downs since operations were begun between Luton and Dublin in 1986. In addition, services are now offered to Cardiff, Liverpool, Brussels, Munich and Knock in western Ireland, from Knock to Birmingham, Luton and Gatwick, from Shannon to Luton and from Galway to Luton. The company also operates charter and holiday flights. In 1987 it acquired the assets of London European Airways, integrating them into the company as the charter wing, Ryanair Europe. The "London European" name was to be restored in 1991 for scheduled services from Luton.
Fleet: eight Rombac One-Eleven 500; two BAe 748; three ATR 42-300. On order ten ATR 42/72

Rombac One-Eleven 500

SkyWest

Utah-based SkyWest is a US commuter airline, formed in 1972. Operating under the Delta Express marketing banner, it feeds Delta Airline's hubs at Los Angeles and Salt Lake City. SkyWest's twin-prop fleet brings in passengers from 42 cities in the mid-west and west of the US.
Fleet: nine Embraer EMB-120 Brasilia; 37 Fairchild Metro. On order 20 Saab 2000; seven Embraer EMB-120 Brasilia

Embraer EMB-120 Brasilia

Sobelair

Société Belge de Transports par Air

The charter subsidiary of Sabena was founded in 1946, flying ad hoc charters and utility flights, mainly in the then Belgian Congo. Today the airline operates passenger charter and inclusive tour flights to Mediterranean and African resort destinations.
Fleet: three Boeing 737-200, one 737-300, one 737-400. On order one Boeing 737-400

Boeing 737-300

Somali Airlines

The national carrier of Somalia was founded in 1964, with Alitalia owning 49% of the shares. In 1977 the airline became entirely state-owned. A network of domestic routes are flown from the capital, Mogadishu, and to Doha, Djibouti, Dubai, Abu Dhabi, Cairo, Frankfurt, Rome, Jeddah and Nairobi.
Fleet: one Airbus A310-300; two Boeing 707-320B; two Dornier Do 228

Airbus Industrie A310-300

Southwest Air Lines

SWAL

SWAL was formed in 1967 to operate a service in the Ryukyu islands, the 300-mile chain stretching southwest from the Japanese home island of Kyushu to Okinawa. Previously the services had been operated by Air America. The airline is based on Okinawa and scheduled passenger services link Naha airport with most of the islands in the Ryukyus and the Sakishima Shoto groups.
Fleet: seven Boeing 737-200; six NAMC YS-11A; four DHC Twin Otter

Boeing 737-200

Southwest Airlines

This Dallas-based airline ranks 38th in the world in terms of annual sales. It was formed in 1967 as Air Southwest to service a growing market for low-fare air travel within Texas. The present name was adopted in 1971. Today the airline flies its large fleet of Boeing 737-200s and -300s to 31 US airports in 14 states.
Fleet: 48 Boeing 737-300, 48 737-200, six 737-500. On order 14 Boeing 737-300, 42 737-500, 42 737-500

Boeing 737-300

Sudan Airways

The national airline of Sudan was founded in 1946. In the 1950s it operated a small fleet of DC-3s and DH Doves on local and regional routes to neighboring countries, with a single Viscount flying between London and Khartoum. Today it operates a domestic network across the country with international links to Middle East capitals and to Kano, Nairobi, Addis Ababa, Tripoli, N'Djamena and Cairo, plus Athens, Frankfurt, London and Rome.
Fleet: six Boeing 707-320C, two Boeing 737-200C; one Fokker F27-200, two F27-600, two Fokker 50

Boeing 707-320C

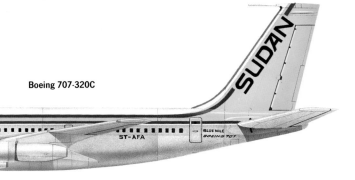

Sun Country Airlines

Formed by former Braniff staff in 1982, this Minneapolis-based charter operator flies largely within North America, and also to holiday destinations in Mexico and the Caribbean, and to Europe with its single DC-10.
Fleet: three Boeing 727-200, one McDonnell Douglas DC-10-40

McDonnell Douglas DC-10-40

Syrianair

Syrian Arab Airlines

The state airline of Syria was restructured in 1961 to succeed Syrian Airways, which had itself been founded in 1946. Following the short-lived union of Egypt and Syria in 1960-61, the two countries had formed United Arab Airlines with an ambitiously modern fleet of Comets and Viscounts. Syrian Arab Airlines, to give it its full title, flies from Damascus to Aleppo, Latakia and Deirezzor, and to major cities in Europe, North Africa, the Middle and Far East.
Fleet: three Boeing 727-200, two Boeing 747SP; two Caravelle 10B; two Dassault Falcon 20F; five Antonov An-26, five Antonov An-24; four Ilyushin Il-76; six Tupolev Tu-154M, six Tupolev Tu-134; seven Yakovlev Yak-40

Boeing 747SP

TAAG-Angola Airlines

Linhas Aéreas de Angola

Angola's national airline was founded in 1940, with the title of Direcçao de Exploraçao dos Transportes Aéreos (DTA). In the 1950s and 1960s it operated a fleet of DC-3s and a DH Rapide on domestic and regional services. After independence in 1973 the airline adopted its present name. A small fleet of aging 707s and Fokker twin-props flies services from the capital, Luanda, to 18 internal destinations. International scheduled passenger services are flown to São Tomé, Kinshasa, Brazzaville, Maputo and Lusaka, and to Paris, Rome, Lisbon, Berlin, Moscow and Rio de Janeiro. There is a subsidiary air charter company with two Boeing 707-320Cs.
Fleet: one Boeing 707-320B, five 707-320C, four Boeing 737-200, one 737-200C; one CASA C212; one Lockheed L-100-30; six Fokker F27; two Ilyushin Il-62; two Yakovlev Yak-40

Taca International Airlines

This El Salvador-based airline was founded in 1939. In the 1960s it operated two Viscounts on a route via Panama and Belize to New Orleans where it had its operating headquarters. Today the airline provides services to New Orleans, Los Angeles, Houston, Miami, San Francisco, New York and Washington, as well as to regional Central American capitals.
Fleet: four Boeing 737-200, one Boeing 767-200. On order two 737-300, one 767-300ER.

Boeing 737-200

TAROM

Transportutile Aeriene Române

The Romanian state airline began operating in 1954 with Soviet-supplied Li-2s and Ilyushin Il-14s. Its current equipment – a mix of eastern, western and home-built (Rombac One-Elevens) aircraft – reflects the former dictatorship's changing relationships with the European power blocs. In spite of post-revolution operating problems, Tarom maintain a network of internal passenger and cargo services, plus international scheduled passenger services to European capitals, to Tripoli, Algiers and Casablanca, Amman, Beirut, Cairo, Damascus, Istanbul, Abu Dhabi, Larnaca and Tel Aviv, Karachi, Bangkok, Singapore, Beijing and New York.

Fleet: four Boeing 707-320C; six BAe One-Eleven-500, four One-Eleven 400; four Rombac One-Eleven-500; 32 Antonov An-24, 12 Antonov An-26; five Ilyushin Il-62/62M, 11 Ilyushin Il -18; 11 Tupolev Tu-154B. On order three Boeing 767-200ER

BAe One-Eleven 500

TAT

Transport Aérien Transrégional

This French airline was formed in 1968 as Touraine Air Transport and grew gradually from air-taxi operator to major regional carrier by taking over other competitors, including Air Paris, Rousseau Aviation, Air Alpes and Air Alsace. An extensive network of scheduled passenger services is operated from Paris (Orly) and from Lyons. A seasonal summer service is flown from Tours and Poitiers in midwestern France to London (Gatwick). In addition, TAT flies a number of services on behalf of Air France.

Fleet: seven Fokker F28-1000, four F28-2000, five F28-4000, one Fokker 100; 14 Fairchild FH-227B, two Fairchild F27A, three Fairchild Metro; two ATR 42-300; five DHC Twin Otter; three Beech 99; one Nord 262. On order six ATR 42, 30 ATR 72; seven Fokker 100

Fokker 100

TNT

The air freight arm of the Australian-controlled TNT transport group began operations in 1968. In 1984 came a move into Europe with the establishment of an operating hub in Cologne with several sub-centers. The workhorse of the operation is a fleet of BAE 146-200QT (Quiet Traders) optimized for flying overnight parcel services from city to city. Joint ventures at the outset of the 1990s with the Hungarian airline Malev and Aeroflot have proved commercially disappointing.

Fleet: 11 BAe 146-200QT two BAe 146-300QT; one Fokker F27-600F. On order ten BAe 146-300QT

British Aerospace 146-200QT

Yemenia

This was formed in 1963 as Yemen Airlines, the national airline of the Yemen Arab Republic. The present name was adopted in 1978 when the airline was reorganized, with the Yemeni government and Saudi Arabia holding respectively 51% and 49% of the capital. In 1990 the airlines of North and South Yemen, Alyemda and Yemenia, agreed to merge. A network of domestic routes is operated from the operating base at Sana'a – with international scheduled passenger services to cities including Amman, Doha, Jeddah, Sharjah, Khartoum, Addis Ababa, Karachi, Damascus, Riyadh, Cairo, Rome, London, Amsterdam, Istanbul, Moscow, Frankfurt, Bombay, and Paris.

Fleet: (Yemenia) four Boeing 727-200, one Boeing 737-200; two Boeing Canada Dash 7. (Alyemda – Democratic Yemen Airlines) two Boeing 707-320C, two Boeing 737-200C; two Boeing Canada Dash 7; one Antonov An-24; one Antonov An-26; one Tupolev Tu-154

Boeing 727-200

Zambia Airways

The national carrier of Zambia was formed in 1967, soon after independence, with initial technical support from Alitalia and then from Aer Lingus. A small fleet operates scheduled passenger and freight services to points within Zambia from the capital, Lusaka. International services are flown to Nairobi, Dar-es-Salaam, Harare, Gaborone, Johannesburg, Jeddah, Entebbe, Frankfurt, London, Rome, New York and Bombay.

Fleet: one Boeing 737-200; two ATR 42-300; one McDonnell Douglas DC-8-71, one McDonnell Douglas DC-10-30. On order one McDonnell Douglas MD-11

McDonnell Douglas DC-10-30

Index

Index

Acknowledgements

All *color photographs* in this book by Mark Wagner, except for the following: Airbus Industrie 12; Boeing 14; David Cooper 59,60; JAL 80 above and below; Avión AeroMexico 138 top; Air BC 140 top; Air Europe 141 top; Air Pacific 144 center; Air Transat 144 bottom; Quadrant/Flight 146 bottom, 179 top, 185 top; Michael Sugden Ltd 147 bottom,156 bottom; Australian Airlines TN 148 center; Malcolm Ginsberg & Associates 151 top; British Aerospace 152 bottom, 178 top; Varig 154 top; Communications in Business 157 bottom; Ethiopian Airlines 158 top; Far Eastern Air Transport Corporation 159 center; Great American Airways 161 center; Charles Barker Traverse-Healy Ltd 163 top; Japan Air Lines 165 top and center, 179 bottom; Aviation Picture Library/Austin J.Brown 165 bottom; Finnair 166 top; Lauda Air 168 bottom; Linjeflyg 170 top; Luxair 171 center; MGM Grand Air 174 top; Midwest Express 175 top; Monarch Airlines 175 center; Nationair 175 bottom; Ontario Express 176 top; Rich International Airways 177 top; Patrick Lennon Associates 177 bottom; Ryanair 178 center; SkyWest Airlines 178 bottom; Somali Embassy 179 center;Sun Country Airlines 180 bottom; Syrianair 181 top; TAT 182 center; TNT Express 182 bottom; Tower Air 183 top; Turkish Airlines 184 bottom; Aviation Picture Library/Mark Wagner 186 bottom; Yemen Airways 187 top. *Black and white photographs:* Christy Campbell, 32, 39, 40, 53, 54, 55, 71, 83, 100, 120. *Color artwork, cutaway drawings and three-view schematics:* copyright Greenborough Associates. *Book design:* Hussain R. Mohamed.

THE COMPLETE GUIDE TO

HOME WIRING

*A Comprehensive Manual,
from Basic Repairs to
Advanced Projects*

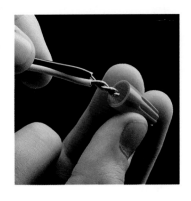

COWLES
Creative Publishing, Inc.

Contents

COWLES
Creative Publishing, Inc.
Minnetonka, Minnesota, USA

Copyright © 1998
Cowles Creative Publishing, Inc.
5900 Green Oak Drive
Minnetonka, Minnesota 55343
1-800-328-3895
All rights reserved
Printed in U.S.A.

President: Iain Macfarlane
Group Executive Director: Zoe Graul
Creative Director: Lisa Rosenthal
Senior Managing Editor: Elaine Perry

ADVANCED HOME WIRING
Created by: The Editors of Cowles Creative Publishing, Inc., in
cooperation with Black & Decker. ● BLACK&DECKER is a trademark
of the Black & Decker Corporation and is used under license.

"Wire-Nut®" is a registered trademark of Ideal Industries, Inc.

Portions of *The Complete Guide to Home Wiring* are from the Black & Decker® books *Basic Wiring & Electrical Repairs* and *Advanced Home Wiring*. Other books in the Black & Decker® Home Improvement Library™ include:

Everyday Home Repairs, Decorating With Paint & Wallcovering, Carpentry: Tools • Shelves • Walls • Doors, Kitchen Remodeling, Building Decks, Home Plumbing Projects & Repairs, Workshop Tips & Techniques, Advanced Home Wiring, Carpentry: Remodeling, Landscape Design & Construction, Bathroom Remodeling, Built-In Projects for the Home, Kitchen & Bathroom Ideas, Refinishing & Finishing Wood, Exterior Home Repairs & Improvements, Home Masonry Repairs & Projects, Building Porches & Patios, Deck & Landscape Ideas, Flooring Projects & Techniques, Advanced Deck Building, Advanced Home Plumbing

Introduction

Electricity and the components that supply it are essential elements of your home life. They provide for necessities from food preparation, illumination, safety, and climate control to entertainment, relaxation, and work. Knowing about your electrical system and how it provides for your needs will give you the power to make sensible, effective, and economical decisions and provide you with a great deal of security. The information in *The Complete Guide to Home Wiring* will help you make quality decisions. From troubleshooting problems to understanding how best to meet your lighting needs when designing a remodeling project, the information you find here will help you make your home a more delightful environment—while you save money.

This book also contains step-by-step instructions, clearly illustrated with color photographs, for any electrical work you will need to do around your house, from basic repairs to advanced wiring projects. Even if you hire professionals to replace fixtures or install new circuits, your increased understanding of what is required will help you work with these contractors and make the best use of your dollars. But as you see how easily you can do the work yourself you can save substantially more. *The Complete Guide to Home Wiring* provides everything you need to know to successfully do electrical work around your house.

The first section of the book covers basic electrical repairs. From lamps to ceiling fixtures, switches and receptacles to thermostats, you learn how to troubleshoot and fix the problems. Each major component of your home's electrical system is thoroughly covered. First you learn how do electrical work safely, with no chance of mistake. Then you see all types of wires and cables, fuse boxes and breaker panels, switches and receptacles to help you identify and work with what is in your house. All the tools and materials necessary for performing the repairs are shown, as well as professional techniques for using them. You also see how mapping your home's electrical system will make it much simpler and safer to do work. And you also get a review of problems that an electrical inspector would point out, and how to fix them.

The second section of the book presents complete wiring projects for your home, whether you are remodeling and working in new construction, or making changes within the existing structure.

You see complete instructions on the tools, materials, and techniques required to perform these projects and how to do the work quickly and safely. Plus you learn how to plan a major wiring project, from what electrical code requirements your project must meet, to how to draw plans and obtain a permit, to making an electrical layout that best serves your needs. Whether your wiring project is for a kitchen, bathroom, basement, or attic remodel, or a room addition, you will find all the information you need.

The photographs and information in the final section show you how to design a lighting scheme. They will help you visualize ideas and make decisions so your wiring projects meet your needs and provide long-lasting satisfaction. You will see how to choose from the wide variety of lamps and light fixtures available and learn how to locate them, individually and in combination, to achieve best results. Using this information when planning your wiring project will make it completely successful.

The Complete Guide to Home Wiring will be a vital resource for you for years to come. As your home environment needs change, and as wear and tear affects your house, you will always find information and solutions that will meet your needs and save you money.

NOTICE TO READERS

This book provides useful instructions, but we cannot anticipate all of your working conditions or the characteristics of your materials and tools. For safety, you should use caution, care, and good judgment when following the procedures described in this book. Consider your own skill level and the instructions and safety precautions associated with the various tools and materials shown. Neither the publisher nor Black & Decker® can assume responsibility for any damage to property or injury to persons as a result of misuse of the information provided.

The instructions in this book conform to "The Uniform Plumbing Code," "The National Electrical Code Reference Book," and "The Uniform Building Code" current at the time of its original publication. Consult your local Building Department for information on building permits, codes, and other laws as they apply to your project.

Faucet

Water flows under pressure

Water supply pipe

Drain pipe

Water returns under no pressure

Understanding Electricity

A household electrical system can be compared with a home's plumbing system. Electrical current flows in wires in much the same way that water flows inside pipes. Both electricity and water enter the home, are distributed throughout the house, do their "work," and then exit.

In plumbing, water first flows through the pressurized water supply system. In electricity, current first flows along hot wires. Current flowing along hot wires also is pressurized. The pressure of electrical current is called **voltage.**

Large supply pipes can carry a greater volume of water than small pipes. Likewise, large electrical wires carry more current than small wires. This current-carrying capacity of wires is called **amperage.**

Water is made available for use through the faucets, spigots, and shower heads in a home. Electricity is made available through receptacles, switches, and fixtures.

Water finally leaves the home through a drain system, which is not pressurized. Similarly, electrical current flows back through neutral wires. The current in neutral wires is not pressurized, and is said to be at zero voltage.

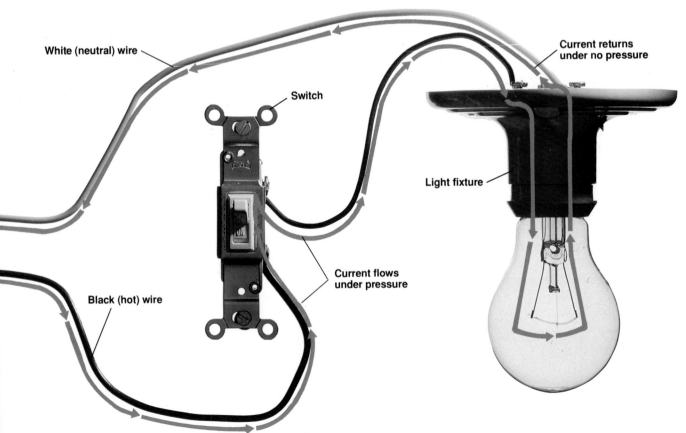

White (neutral) wire

Current returns under no pressure

Switch

Light fixture

Current flows under pressure

Black (hot) wire

Glossary of Electrical Terms

ampere (or **amp**): Refers to the rate at which electrical power flows to a light, tool, or an appliance.

armored cable: Two or more wires that are grouped together and protected by a flexible metal covering.

box: A device used to contain wiring connections.

BX: See **armored cable.**

cable: Two or more wires that are grouped together and protected by a covering or sheath.

circuit: A continuous loop of electrical current flowing along wires or cables.

circuit breaker: A safety device that interrupts an electrical circuit in the event of an overload or short circuit.

conductor: Any material that allows electrical current to flow through it. Copper wire is an especially good conductor.

conduit: A metal or plastic tube used to protect wires.

continuity: An uninterrupted electrical pathway through a circuit or electrical fixture.

current: The movement of electrons along a conductor.

duplex receptacle: A receptacle that provides connections for two plugs.

feed wire: A conductor that carries 120-volt current uninterrupted from the service panel.

fuse: A safety device, usually found in older homes, that interrupts electrical circuits during an overload or short circuit.

Greenfield: See **armored cable.**

grounded wire: See **neutral wire.**

grounding wire: A wire used in an electrical circuit to conduct current to the earth in the event of a short circuit. The grounding wire often is a bare copper wire.

hot wire: Any wire that carries voltage. In an electrical circuit, the hot wire usually is covered with black or red insulation.

insulator: Any material, such as plastic or rubber, that resists the flow of electrical current. Insulating materials protect wires and cables.

junction box: See **box.**

meter: A device used to measure the amount of electrical power being used.

neutral wire: A wire that returns current at zero voltage to the source of electrical power. Usually covered with white or light gray insulation. Also called the grounded wire.

outlet: See **receptacle.**

overload: A demand for more current than the circuit wires or electrical device was designed to carry. Usually causes a fuse to blow or a circuit breaker to trip.

pigtail: A short wire used to connect two or more circuit wires to a single screw terminal.

polarized receptacle: A receptacle designed to keep hot current flowing along black or red wires, and neutral current flowing along white or gray wires.

power: The result of hot current flowing for a period of time. Use of power makes heat, motion, or light.

receptacle: A device that provides plug-in access to electrical power.

Romex: A brand name of plastic-sheathed electrical cable that is commonly used for indoor wiring.

screw terminal: A place where a wire connects to a receptacle, switch, or fixture.

service panel: A metal box usually near the site where electrical power enters the house. In the service panel, electrical current is split into individual circuits. The service panel has circuit breakers or fuses to protect each circuit.

short circuit: An accidental and improper contact between two current-carrying wires, or between a current-carrying wire and a grounding conductor.

switch: A device that controls electrical current passing through hot circuit wires. Used to turn lights and appliances on and off.

UL: An abbreviation for Underwriters Laboratories, an organization that tests electrical devices and manufactured products for safety.

voltage (or **volts**): A measurement of electricity in terms of pressure.

wattage (or **watt**): A measurement of electrical power in terms of total energy consumed. Watts can be calculated by multiplying the voltage times the amps.

wire nut: A device used to connect two or more wires together.

Electricity & Safety

Safety should be the primary concern of anyone working with electricity. Although most household electrical repairs are simple and straightforward, always use caution and good judgment when working with electrical wiring or devices. Common sense can prevent accidents.

The basic rule of electrical safety is: **Always turn off power to the area or device you are working on.** At the main service panel, remove the fuse or shut off the circuit breaker that controls the circuit you are servicing. Then check to make sure the power is off by testing for power with a neon circuit tester (page 18). Restore power only when the repair or replacement project is complete.

Follow the safety tips shown on these pages. Never attempt an electrical project beyond your skill or confidence level. Never attempt to repair or replace your main service panel or service entrance head (pages 12 to 13). These are jobs for a qualified electrician, and require that the power company shuts off power to your house.

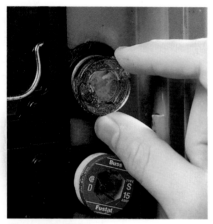

Shut off power to the proper circuit at the fuse box or main service panel before beginning work.

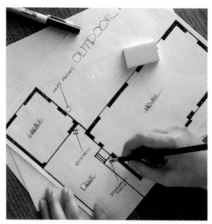

Make a map of your household electrical circuits (pages 30 to 33) to help you turn the proper circuits on and off for electrical repairs.

Close service panel door and post a warning sign to prevent others from turning on power while you are working on electrical projects.

Keep a flashlight near your main service panel. Check flashlight batteries regularly.

Always check for power at the fixture you are servicing before you begin any work.

Use only UL approved electrical parts or devices. These devices have been tested for safety by Underwriters Laboratories.

Wear rubber-soled shoes while working on electrical projects. On damp floors, stand on a rubber mat or dry wooden boards.

Use fiberglass or wood ladders when making routine household repairs near the service head.

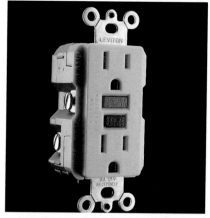

Use GFCI receptacles (ground-fault circuit-interrupters) where specified by local electrical codes (pages 74 to 77).

Protect children with receptacle caps or childproof receptacle covers (page 69).

Use extension cords only for temporary connections. Never place them underneath rugs, or fasten them to walls, baseboards, or other surfaces.

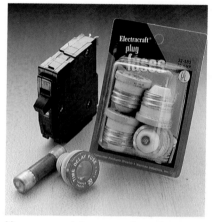

Use correct fuses or breakers in the main service panel (pages 28 to 29). Never install a fuse or breaker that has a higher amperage rating than the circuit wires.

Do not touch metal pipes, faucets, or fixtures while working with electricity. The metal may provide a grounding path, allowing electrical current to flow through your body.

Never alter the prongs of a plug to fit a receptacle. If possible, install a new grounded receptacle.

Do not drill walls or ceilings without first shutting off electrical power to the circuits that may be hidden. Use double-insulated tools.

Your Electrical System

Electrical power that enters the home is produced by large **power plants**. Power plants are located in all parts of the country, and generate electricity with turbines that are turned by water, wind, or steam. From these plants electricity enters large "step-up" transformers that increase voltage to half a million volts or more.

Electricity flows easily at these large voltages, and travels through high-voltage transmission lines to communities that can be hundreds of miles from the power plants. "Step-down" transformers located at **substations** then reduce the voltage for distribution along street lines. On **utility power poles**, smaller transformers further reduce the voltage to ordinary 120-volt current for household use.

Lines carrying current to the house either run underground, or are strung overhead and attached to a post called a **service head**. Most homes built after 1950 have three wires running to the service head: two power lines, each carrying 120 volts of current, and a grounded neutral wire. Power from the two 120-volt lines may be combined at the **service panel** to supply current to large, 240-volt appliances like clothes dryers or electric water heaters.

Many older homes have only two wires running to the service head, with one 120-volt line and a grounded neutral wire. This older two-wire service is inadequate for today's homes. Contact an electrical contractor and your local power utility company to upgrade to a three-wire service.

Incoming power passes through an **electric meter** that measures power consumption. Power then enters the service panel, where it is distributed to circuits that run throughout the house. The service panel also contains fuses or circuit breakers that shut off power to the individual circuits in the event of a short circuit or an overload. Certain high-wattage appliances, like microwave ovens, are usually plugged into their own individual circuits to prevent overloads.

Voltage ratings determined by power companies and manufacturers have changed over the years. Current rated at 110 volts changed to 115 volts, then 120 volts. Current rated at 220 volts changed to 230 volts, then 240 volts. Similarly, ratings for receptacles, tools, light fixtures, and appliances have changed from 115 volts to 125 volts. These changes will not affect the performance of new devices connected to older wiring. For making electrical calculations, such as the ones shown in "Evaluating Circuits for Safe Capacity" (pages 34 to 35), use a rating of 120 volts or 240 volts for your circuits.

Power plants supply electricity to thousands of homes and businesses. Step-up transformers increase the voltage produced at the plant, making the power flow more easily along high-voltage transmission lines.

Substations are located near the communities they serve. A typical substation takes current from high-voltage transmission lines and reduces it for distribution along street lines.

Utility pole transformers reduce the high-voltage current that flows through power lines along neighborhood streets. A utility pole transformer reduces voltage from 10,000 volts to the normal 120-volt current used in households.

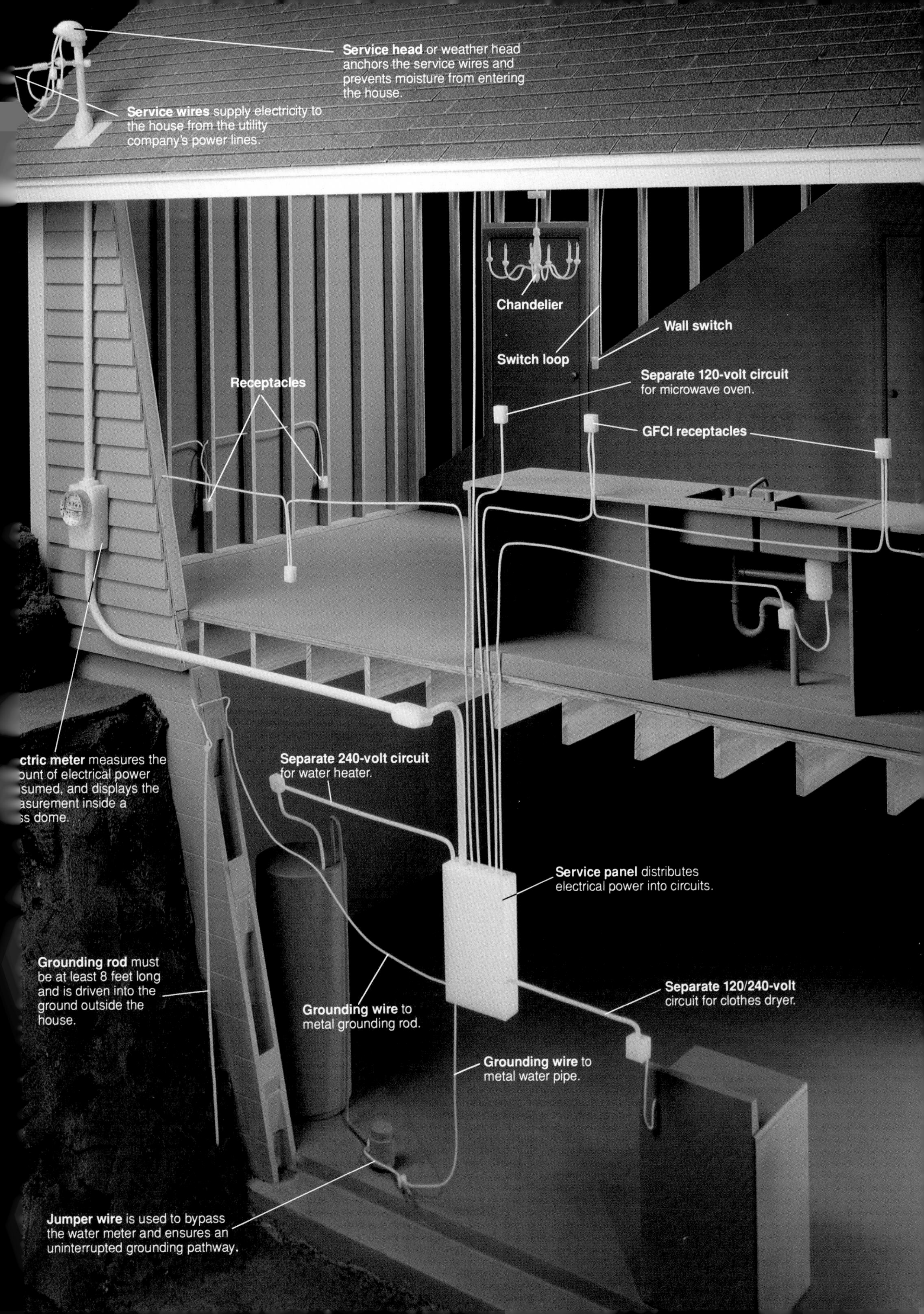

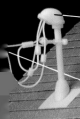

Service wires supply electricity to the house from the utility company's power lines.

Service head or weather head anchors the service wires and prevents moisture from entering the house.

Chandelier

Switch loop

Wall switch

Receptacles

Separate 120-volt circuit for microwave oven.

GFCI receptacles

ctric meter measures the ount of electrical power sumed, and displays the asurement inside a ss dome.

Separate 240-volt circuit for water heater.

Service panel distributes electrical power into circuits.

Grounding rod must be at least 8 feet long and is driven into the ground outside the house.

Grounding wire to metal grounding rod.

Separate 120/240-volt circuit for clothes dryer.

Grounding wire to metal water pipe.

Jumper wire is used to bypass the water meter and ensures an uninterrupted grounding pathway.

Parts of the Electrical System

The service head, sometimes called the weather head, anchors the service wires to the home. Three wires provide the standard 240-volt service necessary for the average home. Older homes may have two-wire service that provides only 120 volts of power. Two-wire service should be upgraded to three-wire service by an electrical contractor.

The electric meter measures the amount of electrical power consumed. It is usually attached to the side of the house, and connects to the service head. A thin metal disc inside the meter rotates when power is used. The electric meter belongs to your local power utility company. If you suspect the meter is not functioning properly, contact the power company.

Grounding wire connects the electrical system to the earth through a cold water pipe and a grounding rod. In the event of an overload or short circuit, the grounding wire allows excess electrical power to find its way harmlessly to the earth.

Light fixtures attach directly to a household electrical system. They are usually controlled with wall switches. The two common types of light fixtures are **incandescent** (page 78) and **fluorescent** (page 88).

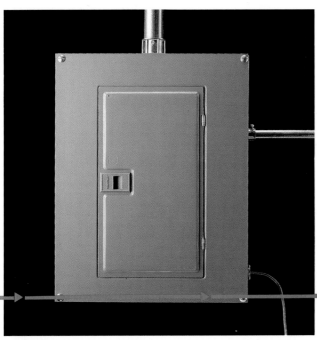

The main service panel, sometimes called a fuse box or **breaker box,** distributes power to individual circuits. Fuses or circuit breakers protect each circuit from short circuits and overloads. Fuses and circuit breakers also are used to shut off power to individual circuits while repairs are made.

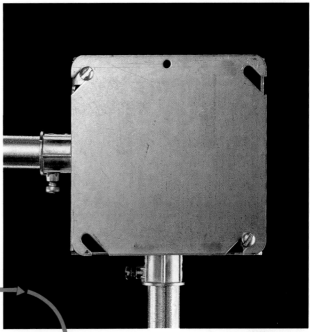

Electrical boxes enclose wire connections. According to the National Electrical Code, all wire splices or connections must be contained entirely in a plastic or metal electrical box.

Switches control electrical current passing through hot circuit wires. Switches can be wired to control light fixtures, ceiling fans, appliances, and receptacles.

Receptacles, sometimes called **outlets,** provide plug-in access to electrical power. A 125-volt, 15-amp receptacle with a grounding hole is the most typical receptacle in wiring systems installed after 1965. Most receptacles have two plug-in locations, and are called **duplex receptacles.**

Understanding Circuits

An electrical circuit is a continuous loop. Household circuits carry power from the main service panel, throughout the house, and back to the main service panel. Several switches, receptacles, light fixtures, or appliances may be connected to a single circuit.

Current enters a circuit loop on hot wires, and returns along neutral wires. These wires are color coded for easy identification. Hot wires are black or red, and neutral wires are white or light gray. For safety, most circuits include a bare copper or green insulated grounding wire. The grounding wire conducts current in the event of a short circuit or overload, and helps reduce the chance of severe electrical shock. The service panel also has a grounding wire connected to a metal water pipe and metal grounding rod buried underground (pages 16 to 17).

If a circuit carries too much power, it can overload. A fuse or a circuit breaker protects each circuit in case of overloads (pages 28 to 29). To calculate how much power any circuit can carry, see "Evaluating Circuits for Safe Capacity" (pages 34 to 35).

Current returns to the service panel along a neutral circuit wire. Current then becomes part of a main circuit and leaves the house on a large neutral service wire that returns it to the utility pole transformer.

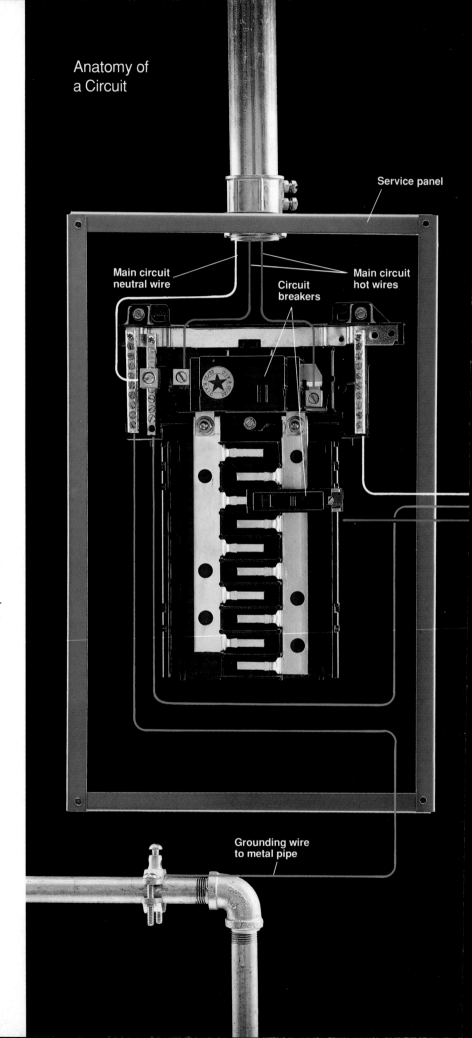

Service panel

Main circuit neutral wire

Circuit breakers

Main circuit hot wires

Grounding wire to metal pipe

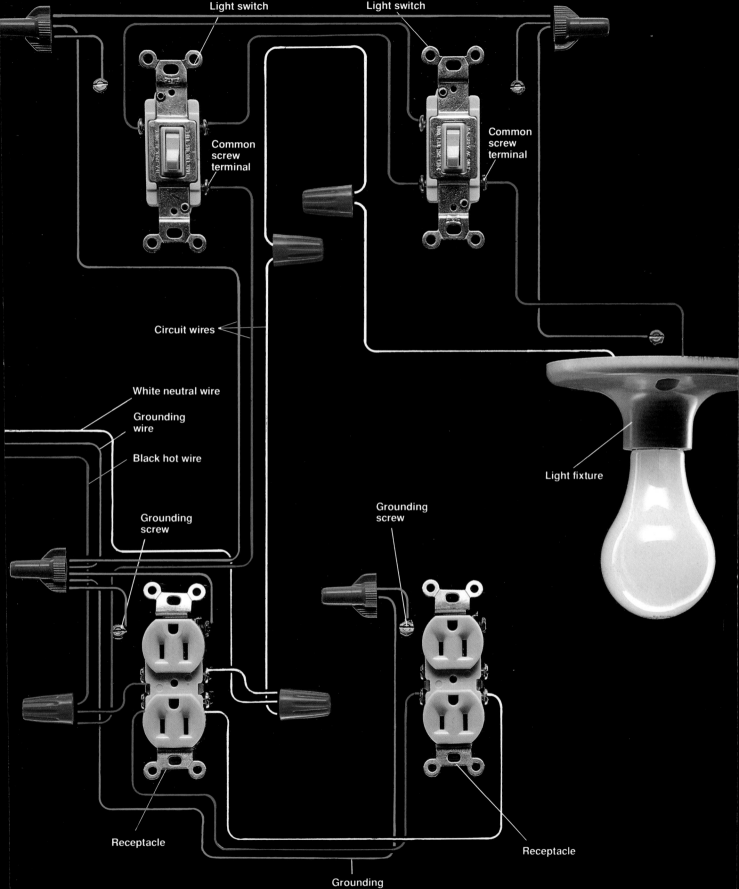

Light switch

Light switch

Common screw terminal

Common screw terminal

Circuit wires

White neutral wire

Grounding wire

Black hot wire

Grounding screw

Grounding screw

Light fixture

Receptacle

Receptacle

Grounding

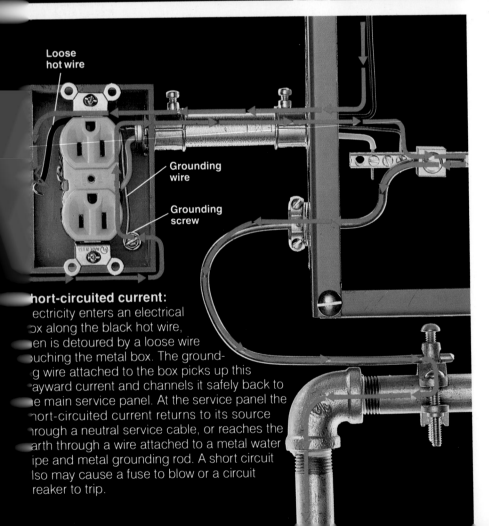

Service panel

Black hot wire

White neutral wire

Grounding wire

Grounding wire to metal cold water pipe

Normal current flow: Electricity enters an electrical box along a black hot wire, then returns to the service panel along a white neutral wire. Excess current reaches the earth through a grounding wire attached to a metal water pipe and metal grounding rod.

Loose hot wire

Grounding wire

Grounding screw

hort-circuited current:
ectricity enters an electrical
ox along the black hot wire,
en is detoured by a loose wire
uching the metal box. The ground-
g wire attached to the box picks up this
ayward current and channels it safely back to
e main service panel. At the service panel the
hort-circuited current returns to its source
rough a neutral service cable, or reaches the
arth through a wire attached to a metal water
ipe and metal grounding rod. A short circuit
lso may cause a fuse to blow or a circuit
reaker to trip.

Grounding & Polarization

Electricity always seeks to return to its source and complete a continuous circuit. In a house-hold wiring system, this return path is provided by white neutral wires that return current to the main service panel. From the ser-vice panel, current returns along a neutral service wire to a power pole transformer.

A **grounding wire** provides an additional return path for electri-cal current. The grounding wire is a safety feature. It is designed to conduct electricity if current seeks to return to the service panel along a path other than the neutral wire, a condition known as a **short circuit**.

A short circuit is a potentially dangerous situation. If an elec-trical box, tool or appliance be-comes short circuited and is touched by a person, the elec-trical current may attempt to return to its source by passing through that person's body.

However, electrical current al-ways seeks to move along the easiest path. A grounding wire provides a safe, easy path for current to follow back to its source. If a person touches an electrical box, tool, or appliance that has a properly installed grounding wire, any chance of receiving a severe electrical shock is greatly reduced.

In addition, household wiring systems are required to be con-nected directly to the earth. The earth has a unique ability to ab-sorb the electrons of electrical current. In the event of a short circuit or overload, any excess electricity will find its way along the grounding wire to the earth, where it becomes harmless.

This additional grounding is completed by wiring the household electrical system to a metal cold water pipe and a metal grounding rod that is buried underground.

After 1920, most American homes included receptacles that accepted **polarized plugs**. While not a true grounding method, the two-slot polarized plug and receptacle was designed to keep hot current flowing along black or red wires, and neutral current flowing along white or gray wires.

Armored cable and metal conduit, widely installed in homes during the 1940s, provided a true grounding path. When connected to metal junction boxes, it provided a metal pathway back to the service panel.

Modern cable includes a bare or green insulated copper wire that serves as the grounding path. This grounding wire is connected to all receptacles and metal boxes to provide a continuous pathway for any short-circuited current. A cable with a grounding wire usually is attached to three-slot receptacles. By plugging a three-prong plug into a grounded three-slot receptacle, appliances and tools are protected from short circuits.

Use a receptacle adapter to plug three-prong plugs into two-slot receptacles, but use it only if the receptacle connects to a grounding wire or grounded electrical box. Adapters have short grounding wires or wire loops that attach to the receptacle's coverplate mounting screw. The mounting screw connects the adapter to the grounded metal electrical box.

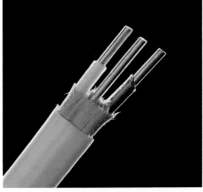

Modern NM (nonmetallic) cable, found in most wiring systems installed after 1965, contains a bare copper wire that provides grounding for receptacle and switch boxes.

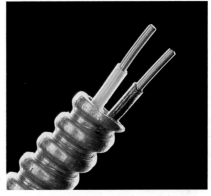

Armored cable, sometimes called BX or Greenfield cable, has a metal sheath that serves as the grounding pathway. Short-circuited current flows through the metal sheath back to the service panel.

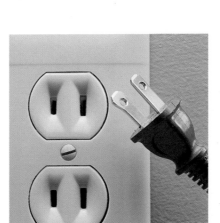

Polarized receptacles have a long slot and a short slot. Used with a polarized plug, the polarized receptacle keeps electrical current directed for safety.

Three-slot receptacles are required by code for new homes. They are usually connected to a standard two-wire cable with ground (above, left).

Receptacle adapter allows three-prong plugs to be inserted into two-slot receptacles. The adapter can be used only with grounded receptacles, and the grounding loop or wire of the adapter must be attached to the coverplate mounting screw of the receptacle.

Double-insulated tools have nonconductive plastic bodies to prevent shocks caused by short circuits. Because of these features, double-insulated tools can be used safely with ungrounded receptacles.

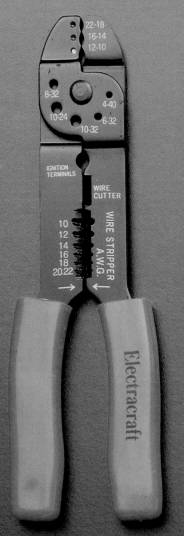

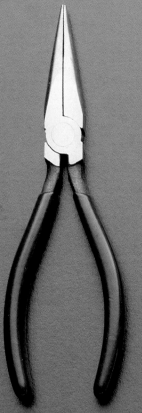

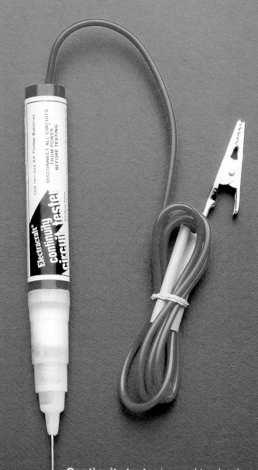

Needlenose pliers bends and shapes wires for making screw terminal connections. Some needlenose pliers also have cutting jaws for clipping wires.

Combination tool is essential for home wiring projects. It cuts cables and individual wires, measures wire gauges, and strips the insulation from wires. It has insulated handles.

Continuity tester is used to check switches, lighting fixtures, and other devices for faults. It has a battery that generates current, and a loop of wire for creating an electrical circuit (page 52).

Cordless screwdriver drives a wide variety of screws and fasteners. It is rechargeable, and can be used in either a power or manual mode. A removable tip allows the cordless screwdriver to drive either slotted or Phillips screws.

Neon circuit tester is used to check circuit wires for power. Testing for power is an essential safety step in any electrical repair project (page 70).

Tools for Electrical Repairs

Home electrical repairs require only a few inexpensive tools. As with any tool purchase, invest in quality when buying tools for electrical repairs.

Keep tools clean and dry, and store them securely. Tools with cutting jaws, like needlenose pliers and combination tools, should be resharpened or discarded if the cutting edges become dull.

Several testing tools are used in electrical repair projects. Neon circuit testers (page 70), continuity testers (page 52), and multi-testers (below) should be checked periodically to make sure they are operating properly. Continuity testers and multi-testers have batteries that should be replaced regularly.

Insulated screwdrivers have rubber-coated handles that reduce the risk of shock if the screwdriver should accidentally touch live wires.

Fuse puller is used to remove cartridge-type fuses from the fuse blocks usually found in older main service panels.

Cable ripper fits over NM (nonmetallic) cable. A small cutting point rips the outer plastic vinyl sheath on NM cable so the sheath can be removed without damaging wires.

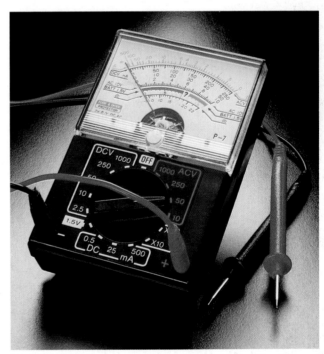

Multi-tester is a versatile, battery-operated tool frequently used to measure electrical voltages. It also is used to test for continuity in switches, light fixtures, and other electrical devices. An adjustable control makes it possible to measure current ranging from 1 to 1000 volts. A multi-tester is an essential tool for measuring current in low-voltage transformers, like those used to power doorbell and thermostat systems (pages 98 to 111).

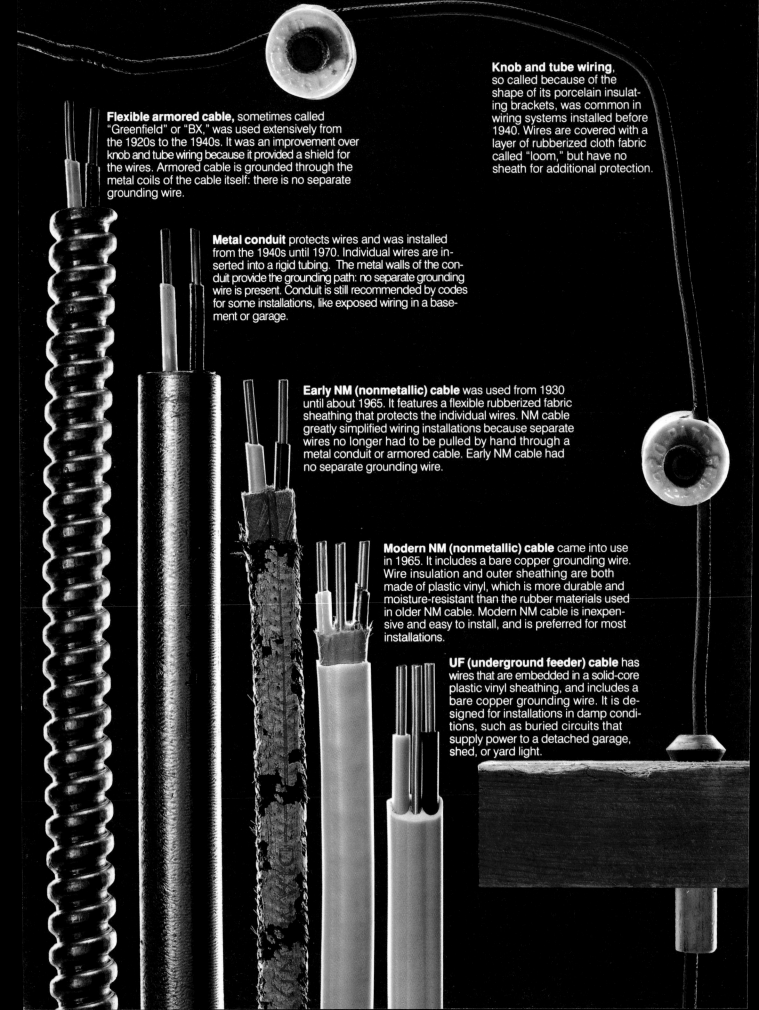

Flexible armored cable, sometimes called "Greenfield" or "BX," was used extensively from the 1920s to the 1940s. It was an improvement over knob and tube wiring because it provided a shield for the wires. Armored cable is grounded through the metal coils of the cable itself: there is no separate grounding wire.

Knob and tube wiring, so called because of the shape of its porcelain insulating brackets, was common in wiring systems installed before 1940. Wires are covered with a layer of rubberized cloth fabric called "loom," but have no sheath for additional protection.

Metal conduit protects wires and was installed from the 1940s until 1970. Individual wires are inserted into a rigid tubing. The metal walls of the conduit provide the grounding path: no separate grounding wire is present. Conduit is still recommended by codes for some installations, like exposed wiring in a basement or garage.

Early NM (nonmetallic) cable was used from 1930 until about 1965. It features a flexible rubberized fabric sheathing that protects the individual wires. NM cable greatly simplified wiring installations because separate wires no longer had to be pulled by hand through a metal conduit or armored cable. Early NM cable had no separate grounding wire.

Modern NM (nonmetallic) cable came into use in 1965. It includes a bare copper grounding wire. Wire insulation and outer sheathing are both made of plastic vinyl, which is more durable and moisture-resistant than the rubber materials used in older NM cable. Modern NM cable is inexpensive and easy to install, and is preferred for most installations.

UF (underground feeder) cable has wires that are embedded in a solid-core plastic vinyl sheathing, and includes a bare copper grounding wire. It is designed for installations in damp conditions, such as buried circuits that supply power to a detached garage, shed, or yard light.

Wires & Cables: Repairs

Wires are made of copper, aluminum, or aluminum covered with a thin layer of copper. Solid copper wires are the best conductors of electricity and are the most widely used. Aluminum and copper-covered aluminum wires require special installation techniques. They are discussed on page 22.

A group of two or more wires enclosed in a metal, rubber, or plastic sheath is called a **cable** (photo, page opposite). The sheath protects the wires from damage. Metal conduit also protects wires, but it is not considered a cable.

Individual wires are covered with rubber or plastic vinyl insulation. An exception is a bare copper grounding wire, which does not need an insulating cover. The insulation is color coded (chart, right) to identify the wire as a hot wire, a neutral wire, or a grounding wire.

In most wiring systems installed after 1965, the wires and cables are insulated with plastic vinyl. This type of insulation is very durable, and can last as long as the house itself.

Before 1965, wires and cables were insulated with rubber. Rubber insulation has a life expectancy of about 25 years (see "Evaluating Old Wiring," pages 124 to 127). Old insulation that is cracked or damaged can be reinforced temporarily by wrapping the wire with plastic electrical tape. However, old wiring with cracked or damaged insulation should be inspected by a qualified electrician to make sure it is safe.

Wires must be large enough for the amperage rating of the circuit (chart, right). A wire that is too small can become dangerously hot. Wire sizes are categorized according to the American Wire Gauge (AWG) system. To check the size of a wire, use the wire stripper openings of a combination tool (page 18) as a guide.

Everything You Need:

Tools: cable ripper, combination tool, screwdriver, needlenose pliers.

Materials: wire nuts, pigtail wires (if needed).

See Inspector's Notebook:
- Common Cable Problems (pages 114 to 115).
- Checking Wire Connections (pages 116 to 117).
- Electrical Box Inspection (pages 118 to 119).

Wire Color Chart

Wire color	Function
White	Neutral wire carrying current at zero voltage.
Black	Hot wire carrying current at full voltage.
Red	Hot wire carrying current at full voltage.
White, black markings	Hot wire carrying current at full voltage.
Green	Serves as a grounding pathway.
Bare copper	Serves as a grounding pathway.

Individual wires are color coded to identify their function. In some circuit installations, the white wire serves as a hot wire that carries voltage. If so, this white wire may be labeled with black tape or paint to identify it as a hot wire.

Wire Size Chart

Wire gauge	Wire capacity & use
#6	60 amps, 240 volts; central air conditioner, electric furnace.
#8	40 amps, 240 volts; electric range, central air conditioner.
#10	30 amps, 240 volts; window air conditioner, clothes dryer.
#12	20 amps, 120 volts; light fixtures, receptacles, microwave oven.
#14	15 amps, 120 volts; light fixtures, receptacles.
#16	Light-duty extension cords.
#18 to 22	Thermostats, doorbells, security systems.

Wire sizes (shown actual size) are categorized by the American Wire Gauge system. The larger the wire size, the smaller the AWG number.

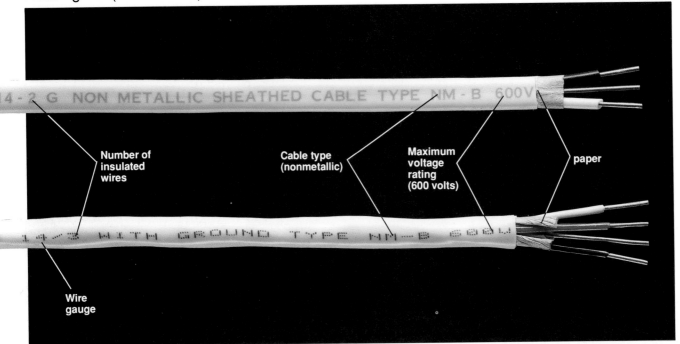

14 - 2 G NON METALLIC SHEATHED CABLE TYPE NM - B 600V

Number of insulated wires

Cable type (nonmetallic)

Maximum voltage rating (600 volts)

paper

14/3 WITH GROUND TYPE NM-B 600V

Wire gauge

NM (nonmetallic) cable is labeled with the number of insulated wires it contains. The bare grounding wire is not counted. For example, a cable marked 14/2 G (or 14/2 WITH GROUND) contains two insulated 14-gauge wires, plus a bare copper grounding wire.

Cable marked 14/3 WITH GROUND has three 14-gauge wires plus a grounding wire. A strip of paper inside the cable protects the individual wires. NM cable also is stamped with a maximum voltage rating, as determined by Underwriters Laboratories (UL).

Aluminum Wire

Inexpensive aluminum wire was used in place of copper in many wiring systems installed during the late 1960s and early 1970s, when copper prices were high. Aluminum wire is identified by its silver color,

2AL/2 WITH GROUND TYPE NM 600V

and by the AL stamp on the cable sheathing. A variation, copper-clad aluminum wire, has a thin coating of copper bonded to a solid aluminum core.

By the early 1970s, all-aluminum wire was found to pose a safety hazard if connected to a switch or receptacle with brass or copper screw terminals. Because aluminum expands and contracts at a different rate than copper or brass, the wire connections could become loose. In some instances, fires resulted.

Existing aluminum wiring in homes is considered safe if proper installation methods have been followed, and if the wires are connected to special switches and receptacles designed to be used with aluminum wire. If you have aluminum wire in your home, have a qualified electrical inspector review the system. Copper-coated aluminum wire is not a hazard.

For a short while, switches and receptacles with an Underwriters Laboratories (UL) wire compatibility

rating of AL-CU were used with both aluminum and copper wiring. However, these devices proved to be hazardous when connected to aluminum wire. AL-CU devices should not be used with aluminum wiring.

In 1971, switches and receptacles designed for use with aluminum wiring were introduced. They are marked CO/ALR. This mark is now the only approved rating for aluminum wires. If your home has aluminum wires connected to a switch or receptacle without a CO/ALR rating stamp, replace the device with a switch or receptacle rated CO/ALR.

A switch or receptacle that has no wire compatibility rating printed on the mounting strap or casing should not be used with aluminum wires. These devices are designed for use with copper wires only.

CO/ALR

REPLACE ONLY WITH CO/ALR DEVICE

How to Strip NM (Nonmetallic) Cable & Wires

1 Measure and mark the cable 8" to 10" from end. Slide the cable ripper onto the cable, and squeeze tool firmly to force cutting point through plastic sheathing.

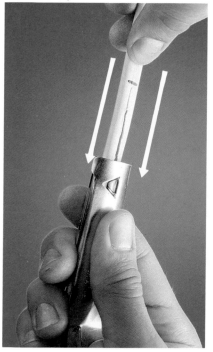

2 Grip the cable tightly with one hand, and pull the cable ripper toward the end of the cable to cut open the plastic sheathing.

3 Peel back the plastic sheathing and the paper wrapping from the individual wires.

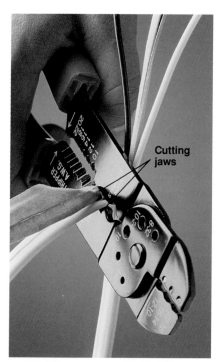

4 Cut away the excess plastic sheathing and paper wrapping, using the cutting jaws of a combination tool.

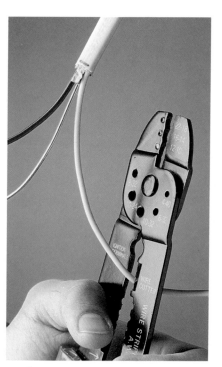

5 Cut the individual wires, if necessary, using the cutting jaws of the combination tool.

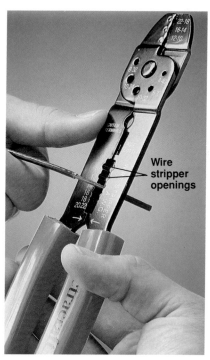

6 Strip insulation from each wire, using the stripper openings. Choose the opening that matches the gauge of the wire, and take care not to nick or scratch the ends of the wires.

How to Connect Wires to Screw Terminals

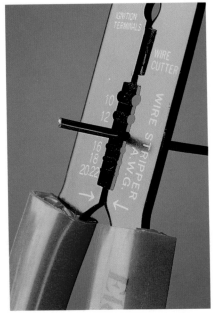

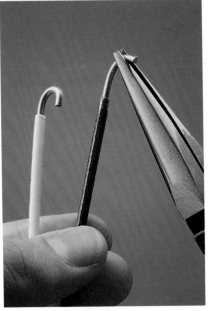

1 Strip about ¾" of insulation from each wire, using a combination tool. Choose the stripper opening that matches the gauge of the wire, then clamp wire in tool. Pull the wire firmly to remove plastic insulation.

2 Form a C-shaped loop in the end of each wire, using a needlenose pliers. The wire should have no scratches or nicks.

3 Hook each wire around the screw terminal so it forms a clockwise loop. Tighten screw firmly. Insulation should just touch head of screw. Never place the ends of two wires under a single screw terminal. Instead, use a pigtail wire (page opposite).

How to Connect Wires with Push-in Fittings

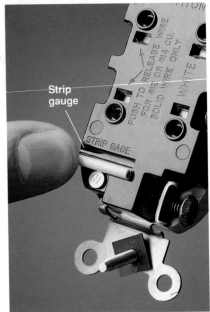

1 Mark the amount of insulation to be stripped from each wire, using the strip gauge on the back of the switch or receptacle. Strip the wires using a combination tool (step 1, above). Never use push-in fittings with aluminum wiring.

2 Insert the bare copper wires firmly into the push-in fittings on the back of the switch or receptacle. When inserted, wires should have no bare copper exposed.

Remove a wire from a push-in fitting by inserting a small nail or screwdriver in the release opening next to the wire. Wire will pull out easily.

24

How to Connect Two or More Wires with a Wire Nut

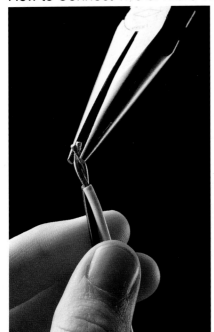

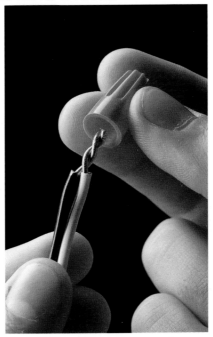

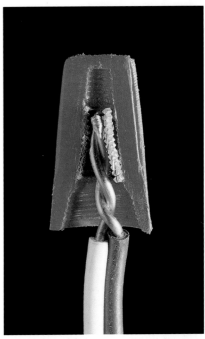

1 Strip about ½" of insulation from each wire. Hold the wires parallel, and twist them together in a clockwise direction, using a needle-nose pliers or combination tool.

2 Screw the wire nut onto the twisted wires. Tug gently on each wire to make sure it is secure. In a proper connection, no bare wire should be exposed past the bottom of the wire nut.

Wire nut (shown in cutaway) has metal threads that grip the bare ends of the wires. When connected, the wire nut should completely cover the bare wires.

How to Pigtail Two or More Wires

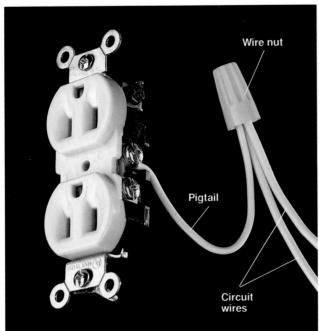

Wire nut

Pigtail

Circuit wires

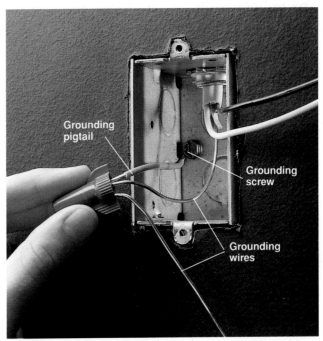

Grounding pigtail

Grounding screw

Grounding wires

Connect two or more wires to a single screw terminal with a pigtail. A pigtail is a short piece of wire. One end of the pigtail connects to a screw terminal, and the other end connects to circuit wires, using a wire nut. A pigtail also can be used to lengthen circuit wires that are too short (page 118).

Grounding pigtail has green insulation, and is available with a preattached grounding screw. This grounding screw connects to the grounded metal electrical box. The end of the pigtail wire connects to the bare copper grounding wires with a wire nut.

25

Service Panels

Every home has a main service panel that distributes electrical current to the individual circuits. The main service panel usually is found in the basement, garage, or utility area, and can be identified by its metal casing. Before making any repair to your electrical system, you must shut off power to the correct circuit at the main service panel. The service panel should be indexed (pages 30 to 33) so circuits can be identified easily.

Service panels vary in appearance, depending on the age of the system. Very old wiring may operate on 30-amp service that has only two circuits. New homes can have 200-amp service with 30 or more circuits. Find the size of the service by reading the amperage rating printed on the main fuse block or main circuit breaker.

Regardless of age, all service panels have **fuses** or **circuit breakers** (pages 28 to 29) that control each circuit and protect them from overloads. In general, older service panels use fuses, while newer service panels use circuit breakers.

In addition to the main service panel, your electrical system may have a subpanel that controls some of the circuits in the home. A subpanel has its own circuit breakers or fuses, and is installed to control circuits that have been added to an existing wiring system.

The subpanel resembles the main service panel, but is usually smaller. It may be located near the main panel, or it may be found near the areas served by the new circuits. Garages and attics that have been updated often have their own subpanels. If your home has a subpanel, make sure that its circuits are indexed correctly.

When handling fuses or circuit breakers, make sure the area around the service panel is dry. Never remove the protective cover on the service panel. After turning off a circuit to make electrical repairs, remember to always test the circuit for power before touching any wires.

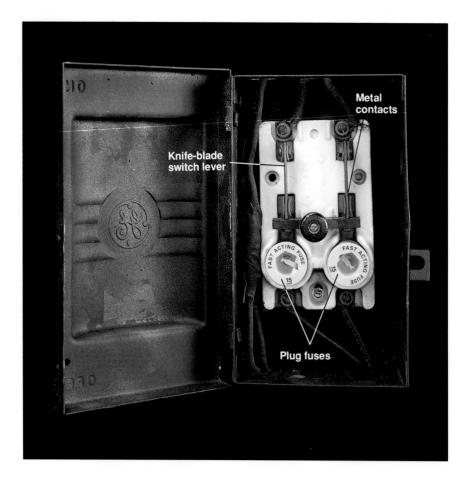

Metal contacts

Knife-blade switch lever

Plug fuses

A 30-amp service panel, common in systems installed before 1950, is identified by a ceramic fuse holder containing two plug fuses and a "knife-blade" switch lever. The fuse holder sometimes is contained in a black metal box mounted in an entryway or basement. This 30-amp service panel provides only 120 volts of power, and now is considered inadequate. For example, most home loan programs, like the FHA (Federal Housing Administration), require that 30-amp service be updated to 100 amps or more before a home can qualify for mortgage financing.

To shut off power to individual circuits in a 30-amp panel, carefully unscrew the plug fuses, touching only the insulated rim of the fuse. To shut off power to the entire house, open the knife-blade switch. Be careful not to touch the metal contacts on the switch.

A 60-amp fuse panel often is found in wiring systems installed between 1950 and 1965. It usually is housed in a gray metal cabinet that contains four individual plug fuses, plus one or two pull-out fuse blocks that hold cartridge fuses. This type of panel is regarded as adequate for a small, 1100-square-foot house that has no more than one 240-volt appliance. Many homeowners update 60-amp service to 100 amps or more so that additional lighting and appliance circuits can be added to the system. Home loan programs also may require that 60-amp service be updated before a home can qualify for financing.

To shut off power to a circuit, carefully unscrew the plug fuse, touching only its insulated rim. To shut off power to the entire house, hold the handle of the main fuse block and pull sharply to remove it. Major appliance circuits are controlled with another cartridge fuse block. Shut off the appliance circuit by pulling out this fuse block.

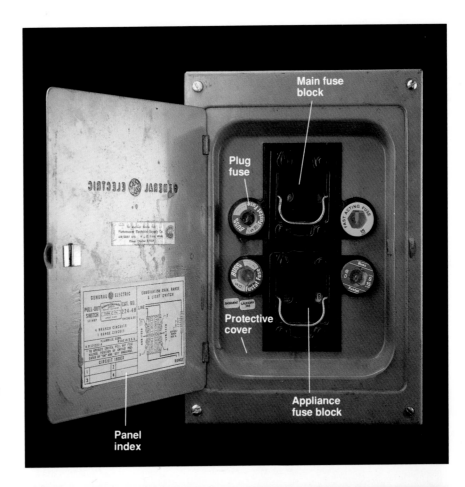

A circuit breaker panel providing 100 amps or more of power is common in wiring systems installed during the 1960s and later. A circuit breaker panel is housed in a gray metal cabinet that contains two rows of individual circuit breakers. The size of the service can be identified by reading the amperage rating of the main circuit breaker, which is located at the top of the main service panel.

A 100-amp service panel is now the minimum standard for most new housing. It is considered adequate for a medium-sized house with no more than three major electric appliances. However, larger houses with more electrical appliances require a service panel that provides 150 amps or more.

To shut off power to individual circuits in a circuit breaker panel, flip the lever on the appropriate circuit breaker to the OFF position. To shut off the power to the entire house, turn the main circuit breaker to the OFF position.

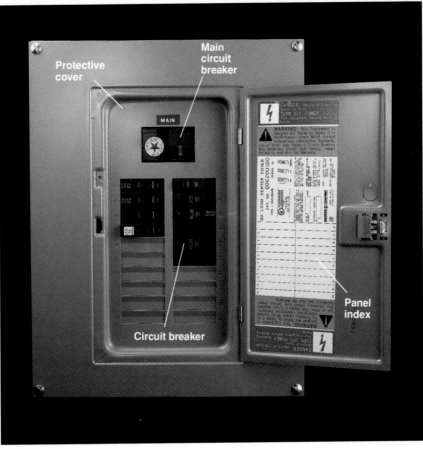

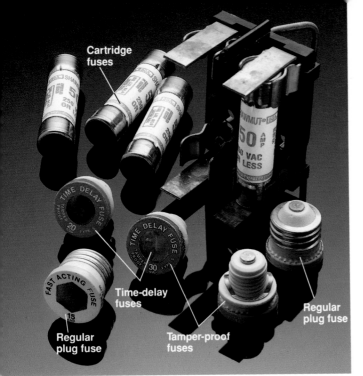

Cartridge
fuses

Time delay fuse

Time-delay
fuses

Fast acting fuse

Regular
plug fuse

Tamper-proof
fuses

Regular
plug fuse

Fuses & Circuit Breakers

Fuses and circuit breakers are safety devices designed to protect the electrical system from short circuits and overloads. Fuses and circuit breakers are located in the main service panel.

Most service panels installed before 1965 rely on fuses to control and protect individual circuits. Screw-in plug fuses protect 120-volt circuits that power lights and receptacles. Cartridge fuses protect 240-volt appliance circuits and the main shutoff of the service panel.

Inside each fuse is a current-carrying metal alloy ribbon. If a circuit is overloaded (pages 34 to 35), the metal ribbon melts and stops the flow of power. A fuse must match the amperage rating of the circuit. Never replace a fuse with one that has a larger amperage rating.

In most service panels installed after 1965, circuit breakers protect and control individual circuits. Single-pole circuit breakers protect 120-volt circuits, and double-pole circuit breakers protect 240-volt circuits. Amperage ratings for circuit breakers range from 15 to 100 amps.

Fuses are used in older service panels. Plug fuses usually control 120-volt circuits rated for 15, 20 or 30 amps. Tamper-proof plug fuses have threads that fit only matching sockets, making it impossible to install a wrong-sized fuse. Time-delay fuses absorb temporary heavy power load without blowing. Cartridge fuses control 240-volt circuits and range from 30 to 100 amps.

Each circuit breaker has a permanent metal strip that heats up and bends when voltage passes through it. If a circuit is overloaded, the metal strip inside the breaker bends enough to "trip" the switch and stop the flow of power. If a circuit breaker trips frequently even though the power demand is small, the mechanism inside the breaker may be worn out. Worn circuit breakers should be replaced by an electrician.

When a fuse blows or a circuit breaker trips, it is usually because there are too many light fixtures and plug-in appliances drawing power through the circuit. Move some of the plug-in appliances to another circuit, then replace the fuse or reset the breaker. If the fuse blows or breaker trips again immediately, there may be a short circuit in the system. Call a licensed electrician if you suspect a short circuit.

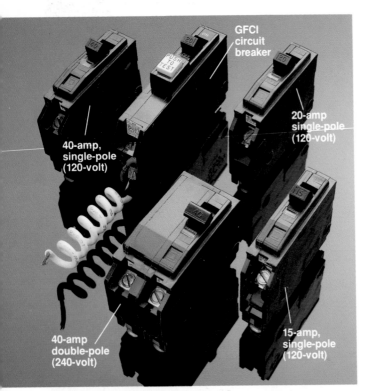

GFCI
circuit
breaker

40-amp,
single-pole
(120-volt)

20-amp
single-pole
(120-volt)

40-amp
double-pole
(240-volt)

15-amp,
single-pole
(120-volt)

Circuit breakers are used in newer service panels. Single-pole breakers rated for 15 or 20 amps control 120-volt circuits. Double-pole breakers rated for 20 to 50 amps control 240-volt circuits. GFCI (ground-fault circuit-interrupter) breakers provide shock protection for the entire circuit.

Everything You Need:

Tools: fuse puller (for cartridge fuses only).

Materials: replacement fuse.

How to Identify & Replace a Blown Plug Fuse

1 Go to the main service panel and locate the blown fuse. If the metal ribbon inside fuse is cleanly melted (right), the circuit was overloaded. If window in fuse is discolored (left), there was a short circuit in the system.

2 Unscrew the fuse, being careful to touch only the insulated rim of the fuse. Replace it with a fuse that has the same amperage rating.

How to Remove, Test & Replace a Cartridge Fuse

1 Remove cartridge fuses by gripping the handle of the fuse block and pulling sharply.

2 Remove the individual cartridge fuses from the block, using a fuse puller.

3 Test each fuse, using a continuity tester. If the tester glows, the fuse is good. If the tester does not glow, replace the fuse with one that has the same amperage rating.

How to Reset a Circuit Breaker

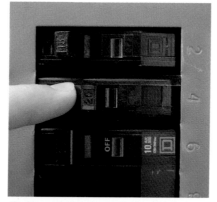

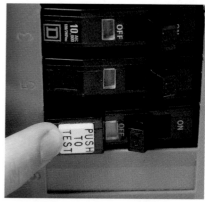

1 Open the service panel and locate the tripped breaker. The lever on the tripped breaker will be either in the OFF position, or in a position between ON and OFF.

2 Reset the tripped circuit breaker by pressing the circuit breaker lever all the way to the OFF position, then pressing it to the ON position.

Test GFCI circuit breakers by pushing TEST button. Breaker should trip to the OFF position. If not, the breaker is faulty and must be replaced by an electrician.

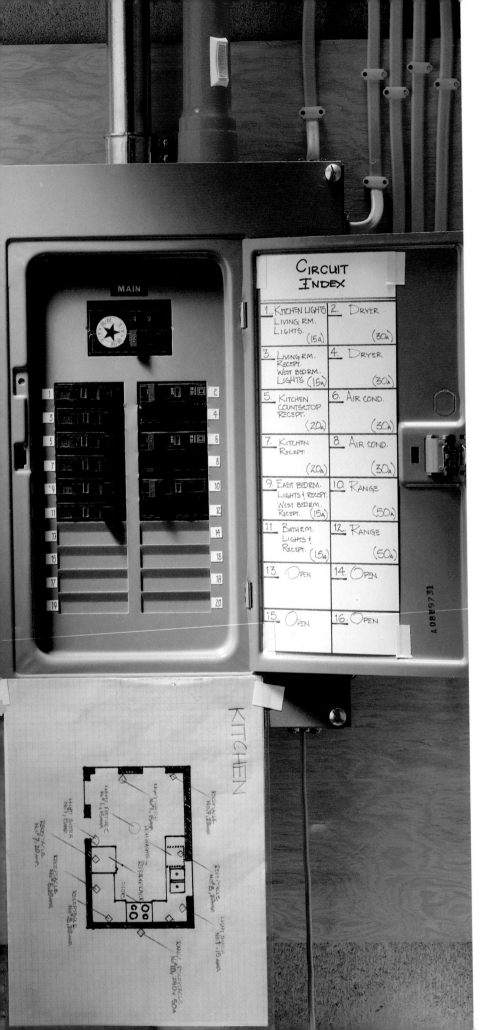

Mapping Circuits & Indexing the Service Panel

Making repairs to an electrical system is easier and safer if you have an accurate, up-to-date map of your home's electrical circuits. A circuit map shows all lights, appliances, switches, and receptacles connected to each circuit. The map allows you to index the main service panel so that the correct circuit can be shut off when repairs are needed.

Mapping all the circuits and indexing the main service panel requires four to six hours. If your service panel was indexed by a previous owner, it is a good idea to make your own circuit map to make sure the old index is accurate. If circuits have been added or changed, the old index will be outdated.

The easiest way to map circuits is to turn on one circuit at a time and check to see which light fixtures, receptacles, and appliances are powered by the circuit. All electrical devices must be in good working condition before you begin.

A circuit map also will help you evaluate the electrical demands on each circuit (pages 34 to 35). This information can help you determine if your wiring system needs to be updated.

Everything You Need:

Tools: pens, circuit tester.

Materials: graph paper, masking tape.

See Inspector's Notebook:

• Service Panel Inspection (page 113).

How to Map Circuits & Index a Service Panel

1 Make a sketch of each room in the house on graph paper. Include the hallways, basement and attic, and all utility areas. Or, use a blueprint of your house.

2 Make a sketch of the outside of the house, the garage, and any other separate structures that are wired for electricity.

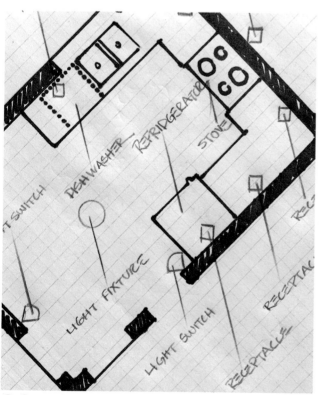

3 On each sketch, indicate the location of all receptacles, light fixtures, switches, appliances, doorbells, thermostats, heaters, fans, and air conditioners.

4 At the main service panel, number each circuit breaker or fuse. Turn off all the circuit breakers or loosen all the fuses, but leave the main shutoff in the ON position.

(continued next page)

5 Turn on one circuit at a time by flipping the circuit breaker lever or tightening the correct fuse. Note the amperage rating printed on the circuit breaker lever, or on the rim of the fuse (page 28).

6 Turn on switches, lights, and appliances throughout the house, and identify those that are powered by the circuit. Write the circuit number and amperage rating on a piece of masking tape. The tape makes a handy temporary reference.

7 Test receptacles for power, using a neon circuit tester. Make sure to check both halves of the receptacle.

8 Indicate which circuit supplies power to each receptacle. Although uncommon, remember that receptacles can be wired so that each half of the receptacle is powered by a different circuit.

9 To check the furnace for power, set thermostat to highest temperature setting. Furnaces and their low-voltage thermostats are on the same circuit. If the circuit is hot, the furnace will begin running. The lowest temperature setting will turn on central air conditioner.

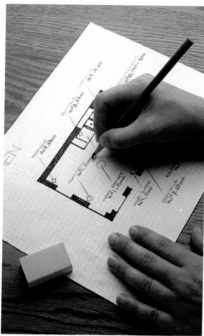

10 Check electric water heater for power by setting its thermostat to highest temperature setting. Water heater will begin to heat if it is powered by the circuit.

11 Check the doorbell system for power by ringing all of the doorbells.

12 On the circuit maps, indicate the circuit number, the voltage, and the amperage rating of each receptacle, switch, light fixture, and appliance.

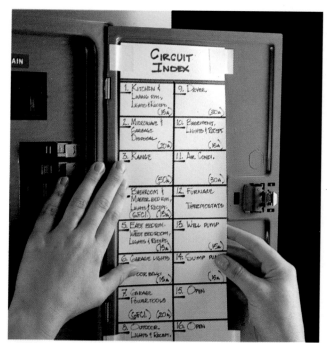

13 On the door of the main service panel, tape an index that provides a brief summary of all the fixtures, receptacles, and appliances that are powered by each circuit.

14 Attach the completed circuit maps to the main service panel, and make sure the power is turned on for all the circuits.

Evaluating Circuits for Safe Capacity

Every electrical circuit in a home has a "safe capacity." Safe capacity is the total amount of power the circuit wires can carry without tripping circuit breakers or blowing fuses. According to the National Electrical Code, the power used by light fixtures, lamps, tools, and appliances, called the "demand," must not exceed the safe capacity of the circuit.

Finding the safe capacity and the demand of a circuit is easy. Make these simple calculations to reduce the chances of tripped circuit breakers or blown fuses, or to help plan the location of new appliances or plug-in lamps.

First, determine the amperage and voltage rating of the circuit. If you have an up-to-date circuit map (pages 30 to 33) these ratings should be indicated on the map. If not, open the service panel door and read the amperage rating printed on the circuit breaker, or on the rim of the fuse. The type of circuit breaker or fuse (page 28) indicates the voltage of the circuit.

Use the amperage and voltage ratings to find the safe capacity of the circuit. Safe capacities of the most common household circuits are given in the table at right.

Safe capacities can be calculated by multiplying the amperage rating by voltage. The answer is the total capacity, expressed in **watts**, a unit of electrical measurement. To find the safe capacity, reduce the total capacity by 20%.

Next, compare the safe capacity of the circuit to the total power demand. To find the demand, add the wattage ratings for all light fixtures, lamps, and appliances on the circuit. For lights, use the wattage rating printed on the light bulbs. Wattage ratings for appliances often are printed on the manufacturer's label. Approximate wattage ratings for many common household items are given in the table on the opposite page. If you are unsure about the wattage rating of a tool or appliance, use the highest number shown in the table to make calculations.

Compare the power demand to the safe capacity. The power demand should not exceed the safe capacity of the circuit. If it does, you must move lamps or appliances to another circuit. Or, make sure that the power demand of the lamps and appliances turned on **at the same time** does not exceed the safe capacity of the circuit.

Amps x Volts	Total Capacity	Safe Capacity
15 A x 120 V =	1800 watts	1440 watts
20 A x 120 V =	2400 watts	1920 watts
25 A x 120 V =	3000 watts	2400 watts
30 A x 120 V =	3600 watts	2880 watts
20 A x 240 V =	4800 watts	3840 watts
30 A x 240 V =	7200 watts	5760 watts

How to Find Wattage & Amperage Ratings

Light bulb wattage ratings are printed on the top of the bulb. If a light fixture has more than one bulb, remember to add the wattages of all the bulbs to find the total wattage of the fixture.

Appliance wattage ratings are often listed on the manufacturer's label. Or, use table of typical wattage ratings on the opposite page.

Amperage rating can be used to find the wattage of an appliance. Multiply the amperage by the voltage of the circuit. For example, a 13-amp, 120-volt circular saw is rated for 1560 watts.

Sample Circuit Evaluation

Circuit # _6_ Amps _20_ Volts _120_ Total capacity _2400_ (watts) Safe capacity _1920_ (watts)

Appliance or fixture	Notes	Wattage rating
Refrigerator	Constant use	480
Ceiling Light	3 - 60 watt bulbs	180
Microwave oven		625
Electric can opener	Occasional use	144
Stereo	Portable boom box	300
Ceiling Light (Hallway)	2 60 watt bulbs	120
	Total demand:	1849 (watts)

Photocopy this sample circuit evaluation to keep a record of the power demand of each circuit. The words and numbers printed in blue will not reproduce on photocopies. In this sample kitchen circuit, the demand on the circuit is very close to the safe capacity. Adding another appliance, such as an electric frying pan, could overload the circuit and cause a fuse to blow or a circuit breaker to trip.

Typical Wattage Ratings (120-volt Circuit Except Where Noted)

Appliance	Amps	Watts	Appliance	Amps	Watts
Air conditioner (central)	21 (240-v)	5040	Hair dryer	5 to 10	600 to 1200
Air conditioner (window)	6 to 13	720 to 1560	Heater (portable)	7 to 12	840 to 1440
Blender	2 to 4	240 to 480	Microwave oven	4 to 7	480 to 840
Broiler	12.5	1500	Range (oven/stove)	16 to 32 (240-v)	3840 to 7680
Can opener	1.2	144	Refrigerator	2 to 4	240 to 480
Circular saw	10 to 12	1200 to 1440	Router	8	960
Coffee maker	4 to 8	480 to 960	Sander (portable)	2 to 5	240 to 600
Clothes dryer	16.5 to 34 (240-v)	3960 to 8160	Saw (table)	7 to 10	840 to 1200
Clothes iron	9	1080	Sewing machine	1	120
Computer	4 to 7	480 to 840	Stereo	2.5 to 4	300 to 480
Dishwasher	8.5 to 12.5	1020 to 1500	Television (b & w)	2	240
Drill (portable)	2 to 4	240 to 480	Television (color)	2.5	300
Fan (ceiling)	3.5	420	Toaster	9	1080
Fan (portable)	2	240	Trash compactor	4 to 8	480 to 960
Freezer	2 to 4	240 to 480	Vacuum cleaner	6 to 11	720 to 1320
Frying pan	9	1080	Waffle iron	7.5	900
Furnace, forced-air gas	6.5 to 13	780 to 1560	Washing machine	12.5	1500
Garbage disposer	3.5 to 7.5	420 to 900	Water heater	10.5 to 21 (240-v)	2520 to 5040

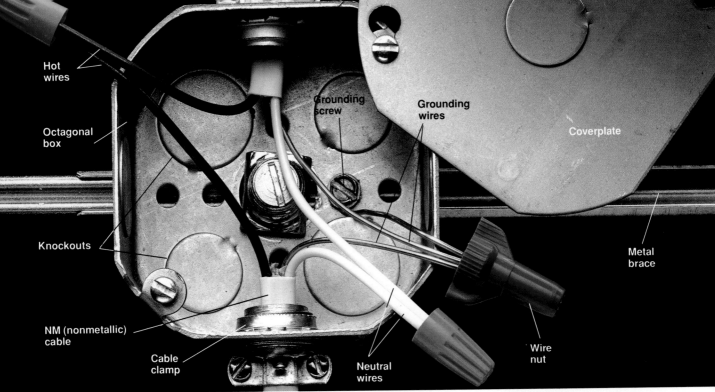

Hot wires

Octagonal box

Grounding screw

Grounding wires

Coverplate

Knockouts

Metal brace

NM (nonmetallic) cable

Cable clamp

Neutral wires

Wire nut

Octagonal boxes usually contain wire connections for ceiling fixtures. Cables are inserted into the box through knockout openings, and are held with cable clamps. Because the ceiling fixture attaches directly to the box, the box should be anchored firmly to a framing member. Often, it is nailed directly to a ceiling joist. However, metal braces are available that allow a box to be mounted between joists or studs. A properly installed octagonal box can support a ceiling fixture weighing up to 35 pounds. Any box must be covered with a tightly fitting coverplate, and the box must not have open knockouts.

Electrical Boxes: Repairs

The National Electrical Code requires that wire connections or cable splices be contained inside an approved metal or plastic box. This shields framing members and other flammable materials from electrical sparks. If you have exposed wire connections or cable splices, protect your home by installing electrical boxes.

Electrical boxes come in several shapes. Rectangular and square boxes are used for switches and receptacles. Rectangular (2" × 3") boxes are used for single switches or duplex receptacles. Square (4" × 4") boxes are used anytime it is convenient for two switches or receptacles to be wired or "ganged" in one box, an arrangement common in kitchens or entry hallways. Octagonal electrical boxes contain wire connections for ceiling fixtures.

All electrical boxes are available in different depths. A box must be deep enough so a switch or receptacle can be removed or installed easily without crimping and damaging the circuit wires. Replace an undersized box with a larger box, using the Electrical Box Chart (right) as a guide. The NEC also says that all electrical boxes must remain accessible. Never cover an electrical box with drywall, paneling, or wallcoverings.

See Inspector's Notebook:
- Electrical Box Inspection (pages 118 to 119).
- Common Cable Problems (pages 114 to 115).

Electrical Box Chart

Box Shape		Maximum number of individual wires in box*	
		14-gauge	12-gauge
2" × 3" rectangular	2½" deep	3	3
	3½" deep	5	4
4" × 4" square	1½" deep	6	5
	2⅛" deep	9	7
Octagonal	1½" deep	4	3
	2⅛" deep	7	6

* Do not count pigtail wires or grounding wires.

Common Electrical Boxes

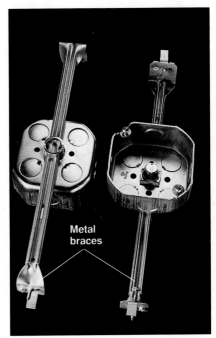

Detachable side

Adapter cover

Metal braces

Rectangular boxes are used with wall switches and duplex receptacles. Single-size rectangular boxes (shown above) may have detachable sides that allow them to be ganged together to form double-size boxes.

Square 4" × 4" boxes are large enough for most wiring applications. They are used for cable splices and ganged receptacles or switches. To install one switch or receptacle in a square box, use an adapter cover.

Braced octagonal boxes fit between ceiling joists. The metal braces extend to fit any joist spacing, and are nailed or screwed to framing members.

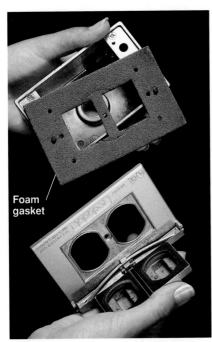

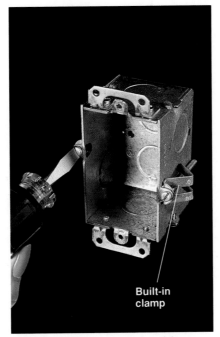

Foam gasket

Built-in clamp

Outdoor boxes have sealed seams and foam gaskets to guard a switch or receptacle against moisture. Corrosion-resistant coatings protect all metal parts.

Retrofit boxes upgrade older boxes to larger sizes. One type (above) has built-in clamps that tighten against the inside of a wall and hold the box in place. A retrofit box with flexible brackets is shown on pages 40 to 41.

Plastic boxes are common in new construction. They can be used only with NM (nonmetallic) cable. Box may include preattached nails for anchoring the box to framing members.

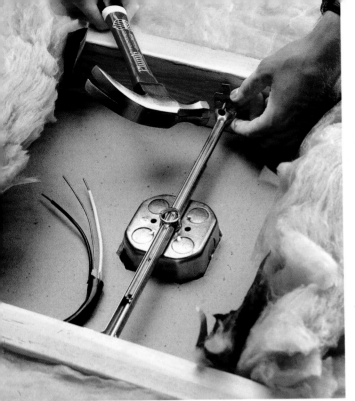

Electrical boxes are required for all wire connections. The box protects wood and other flammable materials from electrical sparks (arcing). Electrical boxes should always be anchored to joists or studs.

Installing an Electrical Box

Install an electrical box any time you find exposed wire connections or cable splices. Exposed connections sometimes can be found in older homes, where wires attach to light fixtures. Exposed splices (page 115) can be found in areas where NM (nonmetallic) cable runs through uncovered joists or wall studs, such as in an unfinished basement or utility room.

When installing an electrical box, make sure there is enough cable to provide about 8" of wire inside the box. If the wires are too short, you can add pigtails to lengthen them (page 118). If the electrical box is metal, make sure the circuit grounding wires are pigtailed to the box.

Everything You Need:

Tools: neon circuit tester, screwdriver, hammer, combination tool.

Materials: screws or nails, electrical box, cable connectors, pigtail wire, wire nuts.

How to Install an Electrical Box for Cable Splices

1 Turn off power to circuit wires at the main service panel. Carefully remove any tape or wire nuts from the exposed splice. Avoid contact with the bare wire ends until the wires have been tested for power.

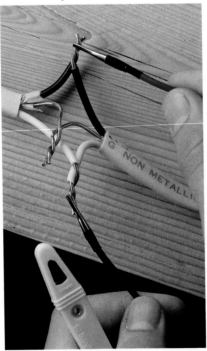

2 Test for power. Touch one probe of a circuit tester to the black hot wires, and touch other probe to the white neutral wires. The tester should not glow. If it does, the wires are still hot. Shut off power to correct circuit at the main service panel. Disconnect the splice wires.

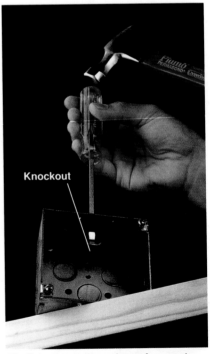

Knockout

3 Open one knockout for each cable that will enter the box, using a hammer and screwdriver. Any unopened knockouts should remain sealed.

4 Anchor the electrical box to a wooden framing member, using screws or nails.

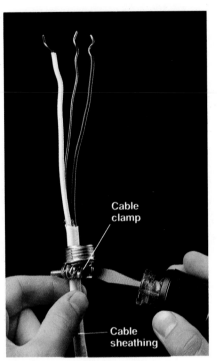

Cable clamp

Cable sheathing

5 Thread each cable through a cable clamp. Tighten the clamp with a screwdriver. Do not overtighten. Overtightening can damage cable sheathing.

Locknut

6 Insert the cables into the electrical box, and screw a locknut onto each cable clamp.

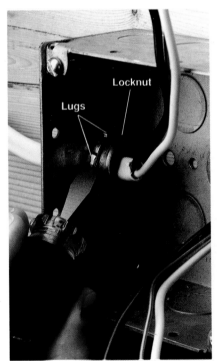

Locknut

Lugs

7 Tighten the locknuts by pushing against the lugs with the blade of a screwdriver.

Grounding screw

8 Use wire nuts to reconnect the wires. Pigtail the copper grounding wires to the green grounding screw in the back of the box.

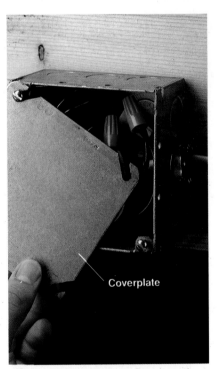

Coverplate

9 Carefully tuck the wires into the box, and attach the coverplate. Turn on the power to the circuit at the main service panel. Make sure the box remains accessible, and is not covered with finished walls or ceilings.

Replacing an Electrical Box

Replace any electrical box that is too small for the number of wires it contains. Forcing wires into an undersized box can damage wires, disturb wire connections, and create a potential fire hazard.

Boxes that are too small often are found when repairing or replacing switches, receptacles, or light fixtures. If you find a box so small that you have difficulty fitting the wires inside, replace it with a larger box. Use the chart on page 36 as a guide when choosing a replacement box.

Metal and plastic retrofit electrical boxes are available in a variety of styles, and can be purchased at any hardware store or home center. Most can be installed without damaging the wall surfaces.

Everything You Need:

Tools: screwdriver, neon circuit tester, reciprocating saw, hammer, needlenose pliers.

Materials: electrical tape, retrofit electrical box with flexible brackets, grounding screw.

How to Replace an Electrical Box

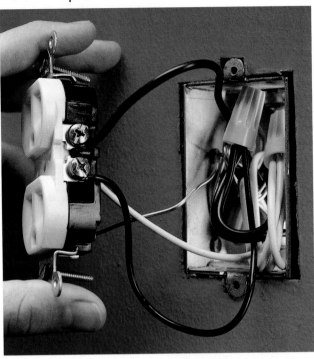

1 Shut off the power to the circuit at the main service panel. Test for power with a neon circuit tester (switches, page 57; receptacles, page 70; light fixtures, page 80). Disconnect and remove receptacle, switch, or fixture from the existing box.

2 Examine the box to determine how it was installed. Most older metal boxes are attached to framing members with nails, and the nail heads will be visible inside the box.

3 Cut through the mounting nails by slipping the metal-cutting blade of a reciprocating saw between the box and framing member. Take care not to damage the circuit wires. Disconnect wires.

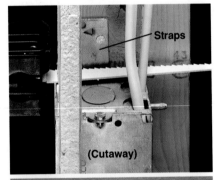

If box is mounted with straps (shown with wall cut away) remove the box by cutting through the straps, using a reciprocating saw and metal-cutting blade. Take care not to damage the wires.

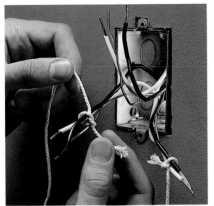

4 To prevent wires from falling into wall cavity, gather wires from each cable and tie them together, using pieces of string.

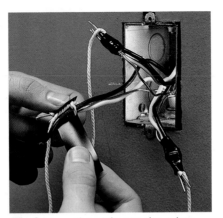

5 Secure the string to the wires, using a piece of plastic electrical tape.

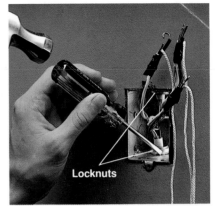

6 Disconnect the internal clamps or locknuts that hold the circuit cables to the box.

7 Pull old electrical box from wall. Take care not to damage insulation on circuit wires, and hold on to string to make sure wires do not fall inside wall cavity.

8 Tape the wires to the edge of the wall cutout.

9 Punch out one knockout for each cable that will enter the new electrical box, using a screwdriver and hammer.

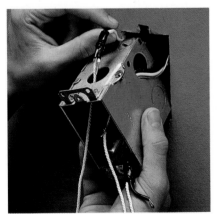

10 Thread cables into the new electrical box, and slide the box into the wall opening. Tighten the internal clamps or locknuts holding the circuit cables to the electrical box. Remove the strings.

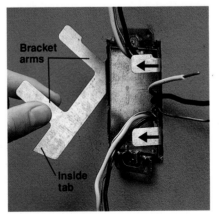

11 Insert flexible brackets into the wall on each side of the electrical box. Pull out bracket arms until inside tab is tight against inside of the wall.

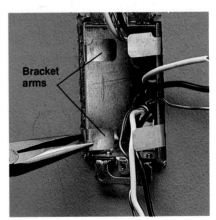

12 Bend bracket arms around walls of box, using needlenose pliers. Reinstall the fixture, and turn on the power to the circuit at the main service panel.

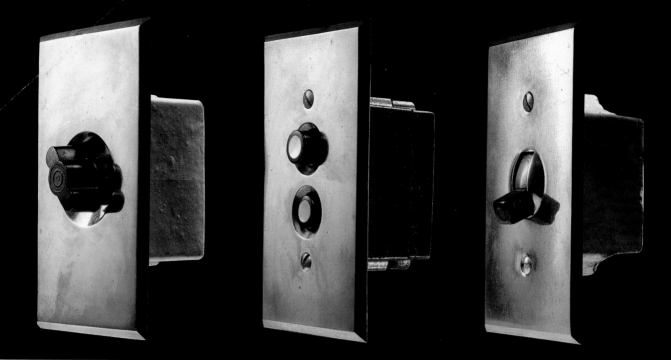

Rotary snap switches are found in many installations completed between 1900 and 1920. Handle is twisted clockwise to turn light on and off. The switch is enclosed in a ceramic housing.

Push-button switches were widely used from 1920 until about 1940. Many switches of this type are still in operation. Reproductions of this switch type are available for restoration projects.

Toggle switches were introduced in the 1930s. This early design has a switch mechanism that is mounted in a ceramic housing sealed with a layer of insulating paper.

Common Wall-switch Problems

An average wall switch is turned on and off more than 1,000 times each year. Because switches receive constant use, wire connections can loosen and switch parts gradually wear out. If a switch no longer operates smoothly, it must be repaired or replaced.

The methods for repairing or replacing a switch vary slightly, depending on the switch type and its location along an electrical circuit. When working on a switch, use the photographs on pages 44 to 51 to identify your switch type and its wiring configuration. Individual switch styles may vary from manufacturer to manufacturer, but the basic switch types are universal.

It is possible to replace most ordinary wall switches with a specialty switch, like a timer switch or an electronic switch. When installing a specialty switch (pages 49 to 51), make sure it is compatible with the wiring configuration of the switch box.

See Inspector's Notebook:
- Common Cable Problems (pages 114 to 115).
- Checking Wire Connections (pages 116 to 117).
- Inspecting Switches (page 123).

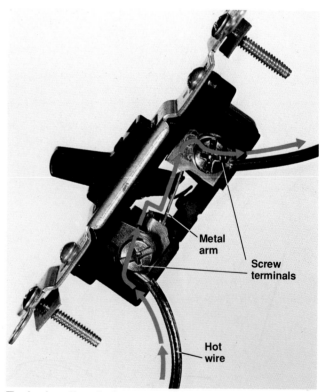

Metal arm

Screw terminals

Hot wire

Typical wall switch has a movable metal arm that opens and closes the electrical circuit. When the switch is ON, the arm completes the circuit and power flows between the screw terminals and through the black hot wire to the light fixture. When the switch is OFF, the arm lifts away to interrupt the circuit, and no power flows. Switch problems can occur if the screw terminals are not tight, or if the metal arm inside the switch wears out.

Toggle switches were improved during the 1950s, and are now the most commonly used type. This switch type was the first to use a sealed plastic housing that protects the inner switch mechanism from dust and moisture.

Mercury switches became common in the early 1960s. They conduct electrical current by means of a sealed vial of mercury. Although more expensive than other types, mercury switches are durable: some are guaranteed for 50 years.

Electronic motion-sensor switch has an infrared eye that senses movement and automatically turns on lights when a person enters a room. Motion-sensor switches can provide added security against intruders.

Problem	Repair
Fuse burns out or circuit breaker trips when the switch is turned on.	1. Tighten any loose wire connections on switch (pages 56 to 57). 2. Move lamps or plug-in appliances to other circuits to prevent overloads (page 34). 3. Test switch (pages 52 to 55), and replace, if needed (pages 56 to 59). 4. Repair or replace faulty fixture (pages 78 to 93) or faulty appliance.
Light fixture or permanently installed appliance does not work.	1. Replace burned-out light bulb. 2. Check for blown fuse or tripped circuit breaker to make sure circuit is operating (pages 28 to 29). 3. Check for loose wire connections on switch (pages 56 to 57). 4. Test switch (pages 52 to 55), and replace, if needed (pages 56 to 59). 5. Repair or replace light fixture (pages 78 to 93) or appliance.
Light fixture flickers.	1. Tighten light bulb in the socket. 2. Check for loose wire connections on switch (pages 56 to 57). 3. Repair or replace light fixture (pages 78 to 93), or switch (pages 56 to 59).
Switch buzzes or is warm to the touch.	1. Check for loose wire connections on switch (pages 56 to 57). .2. Test switch (pages 52 to 55), and replace, if needed (pages 56 to 59). 3. Move lamps or appliances to other circuits to reduce demand (page 34).
Switch lever does not stay in position.	Replace worn-out switch (pages 56 to 59).

Wall-switch Basics

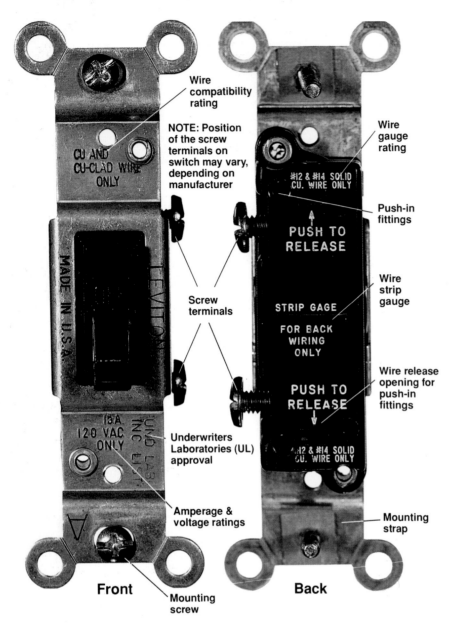

Wire compatibility rating

NOTE: Position of the screw terminals on switch may vary, depending on manufacturer

CU AND CU-CLAD WIRE ONLY

MADE IN U.S.A.

LEVITON

15A. 120 VAC ONLY

UND. LAB. INC. LIST

Screw terminals

Underwriters Laboratories (UL) approval

Amperage & voltage ratings

Front

Mounting screw

Wire gauge rating

#12 & #14 SOLID CU. WIRE ONLY

Push-in fittings

↑ PUSH TO RELEASE

STRIP GAGE
FOR BACK WIRING ONLY

Wire strip gauge

PUSH TO RELEASE ↓

Wire release opening for push-in fittings

#12 & #14 SOLID CU. WIRE ONLY

Mounting strap

Back

Wall switches are available in three general types. To repair or replace a switch, it is important to identify its type.

Single-pole switches are used to control a set of lights from one location. **Three-way switches** are used to control a set of lights from two different locations, and are always installed in pairs. **Four-way switches** are used in combination with a pair of three-way switches to control a set of lights from three or more locations.

Identify switch types by counting the screw terminals. Single-pole switches have two screw terminals, three-way switches have three screw terminals, and four-way switches have four.

Some switches may include a grounding screw terminal, which is identified by its green color. Although grounded switches are not required by most electrical codes, some electricians recommend they be used in bathrooms, kitchens, and basements. When pigtailed to the grounding wires, the grounding screw provides added protection against shock.

When replacing a switch, choose a new switch that has the same number of screw terminals as the old one. The location of the screws on the switch body varies, depending on the manufacturer, but these differences will not affect the switch operation.

Newer switches may have push-in fittings in addition to the screw terminals. Some specialty switches (pages 50 to 51) have wire leads instead of screw terminals. They are connected to circuit wires with wire nuts.

A wall switch is connected to circuit wires with screw terminals or with push-in fittings on the back of the switch. A switch may have a stamped strip gauge that indicates how much insulation must be stripped from the circuit wires to make the connections.

The switch body is attached to a metal mounting strap that allows it to be mounted in an electrical box. Several rating stamps are found on the strap and on the back of the switch. The abbreviation UL or UND. LAB. INC. LIST means that the switch meets the safety standards of the Underwriters Laboratories. Switches also are stamped with maximum voltage and amperage ratings. Standard wall switches are rated 15A, 125V. Voltage ratings of 110, 120, and 125 are considered to be identical for purposes of identification.

For standard wall switch installations, choose a switch that has a wire gauge rating of #12 or #14. For wire systems with solid-core copper wiring, use only switches marked COPPER or CU. For aluminum wiring (page 22), use only switches marked CO/ALR. Switches marked AL/CU can no longer be used with aluminum wiring, according to the National Electrical Code.

Single-pole Wall Switches

A single-pole switch is the most common type of wall switch. It usually has ON-OFF markings on the switch lever, and is used to control a set of lights, an appliance, or a receptacle from a single location. A single-pole switch has two screw terminals. Some types also may have a grounding screw. When installing a single-pole switch, check to make sure the ON marking shows when the switch lever is in the up position.

In a correctly wired single-pole switch, a hot circuit wire is attached to each screw terminal. However, the color and number of wires inside the switch box will vary, depending on the location of the switch along the electrical circuit.

If two cables enter the box, then the switch lies in the middle of the circuit. In this installation, both of the hot wires attached to the switch are black.

If only one cable enters the box, then the switch lies at the end of the circuit. In this installation (sometimes called a switch loop), one of the hot wires is black, but the other hot wire usually is white. A white hot wire sometimes is coded with black tape or paint.

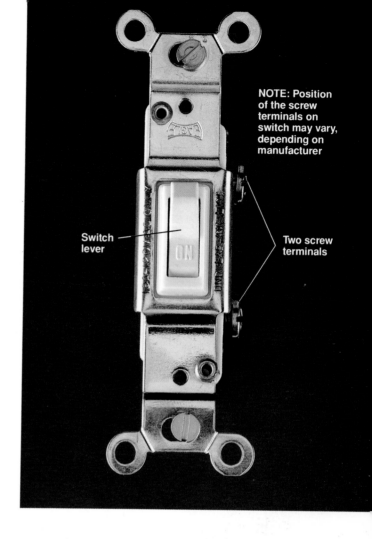

NOTE: Position of the screw terminals on switch may vary, depending on manufacturer

Switch lever

Two screw terminals

Typical Single-pole Switch Installations

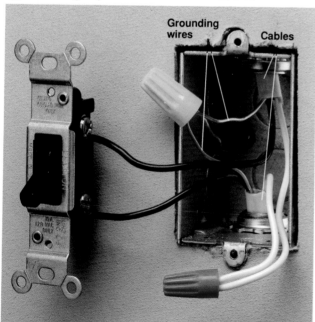

Grounding wires

Cables

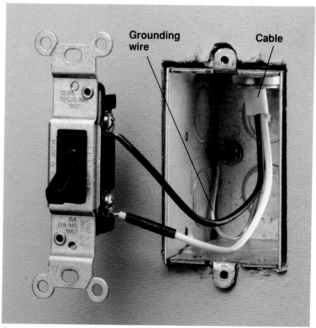

Grounding wire

Cable

Two cables enter the box when a switch is located in the middle of a circuit. Each cable has a white and a black insulated wire, plus a bare copper grounding wire. The black wires are hot, and are connected to the screw terminals on the switch. The white wires are neutral and are joined together with a wire nut. Grounding wires are pigtailed to the grounded box.

One cable enters the box when a switch is located at the end of a circuit. The cable has a white and a black insulated wire, plus a bare copper grounding wire. In this installation, both of the insulated wires are hot. The white wire may be labeled with black tape or paint to identify it as a hot wire. The grounding wire is connected to the grounded metal box.

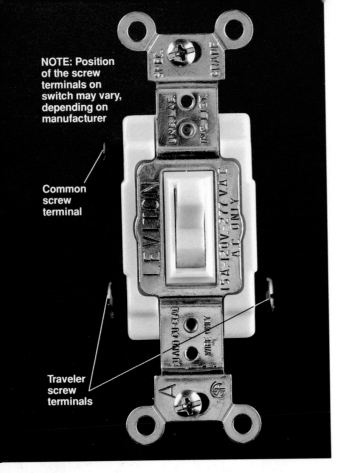

NOTE: Position of the screw terminals on switch may vary, depending on manufacturer

Common screw terminal

Traveler screw terminals

Three-way Wall Switches

Three-way switches have three screw terminals, and do not have ON-OFF markings. Three-way switches are always installed in pairs, and are used to control a set of lights from two locations.

One of the screw terminals on a three-way switch is darker than the others. This screw is the **common screw terminal.** The position of the common screw terminal on the switch body may vary, depending on the manufacturer. Before disconnecting a three-way switch, always label the wire that is connected to the common screw terminal. It must be reconnected to the common screw terminal on the new switch.

The two lighter-colored screw terminals on a three-way switch are called the **traveler screw terminals.** The traveler terminals are interchangeable, so there is no need to label the wires attached to them.

Because three-way switches are installed in pairs, it sometimes is difficult to determine which of the switches is causing a problem. The switch that receives greater use is more likely to fail, but you may need to inspect both switches to find the source of the problem.

Typical Three-way Switch Installations

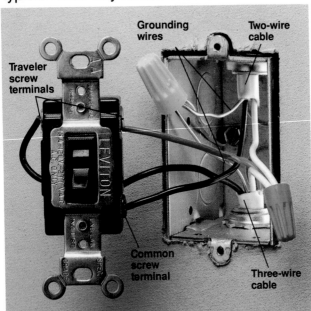

Traveler screw terminals

Grounding wires

Two-wire cable

Common screw terminal

Three-wire cable

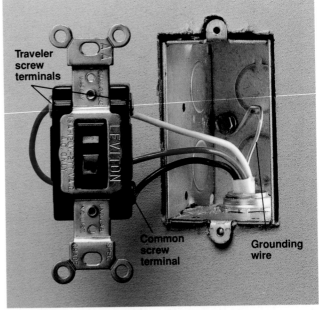

Traveler screw terminals

Common screw terminal

Grounding wire

Two cables enter box if the switch lies in the middle of a circuit. One cable has two wires, plus a bare copper grounding wire; the other cable has three wires, plus a ground. The black wire from the two-wire cable is connected to the dark, common screw terminal. The red and black wires from the three-wire cable are connected to the traveler screw terminals. The white neutral wires are joined together with a wire nut, and the grounding wires are pigtailed to the grounded metal box.

One cable enters the box if the switch lies at the end of the circuit. The cable has a black wire, red wire, and white wire, plus a bare copper grounding wire. The black wire must be connected to the common screw terminal, which is darker than the other two screw terminals. The white and red wires are connected to the two traveler screw terminals. The bare copper grounding wire is connected to the grounded metal box.

Four-way Wall Switches

Four-way switches have four screw terminals, and do not have ON-OFF markings. Four-way switches are always installed between a pair of three-way switches. This switch combination makes it possible to control a set of lights from three or more locations. Four-way switches are not common, but are sometimes found in homes that have very large rooms or long hallways. Switch problems in a four-way installation can be caused by loose connections or worn parts in a four-way switch or in one of the three-way switches (page opposite).

In a typical installation, two pairs of color-matched wires are connected to the four-way switch. To simplify installation, newer four-way switches have screw terminals that are paired by color. One pair of screws usually is copper, while the other pair is brass. When installing the switch, match the wires to the screw terminals by color. For example, if a red wire is connected to one of the brass screw terminals, make sure the other red wire is connected to the remaining brass screw terminal.

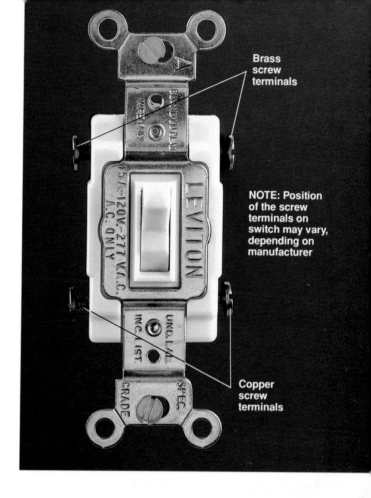

Brass screw terminals

NOTE: Position of the screw terminals on switch may vary, depending on manufacturer

Copper screw terminals

Typical Four-way Switch Installation

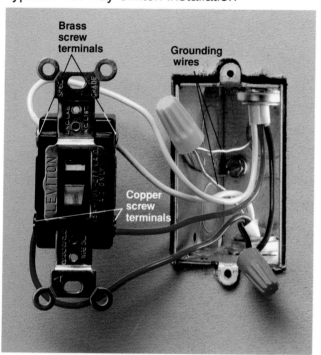

Brass screw terminals

Grounding wires

Copper screw terminals

Four wires are connected to a four-way switch. One pair of color-matched wires is connected to the copper screw terminals, while another pair is connected to the brass screw terminals. A third pair of wires are connected inside the box with a wire nut. The two bare copper grounding wires are pigtailed to the grounded metal box.

Switch variation: Some four-way switches have a wiring guide stamped on the back to help simplify installation. For the switch shown above, one pair of color-matched circuit wires will be connected to the screw terminals marked LINE 1, while the other pair of wires will be attached to the screw terminals marked LINE 2.

47

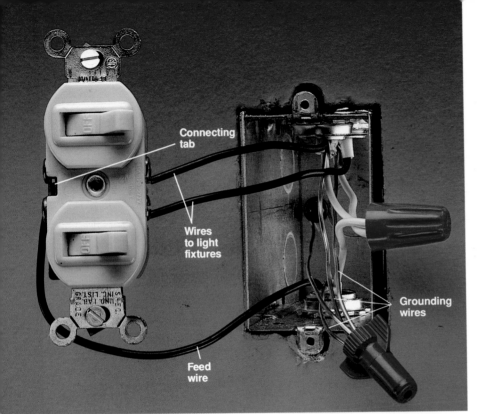

Single-circuit wiring: Three black wires are attached to the switch. The black feed wire bringing power into the box is connected to the side of the switch that has a connecting tab. The wires carrying power out to the light fixtures or appliances are connected to the side of the switch that **does not** have a connecting tab. The white neutral wires are connected together with a wire nut.

Double Switches

A double switch has two switch levers in a single housing. It is used to control two light fixtures or appliances from the same switch box.

In most installations, both halves of the switch are powered by the same circuit. In these **single-circuit** installations, three wires are connected to the double switch. One wire, called the "feed" wire, supplies power to both halves of the switch. The other wires carry power out to the individual light fixtures or appliances.

In rare installations, each half of the switch is powered by a separate circuit. In these **separate-circuit** installations, four wires are connected to the switch, and the metal connecting tab joining two of the screw terminals is removed (photo below).

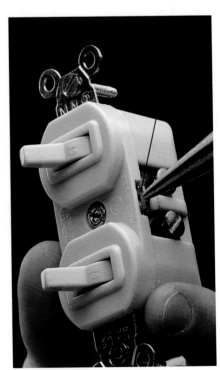

Separate-circuit wiring: Four black wires are attached to the switch. Feed wires from the power source are attached to the side of switch that has a connecting tab, and the connecting tab is removed (photo, right). Wires carrying power from the switch to light fixtures or appliances are connected to the side of the switch that **does not** have a connecting tab. White neutral wires are connected together with a wire nut.

Remove the connecting tab on a double switch when wired in a separate-circuit installation. The tab can be removed with needle-nose pliers or a screwdriver.

Pilot-light Switches

A pilot-light switch has a built-in bulb that glows when power flows through the switch to a light fixture or appliance. Pilot-light switches often are installed for convenience if a light fixture or appliance cannot be seen from the switch location. Basement lights, garage lights, and attic exhaust fans frequently are controlled by pilot-light switches.

A pilot-light switch requires a neutral wire connection. A switch box that contains a single two-wire cable has only hot wires, and cannot be fitted with a pilot-light switch.

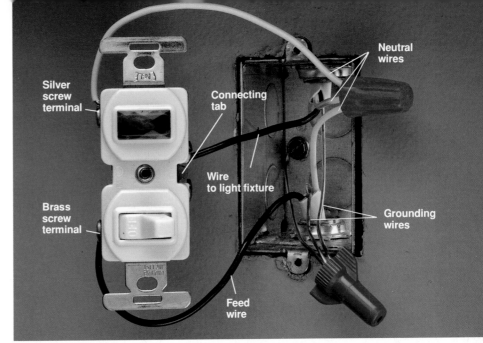

Pilot-light switch wiring: Three wires are connected to the switch. One black wire is the feed wire that brings power into the box. It is connected to the brass screw terminal on the side of the switch that **does not** have a connecting tab. The white neutral wires are pigtailed to the silver screw terminal. Black wire carrying power out to light fixture or appliance is connected to screw terminal on side of the switch that has a connecting tab.

Switch/receptacles

A switch/receptacle combines a grounded receptacle with a single-pole wall switch. In a room that does not have enough wall receptacles, electrical service can be improved by replacing a single-pole switch with a switch/receptacle.

A switch/receptacle requires a neutral wire connection. A switch box that contains a single two-wire cable has only hot wires, and cannot be fitted with a switch/receptacle.

A switch/receptacle can be installed in one of two ways. In the most common installations, the receptacle is hot even when the switch is off (photo, right).

In rare installations, a switch/-receptacle is wired so the receptacle is hot only when the switch is on. In this installation, the hot wires are reversed, so that the feed wire is attached to the brass screw terminal on the side of the switch that does not have a connecting tab.

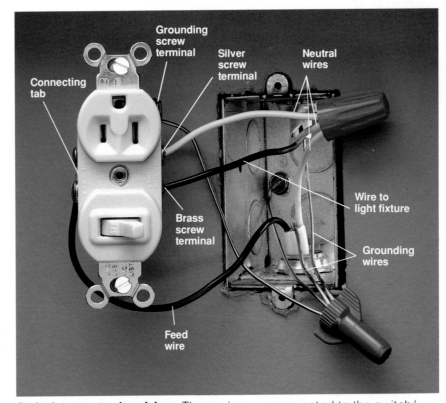

Switch/receptacle wiring: Three wires are connected to the switch/-receptacle. One of the hot wires is the feed wire that brings power into the box. It is connected to the side of the switch that has a connecting tab. The other hot wire carries power out to the light fixture or appliance. It is connected to the brass screw terminal on the side that **does not** have a connecting tab. The white neutral wire is pigtailed to the silver screw terminal. The grounding wires must be pigtailed to the green grounding screw on the switch/receptacle and to the grounded metal box.

Specialty Switches

Specialty switches are available in several types. **Dimmer switches** (pages 60 to 61) are used frequently to control light intensity in dining and recreation areas. **Timer switches** and **time-delay switches** (below) are used to control light fixtures and exhaust fans automatically. New **electronic switches** (page opposite) provide added convenience and home security, and are easy to install. Electronic switches are durable, and they rarely need repair.

Most standard single-pole switches can be replaced with a specialty switch. Most specialty switches have preattached wire leads instead of

screw terminals, and are connected to circuit wires with wire nuts. Some motor-driven timer switches require a neutral wire connection, and cannot be installed in switch boxes that have only one cable with two hot wires.

If a specialty switch is not operating correctly, you may be able to test it with a continuity tester (pages 52 to 55). Timer switches and time-delay switches can be tested for continuity, but dimmer switches cannot be tested. With electronic switches, the manual switch can be tested for continuity (page 55), but the automatic features cannot be tested.

Timer Switches

Timer switches have an electrically powered control dial that can be set to turn lights on and off automatically once each day. They are commonly used to control outdoor light fixtures.

Timer switches have three preattached wire leads. The black wire lead is connected to the hot feed wire that brings power into the box, and the red lead is connected to the wire carrying power out to the light fixture. The remaining wire lead is the neutral lead. It must be connected to any neutral circuit wires. A switch box that contains only one cable has no neutral wires, so it cannot be fitted with a timer switch.

After a power failure, the dial on a timer switch must be reset to the proper time.

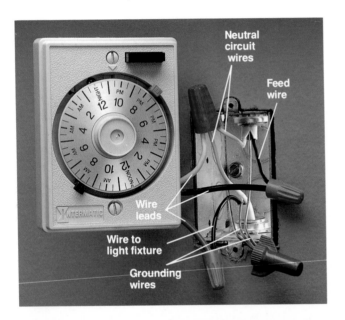

Neutral circuit wires

Feed wire

Wire leads

Wire to light fixture

Grounding wires

Time-delay Switches

A time-delay switch has a spring-driven dial that is wound by hand. The dial can be set to turn off a light fixture after a delay ranging from 1 to 60 minutes. Time-delay switches often are used for exhaust fans, electric space heaters, bathroom vent fans, and heat lamps.

The black wire leads on the switch are connected to the hot circuit wires. If the switch box contains white neutral wires, these are connected together with a wire nut. The bare copper grounding wires are pigtailed to the grounded metal box.

A time-delay switch needs no neutral wire connection, so it can be fitted in a switch box that contains either one or two cables.

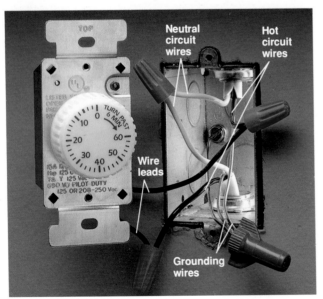

Neutral circuit wires

Hot circuit wires

Wire leads

Grounding wires

Automatic Switches

An automatic switch uses a narrow infrared beam to detect movement. When a hand passes within a few inches of the beam, an electronic signal turns the switch on or off. Some automatic switches have a manual dimming feature.

Automatic switches can be installed wherever a standard single-pole switch is used. Automatic switches are especially convenient for children and handicapped individuals.

Automatic switches require no neutral wire connections. For this reason, an automatic switch can be installed in a switch box containing either one or two cables. The wire leads on the switch are connected to hot circuit wires with wire nuts.

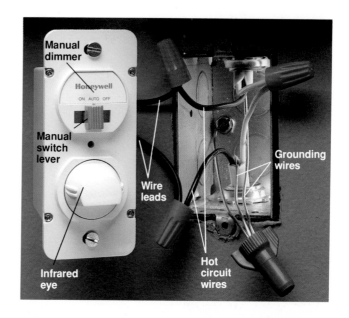

Motion-sensor Security Switches

A motion-sensor switch uses a wide-angle infrared beam to detect movement over a large area, and turns on a light fixture automatically. A time-delay feature turns off lights after movement stops.

Most motion-sensor switches have an override feature that allows the switch to be operated manually. Better switches include an adjustable sensitivity control, and a variable time-delay shutoff control.

Motion-sensor switches require no neutral wire connections. They can be installed in switch boxes containing either one or two cables. The wire leads on the switch are connected to hot circuit wires with wire nuts.

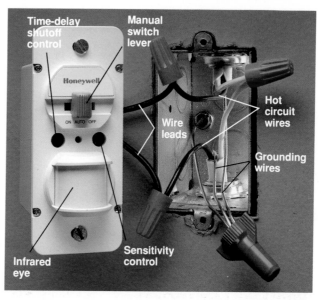

Programmable Switches

Programmable switches represent the latest in switch design. They have digital controls, and can provide four on-off cycles each day.

Programmable switches frequently are used to provide security when a homeowner is absent from the house. Law enforcement experts say that programmed lighting is a proven crime deterrent. For best protection, programmable switches should be set to a random on-off pattern.

Programmable switches require no neutral wire connections. They can be installed in switch boxes containing either one or two cables. The wire leads on the switch are connected to hot circuit wires with wire nuts.

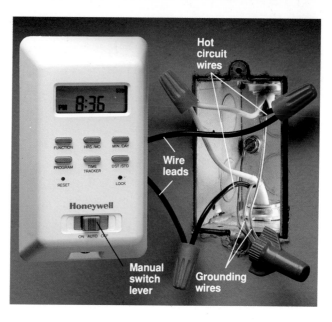

Testing Switches for Continuity

A switch that does not work properly may have worn or broken internal parts. Test for internal wear with a battery-operated continuity tester. The continuity tester detects any break in the metal pathway inside the switch. Replace the switch if the continuity tester shows the switch to be faulty.

Never use a continuity tester on wires that might carry live current. Always shut off the power and disconnect the switch before testing for continuity.

Some specialty switches, like dimmers, cannot be tested for continuity. Electronic switches can be tested for manual operation using a continuity tester, but the automatic operation of these switches cannot be tested.

Everything You Need:
Tools: continuity tester.

How to Test a Single-pole Wall Switch

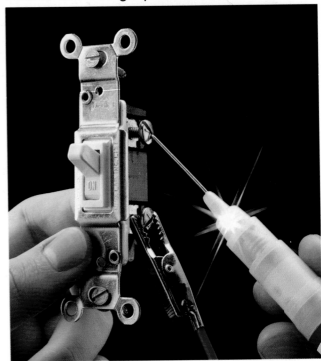

Attach clip of tester to one of the screw terminals. Touch the tester probe to the other screw terminal. Flip switch lever from ON to OFF. If switch is good, tester glows when lever is ON, but not when OFF.

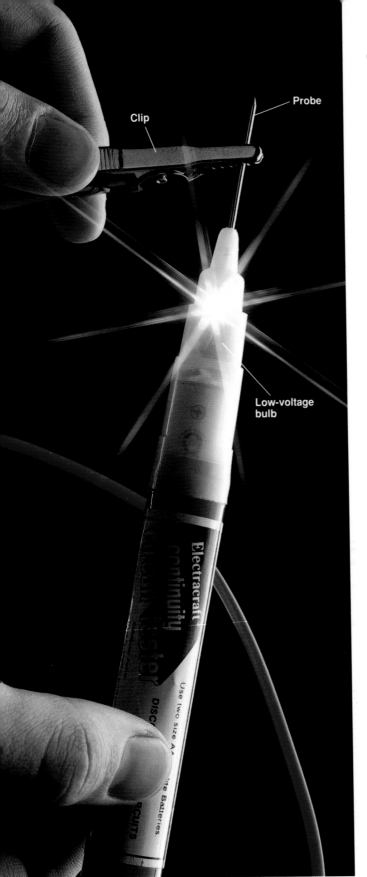

Continuity tester uses battery-generated current to test the metal pathways running through switches and other electrical fixtures. Always "test" the tester before use. Touch the tester clip to the metal probe. The tester should glow. If not, then the battery or light bulb is dead and must be replaced.

How to Test a Three-way Wall Switch

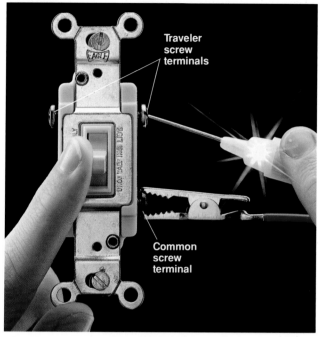

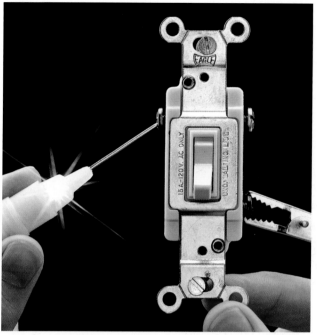

1 Attach tester clip to the dark common screw terminal. Touch the tester probe to one of the traveler screw terminals, and flip switch lever back and forth. If switch is good, the tester should glow when the lever is in one position, but not both.

2 Touch probe to the other traveler screw terminal, and flip the switch lever back and forth. If switch is good, the tester will glow only when the switch lever is in the position opposite from the positive test in step 1.

How to Test a Four-way Wall Switch

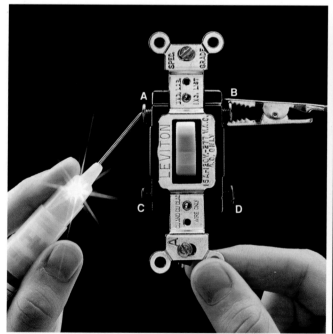

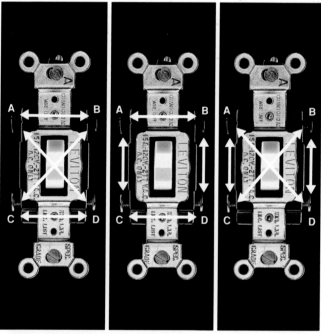

1 Test switch by touching probe and clip of continuity tester to each pair of screw terminals (A-B, C-D, A-D, B-C, A-C, B-D). The test should show continuous pathways between two different pairs of screw terminals. Flip lever to opposite position, and repeat test. Test should show continuous pathways between two different pairs of screw terminals.

2 If switch is good, test will show a total of four continuous pathways between screw terminals — two pathways for each lever position. If not, then switch is faulty and must be replaced. (The arrangement of the pathways may differ, depending on the switch manufacturer. The photo above shows the three possible pathway arrangements.)

How to Test a Pilot-light Switch

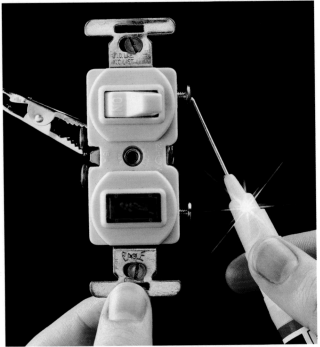

1 Test pilot light by flipping the switch lever to the ON position. Check to see if the light fixture or appliance is working. If the pilot light does not glow even though the switch operates the light fixture or appliance, then the pilot light is defective and the unit must be replaced.

2 Test the switch by disconnecting the unit. With the switch lever in the ON position, attach the tester clip to the top screw terminal on one side of the switch. Touch tester probe to top screw terminal on opposite side of the switch. If switch is good, tester will glow when switch is ON, but not when OFF.

How to Test a Timer Switch

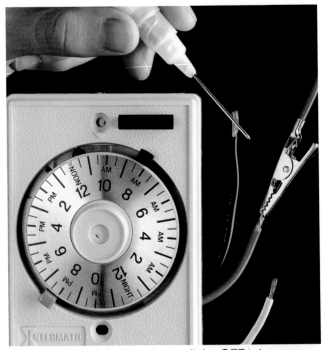

1 Attach the tester clip to the red wire lead on the timer switch, and touch the tester probe to the black hot lead. Rotate the timer dial clockwise until the ON tab passes the arrow marker. Tester should glow. If it does not, the switch is faulty and must be replaced.

2 Rotate the dial clockwise until the OFF tab passes the arrow marker. Tester should not glow. If it does, the switch is faulty and must be replaced.

How to Test Switch/receptacle

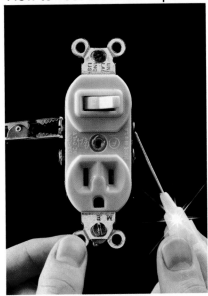

Attach tester clip to one of the top screw terminals. Touch the tester probe to the top screw terminal on the opposite side. Flip the switch lever from ON to OFF position. If the switch is working correctly, the tester will glow when the switch lever is ON, but not when OFF.

How to Test a Double Switch

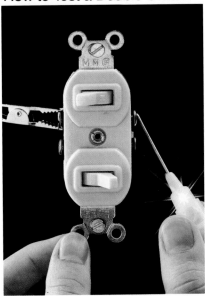

Test each half of switch by attaching the tester clip to one screw terminal, and touching the probe to the opposite side. Flip switch lever from ON to OFF position. If switch is good, tester glows when the switch lever is ON, but not when OFF. Repeat test with the remaining pair of screw terminals. If either half tests faulty, replace the unit.

How to Test a Time-delay Switch

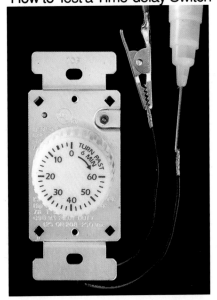

Attach tester clip to one of the wire leads, and touch the tester probe to the other lead. Set the timer for a few minutes. If switch is working correctly, the tester will glow until the time expires.

How to Test Manual Operation of Electronic Switches

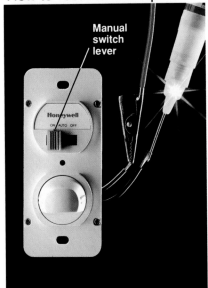

Automatic switch: Attach the tester clip to a black wire lead, and touch the tester probe to the other black lead. Flip the manual switch lever from ON to OFF position. If switch is working correctly, tester will glow when the switch lever is ON, but not when OFF.

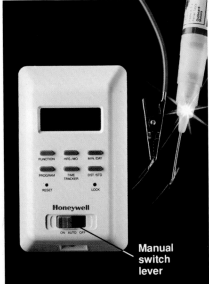

Programmable switch: Attach the tester clip to a wire lead, and touch the tester probe to the other lead. Flip the manual switch lever from ON to OFF position. If the switch is working correctly, the tester will glow when the switch lever is ON, but not when OFF.

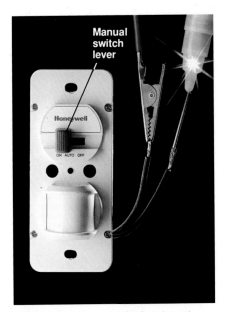

Motion-sensor switch: Attach the tester clip to a wire lead, and touch the tester probe to the other lead. Flip the manual switch lever from ON to OFF position. If the switch is working correctly, the tester will glow when the switch lever is ON, but not when OFF.

Fixing & Replacing Wall Switches

Most switch problems are caused by loose wire connections. If a fuse blows or a circuit breaker trips when a switch is turned on, a loose wire may be touching the metal box. Loose wires also can cause switches to overheat or buzz.

Switches sometimes fail because internal parts wear out. To check for wear, the switch must be removed entirely and tested for continuity (pages 52 to 55). If the continuity test shows the switch is faulty, replace it.

Everything You Need:

Tools: screwdriver, neon circuit tester, continuity tester, combination tool.

Materials: fine sandpaper, anti-oxidant paste (for aluminum wiring).

See Inspector's Notebook:
- Common Cable Problems (pages 114 to 115).
- Checking Wire Connections (pages 116 to 117).
- Electrical Box Inspection (pages 118 to 119).
- Inspecting Switches (page 123).

How to Fix or Replace a Single-pole Wall Switch

1 Turn off the power to the switch at the main service panel, then remove the switch coverplate.

2 Remove the mounting screws holding the switch to the electrical box. Holding the mounting straps carefully, pull the switch from the box. Be careful not to touch any bare wires or screw terminals until the switch has been tested for power.

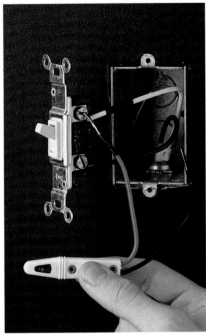

3 Test for power by touching one probe of the neon circuit tester to the grounded metal box or to the bare copper grounding wire, and touching other probe to each screw terminal. Tester should not glow. If it does, there is still power entering the box. Return to service panel and turn off correct circuit.

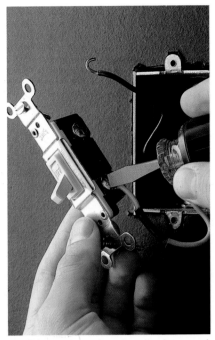

4 Disconnect the circuit wires and remove the switch. Test the switch for continuity (page 52), and buy a replacement if the switch is faulty. If circuit wires are too short, lengthen them by adding pigtail wires (page 118).

5 If wires are broken or nicked, clip off damaged portion, using a combination tool. Strip wires so there is about ¾" of bare wire at the end of each wire.

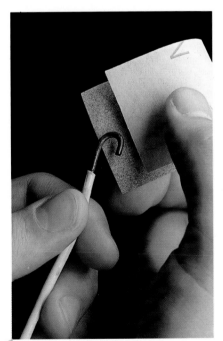

6 Clean the bare copper wires with fine sandpaper if they appear darkened or dirty. If wires are aluminum, apply an anti-oxidant paste before connecting the wires.

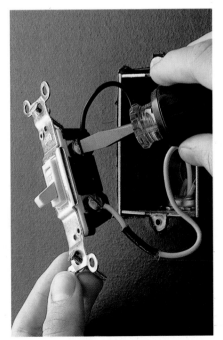

7 Connect the wires to the screw terminals on the switch. Tighten the screws firmly, but do not overtighten. Overtightening may strip the screw threads

8 Remount the switch, carefully tucking the wires inside the box. Reattach the switch coverplate and turn on the power to the switch at the main service panel.

How to Fix or Replace a Three-way Wall Switch

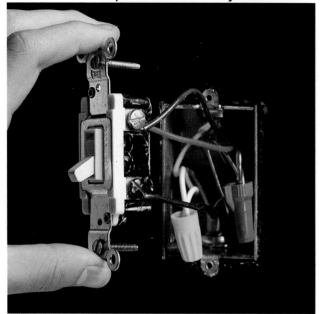

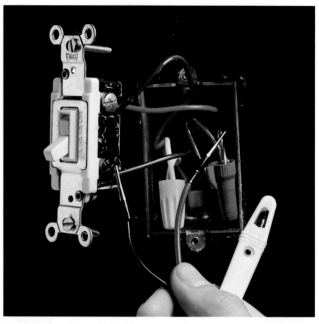

1 Turn off power to the switch at the main service panel, then remove the switch coverplate and mounting screws. Holding the mounting strap carefully, pull the switch from the box. Be careful not to touch the bare wires or screw terminals until they have been tested for power.

2 Test for power by touching one probe of the neon circuit tester to the grounded metal box or to the bare copper grounding wire, and touching the other probe to each screw terminal. Tester should not glow. If it does, there is still power entering the box. Return to the service panel and turn off the correct circuit.

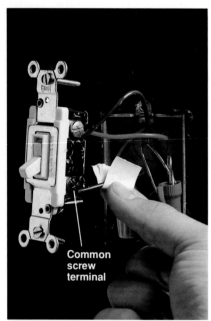

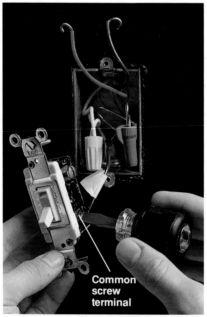

3 Locate dark common screw terminal, and use masking tape to label the "common" wire attached to it. Disconnect wires and remove switch. Test switch for continuity (page 53). If it tests faulty, buy a replacement. Inspect wires for nicks and scratches. If necessary, clip damaged wires and strip them (page 23).

4 Connect the common wire to the dark common screw terminal on the switch. On most three-way switches the common screw terminal is copper. Or, it may be labeled with the word COMMON stamped on the back of the switch.

5 Connect the remaining wires to the brass or silver screw terminals. These wires are interchangeable, and can be connected to either screw terminal. Carefully tuck the wires into the box. Remount the switch, and attach the coverplate. Turn on the power at the main service panel.

How to Fix or Replace a Four-way Wall Switch

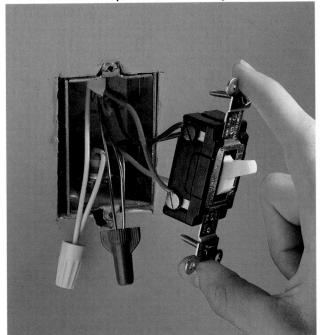

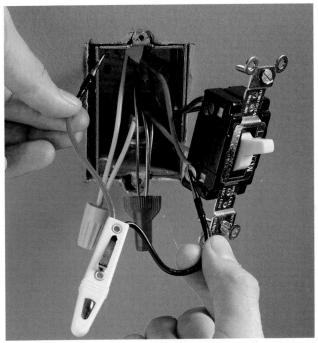

1 Turn off the power to the switch at the main service panel, then remove the switch coverplate and mounting screws. Holding the mounting strap carefully, pull the switch from the box. Be careful not to touch any bare wires or screw terminals until they have been tested for power.

2 Test for power by touching one probe of the circuit tester to the grounded metal box or bare copper grounding wire, and touching the other probe to each of the screw terminals. Tester should not glow. If it does, there is still power entering the box. Return to the service panel and turn off the correct circuit.

3 Disconnect the wires and inspect them for nicks and scratches. If necessary, clip damaged wires and strip them (page 23). Test the switch for continuity (page 53). Buy a replacement if the switch tests faulty.

4 Connect two wires of the same color to the brass screw terminals. On the switch shown above, the brass screw terminals are labeled LINE 1.

5 Attach remaining wires to copper screw terminals, marked LINE 2 on some switches. Carefully tuck the wires inside the switch box, then remount the switch and attach the coverplate. Turn on the power at the main service panel.

Toggle-type dimmer resembles standard switches. Toggle dimmers are available in both single-pole and three-way designs.

Dial-type dimmer is the most common style. Rotating the dial changes the light intensity.

Slide-action dimmer has an illuminated face that makes the switch easy to locate in the dark.

Automatic dimmer has an electronic sensor that adjusts the light fixture to compensate for the changing levels of natural light. An automatic dimmer also can be operated manually.

Dimmer Switches

A dimmer switch makes it possible to vary the brightness of a light fixture. Dimmers are often installed in dining rooms, recreation areas, or bedrooms.

Any standard single-pole switch can be replaced with a dimmer, as long as the switch box is of adequate size. Dimmer switches have larger bodies than standard switches. They also generate a small amount of heat that must dissipate. For these reasons, dimmers should not be installed in undersized electrical boxes, or in boxes that are crowded with circuit wires. Always follow the manufacturer's specifications for installation.

In lighting configurations that use three-way switches (pages 46 to 47), one of the three-way switches can be replaced with a special three-way dimmer. In this arrangement, all switches will turn the light fixture on and off, but light intensity will be controlled only from the dimmer switch.

Dimmer switches are available in several styles (photo, left). All types have wire leads instead of screw terminals, and they are connected to circuit wires using wire nuts. A few types have a green grounding lead that should be connected to the grounded metal box or to the bare copper grounding wires.

Everything You Need:

Tools: screwdriver, neon circuit tester, needlenose pliers.

Materials: wire nuts, masking tape.

See Inspector's Notebook:
• Electrical Box Inspection (pages 118 to 119).

How to Install a Dimmer Switch

1 Turn off power to switch at the main service panel, then remove the coverplate and mounting screws. Holding the mounting straps carefully, pull switch from the box. Be careful not to touch bare wires or screw terminals until they have been tested for power.

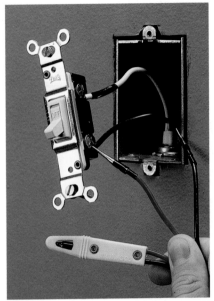

2 Test for power by touching one probe of neon circuit tester to the grounded metal box or to the bare copper grounding wires, and touching other probe to each screw terminal. Tester should not glow. If it does, there is still power entering the box. Return to the service panel and turn off the correct circuit.

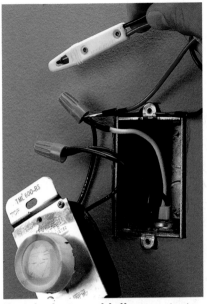

If replacing an old dimmer, test for power by touching one probe of circuit tester to the grounded metal box or bare copper grounding wires, and inserting the other probe into each wire nut. Tester should not glow. If it does, there is still power entering the box. Return to the service panel and turn off the correct circuit.

3 Disconnect the circuit wires and remove the switch. Straighten the circuit wires, and clip the ends, leaving about ½" of the bare wire end exposed.

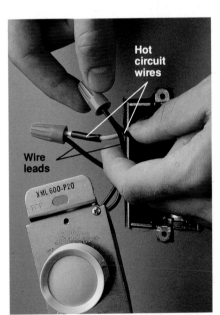

4 Connect the wire leads on the dimmer switch to the circuit wires, using wire nuts. The switch leads are interchangeable, and can be attached to either of the two circuit wires.

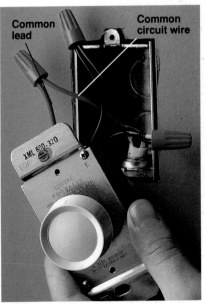

Three-way dimmer has an additional wire lead. This "common" lead is connected to the common circuit wire. When replacing a standard three-way switch with a dimmer, the common circuit wire is attached to the darkest screw terminal on the old switch (page 58).

The earliest receptacles were modifications of the screw-in type light bulb. This receptacle was used in the early 1900s.

The polarized receptacle became standard in the 1920s. The different sized slots direct current flow for safety.

The ground-fault circuit-interrupter, or GFCI receptacle, is a modern safety device. When it detects slight changes in current, it instantly shuts off power.

Common Receptacle Problems

Household receptacles, also called outlets, have no moving parts to wear out, and usually last for many years without servicing. Most problems associated with receptacles are actually caused by faulty lamps and appliances, or their plugs and cords. However, the constant plugging in and removal of appliance cords can wear out the metal contacts inside a receptacle. Any receptacle that does not hold plugs firmly should be replaced.

A loose wire connection is another possible problem. A loose connection can spark (called arcing), trip a circuit breaker, or cause heat to build up in the receptacle box, creating a potential fire hazard.

Wires can come loose for a number of reasons. Everyday vibrations caused by walking across floors, or from nearby street traffic, may cause a connection to shake loose. In addition, because wires heat and cool with normal use, the ends of the wires will expand and contract slightly. This movement also may cause the wires to come loose from the screw terminal connections.

See Inspector's Notebook:
- Checking Wire Connections (pages 116 to 117).
- Electrical Box Inspection (pages 118 to 119).
- Inspecting Receptacles (page 122).

Problem	Repair
Circuit breaker trips repeatedly, or fuse burns out immediately after being replaced.	1. Repair or replace worn or damaged lamp or appliance cord. 2. Move lamps or appliances to other circuits to prevent overloads (page 34). 3. Tighten any loose wire connections (pages 72 to 73). 4. Clean dirty or oxidized wire ends (page 72).
Lamp or appliance does not work.	1. Make sure lamp or appliance is plugged in. 2. Replace burned-out bulbs. 3. Repair or replace worn or damaged lamp or appliance cord. 4. Tighten any loose wire connections (pages 72 to 73). 5. Clean dirty or oxidized wire ends (page 72). 6. Repair or replace any faulty receptacle (pages 72 to 73).
Receptacle does not hold plugs firmly.	1. Repair or replace worn or damaged plugs (pages 94 to 95). 2. Replace faulty receptacle (pages 72 to 73).
Receptacle is warm to the touch, buzzes, or sparks when plugs are inserted or removed.	1. Move lamps or appliances to other circuits to prevent overloads (page 34). 2. Tighten any loose wire connections (pages 72 to 73). 3. Clean dirty or oxidized wire ends (page 72). 4. Replace faulty receptacle (pages 72 to 73).

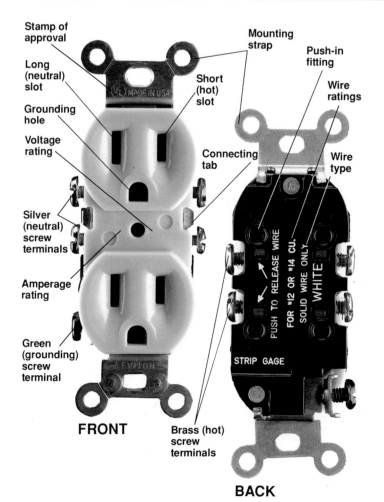

FRONT

BACK

Stamp of approval
Long (neutral) slot
Grounding hole
Voltage rating
Silver (neutral) screw terminals
Amperage rating
Green (grounding) screw terminal
Mounting strap
Short (hot) slot
Connecting tab
Brass (hot) screw terminals
Push-in fitting
Wire ratings
Wire type

The standard duplex receptacle has two halves for receiving plugs. Each half has a long (neutral) slot, a short (hot) slot, and a U-shaped grounding hole. The slots fit the wide prong, narrow prong, and grounding prong of a three-prong plug. This ensures that the connection between receptacle and plug will be polarized and grounded for safety (page 16).

Wires are attached to the receptacle at screw terminals or push-in fittings. A connecting tab between the screw terminals allows a variety of different wiring configurations. Receptacles also include mounting straps for attaching to electrical boxes.

Stamps of approval from testing agencies are found on the front and back of the receptacle. Look for the symbol UL or UND. LAB. INC. LIST to make sure the receptacle meets the strict standards of Underwriters Laboratories.

The receptacle is marked with ratings for maximum volts and amps. The common receptacle is marked 15A, 125V. Receptacles marked CU or COPPER are used with solid copper wire. Those marked CU-CLAD ONLY are used with copper-coated aluminum wire. Only receptacles marked CO/ALR may be used with solid aluminum wiring (page 22). Receptacles marked AL/CU no longer may be used with aluminum wire according to code.

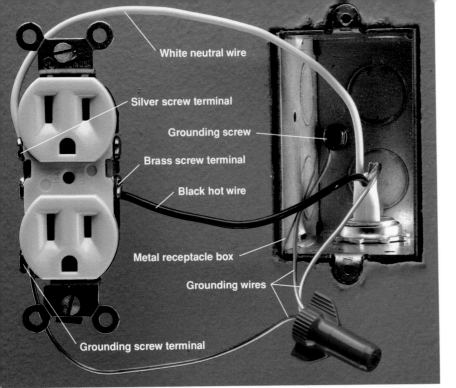

White neutral wire

Silver screw terminal

Grounding screw

Brass screw terminal

Black hot wire

Metal receptacle box

Grounding wires

Grounding screw terminal

Single cable entering the box indicates end-of-run wiring. The black hot wire is attached to a brass screw terminal, and the white neutral wire is connected to a silver screw terminal. If the box is metal, the grounding wire is pigtailed to the grounding screws of the receptacle and the box. In a plastic box, the grounding wire is attached directly to the grounding screw terminal of the receptacle.

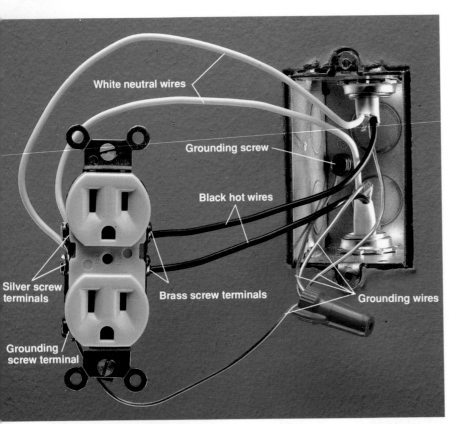

White neutral wires

Grounding screw

Black hot wires

Silver screw terminals

Brass screw terminals

Grounding wires

Grounding screw terminal

Two cables entering the box indicate middle-of-run wiring. Black hot wires are connected to brass screw terminals, and white neutral wires to silver screw terminals. The grounding wire is pigtailed to the grounding screws of the receptacle and the box.

Receptacle Wiring

A 125-volt duplex receptacle can be wired to the electrical system in a number of ways. The most common are shown on these pages.

Wiring configurations may vary slightly from these photographs, depending on the kind of receptacle used, the type of cable, or the technique of the electrician who installed the wiring. To make dependable repairs or replacements, use masking tape and label each wire according to its location on the terminals of the existing receptacle.

Receptacles are wired as either **end-of-run** or **middle-of-run**. These two basic configurations are easily identified by counting the number of cables entering the receptacle box. End-of-run wiring has only one cable, indicating that the circuit ends. Middle-of-run wiring has two cables, indicating that the circuit continues on to other receptacles, switches, or fixtures.

A **split-circuit receptacle** is shown on the opposite page. Each half of a split-circuit receptacle is wired to a separate circuit. This allows two appliances of high wattage to be plugged into the same receptacle without blowing a fuse or tripping a breaker. This wiring configuration is similar to a receptacle that is controlled by a wall switch. Code requires a **switch-controlled receptacle** in any room that does not have a built-in light fixture operated by a wall switch.

Split-circuit and switch-controlled receptacles are connected to two hot wires, so use caution during repairs or replacements. Make sure the connecting tab between the hot screw terminals is removed.

Two-slot receptacles are common in older homes. There is no grounding wire attached to the receptacle, but the box may be grounded with armored cable or conduit (page 20).

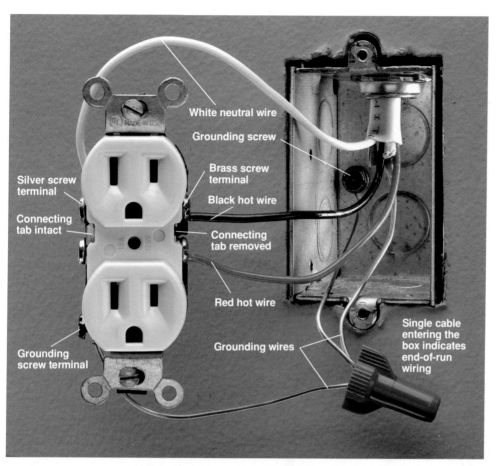

Split-circuit receptacle is attached to a black hot wire, a red hot wire, a white neutral wire, and a bare grounding wire. The wiring is similar to a switch-controlled receptacle.

The hot wires are attached to the brass screw terminals, and the connecting tab or fin between the brass terminals is removed. The white wire is attached to a silver screw terminal, and the connecting tab on the neutral side remains intact. The grounding wire is pig-tailed to the grounding screw terminal of the receptacle, and to the grounding screw attached to the box.

White neutral wire

Grounding screw

Brass screw terminal

Black hot wire

Connecting tab removed

Red hot wire

Silver screw terminal

Connecting tab intact

Grounding screw terminal

Grounding wires

Single cable entering the box indicates end-of-run wiring

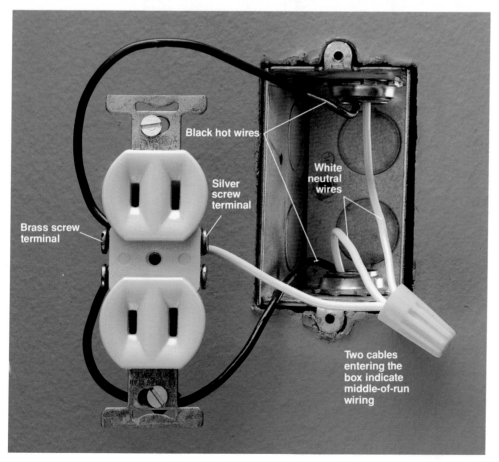

Two-slot receptacle is often found in older homes. The black hot wires are connected to the brass screw termi-nals, and the white neutral wires are pigtailed to a silver screw terminal.

Two-slot receptacles may be replaced with three-slot types, but only if a means of grounding ex-ists at the receptacle box.

Black hot wires

Silver screw terminal

White neutral wires

Brass screw terminal

Two cables entering the box indicate middle-of-run wiring

Basic Types of Receptacles

Several different types of receptacles are found in the typical home. Each has a unique arrangement of slots that accepts only a certain kind of plug, and each is designed for a specific job.

Household receptacles provide two types of voltage: normal and high voltage. Although voltage ratings have changed slightly over the years, normal receptacles should be rated for 110, 115, 120, or 125 volts. For purposes of replacement, these ratings are considered identical. High-voltage receptacles are rated at 220, 240, or 250 volts. These ratings are considered identical.

When replacing a receptacle, check the amperage rating of the circuit at the main service panel, and buy a receptacle with the correct amperage rating (page 28).

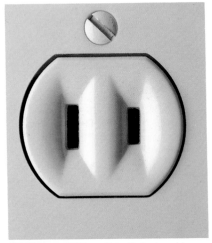

15 amps, 125 volts. Polarized two-slot receptacle is common in homes built before 1960. Slots are different sizes to accept polarized plugs.

15 amps, 125 volts. Three-slot grounded receptacle has two different size slots and a U-shaped hole for grounding. It is required in all new wiring installations.

20 amps, 125 volts. This three-slot grounded receptacle features a special T-shaped slot. It is installed for use with large appliances or portable tools that require 20 amps of current.

15 amps, 250 volts. This receptacle is used primarily for window air conditioners. It is available as a single unit, or as half of a duplex receptacle, with the other half wired for 125 volts.

30 amps, 125/250 volts. This receptacle is used for clothes dryers. It provides high-voltage current for heating coils, and 125-volt current to run lights and timers.

50 amps, 125/250 volts. This receptacle is used for ranges. The high-voltage current powers heating coils, and the 125-volt current runs clocks and lights.

Older Receptacles

Older receptacles may look different from more modern types, but most will stay in good working order. Follow these simple guidelines for evaluating or replacing older receptacles:

• Never replace an older receptacle with one of a different voltage or higher amperage rating.
• Any two-slot, unpolarized receptacle should be replaced with a two- or three-slot polarized receptacle.
• If no means of grounding is available at the receptacle box, install a GFCI (pages 74 to 77).
• If in doubt, seek the advice of a qualified electrician.

Never alter the prongs of a plug to fit an older receptacle. Altering the prongs may remove the grounding or polarizing features of the plug.

Unpolarized receptacles have slots that are the same length. Modern plug types may not fit these receptacles. Never modify the prongs of a polarized plug to fit the slots of an unpolarized receptacle.

Surface-mounted receptacles were popular in the 1940s and 1950s for their ease of installation. Wiring often ran in the back of hollowed-out base moldings. Surface-mounted receptacles are usually ungrounded.

Ceramic duplex receptacles were manufactured in the 1930s. They are polarized but ungrounded, and they can be wired for either 125 volts or 250 volts.

Twist-lock receptacles are designed to be used with plugs that are inserted and rotated. A small tab on the end of one of the prongs prevents the plug from being pulled from the receptacle.

Ceramic duplex receptacle has a unique hourglass shape. The receptacle shown above is rated for 250 volts but only 5 amps, and would not be allowed by today's electrical codes.

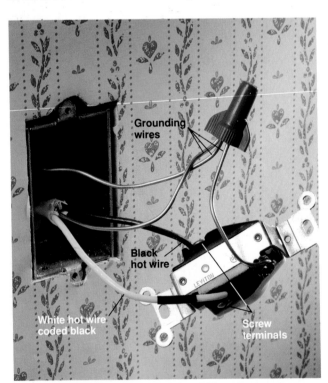

A receptacle rated for 125/250 volts has two incoming hot wires, each carrying 125 volts, and a white neutral wire. A grounding wire is attached to the metal receptacle box. Connections are made with setscrew terminals at the back of the receptacle.

High-voltage Receptacles

High-voltage receptacles provide current to large appliances like clothes dryers, ranges, water heaters, and air conditioners. The slot configuration of a high-voltage receptacle (page 66) will not accept a plug rated for 125 volts.

A high-voltage receptacle can be wired in one of two ways. In a standard high-voltage receptacle, voltage is brought to the receptacle with two hot wires, each carrying a maximum of 125 volts. No white neutral wire is necessary, but a grounding wire should be attached to the receptacle and to the metal receptacle box.

A clothes dryer or range also may require normal current (a maximum of 125 volts) to run lights, timers and clocks. If so, a white neutral wire will be attached to the receptacle. The appliance itself will split the incoming current into a 125-volt circuit and a 250-volt circuit.

Repair or replace a high-voltage receptacle using the techniques shown on pages 72 to 73. It is important to identify and tag all wires on the existing receptacle so that the new receptacle will be properly wired.

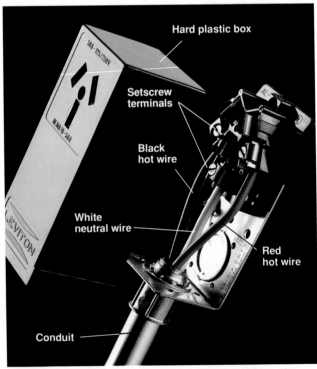

Standard receptacle rated for 250 volts has two incoming hot wires and no neutral wire. A grounding wire is pigtailed to the receptacle and to the metal receptacle box.

Surface-mounted receptacle rated for 250 volts has a hard plastic box that can be installed on concrete or block walls. Surface-mounted receptacles are often found in basements and utility rooms.

Childproof Receptacles & Other Accessories

Childproof your receptacles or adapt them for special uses by adding receptacle accessories. Before installing an accessory, be sure to read the manufacturer's instructions.

Homeowners with small children should add inexpensive caps or covers to guard against accidental electric shocks.

Plastic caps do not conduct electricity and are virtually impossible for small children to remove. A receptacle cover attaches directly to the receptacle and fits over plugs, preventing the cords from being removed.

Protect children against the possibility of electrical shock. Place protective caps in any receptacles that are not being used.

Prevent accidents by installing a receptacle cover to prevent cords and plugs from being removed.

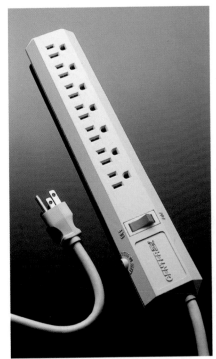

Install more than two plugs in a single duplex receptacle by using a multi-outlet power strip. A multi-outlet strip should have a built-in circuit breaker or fuse to protect against overloads.

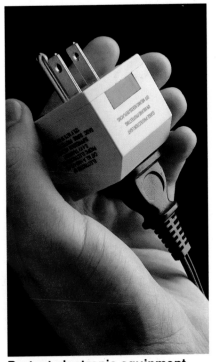

Protect electronic equipment, such as a home computer or stereo, with a surge protector. The surge protector prevents any damage to sensitive wiring or circuitry caused by sudden drops or surges in power.

Recessed wall receptacle permits a plug-in clock to be hung flush against a wall surface.

Metal probes

Insulated handles

Bulb

Testing Receptacles for Power, Grounding & Polarity

Test for power to make sure that live voltage is not reaching the receptacle during a repair or replacement project.

Test for grounding to plan receptacle replacements. The test for grounding will indicate how an existing receptacle is wired, and whether a replacement receptacle should be a two-slot polarized receptacle, a grounded three-slot receptacle, or a GFCI.

If the test indicates that the hot and neutral wires are reversed (page 123), make sure the wires are installed correctly on the replacement receptacle.

Test for hot wires if you need to confirm which wire is carrying live voltage.

An inexpensive neon circuit tester makes it easy to perform these tests. It has a small bulb that glows when electrical power flows through it.

Remember that the tester only glows when it is part of a complete circuit. For example, if you touch one probe to a hot wire and do not touch anything with the other probe, the tester will not glow, even though the hot wire is carrying power. When using the tester, take care not to touch the metal probes.

When testing for power or grounding, always confirm any negative (tester does not glow) results by removing the coverplate and examining the receptacle to make sure all wires are intact and properly connected. Do not touch any wires without first turning off the power at the main service panel.

> **Everything You Need:**
>
> Tools: neon circuit tester, screwdriver.

How to Test a Receptacle for Power

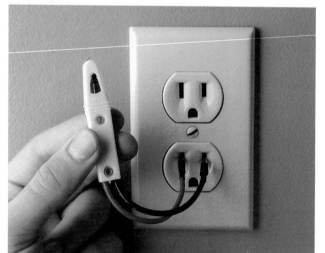

1 Turn off power at the main service panel. Place one probe of the tester in each slot of the receptacle. The tester should not glow. If it does glow, the correct circuit has not been turned off at the main service panel. Test both ends of a duplex receptacle. Remember that this is a preliminary test. You must confirm that power is off by removing the coverplate and testing for power at the receptacle wires (step 2).

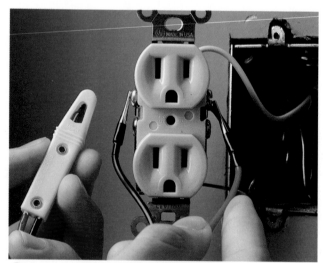

2 Remove the receptacle coverplate. Loosen the mounting screws and carefully pull the receptacle from its box. Take care not to touch any wires. Touch one probe of the neon tester to a brass screw terminal, and one probe to a silver screw terminal. The tester should not glow. If it does, you must shut off the correct circuit at the service panel. If wires are connected to both sets of terminals, test both sets.

70

This photo shows hot and neutral wires that are reversed.

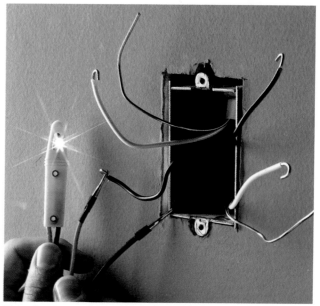

Test a three-slot receptacle for grounding. With the power on, place one probe of the tester in the short (hot) slot, and the other in the U-shaped grounding hole. The tester should glow. If it does not glow, place a probe in the long (neutral) slot and one in the grounding hole. If the tester glows, the hot and neutral wires are reversed (page 123). If tester dows not glow in either position, the receptacle is not grounded.

Test for hot wires. Occasionally, you may need to determine which wire is hot. With the power turned off, carefully separate all ends of wires so that they do not touch each other or anything else. Restore power to the circuit at the main service panel. Touch one probe of the neon tester to the bare grounding wire or grounded metal box, and the other probe to the ends of each of the wires. Check all wires. If the tester glows, the wire is hot. Label the hot wire for identification, and turn off power at the service panel before continuing work.

How to Test a Two-slot Receptacle for Grounding

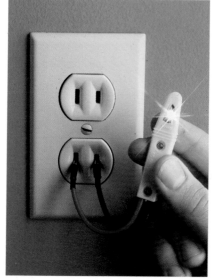

1 With the power turned on, place one probe of the neon tester in each slot. The tester should glow. If it does not glow, then there is no power to the receptacle.

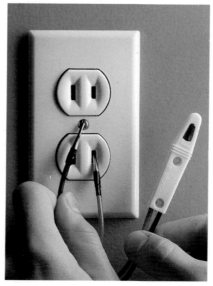

2 Place one probe of the tester in the short (hot) slot, and touch the other probe to the coverplate screw. The screw head must be free of paint, dirt, and grease. If the tester glows, the receptacle box is grounded If it does not glow, proceed to step 3.

3 Place one probe of the tester in the long (neutral) slot, and touch the other to the coverplate screw. If the tester glows, the receptacle box is grounded but hot and neutral wires are reversed (page 123). If tester does not glow, the box is not grounded.

Repairing & Replacing Receptacles

Receptacles are easy to repair. After shutting off power to the receptacle circuit, remove the coverplate and inspect the receptacle for any obvious problems such as a loose or broken connection, or wire ends that are dirty or oxidized. Remember that a problem at one receptacle may affect other receptacles in the same circuit. If the cause of a faulty receptacle is not readily apparent, test other receptacles in the circuit for power (page 70).

When replacing a receptacle, check the amperage rating of the circuit at the main service panel, and buy a replacement receptacle with the correct amperage rating (page 34).

When installing a new receptacle, always test for grounding (pages 70 to 71). Never install a three-slot receptacle where no grounding exists. Instead, install a two-slot polarized, or GFCI receptacle.

Everything You Need:

Tools: neon circuit tester, screwdriver, vacuum cleaner (if needed).

Materials: fine sandpaper, anti-oxidant paste (if needed).

See Inspector's Notebook:
• Electrical Box Inspection (pages 118 to 119).
• Inspecting Switches and Receptacles (page 122).

How to Repair a Receptacle

1 Turn off power at the main service panel. Test the receptacle for power with a neon circuit tester (page 70). Test both ends of a duplex receptacle. Remove the coverplate, using a screwdriver.

2 Remove the mounting screws that hold the receptacle to the box. Carefully pull the receptacle from the box. Take care not to touch any bare wires.

3 Confirm that the power to the receptacle is off (page 70), using a neon circuit tester. If wires are attached to both sets of screw terminals, test both sets. The tester should not glow. If it does, you must turn off the correct circuit at the service panel.

4 If the ends of the wires appear darkened or dirty, disconnect them one at a time, and clean them with fine sandpaper. If the wires are aluminum, apply an anti-oxidant paste before reconnecting. Anti-oxidant paste is available at hardware stores.

5 Tighten all connections, using a screwdriver. Take care not to overtighten and strip the screws.

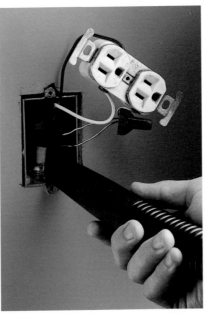

6 Check the box for dirt or dust and, if necessary, clean it with a vacuum cleaner and narrow nozzle attachment.

7 Reinstall the receptacle, and turn on power at the main service panel. Test the receptacle for power with a neon circuit tester. If the receptacle does not work, check other receptacles in the circuit before making a replacement.

How to Replace a Receptacle

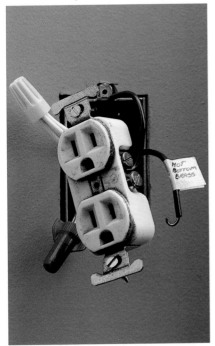

1 To replace a receptacle, repeat steps 1 to 3 on the opposite page. With the power off, label each wire for its location on the receptacle screw terminals, using masking tape and a felt-tipped pen.

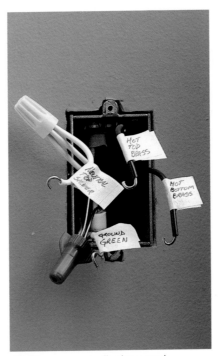

2 Disconnect all wires and remove the receptacle.

3 Replace the receptacle with one rated for the correct amperage and voltage (page 28). Replace coverplate, and turn on power. Test receptacle with a neon circuit tester (pages 70 to 71).

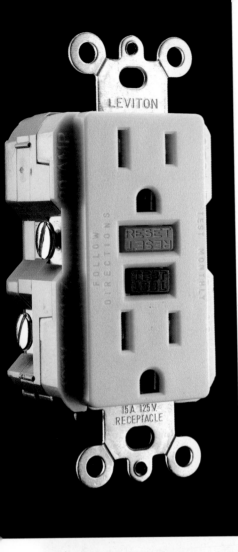

GFCI Receptacles

The ground-fault circuit-interrupter (GFCI) receptacle is a safety device. It protects against electrical shock caused by a faulty appliance, or a worn cord or plug. The GFCI senses small changes in current flow and can shut off power in as little as 1/40 of a second.

When you are updating wiring, installing new circuits, or replacing receptacles, GFCIs are now required in bathrooms, kitchens, garages, crawl spaces, unfinished basements, and outdoor receptacle locations. GFCIs are easily installed as safety replacements for any standard duplex receptacle. Consult your local codes for any requirements regarding the installation of GFCI receptacles.

The GFCI receptacle may be wired to protect only itself (single location), or it can be wired to protect all receptacles, switches, and light fixtures from the GFCI "forward" to the end of the circuit (multiple locations). The GFCI cannot protect those devices that exist between the GFCI location and the main service panel.

Because the GFCI is so sensitive, it is most effective when wired to protect a single location. The more receptacles any one GFCI protects, the more susceptible it is to "phantom tripping," shutting off power because of tiny, normal fluctuations in current flow.

Everything You Need:

Tools: neon circuit tester, screwdriver.

Materials: wire nuts, masking tape.

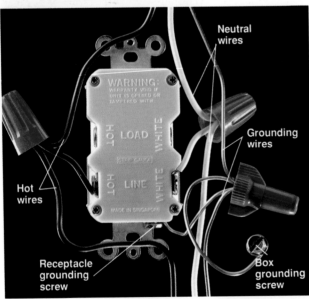

A GFCI wired for single-location protection (shown from the back) has hot and neutral wires connected only to the screw terminals marked LINE. A GFCI connected for single-location protection may be wired as either an end-of-run or middle-of-run configuration (page 64).

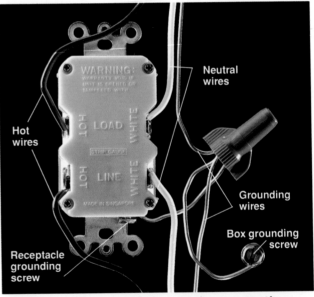

A GFCI wired for multiple-location protection (shown from the back) has one set of hot and neutral wires connected to the LINE pair of screw terminals, and the other set connected to the LOAD pair of screw terminals. A GFCI receptacle connected for multiple-location protection may be wired only as a middle-of-run configuration.

How to Install a GFCI for Single-location Protection

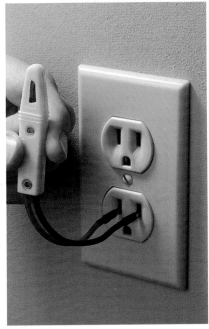

1 Shut off power to the receptacle at the main service panel. Test for power with a neon circuit tester (page 70). Be sure to check both halves of the receptacle.

2 Remove coverplate. Loosen mounting screws, and gently pull receptacle from the box. Do not touch wires. Confirm power is off with a circuit tester (page 70).

3 Disconnect all white neutral wires from the silver screw terminals of the old receptacle.

4 Pigtail all the white neutral wires together, and connect the pigtail to the terminal marked WHITE LINE on the GFCI (see photo on opposite page).

5 Disconnect all black hot wires from the brass screw terminals of the old receptacle. Pigtail these wires together and connect them to the terminal marked HOT LINE on the GFCI.

6 If a grounding wire is available, disconnect it from the old receptacle, and reconnect it to the green grounding screw terminal of the GFCI. Mount the GFCI in the receptacle box, and reattach the coverplate. Restore power and test the GFCI according to the manufacturer's instructions.

How to Install a GFCI for Multiple-location Protection

1 Use a map of your house circuits (pages 30 to 33) to determine a location for your GFCI. Indicate all receptacles that will be protected by the GFCI installation.

2 Turn off power to the correct circuit at the main service panel. Test all the receptacles in the circuit with a neon circuit tester to make sure the power is off. Always check both halves of each duplex receptacle.

3 Remove the coverplate from the receptacle that will be replaced with the GFCI. Loosen the mounting screws and gently pull the receptacle from its box. Take care not to touch any bare wires. Confirm the power is off with a neon circuit tester (page 70).

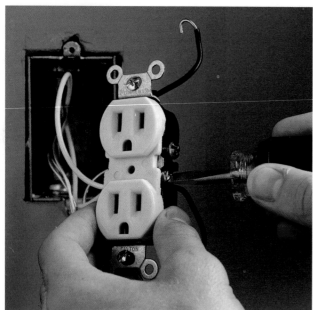

4 Disconnect all black hot wires. Carefully separate the hot wires and position them so that the bare ends do not touch anything. Restore power to the circuit at the main service panel. Determine which black wire is the "feed" wire by testing for hot wires (page 71). The feed wire brings power to the receptacle from the service panel. Use caution: This is a "live" wire test, and power will be turned on temporarily.

5 When you have found the hot feed wire, turn off power at the main service panel. Identify the feed wire by marking it with masking tape.

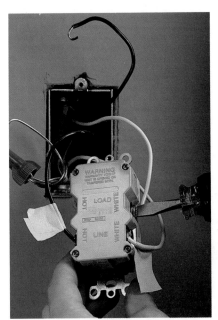

6 Disconnect the white neutral wires from the old receptacle. Identify the white feed wire and label it with masking tape. The white feed wire will be the one that shares the same cable as the black feed wire.

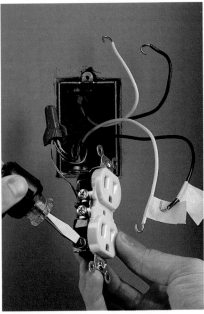

7 Disconnect the grounding wire from the grounding screw terminal of the old receptacle. Remove the old receptacle. Connect the grounding wire to the grounding screw terminal of the GFCI.

8 Connect the white feed wire to the terminal marked WHITE LINE on the GFCI. Connect the black feed wire to the terminal marked HOT LINE on the GFCI.

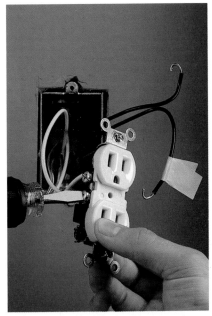

9 Connect the other white neutral wire to the terminal marked WHITE LOAD on the GFCI.

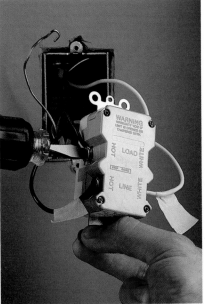

10 Connect the other black hot wire to the terminal marked HOT LOAD on the GFCI.

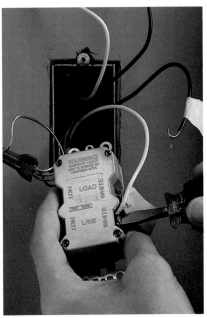

11 Carefully tuck all wires into the receptacle box. Mount the GFCI in the box and attach the coverplate. Turn on power to the circuit at the main service panel. Test the GFCI according to the manufacturer's instructions.

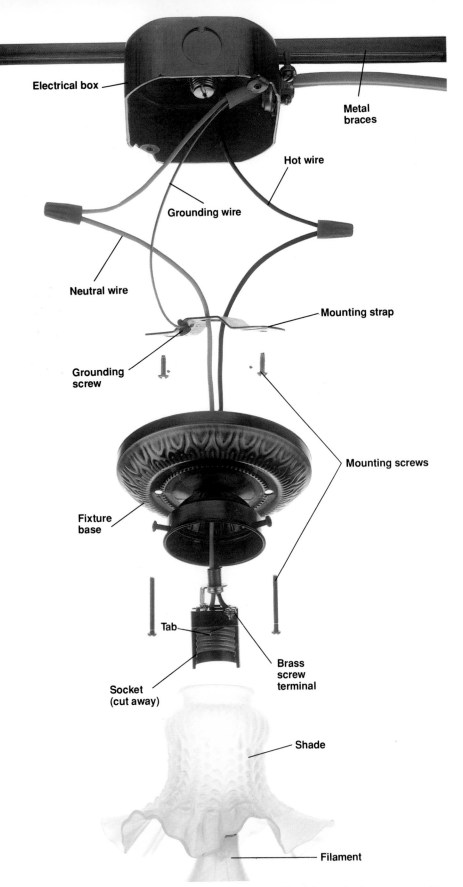

Electrical box

Metal braces

Hot wire

Grounding wire

Neutral wire

Mounting strap

Grounding screw

Mounting screws

Fixture base

Tab

Brass screw terminal

Socket (cut away)

Shade

Filament

In a typical incandescent light fixture, a black hot wire is connected to a brass screw terminal on the socket. Power flows to a small tab at the bottom of the metal socket and through a metal filament inside the bulb. The power heats the filament and causes it to glow. The current then flows through the threaded portion of the socket and through the white neutral wire back to the main service panel.

Repairing & Replacing Incandescent Light Fixtures

Incandescent light fixtures are attached permanently to ceilings or walls. They include wall-hung sconces, ceiling-hung globe fixtures, recessed light fixtures, and chandeliers. Most incandescent light fixtures are easy to repair, using basic tools and inexpensive parts.

Track lights, another type of incandescent light fixture, are difficult to fix and should be repaired or replaced by an electrician.

If a light fixture fails, always make sure the light bulb is screwed in tightly and is not burned out. A faulty light bulb is the most common cause of light fixture failure. If the light fixture is controlled by a wall switch, also check the switch as a possible source of problems (pages 42 to 61).

Light fixtures can fail because the sockets or built-in switches wear out. Some fixtures have sockets and switches that can be removed for minor repairs. These parts are held to the base of the fixture with mounting screws or clips. Other fixtures have sockets and switches that are joined permanently to the base. If this type of fixture fails, purchase and install a new light fixture.

Damage to light fixtures often occurs because homeowners install light bulbs with wattage ratings that are too high. Prevent overheating and light fixture failures by using only light bulbs that match the wattage ratings printed on the fixtures.

Techniques for repairing fluorescent lights are different from those for incandescent lights. Refer to pages 88 to 93 to repair or replace a fluorescent light fixture.

Everything You Need:

Tools: neon circuit tester, screwdrivers, continuity tester, combination tool.

Materials: replacement parts, as needed.

See Inspector's Notebook:
- Common Cable Problems (pages 114 to 115).
- Checking Wire Connections (pages 116 to 117).
- Electrical Box Inspection (pages 118 to 119).

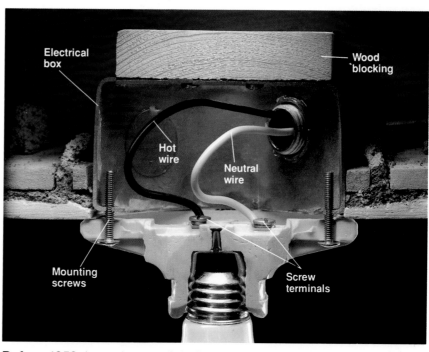

Before 1959, incandescent light fixtures (shown cut away) often were mounted directly to an electrical box or to plaster lath. Electrical codes now require that fixtures be attached to mounting straps that are anchored to the electrical boxes (page opposite). If you have a light fixture attached to plaster lath, install an approved electrical box with a mounting strap to support the fixture (pages 38 to 41).

Problem	Repair
Wall- or ceiling-mounted fixture flickers, or does not light.	1. Check for faulty light bulb. 2. Check wall switch, and repair or replace, if needed (pages 42 to 61). 3. Check for loose wire connections in electrical box . 4. Test socket, and replace if needed (pages 80 to 81). 5. Replace light fixture (page 82).
Built-in switch on fixture does not work.	1. Check for faulty light bulb. 2. Check for loose wire connections on switch . 3. Replace switch (page 81). 4. Replace light fixture (page 82).
Chandelier flickers or does not light.	1. Check for faulty light bulb. 2. Check wall switch, and repair or replace, if needed (pages 42 to 61). 3. Check for loose wire connections in electrical box. 4. Test sockets and fixture wires, and replace if needed (pages 86 to 87).
Recessed fixture flickers or does not light.	1. Check for faulty light bulb. 2. Check wall switch, and repair or replace, if needed (pages 42 to 61). 3. Check for loose wire connections in electrical box. 4. Test fixture, and replace if needed (pages 83 to 85).

How to Remove a Light Fixture & Test a Socket

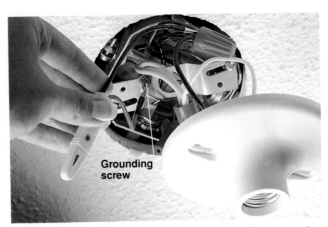

1 Turn off the power to the light fixture at the main service panel. Remove the light bulb and any shade or globe, then remove the mounting screws holding the fixture base to the electrical box or mounting strap. Carefully pull the fixture base away from box.

2 Test for power by touching one probe of a neon circuit tester to green grounding screw, then inserting other probe into each wire nut. Tester should not glow. If it does, there is still power entering box. Return to the service panel and turn off power to correct circuit.

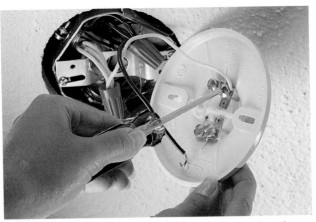

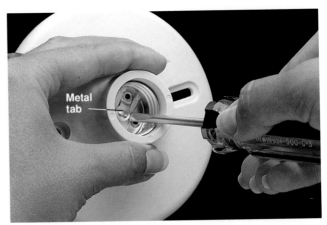

3 Disconnect the light fixture base by loosening the screw terminals. If fixture has wire leads instead of screw terminals, remove the light fixture base by unscrewing the wire nuts.

4 Adjust the metal tab at the bottom of the fixture socket by prying it up slightly with a small screwdriver. This adjustment will improve the contact between the socket and the light bulb.

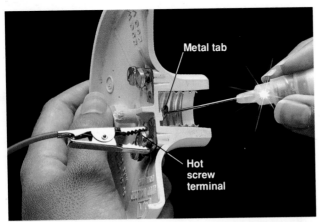

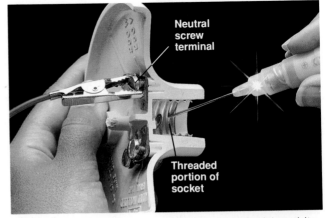

5 Test the socket (shown cut away) by attaching the clip of a continuity tester to the hot screw terminal (or black wire lead), and touching probe of tester to metal tab in bottom of socket. Tester should glow. If not, socket is faulty and must be replaced.

6 Attach tester clip to neutral screw terminal (or white wire lead), and touch probe to threaded portion of socket. Tester should glow. If not, socket is faulty and must be replaced. If socket is permanently attached, replace the fixture (page 82).

How to Replace a Socket

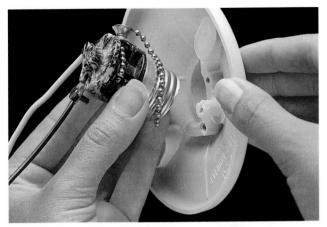

1 Remove light fixture (steps 1 to 3, page opposite). Remove the socket from the fixture. Socket may be held by a screw, clip, or retaining ring. Disconnect wires attached to the socket.

2 Purchase an identical replacement socket. Connect white wire to silver screw terminal on socket, and connect black wire to brass screw terminal. Attach socket to fixture base, and reinstall fixture.

How to Test & Replace a Built-in Light Switch

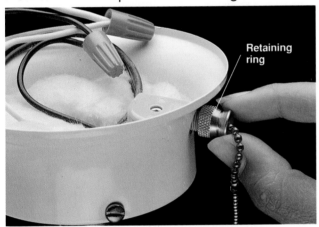

Retaining ring

1 Remove light fixture (steps 1 to 3, page opposite). Unscrew the retaining ring holding the switch.

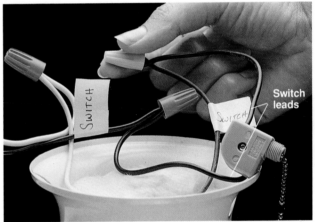

Switch leads

2 Label the wires connected to the switch leads. Disconnect the switch leads and remove switch.

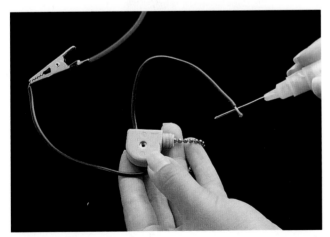

3 Test switch by attaching clip of continuity tester to one of the switch leads, and holding tester probe to the other lead. Operate switch control. If switch is good, tester will glow when switch is in one position, but not both.

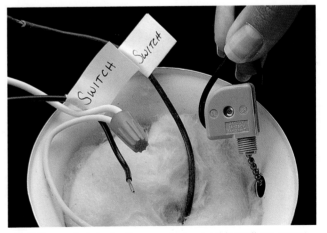

4 If the switch is faulty, purchase and install an exact duplicate switch. Remount the light fixture, and turn on the power at the main service panel.

How to Replace an Incandescent Light Fixture

1 Turn off the power and remove the old light fixture, following the directions for standard light fixtures (page 80, steps 1 to 3) or chandeliers (pages 86 to 87, steps 1 to 4).

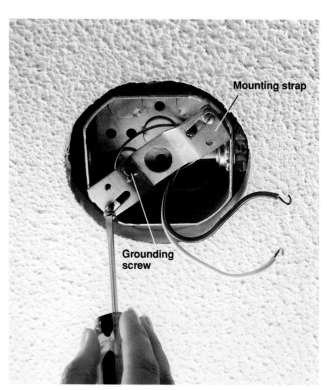

2 Attach a mounting strap to the electrical box, if box does not already have one. The mounting strap, included with the new light fixture, has a preinstalled grounding screw.

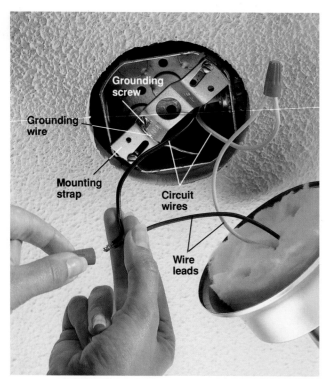

3 Connect the circuit wires to the base of new fixture, using wire nuts. Connect the white wire lead to the white circuit wire, and the black wire lead to the black circuit wire. Pigtail the bare copper grounding wire to the grounding screw on the mounting strap.

4 Attach the light fixture base to the mounting strap, using the mounting screws. Attach the globe, and install a light bulb with a wattage rating that is the same or lower than the rating indicated on the fixture. Turn on the power at the main service panel.

Repairing & Replacing Recessed Light Fixtures

Most problems with recessed light fixtures occur because heat builds up inside the metal canister and melts the insulation on the socket wires. On some recessed light fixtures, sockets with damaged wires can be removed and replaced. However, most newer fixtures have sockets that cannot be removed. With this type, you will need to buy a new fixture if the socket wires are damaged.

When buying a new recessed light fixture, choose a replacement that matches the old fixture. Install the new fixture in the metal mounting frame that is already in place.

Make sure building insulation is at least 3" away from the metal canister on a recessed light fixture. Insulation that fits too closely traps heat and can damage the socket wires.

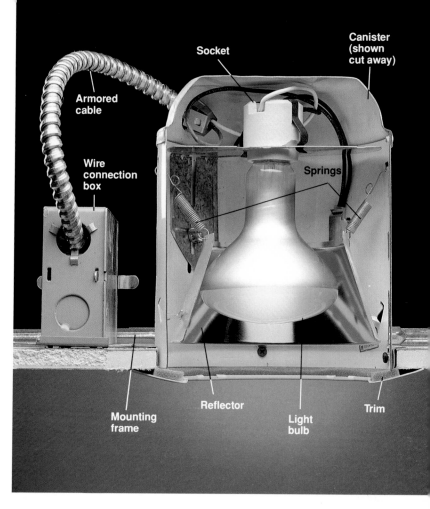

How to Remove & Test a Recessed Light Fixture

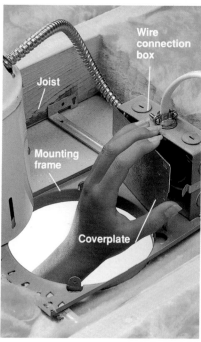

1 Turn off the power to the light fixture at the main service panel. Remove the trim, light bulb, and reflector. The reflector is held to the canister with small springs or mounting clips.

2 Loosen the screws or clips holding the canister to the mounting frame. Carefully raise the canister and set it away from the frame opening.

3 Remove the coverplate on the wire connection box. The box is attached to the mounting frame between the ceiling joists.

(continued next page)

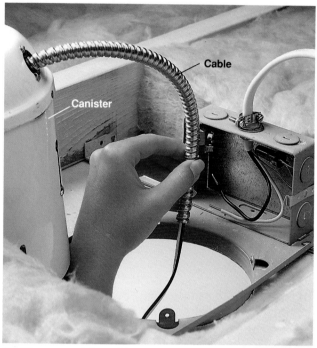

4 Test for power by touching one probe of neon circuit tester to grounded wire connection box, and inserting other probe into each wire nut. Tester should not glow. If it does, there is still power entering box. Return to the service panel and turn off correct circuit.

5 Disconnect the white and black circuit wires by removing the wire nuts. Pull the armored cable from the wire connection box. Remove the canister through the frame opening.

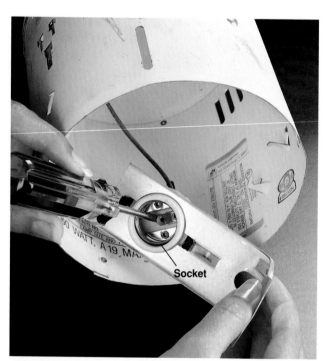

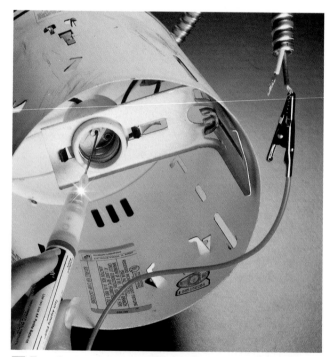

6 Adjust the metal tab at the bottom of the fixture socket by prying it up slightly with a small screwdriver. This adjustment will improve contact with the light bulb.

7 Test the socket by attaching the clip of a continuity tester to the black fixture wire and touching tester probe to the metal tab in bottom of the socket. Attach the tester clip to white fixture wire, and touch probe to the threaded metal socket. Tester should glow for both tests. If not, then socket is faulty. Replace the socket (page 81), or install a new light fixture (page opposite).

How to Replace a Recessed Light Fixture

1 Remove the old light fixture (pages 83 to 84). Buy a new fixture that matches the old fixture. Although new light fixture comes with its own mounting frame, it is easier to mount the new fixture using the frame that is already in place.

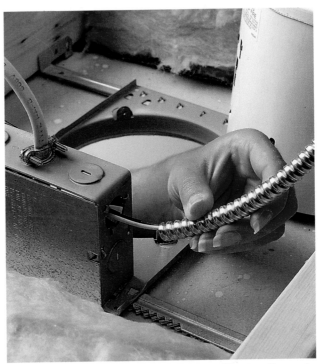

2 Set the fixture canister inside the ceiling cavity, and thread the fixture wires through the opening in the wire connection box. Push the armored cable into the wire connection box to secure it.

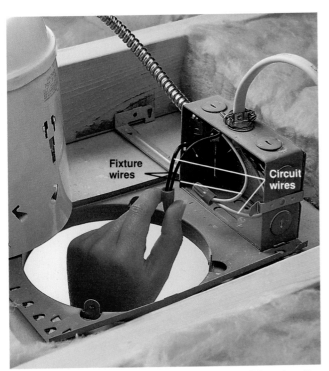

3 Connect the white fixture wire to the white circuit wire, and the black fixture wire to the black circuit wire, using wire nuts. Attach the coverplate to the wire connection box. Make sure any building insulation is at least 3" from canister and wire connection box.

4 Position the canister inside the mounting frame, and attach the mounting screws or clips. Attach the reflector and trim. Install a light bulb with a wattage rating that is the same or lower than rating indicated on the fixture. Turn on power at main service panel.

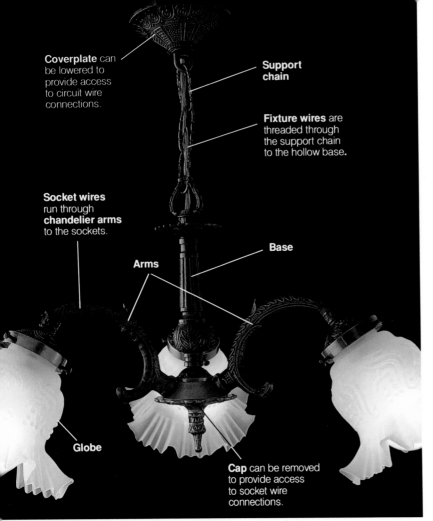

Coverplate can be lowered to provide access to circuit wire connections.

Support chain

Fixture wires are threaded through the support chain to the hollow base.

Socket wires run through chandelier arms to the sockets.

Base

Arms

Globe

Cap can be removed to provide access to socket wire connections.

Repairing Chandeliers

Repairing a chandelier requires special care. Because chandeliers are heavy, it is a good idea to work with a helper when removing a chandelier. Support the fixture to prevent its weight from pulling against the wires.

Chandeliers have two fixture wires that are threaded through the support chain from the electrical box to the hollow base of the chandelier. The socket wires connect to the fixture wires inside this base.

Fixture wires are identified as hot and neutral. Look closely for printed lettering or a colored stripe on one of the wires. This is the neutral wire that is connected to the white circuit wire and white socket wire. The other, unmarked, fixture wire is hot, and is connected to the black wires.

If you have a new chandelier, it may have a grounding wire that runs through the support chain to the electrical box. If this wire is present, make sure it is connected to the grounding wires in the electrical box.

How to Repair a Chandelier

1 Label any lights that are not working, using masking tape. Turn off power to the fixture at the main service panel. Remove light bulbs and all shades or globes.

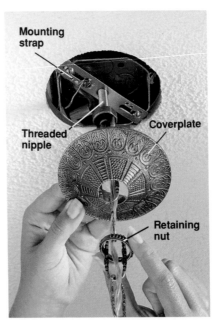

Mounting strap

Threaded nipple

Coverplate

Retaining nut

2 Unscrew the retaining nut and lower the decorative coverplate away from the electrical box. Most chandeliers are supported by a threaded nipple attached to a mounting strap.

Mounting strap

Mounting bolt

Bolt cap nut

Mounting variation: Some chandeliers are supported only by the coverplate that is bolted to the electrical box mounting strap. These types do not have a threaded nipple.

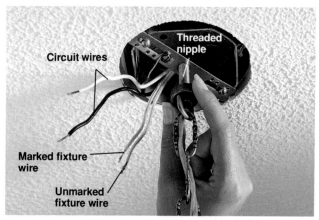

3 Test for power by touching one probe of neon circuit tester to the green grounding screw, and inserting other probe into each wire nut. Tester should not glow. If it does, there is still power entering box. Return to service panel and turn off power to correct circuit.

4 Disconnect fixture wires by removing the wire nuts. Marked fixture wire is neutral, and is connected to white circuit wire. Unmarked fixture wire is hot, and is connected to black circuit wire. Unscrew threaded nipple and carefully place chandelier on a flat surface.

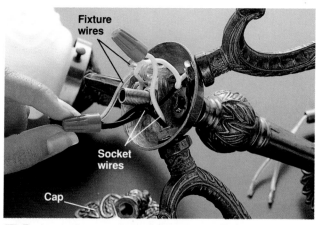

5 Remove the cap from the bottom of the chandelier, exposing the wire connections inside the hollow base. Disconnect the black socket wires from the unmarked fixture wire, and disconnect the white socket wires from the marked fixture wire.

6 Test socket by attaching clip of continuity tester to black socket wire, and touching probe to tab in socket. Repeat test with threaded portion of socket and white socket wire. Tester should glow for both tests. If not, the socket is faulty and must be replaced.

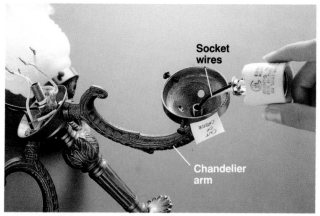

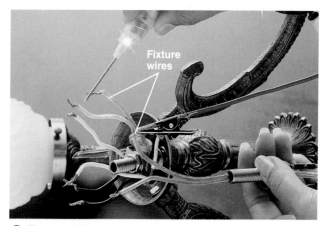

7 Remove a faulty socket by loosening any mounting screws or clips, and pulling the socket and socket wires out of the fixture arm. Purchase and install a new chandelier socket, threading the socket wires through the fixture arm.

8 Test each fixture wire by attaching clip of continuity tester to one end of wire, and touching probe to other end. If tester does not glow, wire is faulty and must be replaced. Install new wires, if needed, then reassemble and rehang the chandelier.

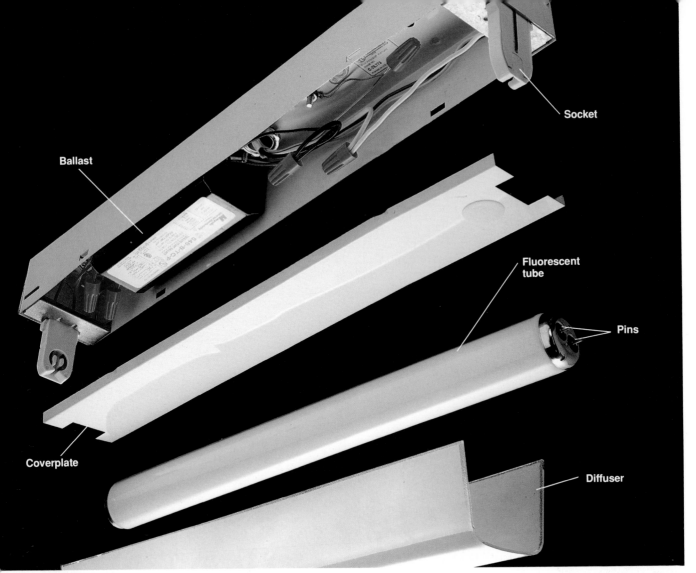

Ballast

Socket

Fluorescent tube

Pins

Coverplate

Diffuser

A fluorescent light works by directing electrical current through a special gas-filled **tube** that glows when energized. A white transluscent **diffuser** protects the fluorescent tube and softens the light. A **coverplate** protects a special transformer, called a **ballast**. The ballast regulates the flow of 120-volt household current to the **sockets**. The sockets transfer power to metal **pins** that extend into the tube.

Repairing & Replacing Fluorescent Lights

Fluorescent lights are relatively trouble-free, and use less energy than incandescent lights. A typical fluorescent tube lasts about three years, and produces two to four times as much light per watt as a standard incandescent light bulb.

The most frequent problem with a fluorescent light fixture is a worn-out tube. If a fluorescent light fixture begins to flicker, or does not light fully, remove and examine the tube. If the tube has bent or broken pins, or black discoloration near the ends, replace it. Light gray discoloration is normal in working fluorescent tubes. When replacing an old tube, read the wattage rating printed on the glass surface, and buy a new tube with a matching rating.

Never dispose of old tubes by breaking them. Fluorescent tubes contain a small amount of hazardous mercury. Check with your local environmental control agency or health department for disposal guidelines.

Fluorescent light fixtures also can malfunction if the sockets are cracked or worn. Inexpensive replacement sockets are available at any hardware store, and can be installed in a few minutes.

If a fixture does not work even after the tube and sockets have been serviced, the ballast probably is defective. Faulty ballasts may leak a black, oily substance, and can cause a fluorescent light

Problem	Repair
Tube flickers, or lights partially.	1. Rotate tube to make sure it is seated properly in the sockets. 2. Replace tube (page 90) and the starter (where present) if tube is discolored or if pins are bent or broken. 3. Replace the ballast (page 92) if replacement cost is reasonable. Otherwise, replace the entire fixture (page 93).
Tube does not light.	1. Check wall switch, and repair or replace, if needed (pages 42 to 61). 2. Rotate the tube to make sure it is seated properly in sockets. 3. Replace tube (page 90) and the starter (where present) if tube is discolored or if pins are bent or broken. 4. Replace sockets if they are chipped, or if tube does not seat properly (page 91). 5. Replace the ballast (page 92) or the entire fixture (page 93).
Noticeable black substance around ballast.	Replace ballast (page 92) if replacement cost is reasonable. Otherwise, replace the entire fixture (page 93).
Fixture hums.	Replace ballast (page 92) if replacement cost is reasonable. Otherwise, replace the entire fixture (page 93).

fixture to make a loud humming sound. Although ballasts can be replaced, always check prices before buying a new ballast. It may be cheaper to purchase and install a new fluorescent fixture rather than to replace the ballast in an old fluorescent light fixture.

Everything You Need:

Tools: screwdriver, ratchet wrench, combination tool, neon circuit tester.

Materials: replacement tubes, starters, or ballast (if needed); replacement fluorescent light fixture (if needed).

See Inspector's Notebook:

- Common Cable Problems (pages 114 to 115).
- Checking Wire Connections (pages 116 to 117).
- Electrical Box Inspection (pages 118 to 119).

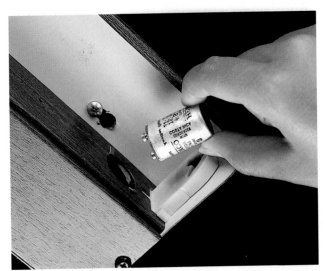

Older fluorescent lights may have a small cylindrical device, called a starter, located near one of the sockets. When a tube begins to flicker, replace both the tube and the starter. Turn off the power, then remove the starter by pushing it slightly and turning counterclockwise. Install a replacement that matches the old starter.

How to Replace a Fluorescent Tube

1 Turn off power to the light fixture at the main service panel. Remove the diffuser to expose the fluorescent tube.

2 Remove the fluorescent tube by rotating it ¼ turn in either direction and sliding the tube out of the sockets. Inspect the pins at the end of the tube. Tubes with bent or broken pins should be replaced.

3 Inspect the ends of the fluorescent tube for discoloration. New tube in good working order (top) shows no discoloration. Normal, working tube (middle) may have gray color. A worn-out tube (bottom) shows black discoloration.

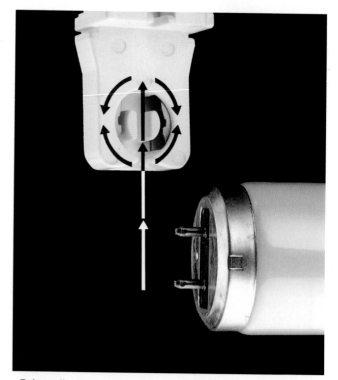

4 Install a new tube with the same wattage rating as the old tube. Insert the tube so that pins slide fully into sockets, then twist tube ¼ turn in either direction until it is locked securely. Reattach the diffuser, and turn on the power at the main service panel.

How to Replace a Socket

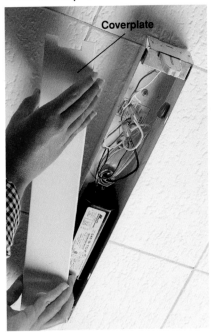

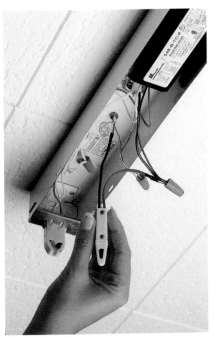

1 Turn off the power at the main service panel. Remove the diffuser, fluorescent tube, and the coverplate.

2 Test for power by touching one probe of a neon circuit tester to the grounding screw, and inserting the other probe into each wire nut. Tester should not glow. If it does, power is still entering the box. Return to the service panel and turn off correct circuit.

3 Remove the faulty socket from the fixture housing. Some sockets slide out, while others must be unscrewed.

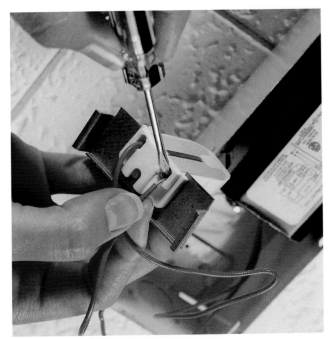

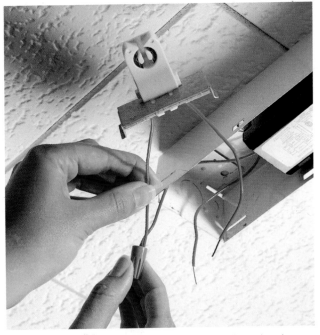

4 Disconnect wires attached to socket. For push-in fittings (above) remove the wires by inserting a small screwdriver into the release openings. Some sockets have screw terminal connections, while others have preattached wires that must be cut before the socket can be removed.

5 Purchase and install a new socket. If socket has preattached wire leads, connect the leads to the ballast wires using wire nuts. Replace coverplate and diffuser, then turn on power at the main service panel.

How to Replace a Ballast

  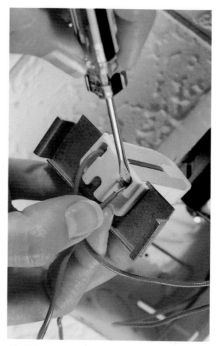

1 Turn off the power at the main service panel, then remove the diffuser, fluorescent tube, and coverplate. Test for power, using a neon circuit tester (step 2, page 91).

2 Remove the sockets from the fixture housing by sliding them out, or by removing the mounting screws and lifting the sockets out.

3 Disconnect the wires attached to the sockets by pushing a small screwdriver into the release openings (above), by loosening the screw terminals, or by cutting wires to within 2" of sockets.

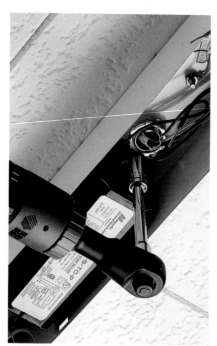 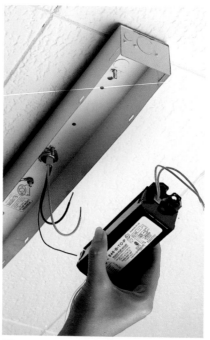 

4 Remove the old ballast, using a ratchet wrench or screwdriver. Make sure to support the ballast so it does not fall.

5 Install a new ballast that has the same ratings as the old ballast.

6 Attach the ballast wires to the socket wires, using wire nuts, screw terminal connections, or push-in fittings. Reinstall the coverplate, fluorescent tube, and diffuser. Turn on power to the light fixture at the main service panel.

How to Replace a Fluorescent Light Fixture

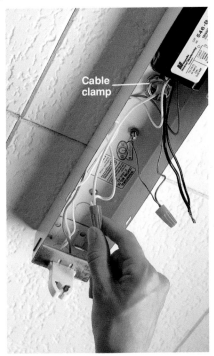

1 Turn off power to the light fixture at the main service panel. Remove diffuser, tube, and coverplate. Test for power, using a neon circuit tester (step 2, page 91).

2 Disconnect the insulated circuit wires and the bare copper grounding wire from the light fixture. Loosen the cable clamp holding the circuit wires.

3 Unbolt the fixture from the wall or ceiling, and carefully remove it. Make sure to support the fixture so it does not fall.

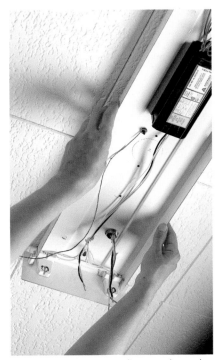

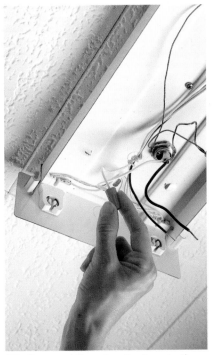

4 Position the new fixture, threading the circuit wires through the knockout opening in the back of the fixture. Bolt the fixture in place so it is firmly anchored to framing members.

5 Connect the circuit wires to the fixture wires, using wire nuts. Follow the wiring diagram included with the new fixture. Tighten the cable clamp holding the circuit wires.

6 Attach the fixture coverplate, then install the fluorescent tubes, and attach the diffuser. Turn on power to the fixture at the main service panel.

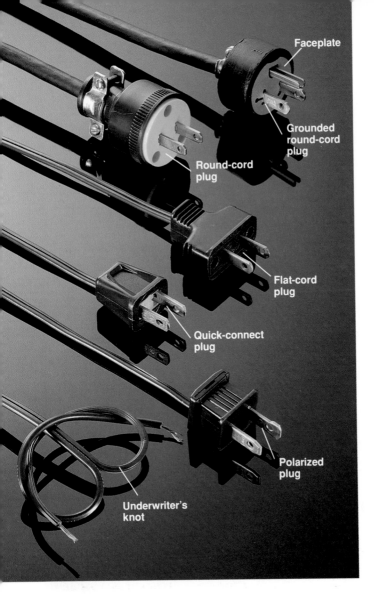

Faceplate

Grounded round-cord plug

Round-cord plug

Flat-cord plug

Quick-connect plug

Polarized plug

Underwriter's knot

Replacing a Plug

Replace an electrical plug whenever you notice bent or loose prongs, a cracked or damaged casing, or a missing insulating faceplate. A damaged plug poses a shock and fire hazard.

Replacement plugs are available in different styles to match common appliance cords. Always choose a replacement that is similar to the original plug. Flat-cord and quick-connect plugs are used with light-duty appliances, like lamps and radios. Round-cord plugs are used with larger appliances, including those that have three-prong grounding plugs.

Some appliances use polarized plugs. A polarized plug has one wide prong and one narrow prong, corresponding to the hot and neutral slots found in a standard receptacle. Polarization (page 16) ensures that the cord wires are aligned correctly with the receptacle slots.

If there is room in the plug body, tie the individual wires in an underwriter's knot to secure the plug to the cord.

Everything You Need:

Tools: combination tool, needlenose pliers, screwdriver.

Materials: replacement plug.

How to Install a Quick-connect Plug

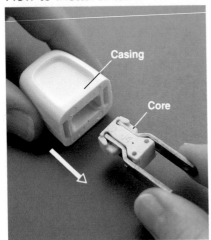

Casing

Core

1 Squeeze the prongs of the new quick-connect plug together slightly and pull the plug core from the casing. Cut the old plug from the flat-cord wire with a combination tool, leaving a clean-cut end.

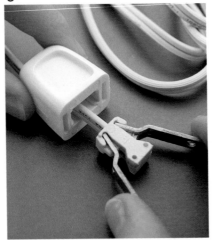

2 Feed unstripped wire through rear of plug casing. Spread prongs, then insert wire into opening in rear of core. Squeeze prongs together; spikes inside core penetrate cord. Slide casing over core until it snaps into place.

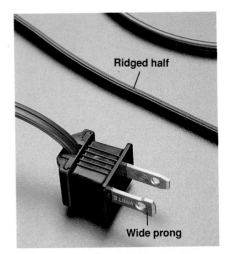

Ridged half

Wide prong

When replacing a polarized plug, make sure that the ridged half of the cord lines up with the wider (neutral) prong of the plug.

How to Replace a Round-cord Plug

1 Cut off round cord near the old plug, using a combination tool. Remove the insulating faceplate on the new plug, and feed cord through rear of plug. Strip about 3" of outer insulation from the round cord. Strip ¾" insulation from the individual wires.

Underwriter's knot

2 Tie an underwriter's knot with the black and white wires. Make sure the knot is located close to the edge of the stripped outer insulation. Pull the cord so that the knot slides into the plug body.

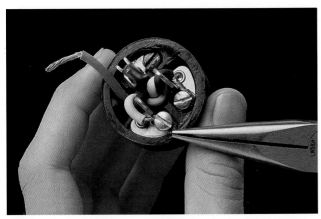

3 Hook end of black wire clockwise around brass screw, and white wire around silver screw. On a three-prong plug, attach third wire to grounding screw. If necessary, excess grounding wire can be cut away.

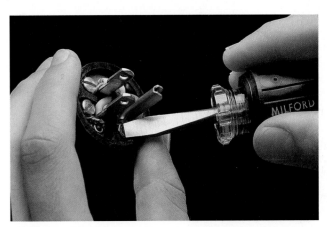

4 Tighten the screws securely, making sure the copper wires do not touch each other. Replace the insulating faceplate.

How to Replace a Flat-cord Plug

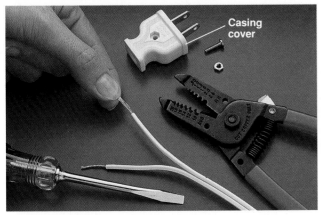

Casing cover

1 Cut old plug from cord using a combination tool. Pull apart the two halves of the flat cord so that about 2" of wire are separated. Strip ¾" insulation from each half. Remove casing cover on new plug.

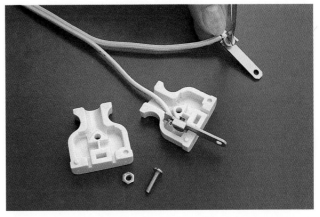

2 Hook ends of wires clockwise around the screw terminals, and tighten the screw terminals securely. Reassemble the plug casing. Some plugs may have an insulating faceplate that must be installed.

Replacing a Lamp Socket

Next to the cord plug, the most common source of trouble in a lamp is a worn light bulb socket. When a lamp socket assembly fails, the problem is usually with the socket-switch unit, although replacement sockets may include other parts you do not need.

Lamp failure is not always caused by a bad socket. You can avoid unnecessary repairs by checking the lamp cord, plug and light bulb before replacing the socket.

Before You Start:

Tools & Materials: replacement socket, continuity tester, screwdriver.

Tip: When replacing a lamp socket, you can improve a standard ON-OFF lamp by installing a three-way socket.

Types of Sockets

Socket-mounted switch types are usually interchangeable: choose a replacement you prefer. Clockwise from top left: twist knob, remote switch, pull chain, push lever.

How to Repair or Replace a Lamp Socket

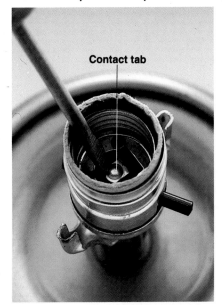

1 Unplug lamp. Remove shade, light bulb and harp (shade bracket). Scrape contact tab clean with a small screwdriver, Pry contact tab up slightly if flattened inside socket. Replace bulb, plug in lamp and test. If lamp does not work, unplug, remove bulb and continue with next step.

2 Squeeze outer shell of socket near PRESS marking, and lift it off. On older lamps, socket may be held by screws found at the base of the screw socket. Slip off cardboard insulating sleeve. If sleeve is damaged, replace entire socket.

3 Check for loose wire connections on screw terminals. Refasten any loose connections, then reassemble lamp and test. If connections are not loose, remove the wires, lift out the socket and continue with the next step.

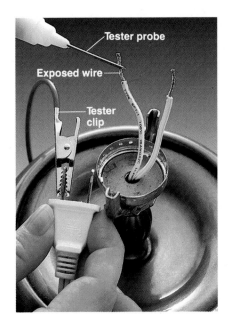

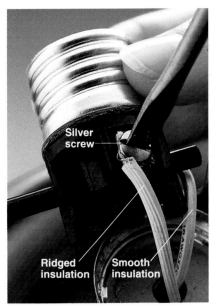

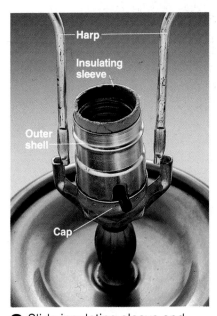

4 Test for lamp cord problems with continuity tester. Place clip of tester on one prong of plug. Touch probe to one exposed wire, then to the other wire. Repeat test with other prong of plug. If tester fails to light for either prong, then replace the cord and plug. Retest the lamp.

5 If cord and plug are functional, then choose a replacement socket marked with the same amp and volt ratings as the old socket. One half of flat-cord lamp wire is covered by insulation that is ridged or marked: attach this wire to the silver screw terminal. Connect other wire to brass screw.

6 Slide insulating sleeve and outer shell over socket so that socket and screw terminals are fully covered and switch fits into sleeve slot. Press socket assembly down into cap until socket locks into place. Replace harp, light bulb and shade.

Home doorbell system is powered by a transformer that reduces 120-volt current to low-voltage current of 20 volts or less. Current flows from the transformer to one or more push-button switches. When pushed, the switch activates a magnetic coil inside the chime unit, causing a plunger to strike a musical tuning bar.

Fixing & Replacing Doorbells

Most doorbell problems are caused by loose wire connections or worn-out switches. Reconnecting loose wires or replacing a switch requires only a few minutes. Doorbell problems also can occur if the chime unit becomes dirty or worn, or if the low-voltage transformer burns out. Both parts are easy to replace. Because doorbells operate at low voltage, the switches and the chime unit can be serviced without turning off power to the system. However, when replacing a transformer, always turn off the power at the main service panel.

Most houses have other low-voltage transformers in addition to the doorbell transformer. These transformers control heating and air-conditioning thermostats (pages 104 to 111), or other low-voltage systems. When testing and repairing a doorbell system, it is important to identify the correct transformer. A doorbell transformer has a voltage rating of 20 volts or less. This rating is printed on the face of the transformer. A doorbell transformer often is located near the main service panel, and in some homes is attached directly to the service panel.

The transformer that controls a heating/air-conditioning thermostat system is located near the furnace, and has a voltage rating of 24 volts or more.

Occasionally, a doorbell problem is caused by a broken low-voltage wire somewhere in the system. You can test for wire breaks with a battery-operated multi-tester. If the test indicates a break, new low-voltage wires must be installed between the transformer and the switches, or between the switches and chime unit. Replacing low-voltage wires is not a difficult job, but it can be time-consuming. You may choose to have an electrician do this work.

Everything You Need:

Tools: continuity tester, screwdriver, multi-tester, needlenose pliers.

Materials: cotton swab, rubbing alcohol, replacement doorbell switch (if needed), masking tape, replacement chime unit (if needed).

How to Test a Doorbell System

1 Remove the mounting screws holding the doorbell switch to the house.

2 Carefully pull the switch away from the wall.

3 Check wire connections on the switch. If wires are loose, reconnect them to the screw terminals. Test the doorbell by pressing the button. If the doorbell still does not work, disconnect the switch and test it with a continuity tester.

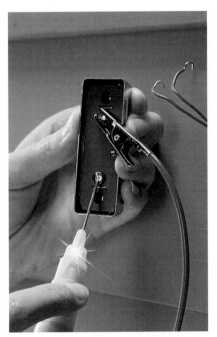

4 Test the switch by attaching the clip of a continuity tester to one screw terminal, and touching the probe to the other screw terminal. Press the switch button. Tester should glow. If not, then the switch is faulty and must be replaced (page 102).

5 Twist the doorbell switch wires together temporarily to test the other parts of the doorbell system.

6 Locate the doorbell transformer, often located near the main service panel. Transformer may be attached to an electrical box, or may be attached directly to the side of the service panel.

(continued next page)

7 Identify the doorbell transformer by reading its voltage rating. Doorbell transformers have a voltage rating of 20 volts or less.

8 Turn off power to transformer at main service panel. Remove cover on electrical box, and test wires for power (step 3, page 109). Reconnect any loose wires. Replace taped connections with wire nut connections. Reattach coverplate.

9 Inspect the low-voltage wire connections, and reconnect any loose wires, using needlenose pliers. Turn on power to the transformer at the main service panel.

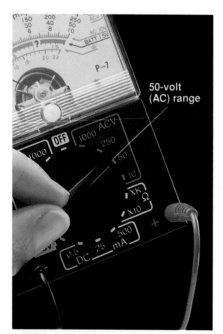

10 Set the dial of multi-tester to the 50-volt (AC) range.

11 Touch the probes of the multi-tester to the low-voltage screw terminals on the transformer.

12 If transformer is operating properly, multi-tester will detect power that is within 2 volts of transformer's rating. If not, the transformer is faulty and must be replaced (page 109).

13 Remove the coverplate on the doorbell chime unit.

14 Inspect the low-voltage wire connections, and reconnect any loose wires.

15 Test to make sure chime unit is receiving proper current with a multi-tester set to 50-volt (AC) range. Touch probes of tester to screw terminals marked TRANS-FORMER (or TRANS) and FRONT.

16 If the multi-tester detects power within 2 volts of the transformer rating, then the chime unit is receiving proper current. If multi-tester detects no power, or very low power, then there is a break in the low-voltage wiring, and new wires must be installed.

17 If necessary, repeat test for rear doorbell wires. Hold probes to terminals marked TRANS-FORMER (or TRANS) and REAR. Multi-tester should detect power within 2 volts of transformer's rating. If not, there is a break in wiring, and new wires must be installed.

18 Clean the chime plungers with a cotton swab dipped in rubbing alcohol. Reassemble doorbell switches, then test the system by pushing one of the switches. If doorbell still does not work, then the chime unit is faulty and must be replaced (page 102).

101

How to Replace a Doorbell Switch

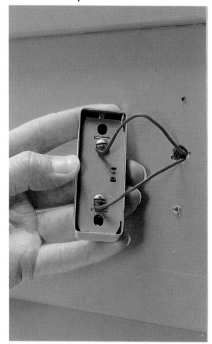

1 Remove the doorbell switch mounting screws, and carefully pull the switch away from the wall.

2 Disconnect wires from switch. Tape wires to the wall to prevent them from slipping into the wall cavity. Purchase a new doorbell switch, and connect wires to screw terminals on new switch. (Wires are interchangeable, and can be connected to either screw terminal.)

3 Anchor the switch to the wall with the mounting screws.

How to Replace a Doorbell Chime Unit

1 Turn off power to the doorbell system at the main service panel. Remove the coverplate from the old chime unit.

2 Using masking tape, label the low-voltage wires FRONT, REAR, or TRANS to identify their screw terminal locations. Disconnect the low-voltage wires.

3 Unscrew the mounting screws, and remove the old chime unit.

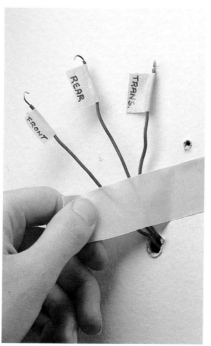

4 Tape the wires to the wall to prevent them from slipping into the wall cavity.

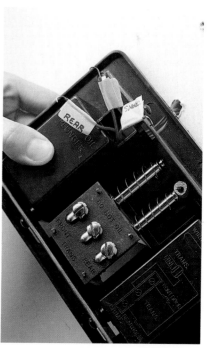

5 Purchase a new chime unit that matches the voltage rating of the old unit. Thread the low-voltage wires through the base of the new chime unit.

6 Attach the chime unit to the wall, using the mounting screws included with the installation kit.

7 Connect the low-voltage wires to the screw terminals on the new chime unit.

8 Attach the coverplate and turn on the power at the main service panel.

Electronic programmable thermostats can be set to make up to four temperature changes each day. They are available in low-voltage designs (right) for central heating/cooling systems, and in line-voltage designs (left) for electric baseboard heating. Most electronic programmable thermostats have an internal battery that saves the program in case of a power failure.

Fixing & Replacing Thermostats

A thermostat is a temperature-sensitive switch that automatically controls home heating and air-conditioning systems. There are two types of thermostats used to control heating and air-conditioning systems. **Low-voltage thermostats** control whole-house heating and air conditioning from one central location. **Line-voltage thermostats** are used in zone heating systems, where each room has its own heating unit and thermostat.

A low-voltage thermostat is powered by a transformer that reduces 120-volt current to about 24 volts. A low-voltage thermostat is very durable, but failures can occur if wire connections become loose or dirty, if thermostat parts become corroded, or if a transformer wears out. Some thermostat systems have two transformers. One transformer controls the heating unit, and the other controls the air-conditioning unit.

Line-voltage thermostats are powered by the same circuit as the heating unit, usually a 240-volt circuit. Always make sure to turn off the power before servicing a line-voltage thermostat.

A thermostat can be replaced in about one hour. Many homeowners choose to replace standard low-voltage or line-voltage thermostats with programmable setback thermostats. These programmable thermostats can cut energy use by up to 35%.

When buying a new thermostat, make sure the new unit is compatible with your heating/air-conditioning system. For reference, take along the brand name and model number of the old thermostat and of your heating/air-conditioning units. When buying a new low-voltage transformer, choose a replacement with voltage and amperage ratings that match the old thermostat.

Everything You Need:

Tools: soft-bristled paint brush, multi-tester, screwdriver, combination tool, neon circuit tester, continuity tester.

Materials: masking tape, short piece of wire.

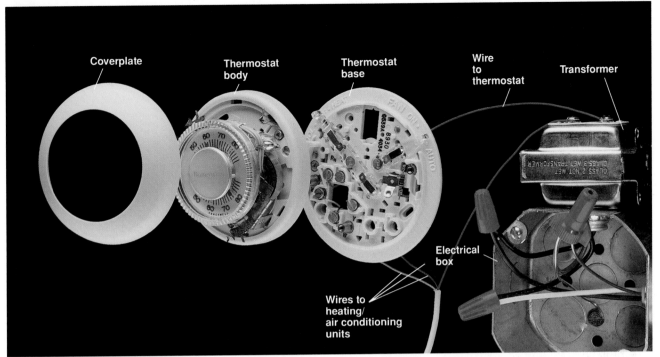

Low-voltage thermostat system has a transformer that is either connected to an electrical junction box or mounted inside a furnace access panel. Very thin wires (18 to 22 gauge) send current to the **thermostat**. The thermostat constantly monitors room temperatures, and sends electrical signals to the heating/cooling unit through additional wires. The number of wires connected to the thermostat varies from two to six, depend-

ing on the type of heating/air-conditioning system. In the common four-wire system shown above, power is supplied to the thermostat through a single wire attached to screw terminal R. Wires attached to other screw terminals relay signals to the furnace heating unit, the air-conditioning unit, and the blower unit. Before removing a thermostat, make sure to label each wire to identify its screw terminal location.

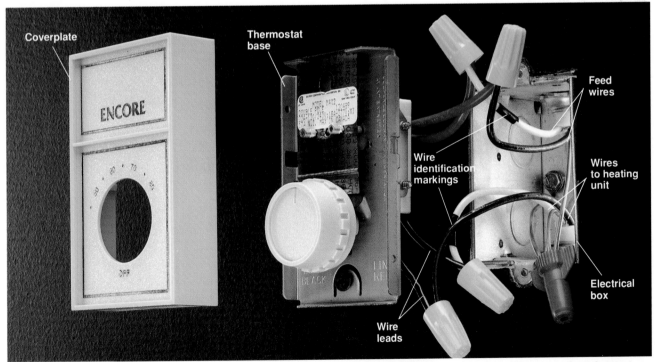

Line-voltage thermostat for 240-volt baseboard heating unit usually has four wire leads, although some models have only two leads. On a four-wire thermostat, the two red wire leads (sometimes marked LINE

or L) are attached to the two hot feed wires bringing power into the box from the service panel. The black wire leads (sometimes marked LOAD) are connected to the circuit wires that carry power to the heating unit.

How to Inspect & Test a Low-voltage Thermostat System

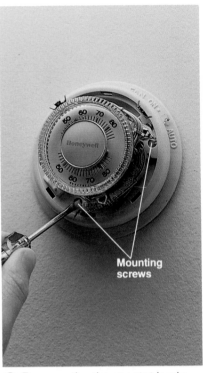

1 Turn off power to the heating/air-conditioning system at the main service panel. Remove the thermostat coverplate.

2 Clean dust from the thermostat parts using a small, soft-bristled paint brush.

3 Remove the thermostat body by loosening the mounting screws with a screwdriver.

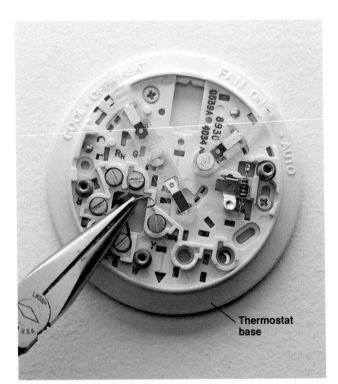

4 Inspect the wire connections on the thermostat base. Reattach any loose wires. If wires are broken or corroded, they should be clipped, stripped, and re-attached to the screw terminals (page 24).

5 Locate the low-voltage transformer that powers the thermostat. This transformer usually is located near the heating/air-conditioning system, or inside a furnace access panel. Tighten any loose wire connections.

6 Set the control dial of multi-tester meter to the 50-volt (AC) range. Turn on power to the heating/air-conditioning system at the main service panel.

7 Touch one probe of multi-tester to each of the low-voltage screw terminals. If tester does not detect current, then the transformer is defective and must be replaced (page 109).

8 Turn on power to heating system. Set thermostat control levers to AUTO and HEAT.

9 Strip ½" from each end of a short piece of insulated wire. Touch one end of the wire to terminal marked W and the other end to terminal marked R. If heating system begins to run, then the thermostat is faulty, and must be replaced (page 108).

How to Install a Programmable Low-voltage Thermostat

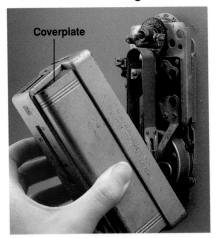

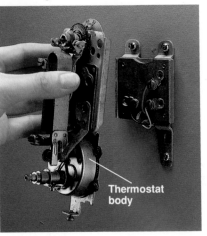

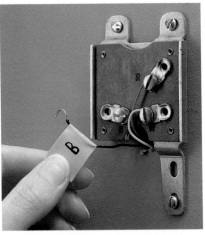

1 Turn off the power to the heating/air-conditioning system at the main service panel. Remove the thermostat coverplate.

2 Unscrew the thermostat mounting screws and remove the thermostat body.

3 Label the low-voltage wires to identify their screw terminal locations, using masking tape. Disconnect all low-voltage wires.

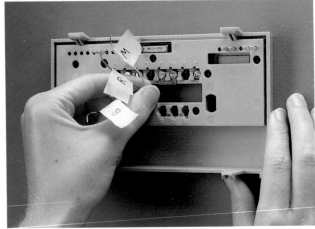

4 Remove the thermostat base by loosening the mounting screws. Tape the wires against the wall to make sure they do not fall into the wall cavity.

5 Thread the low-voltage wires through base of new thermostat. Mount the thermostat base on the wall, using the screws included with the thermostat.

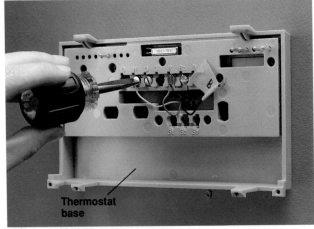

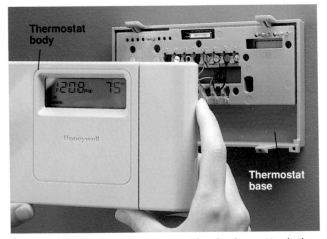

6 Connect the low-voltage wires to the screw terminals on the thermostat base. Use the manufacturer's connection chart as a guide.

7 Install batteries in thermostat body, then attach the body to thermostat base. Turn on power and program the thermostat as desired.

How to Replace a Low-voltage Transformer

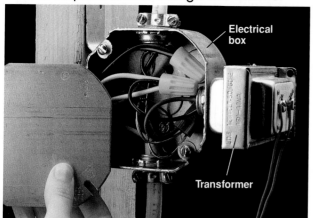

1 Turn off the power to the heating/air-conditioning system at the main service panel. Remove the coverplate on the transformer electrical box.

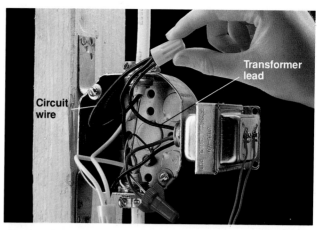

2 Carefully remove the wire nut connecting the black circuit wire to the transformer lead. Be careful not to touch bare wires.

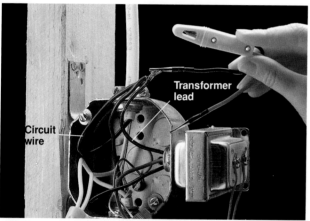

3 Test for power by touching one probe of neon circuit tester to grounded metal box and other probe to exposed wires. Remove wire nut from white wires and repeat test. Tester should not glow for either test. If it does, power is still entering box. Return to service panel and turn off correct circuit.

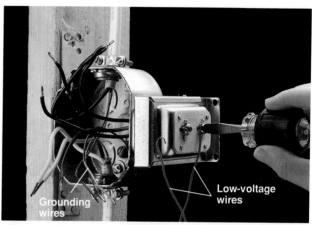

4 Disconnect the grounding wires inside the box, then disconnect low-voltage wires attached to the screw terminals on the transformer. Unscrew the transformer mounting bracket inside the box, and remove transformer. Purchase a new transformer with the same voltage rating as the old transformer.

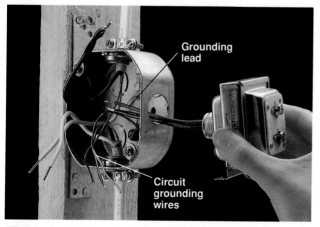

5 Attach new transformer to electrical box. Reconnect circuit wires to transformer leads. Connect circuit grounding wires to transformer grounding lead.

6 Connect the low-voltage wires to the transformer, and reattach the electrical box coverplate. Turn on the power at the main service panel.

How to Test & Replace a Line-voltage Thermostat

1 Turn off the power to the heating unit at the main service panel. Remove the thermostat coverplate.

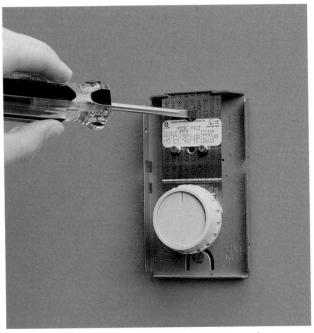

2 Loosen the thermostat mounting screws, and carefully pull the thermostat from the electrical box.

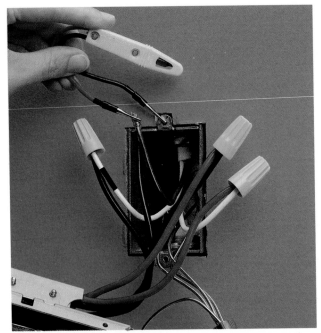

3 Unscrew one wire nut. Test for power by touching one probe of neon circuit tester to grounded metal box and touching other probe to exposed wires. Tester should not glow. Repeat test with other wire connections. Tester should not glow. If it does, then power is still entering box. Return to service panel and turn off correct circuit.

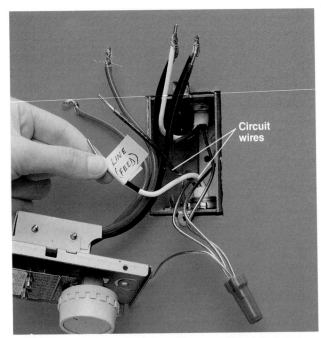

4 Identify the two circuit wires that are attached to the thermostat leads marked LINE. These leads are often red. The circuit wires attached to the LINE leads bring power into the box, and are known as feed wires. Label the feed wires with masking tape, then disconnect all wires.

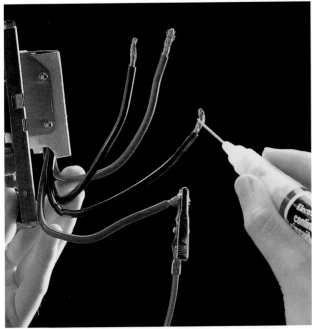

5 Test thermostat by attaching the clip of a continuity tester to one of the red wire leads, then touching probe to black wire lead on same side of thermostat. Turn temperature dial from HIGH to LOW. Tester should glow in both positions. Repeat test with other pair of wire leads. If tester does not glow for both positions, thermostat is faulty and must be replaced.

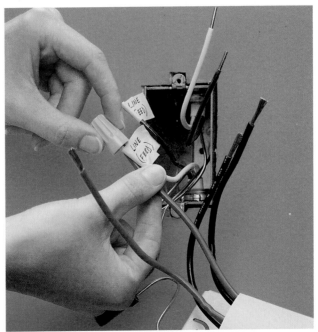

6 Replace a faulty thermostat with a new thermostat that has the same voltage and amperage ratings as the old one. Connect the new thermostat by attaching the circuit feed wires to the wire leads marked LINE, using wire nuts.

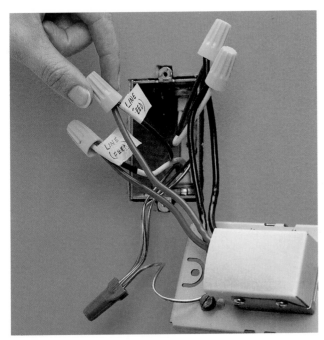

7 Connect the remaining circuit wires to the thermostat leads marked LOAD, using wire nuts. Connect the grounding wires together with a wire nut.

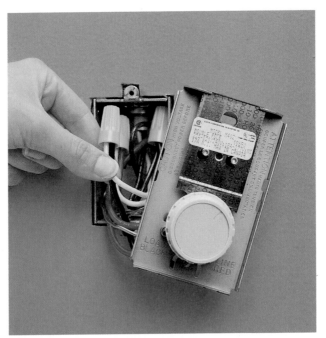

8 Carefully fold the wires inside the electrical box, then attach the thermostat mounting screws and the coverplate. Turn on the power at the main service panel. If new thermostat is programmable (page 104), set the program as desired.

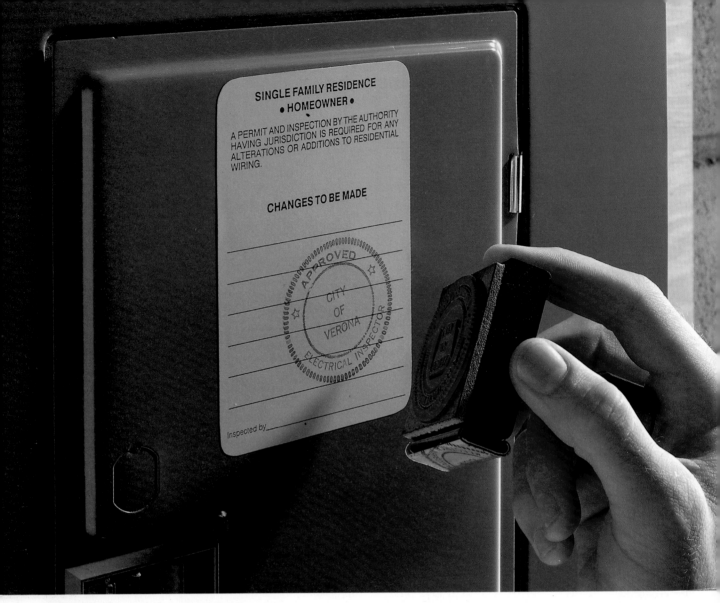

Inspector's Notebook

An electrical inspector visiting your home might identify a number of situations that are not "up to code." These situations may not be immediate problems. In fact, it is possible that the wiring in your home has remained trouble-free for many years.

Nevertheless, any wiring or device that is not up to code carries the potential for problems, often at risk to your home and your family. In addition, you may have trouble selling your home if it is not wired according to accepted methods.

Most local electrical codes are based on the National Electrical Code (NEC), a book updated and published every three years by the National Fire Protection Agency. This code book contains rules and regulations for the proper installation of electrical wiring and devices. Most public libraries carry reference copies of the NEC.

All electrical inspectors are required to be well versed in the NEC. Their job is to know the NEC regulations, and to make sure these rules are followed in order to prevent fires and ensure safety. If you have questions regarding your home wiring system, your local inspector will be happy to answer them.

While a book like *The Complete Guide to Home Wiring* cannot possibly identify all potential wiring problems in your house, we have created the "Inspector's Notebook" to help you identify some of the most common wiring defects and show you how to correct them. When working on home wiring repair or replacement projects, refer to this section to help identify any conditions that may be hazardous.

Service Panel Inspection

Problem: Rust stains are found inside the main service panel. This problem occurs because water seeps into the service head outside the house and drips down into the service panel.

Solution: Have an electrician examine the service head and the main service panel. If the panel or service wires have been damaged, new electrical service must be installed.

Inspecting the Grounding Jumper Wire

Problem: Grounding system jumper wire is missing or is disconnected. In most homes the grounding jumper wire attaches to water pipes on either side of the water meter. Because the ground pathway is broken, this is a dangerous situation that should be fixed immediately.

Solution: Attach a jumper wire to the water pipes on either side of the water meter, using pipe clamps. Use #6-gauge or #4-gauge bare copper wire for the jumper wire.

Common Cable Problems

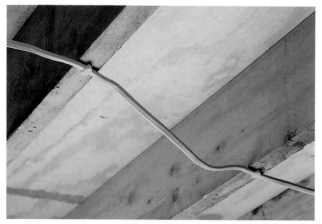

Problem: Cable running across joists or studs is attached to the edge of framing members. Electrical codes forbid this type of installation in exposed areas, like unfinished basements or walk-up attics.

Solution: Protect cable by drilling holes in framing members at least 2" from exposed edges, and threading the cable through the holes.

Problem: Cable running along joists or studs hangs loosely. Loose cables can be pulled accidentally, causing damage to wires.

Solution: Anchor the cable to the side of the framing members at least 1¼" from the edge, using plastic staples. NM (nonmetallic) cable should be stapled every 4½ feet, and within 12" of each electrical box.

Cable
shown
cut away

Problem: Cable threaded through studs or joists lies close to the edge of the framing members. NM (non-metallic) cable (shown cut away) can be damaged easily if nails or screws are driven into the framing members during remodeling projects.

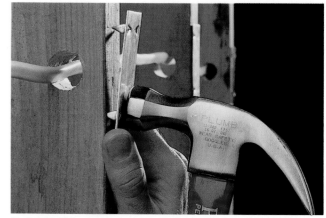

Solution: Install metal nail guards to protect cable from damage. Nail guards are available at hardware stores and home centers.

Problem: Unclamped cable enters a metal electrical box. Edges of the knockout can rub against the cable sheathing and damage the wires. (Note: with plastic boxes, clamps are not required if cables are anchored to framing members within 12" of box.)

Solution: Anchor the cable to the electrical box with a cable clamp (pages 38 to 39). Several types of cable clamps are available at hardware stores and home centers.

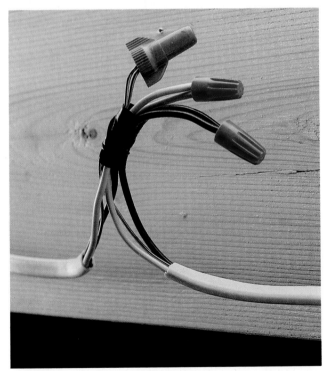

Problem: Cables are spliced outside an electrical box. Exposed splices can spark and create a risk of shock or fire.

Solution: Bring installation "up to code" by enclosing the splice inside a metal or plastic electrical box (pages 36 to 39). Make sure the box is large enough for the number of wires it contains.

Checking Wire Connections

Problem: Two or more wires are attached to a single screw terminal. This type of connection is seen in older wiring, but is now prohibited by the National Electrical Code.

Pigtail

Solution: Disconnect the wires from the screw terminal, then join them to a short length of wire (called a pigtail), using a wire nut (page 25). Connect the other end of the pigtail to the screw terminal.

Exposed wire

Problem: Bare wire extends past a screw terminal. Exposed wire can cause a short circuit if it touches the metal box or another circuit wire.

Solution: Clip the wire and reconnect it to the screw terminal. In a proper connection, the bare wire wraps completely around the screw terminal, and the plastic insulation just touches the screw head (page 24).

Problem: Wires are connected with electrical tape. Electrical tape was used frequently in older installations, but it can deteriorate over time, leaving bare wires exposed inside the electrical box.

Solution: Replace electrical tape with wire nuts (page 25). You may need to clip away a small portion of the wire so the bare end will be covered completely by the wire nut.

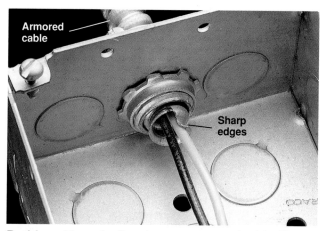

Problem: No protective sleeve on armored cable. Sharp edges of the cable can damage the wire insulation, creating a shock hazard and fire risk.

Solution: Protect the wire insulation by installing plastic or fiber sleeves around the wires. Sleeves are available at hardware stores. Wires that are damaged must be replaced.

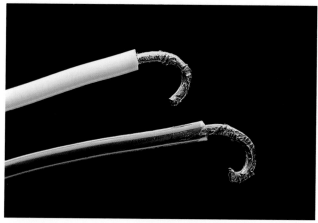

Problem: Nicks and scratches in bare wires interfere with the flow of current. This can cause the wires to overheat.

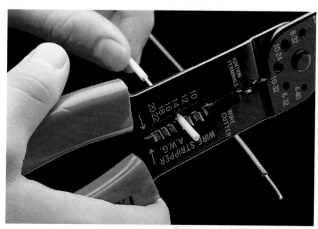

Solution: Clip away damaged portion of wire, then restrip about ¾" of insulation and reconnect the wire to the screw terminal (page 24).

Problem: Insulation on wires is cracked or damaged. If damaged insulation exposes bare wire, a short circuit can occur, posing a shock hazard and fire risk.

Solution: Wrap damaged insulation temporarily with plastic electrical tape. Damaged circuit wires should be replaced by an electrician.

Electrical Box Inspection

Problem: Open electrical boxes create a fire hazard if a short circuit causes sparks (arcing) inside the box.

Solution: Cover the open box with a solid metal coverplate, available at any hardware store. Electrical boxes must remain accessible, and cannot be sealed inside ceilings or walls.

Problem: Short wires are difficult to handle. The National Electrical Code (NEC) requires that each wire in an electrical box have at least 6" of workable length.

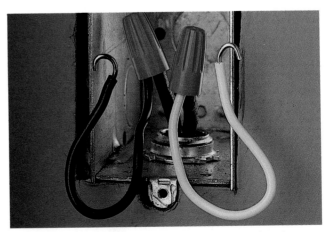

Solution: Lengthen circuit wires by connecting them to short pigtail wires, using wire nuts (page 25). Pigtails can be cut from scrap wire, but should be the same gauge and color as the circuit wires.

Problem: Recessed electrical box is hazardous, especially if the wall or ceiling surface is made from a flammable material, like wood paneling. The National Electrical Code prohibits this type of installation.

Solution: Add an extension ring to bring the face of the electrical box flush with the surface. Extension rings come in several sizes, and are available at hardware stores.

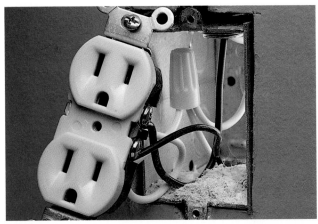

Problem: Dust and dirt in electrical box can cause hazardous high-resistance short circuits (pages 124 to 127). When making routine electrical repairs, always check the electrical boxes for dust and dirt buildup.

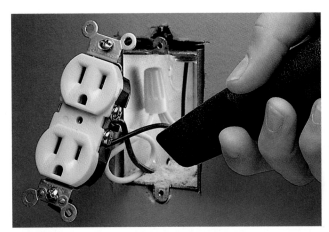

Solution: Vacuum electrical box clean, using a narrow nozzle attachment. Make sure power to box is turned off at main service panel before vacuuming.

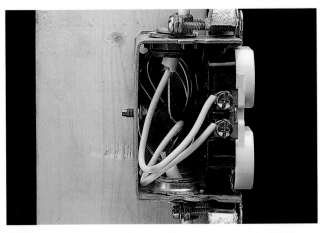

Problem: Crowded electrical box (shown cut away) makes electrical repairs difficult. This type of installation is prohibited because wires can be damaged easily when a receptacle or switch is installed.

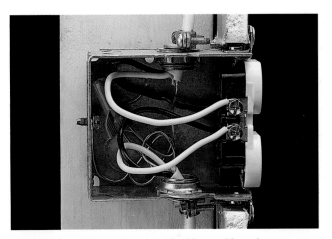

Solution: Replace the electrical box with a deeper electrical box (pages 36 to 39).

Problem: Light fixture is installed without an electrical box. This installation exposes the wiring connections, and provides no support for the light fixture.

Solution: Install an approved electrical box (pages 36 to 39) to enclose the wire connections and support the light fixture.

Common Electrical Cord Problems

Problem: Lamp or appliance cord runs underneath a rug. Foot traffic can wear off insulation, creating a short circuit that can cause fire or shock.

Solution: Reposition the lamp or appliance so the cord is visible. Replace worn cords.

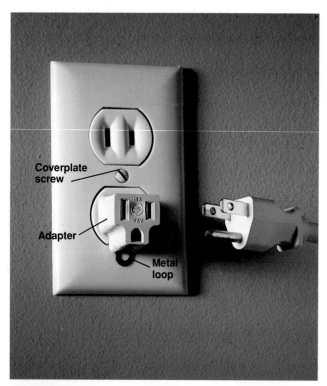

Coverplate screw

Adapter

Metal loop

GFCI receptacle

Problem: Three-prong appliance plugs do not fit two slot receptacle. Do not use three-prong adapters unless the metal loop on the adapter is tightly connected to the coverplate screw on receptacle (page 17).

Solution: Install a three-prong grounded receptacle if a means of grounding exists at the box (pages 70 to 71). Install a GFCI (ground-fault circuit-interrupter) receptacle (pages 74 to 77) in kitchens and bathrooms, or if the electrical box is not grounded.

Problem: Lamp or appliance plug is cracked, or electrical cord is frayed near plug. Worn cords and plugs create a fire and shock hazard.

Solution: Cut away damaged portion of wire and install a new plug (pages 94 to 95). Replacement plugs are available at appliance stores and home centers.

Problem: Extension cord is too small for the power load drawn by a tool or appliance. Undersized extension cords can overheat, melting the insulation and leaving bare wires exposed.

Solution: Use an extension cord with wattage and amperage ratings that meet or exceed the rating of the tool or appliance. Extension cords are for temporary use only. Never use an extension cord for a permanent installation.

Inspecting Receptacles & Switches

Problem: Octopus receptacle attachments used permanently can overload a circuit and cause overheating of the receptacle.

Solution: Use a multi-receptacle power strip with built-in overload protection. This is for temporary use only. If the need for extra receptacles is frequent, upgrade the wiring system.

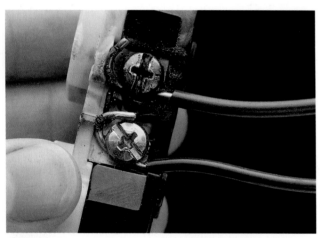

Problem: Scorch marks near screw terminals indicate that electrical arcing has occurred. Arcing usually is caused by loose wire connections.

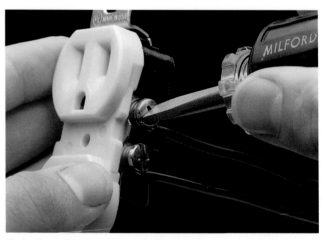

Solution: Clean wires with fine sandpaper, and replace the receptacle if it is badly damaged. Make sure wires are connected securely to screw teminals.

Problem: Two-slot receptacle in outdoor installation is hazardous because it has no grounding slot. In case of a short circuit, a person plugging in a cord becomes a conductor for current to follow to ground.

Solution: Install a GFCI (ground-fault circuit-interrupter) receptacle. Electrical codes now require that GFCIs be used for all outdoor receptacles, as well as for basement, kitchen, and bathroom receptacles.

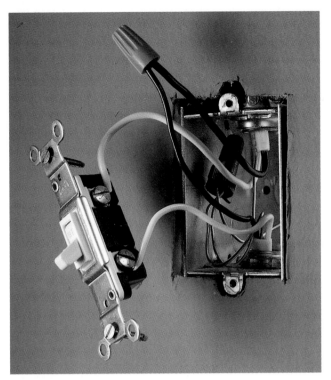

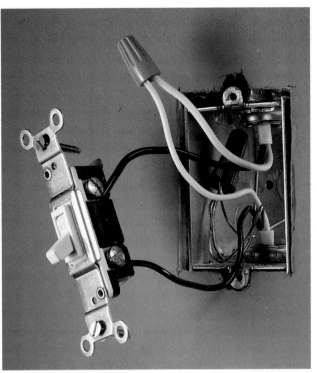

Problem: White neutral wires are connected to switch. Although switch appears to work correctly in this installation, it is dangerous because light fixture carries voltage when the switch is off.

Solution: Connect the black hot wires to the switch, and join the white wires together with a wire nut.

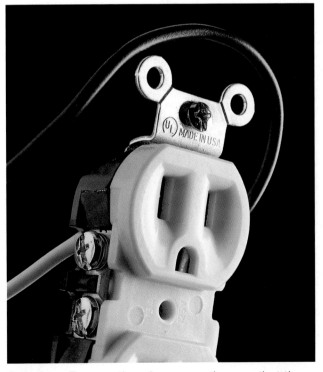

Problem: White neutral wires are connected to the brass screw terminals on the receptacle, and black hot wires are attached to silver screw terminals. This installation is hazardous because live voltage flows into the long neutral slot on the receptacle.

Solution: Reverse the wire connections so that the black hot wires are attached to brass screw terminals and white neutral wires are attached to silver screw terminals. Live voltage now flows into the short slot on the receptacle.

Evaluating Old Wiring

If the wiring in your home is more than 30 years old, it may have a number of age-related problems. Many problems associated with older wiring can be found by inspecting electrical boxes for dirty wire connections (page 72), signs of arcing (page 122), cracked or damaged wire insulation (page 117), or dirt buildup (page 119).

However, it is difficult to identify problems with wiring that is hidden inside the walls. If old wires are dusty and have damaged insulation, they can "leak" electrical current. The amount of current that leaks through dust usually is very small, too small to trip a breaker or blow a fuse. Nevertheless, by allowing current to leave its normal path, these leaks consume power in much the same way that a dripping faucet wastes water.

This kind of electrical leak is called a high-resistance short circuit. A high-resistance short circuit can produce heat, and should be considered a fire hazard.

It is possible to check for high-resistance short circuits by using your electric meter to test the wires of each circuit. The goal of the test is to determine if electricity is being consumed even if none of the lights and appliances are drawing power. To do this, you must turn on all wall switches to activate the hot circuit wires, then stop power consumption by removing light bulbs and fluorescent tubes, and disconnecting all lamps and appliances.

Then examine the electric meter, usually located on the outside of the house near the service head (page 12). If the flat, circular rotor inside the meter is turning, it means that a high-resistance short circuit is causing an electrical leak somewhere in the wiring. High-resistance short circuits consume very small amounts of power, so you should watch the rotor for a full minute to detect any movement.

If the test shows there is a high-resistance short circuit in your wiring, contact a licensed electrician to have it repaired.

Everything You Need:

Tools: screwdriver.

Materials: wire nuts, masking tape, pen.

How to Evaluate Old Wiring for High-resistance Short Circuits

1 Switch on all light fixtures. Remember to turn on closet lights, basement lights, and exterior lights.

2 Stop all power consumption by removing all light bulbs and fluorescent tubes. Turn off all thermostats.

3 Disconnect all plug-in lamps and appliances from the receptacles.

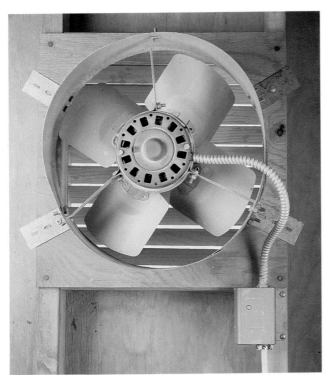

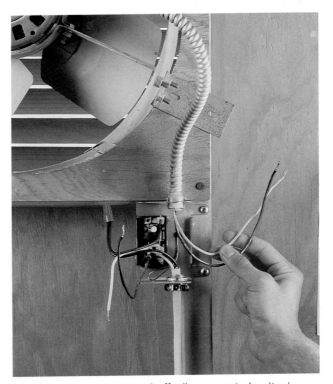

4 Shut off power to all permanently wired appliances by turning off the correct breakers or removing the correct fuses at the service panel. Permanently wired appliances include attic fans, water heaters, garage door openers, and ceiling fans.

5 With the power turned off, disconnect circuit wires from each permanently wired appliance. Cap the wire ends with wire nuts. Next, turn on power and make sure all appliance wall switches are turned on.

(continued next page)

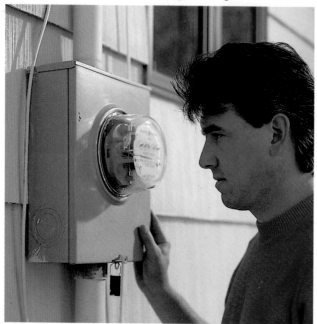

6 Watch the circular rotor located inside the electric meter for at least one minute. If the rotor does not move, then your wiring is in good condition. If the rotor moves, it means there is a high-resistance short circuit somewhere in the wiring system: proceed to step 7.

7 Turn off power to all circuits at the main service panel by switching off circuit breakers or removing fuses. Do not turn off main shutoff. Watch the rotor inside the meter. If rotor moves, then the high-resistance short circuit is located in the main service panel or service wiring. In this case, consult a licensed electrician. If rotor does not move, proceed to step 8.

8 Turn on individual circuits, one at a time, by switching on the circuit breaker or inserting the fuse. Watch for rotor movement in the electric meter. If rotor does not move, wiring is in good condition. Turn off power to the circuit, then proceed to the next circuit.

9 If the rotor is moving, then use masking tape to mark the faulty circuit. Turn off power to the circuit, then proceed to the next circuit.

10 If circuit contains three-way or four-way switches, flip the lever on each switch individually, and watch for rotor movement after each flip of a switch.

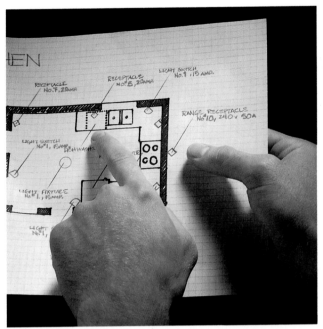

11 For each faulty circuit, identify the appliances, lights, switches, receptacles, and electrical junction boxes powered by the circuit. Use a map of your home wiring system as a guide (pages 30 to 33).

12 Recheck all lights and appliances along each faulty circuit to make sure they are not consuming power. If they are, disconnect them and repeat test.

13 Inspect the electrical boxes along each faulty circuit for dirty wire connections (page 72), damaged wire insulation (page 117), dirt buildup (page 119), or signs of arcing (page 122).

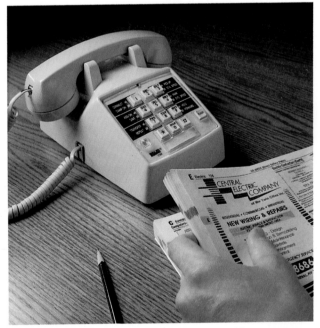

14 If no problems are found in electrical boxes, then the high-resistance short circuit is in wiring contained inside the walls. In this case, consult a licensed electrician.

1. Examine your main service (page 130). The amp rating of the electrical service and the size of the circuit breaker panel will help you determine if a service upgrade is needed.

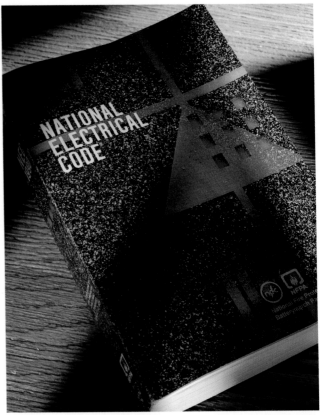

2. Learn about codes (pages 131 to 133). The National Electrical Code, and local Electrical Codes and Building Codes, provide guidelines for determining how much power and how many circuits your home needs. Your local electrical inspector can tell you which regulations apply to your job.

Planning a Wiring Project

Careful planning of a wiring project ensures you will have plenty of power for present and future needs. Whether you are adding circuits in a room addition, wiring a remodeled kitchen, or adding an outdoor circuit, consider all possible ways the space might be used, and plan for enough electrical service to meet peak needs.

For example, when wiring a room addition, remember that the way a room is used can change. In a room used as a spare bedroom, a single 15-amp circuit provides plenty of power, but if you ever choose to convert the same room to a family recreation space, it will need at least two 20-amp circuits.

When wiring a remodeled kitchen, it is a good idea to install circuits for an electric oven and countertop range, even if you do not have these electric appliances. Installing these circuits now makes it easy to convert from gas to electric appliances at a later date.

A large wiring project adds a considerable load to your main electrical service. In about 25% of all homes, some type of service upgrade is needed before new wiring can be installed. For example, many homeowners will need to replace an older 60-amp electrical service with a new service rated for 100 amps or more. This is a job for a licensed electrician, but is well worth the investment. In other cases, the existing main service provides adequate power, but the main circuit breaker panel is too full to hold any new circuit breakers. In this case, it is necessary to install a circuit breaker subpanel to provide room for hooking up added circuits. Installing a subpanel is a job most homeowners can do themselves (pages 180 to 183).

This chapter gives an easy five-step method for determining your electrical needs and planning new circuits.

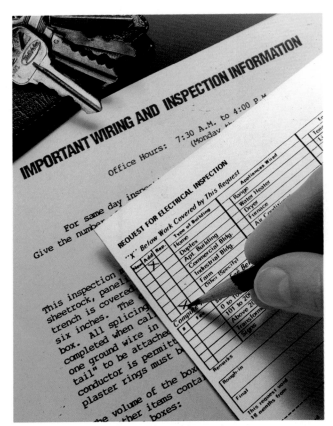

3. Prepare for inspections (pages 134 to 135). Remember that your work must be reviewed by your local electrical inspector. When planning your wiring project, always follow the inspector's guidelines for quality workmanship.

4. Evaluate electrical loads (pages 136 to 139). New circuits put an added load on your electrical service. Make sure the total load of the existing wiring and the planned new circuits does not exceed the main service capacity.

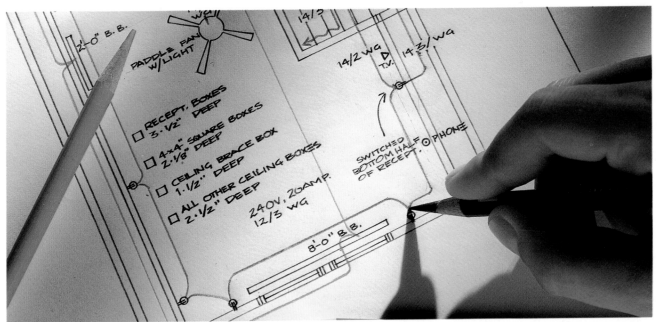

5. Draw a wiring diagram and get a permit (pages 140 to 141). Your inspector needs to see an accurate wiring diagram and materials list before he will issue a work permit for your project. This wiring plan also helps you organize your work.

1: Examine Your Main Service

The first step in planning a new wiring project is to look in your main circuit breaker panel and find the size of the service by reading the amperage rating on the main circuit breaker. As you plan new circuits and evaluate electrical loads, knowing the size of the main service helps you determine if you need a service upgrade.

Also look for open circuit breaker slots in the panel. The number of open slots will determine if you need to add a circuit breaker subpanel.

Find the service size by opening the main service panel and reading the amp rating printed on the main circuit breaker. In most cases, 100-amp service provides enough power to handle the added loads of projects like the ones shown in this book. A service rated for 60 amps or less may need to be upgraded.

Older service panels use fuses instead of circuit breakers. Have an electrician replace this type of panel with a circuit breaker panel that provides enough power and enough open breaker slots for the new circuits you are planning.

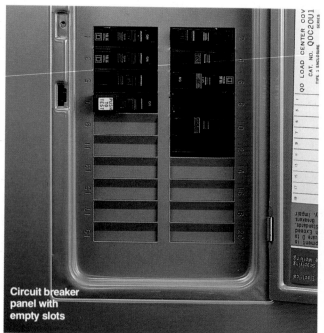

Circuit breaker panel with empty slots

Circuit breaker panel with no empty slots

Look for open circuit breaker slots in the main circuit breaker panel, or in a circuit breaker subpanel, if your home already has one. You will need one open slot for each 120-volt circuit you plan to install, and two slots for each 240-volt circuit. If your main circuit breaker panel has no open breaker slots, install a subpanel (pages 180 to 183) to provide room for connecting new circuits.

2: Learn about Codes

To ensure public safety, your community requires that you get a permit to install new wiring and have the completed work reviewed by an appointed inspector. Electrical inspectors use the National Electrical Code (NEC) as the primary authority for evaluating wiring, but they also follow the local Building Code and Electrical Code standards.

As you begin planning new circuits, call or visit your local electrical inspector and discuss the project with him. The inspector can tell you which of the national and local Code requirements apply to your job, and may give you a packet of information summarizing these regulations. Later, when you apply to the inspector for a work permit, he will expect you to understand the local guidelines as well as a few basic National Electrical Code requirements.

The National Electrical Code is a set of standards that provides minimum safety requirements for wiring installations. It is revised every three years. The national Code requirements for the projects shown in this book are thoroughly explained on the following pages. For more information, you can find copies of the current NEC, as well as a number of excellent handbooks based on the NEC, at libraries and bookstores.

In addition to being the final authority on Code requirements, inspectors are electrical professionals with years of experience. Although they have busy schedules, most inspectors are happy to answer questions and help you design well-planned circuits.

Basic Electrical Code Requirements

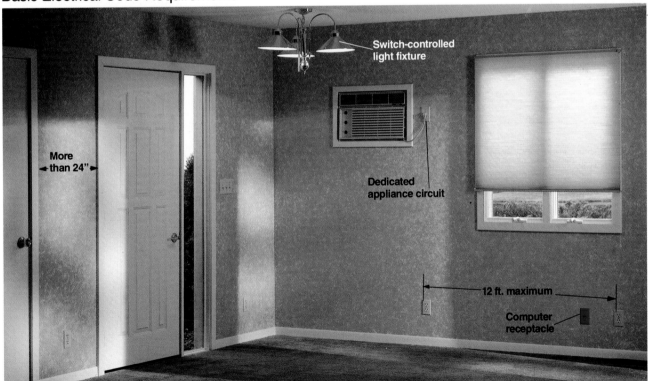

Electrical Code requirements for living areas:
Living areas need at least one 15-amp or 20-amp basic lighting/receptacle circuit for each 600 square feet of living space, and should have a "dedicated" circuit for each type of permanent appliance, like an air conditioner, computer, or a group of baseboard heaters. Receptacles on basic lighting/receptacle circuits should be spaced no more than 12 ft. apart. Many electricians and electrical inspectors recommend even closer spacing. Any wall more than 24" wide also needs a receptacle. Every room should have a wall switch at the point of entry to control either a ceiling light or plug-in lamp. Kitchens and bathrooms must have a ceiling-mounted light fixture.

(continued next page)

Measure the living areas of your home, excluding closets and unfinished spaces. A sonic measuring tool gives room dimensions quickly, and contains a built-in calculator for figuring floor area. You will need a minimum of one basic lighting/receptacle circuit for every 600 sq. ft. of living space. The total square footage also helps you determine heating and cooling needs for new room additions (page 135).

Stairways with six steps or more must have lighting that illuminates each step. The light fixture must be controlled by three-way switches at the top and bottom landings.

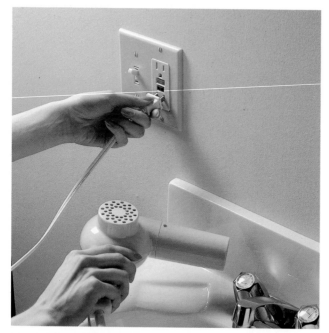

Kitchen and bathroom receptacles must be protected by a ground-fault circuit-interrupter (GFCI). Also, all outdoor receptacles and general-use receptacles in an unfinished basement or crawl space must be protected by a GFCI.

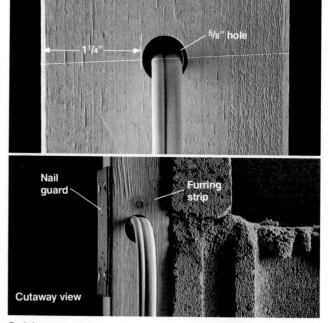

Cables must be protected against damage by nails and screws by at least 1¼" of wood (top). When cables pass through 2 × 2 furring strips (bottom), protect the cables with metal nail guards.

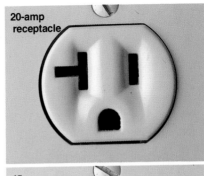

Closets and other storage spaces need at least one light fixture that is controlled by a wall switch near the entrance. Prevent fire hazards by positioning the light fixtures so the outer globes are at least 12" away from all shelf areas.

Hallways more than 10 ft. long need at least one receptacle. All hallways should have a switch-controlled light fixture.

Amp ratings of receptacles must match the size of the circuit. A common mistake is to use 20-amp receptacles (top) on 15-amp circuits—a potential cause of dangerous circuit overloads.

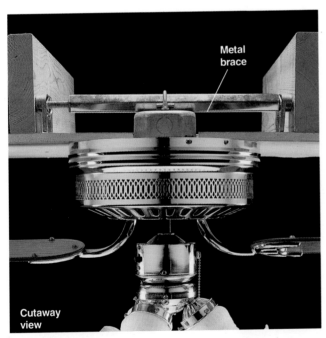

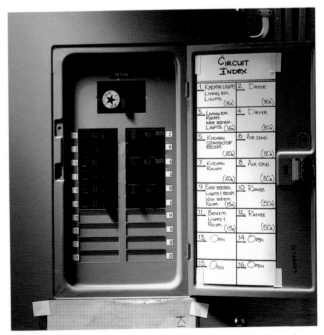

A metal brace attached to framing members is required for ceiling fans and large light fixtures that are too heavy to be supported by an electrical box.

Label new circuits on an index attached to the circuit breaker panel. List the rooms and appliances controlled by each circuit. Make sure the area around the panel is clean, well lighted, and accessible.

3: Prepare for Inspections

The electrical inspector who issues the work permit for your wiring project will also visit your home to review the work. Make sure to allow time for these inspections as you plan the project. For most projects, an inspector makes two visits.

The first inspection, called the "rough-in," is done after the cables are run between the boxes, but before the insulation, wallboard, switches, and fixtures are installed. The second inspection, called the "final," is done after the walls and ceilings are finished and all electrical connections are made.

When preparing for the rough-in inspection, make sure the area is neat. Sweep up sawdust and clean up any pieces of scrap wire or cable insulation. Before inspecting the boxes and cables, the inspector will check to make sure all plumbing and other mechanical work is completed. Some electrical inspectors will ask to see your building and plumbing permits.

At the final inspection, the inspector checks random boxes to make sure the wire connections are correct. If he sees good workmanship at the selected boxes, the inspection will be over quickly. However, if he spots a problem, the inspector may choose to inspect every connection.

Inspectors have busy schedules, so it is a good idea to arrange for an inspection several days or weeks in advance. In addition to basic compliance with Code, the inspector wants your work to meet his own standards for workmanship. When you apply for a work permit, make sure you understand what the inspector will look for during inspections.

You cannot put new circuits into use legally until the inspector approves them at the final inspection. Because the inspector is responsible for the safety of all wiring installations, his approval means that your work meets professional standards. If you have planned carefully and done your work well, electrical inspections are routine visits that give you confidence in your own skills.

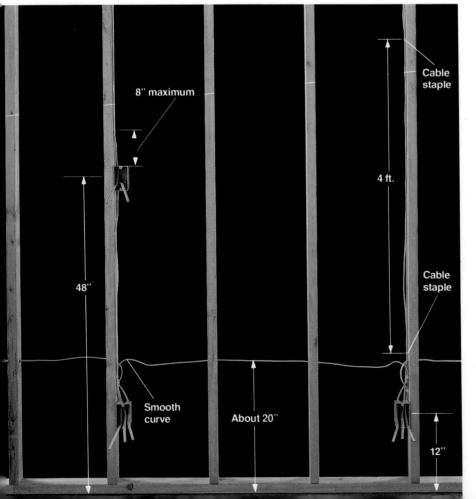

8" maximum

48"

Smooth curve

About 20"

Cable staple

4 ft.

Cable staple

12"

Inspectors measure to see that electrical boxes are mounted at consistent heights. Measured from the center of the boxes, receptacles in living areas typically are located 12" above the finished floor, and switches at 48". For special circumstances, inspectors allow you to alter these measurements. For example, you can install switches at 36" above the floor in a child's bedroom, or set receptacles at 24" to make them more convenient for someone in a wheelchair.

Your inspector will check cables to see that they are anchored by cable staples driven within 8" of each box, and every 4 ft. thereafter when they run along studs. When bending cables, form the wire in a smooth curve. Do not crimp cables sharply or install them diagonally between framing members. Some inspectors specify that cables running between receptacle boxes should be about 20" above the floor.

What Inspectors Look For

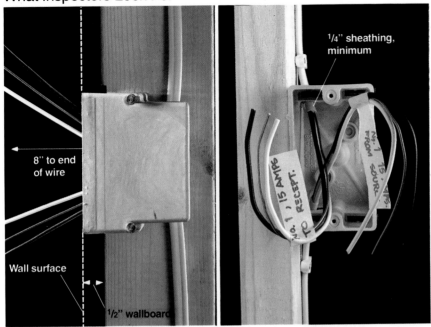

Electrical box faces should extend past the front of framing members so the boxes will be flush with finished walls (left). The inspector will check to see that all boxes are large enough for the wires they contain. Cables should be cut and stripped back so that 8" of usable length extends past the front of the box, and so that at least 1/4" of sheathing reaches into the box (right). Label all cables to show which circuits they serve: inspectors recognize this as a mark of careful work. The labels also simplify the final hookups after the wallboard is installed.

Install an isolated-ground circuit and receptacle if recommended by your inspector. An isolated-ground circuit protects sensitive electronic equipment, like a computer, against tiny current fluctuations. Computers also should be protected by a standard surge protector.

Heating & Air Conditioning Chart (compiled from manufacturers' literature)

Room Addition Living Area	Recommended Total Heating Rating	Recommended Circuit Size	Recommended Air-Conditioner Rating	Recommended Circuit Size
100 sq. feet	900 watts		5,000 BTU	
150 sq. feet	1,350 watts	15-amp (240 volts)	6,000 BTU	
200 sq. feet	1,800 watts		7,000 BTU	15-amp (120 volts)
300 sq. feet	2,700 watts		9,000 BTU	
400 sq. feet	3,600 watts	20-amp (240 volts)	10,500 BTU	
500 sq. feet	4,500 watts	30-amp (240 volts)	11,500 BTU	20-amp (120 volts)
800 sq. feet	7,200 watts	two 20-amp	17,000 BTU	15-amp (240 volts)
1,000 sq. feet	9,000 watts	two 30-amp	21,000 BTU	20-amp (240 volts)

Electric heating and air-conditioning for a new room addition will be checked by the inspector. Determine your heating and air-conditioning needs by finding the total area of the living space. Choose electric heating units with a combined wattage rating close to the chart recommendation above. Choose an air conditioner with a BTU rating close to the

chart recommendation for your room size. NOTE: These recommendations are for homes in moderately cool climates, sometimes referred to as "Zone 4" regions. Cities in Zone 4 include Denver, Chicago, and Boston. In more severe climates, check with your electrical inspector or energy agency to learn how to find heating and air-conditioning needs.

Planning a Wiring Project
4: Evaluate Electrical Loads

Before drawing a plan and applying for a work permit, make sure your home's electrical service provides enough power to handle the added load of the new circuits. In a safe wiring system, the current drawn by fixtures and appliances never exceeds the main service capacity.

To evaluate electrical loads, use the work sheet on page 139, or whatever evaluation method is recommended by your electrical inspector. Include the load for all existing wiring as well as that for proposed new wiring when making your evaluation.

Most of the light fixtures and plug-in appliances in your home are evaluated as part of general allowances for basic lighting/receptacle circuits (page 131) and small-appliance circuits. However, appliances that are permanently installed require their own "dedicated" circuits. The electrical loads for these appliances are added in separately when evaluating wiring.

If your evaluation shows that the load exceeds the main service capacity, you must have an electrician upgrade the main service before you can install new wiring. An electrical service upgrade is a worthwhile investment that improves the value of your home and provides plenty of power for present and future wiring projects.

Tips for Evaluating Appliance Loads

Add 1500 watts for each small appliance circuit required by the local Electrical Code. In most communities, three such circuits are required—two in the kitchen and one for the laundry—for a total of 4500 watts. No further calculations are needed for appliances that plug into small-appliance or basic lighting/receptacle circuits.

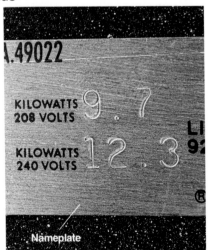

Find wattage ratings for permanent appliances by reading the manufacturer's nameplate. If the nameplate gives the rating in kilowatts, find the watts by multiplying kilowatts times 1000. If an appliance lists only amps, find watts by multiplying the amps times the voltage—either 120 or 240 volts.

Electric water heaters are permanent appliances that require their own dedicated 30-amp, 240-volt circuits. Most water heaters are rated between 3500 and 4500 watts. If the nameplate lists several wattage ratings, use the one labeled "total connected wattage" when figuring electrical loads.

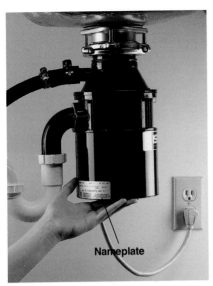

Food disposers are considered permanent appliances and require their own dedicated 15-amp, 120-volt circuits. Most disposers are rated between 500 and 900 watts.

Dishwashers installed permanently under a countertop need dedicated 15-amp, 120-volt circuits. Dishwasher ratings are usually between 1000 and 1500 watts. Portable dishwashers are regarded as part of small appliance circuits, and are not added in when figuring loads.

Electric ranges can be rated for as little as 3000 watts or as much as 12,000 watts. They require dedicated 120/240-volt circuits. Find the exact wattage rating by reading the nameplate, found inside the oven door or on the back of the unit.

Microwave ovens are regarded by many local Codes as permanent appliances. If your inspector asks you to install a separate 20-amp, 120-volt circuit for the microwave oven, add in its wattage rating when calculating loads. The nameplate is found on the back of the cabinet or inside the front door. Most microwave ovens are rated between 500 and 800 watts.

Freezers are permanent appliances that require dedicated 15-amp, 120-volt circuits. Freezer ratings are usually between 500 and 600 watts. But combination refrigerator-freezers rated for 1000 watts or less are plugged into small appliance circuits and do not need their own dedicated circuits. The nameplate for a freezer is found inside the door or on the back of the unit, just below the door seal.

Electric clothes dryers are permanent appliances that need dedicated 30-amp, 120/240-volt circuits. The wattage rating, usually between 4500 and 5500 watts, is printed on the nameplate inside the dryer door. Washing machines, and gas-heat clothes dryers with electric tumbler motors, do not need dedicated circuits. They plug into the 20-amp small-appliance circuit in the laundry.

(continued next page)

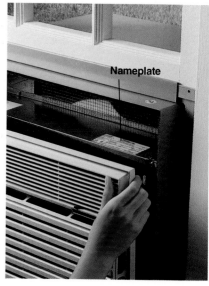

Forced-air furnaces have electric fans, and are considered permanent appliances. They require dedicated 15-amp, 120-volt circuits. Include the fan wattage rating, printed on a nameplate inside the control panel, when figuring wattage loads for heating.

A central air conditioner requires a dedicated 240-volt circuit. Its wattage rating, usually between 2300 and 5500 watts, is printed on a metal plate near the electrical hookup panel. If the air conditioner relies on a furnace fan for circulation, add the fan wattage rating to the air-conditioner rating.

Window air conditioners, both 120-volt and 240-volt types, are permanent appliances that require dedicated 15-amp or 20-amp circuits. The wattage rating, which can range from 500 to 2000 watts, is found on the nameplate located inside the front grill. Make sure to include all window air conditioners in your evaluation.

Electric room heaters that are permanently installed require a dedicated circuit, and must be figured into the load calculations. Use the maximum wattage rating printed inside the cover. As a general rule, 240-volt baseboard-type heaters are rated for about 250 watts for each linear foot.

Air-conditioning and heating appliances are not used at the same time, so figure in only the larger of these two numbers when evaluating your home's electrical load.

Outdoor receptacles and fixtures are not included in basic lighting calculations. When evaluating electrical loads, add in the nameplate wattage rating for each outdoor light fixture, and add in 180 watts for each outdoor receptacle. Receptacles and light fixtures in garages also are considered to be outdoor fixtures when evaluating loads.

How to Evaluate Electrical Loads (photocopy this work sheet as a guide; blue sample calculations will not reproduce)

1. Find the basic lighting/receptacle load by multiplying the square footage of all living areas (including any room additions) times 3 watts.	Existing space: _1100_ square ft. New additions: _400_ square ft. _1500_ total square ft. × 3 watts =	4500 watts
2. Add 1500 watts for each kitchen small-appliance circuit and for the laundry circuit.	_3_ circuits × 1500 watts =	4500 watts
3. Add ratings for permanent electrical appliances, including: range, food disposer, dishwasher, freezer, water heater, and clothes dryer.	RANGE 12.3 K.W. = 12,300 WATTS	12,300 watts
	DRYER 5000	5,000 watts
	DISHWASHER 1200	1,200 watts
	FREEZER 550	550 watts
	FOOD DISPOSER 800	800 watts
Find total wattages for the furnace and heating units, and for air conditioners. Add in only the larger of these numbers.	Furnace heat: _1,200_ watts Space heaters: _5,450_ watts Total heating = _6,650_ watts	6,650 watts
	Central air conditioner: _3500_ watts Window air conditioners: _1,100_ watts Total cooling = _4,600_ watts	
4. For outdoor fixtures (including those in garages) find the nameplate wattage ratings.	Total fixture watts =	650 watts
Multiply the number of outdoor receptacles (including those in garages) times 180 watts.	_3_ receptacles × 180 watts =	540 watts
5. Total the wattages to find the gross load.		36,690 watts
6. Figure the first 10,000 watts of the gross load at 100%.	100% × 10,000 = 10,000	10,000 watts
7. Subtract 10,000 watts from the gross load, then figure the remaining load at 40%.	_36,690_ watts - 10,000 = _26,690_ watts _26,690_ watts × .40 =	10,676 watts
8. Add steps 6 and 7 to estimate the true electrical load.		20,676 watts
9. Convert the estimated true electrical load to amps by dividing by 230.	_20,676_ watts ÷ 230 =	89.9 amps
10. Compare the load with the amp rating of your home's electrical service, printed on the main circuit breaker (page 130). If the load is less than main circuit breaker rating, the system is safe. If the load exceeds the main circuit breaker rating, your service should be upgraded.	OK ☑ Upgrade ☐	

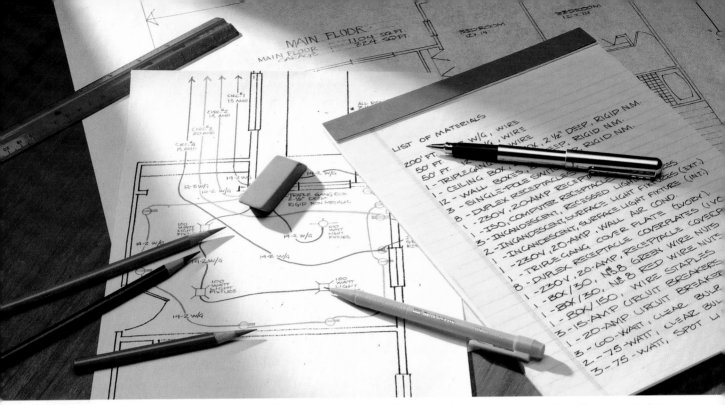

A detailed wiring diagram and a list of materials is required before your electrical inspector will issue a work permit. If blueprints exist for the space you are remodeling, start your electrical diagram by tracing the wall outlines from the blueprint. Use standard electrical symbols (page opposite) to clearly show all the receptacles, switches, light fixtures, and permanent appliances. Make a copy of the symbol key, and attach it to the wiring diagram for the inspector's convenience. Show each cable run, and label its wire size and circuit amperage.

Planning a Wiring Project

5: Draw a Wiring Diagram & Get a Permit

Drawing a wiring diagram is the last step in planning a circuit installation. A detailed wiring diagram helps you get a work permit, makes it easy to create a list of materials, and serves as a guide for laying out circuits and installing cables and fixtures. Use the circuit maps on pages 142 to 153 as a guide for planning wiring configurations and cable runs. Bring the diagram and materials list when you visit the electrical inspector to apply for a work permit.

Never install new wiring without following your community's permit and inspection procedure. A work permit is not expensive, and it ensures that your work will be reviewed by a qualified inspector to guarantee its safety. If you install new wiring without the proper permit, an accident or fire traced to faulty wiring could cause your insurance company to discontinue your policy, and can hurt the resale value of your home.

When the electrical inspector looks over your wiring diagram, he will ask questions to see if you have a basic understanding of the Electrical Code and fundamental wiring skills. Some inspectors ask these questions informally, while others give a short written test. The inspector may allow you to do some, but not all, of the work. For example, he may ask that all final circuit connections at the circuit breaker panel be made by a licensed electrician, while allowing you to do all other work.

A few communities allow you to install wiring only when supervised by an electrician. This means you can still install your own wiring, but must hire an electrician to apply for the work permit and to check your work before the inspector reviews it. The electrician is held responsible for the quality of the job.

Remember that it is your inspector's responsibility to help you do a safe and professional job. Feel free to call him with questions about wiring techniques or materials.

How to Draw a Wiring Plan

1 Draw a scaled diagram of the space you will be wiring, showing walls, doors, windows, plumbing pipes and fixtures, and heating and cooling ducts. Find the floor space by multiplying room length by width, and indicate this on the diagram. Do not include closets or storage areas when figuring space.

2 Mark the location of all switches, receptacles, light fixtures, and permanent appliances, using the electrical symbols shown below. Where you locate these devices along the cable run determines how they are wired. Use the circuit maps on pages 142 to 153 as a guide for drawing wiring diagrams.

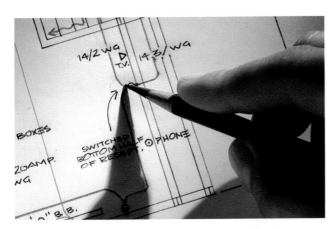

3 Draw in cable runs between devices. Indicate cable size and type, and the amperage of the circuits. Use a different-colored pencil for each circuit.

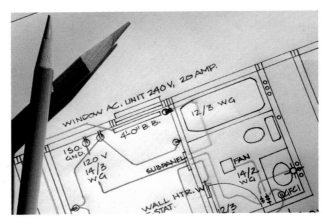

4 Identify the wattages for light fixtures and permanent appliances, and the type and size of each electrical box. On another sheet of paper, make a detailed list of all materials you will use.

Electrical Symbol Key (copy this key and attach it to your wiring plan)

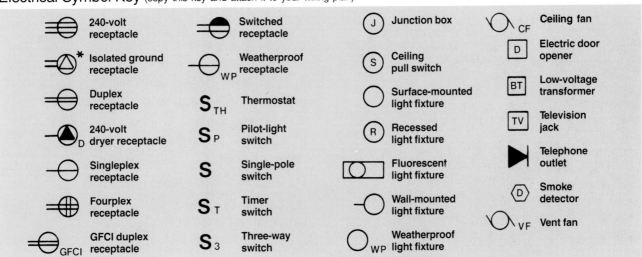

240-volt receptacle	Switched receptacle	J Junction box
Isolated ground receptacle *	Weatherproof receptacle WP	S Ceiling pull switch
Duplex receptacle	S TH Thermostat	Surface-mounted light fixture
240-volt dryer receptacle D	S P Pilot-light switch	R Recessed light fixture
Singleplex receptacle	S Single-pole switch	Fluorescent light fixture
Fourplex receptacle	S T Timer switch	Wall-mounted light fixture
GFCI duplex receptacle GFCI	S 3 Three-way switch	Weatherproof light fixture WP

Ceiling fan CF
D Electric door opener
BT Low-voltage transformer
TV Television jack
Telephone outlet
D Smoke detector
VF Vent fan

141

Ampacity: A measurement of how many amps can be safely carried by a wire or cable. Ampacity varies according to the diameter of the wire (page 163).

Common wire: The hot circuit wire that brings current from the power source to a three-way switch, or that carries current from a three-way switch to a light fixture. A common wire is always connected to the darker screw terminal on the switch, sometimes labeled COMMON.

Dedicated circuit: An electrical circuit that serves only one appliance or series of electric heaters.

EMT: *Electrical Metallic Tubing.* A type of metal conduit used for exposed indoor wiring installations, such as wiring in an unfinished basement.

Feeder cable: The length of cable that carries power from the main circuit breaker panel to the first electrical box in a circuit, or from the main panel to a circuit breaker subpanel. Also known as a *home run.*

GFCI: A duplex receptacle or circuit breaker rated as a *Ground-Fault Circuit-Interrupter.* GFCI receptacles provide extra protection against shock and are required by Code in some locations.

Home run: See *Feeder cable*

IMC: *Intermediate Metallic Conduit.* Sturdier than EMT, IMC conduit is used for exposed wiring both indoors and outdoors.

Isolated-ground circuit: A 120-volt circuit installed with three-wire cable that protects sensitive electronic equipment, like a computer, against power surges.

Isolated-ground receptacle: A special-use receptacle, orange in color, with an insulated grounding screw. Used to protect computers or other sensitive electronic equipment against power surges.

Line side wires: Circuit wires that extend "upstream" from an electrical box, toward the power source.

Load side wires: Circuit wires extending "downstream" from an electrical box toward end of circuit.

NM cable: *Non-Metallic sheathed cable.* The standard cable used for indoor wiring inside finished walls.

Pigtail: A short length of wire used to join two or more circuit wires to the same screw terminal on a receptacle, switch, or metal electrical box. Pigtails are color-coded to match the wires they are connected to.

PVC: *Poly-Vinyl Chloride.* A durable plastic used for electrical boxes and conduit. Can be used instead of metal conduit to protect outdoor wiring.

Shared Neutral: When two 120-volt small-appliance circuits are wired using a single three-wire cable, the white circuit wire is a *shared neutral* that serves both circuits.

Split receptacle: A duplex receptacle in which the connecting tab linking the brass screw terminals has been broken. A split receptacle is required when one half of a duplex receptacle is controlled by a switch, or when each half is controlled by a different circuit.

THHN/THWN wires: The type of wire that is recommended for installation inside metal or plastic conduit. Available as individual conductors with color-coded insulation.

Three-wire cable: Sheathed cable with one black, one white, and one red insulated conductor, plus a bare copper grounding wire.

Traveler wires: In a three-way switch configuration, two *traveler wires* run between the pairs of traveler screw terminals on the three-way switches.

Two-wire cable: Sheathed cable with one black and one white insulated conductor plus a bare copper grounding wire.

UF Cable: *Underground Feeder* cable. Used for outdoor wiring, UF cable is rated for direct contact with soil.

Circuit Maps for 24 Common Wiring Layouts

The arrangement of switches and appliances along an electrical circuit differs for every project. This means that the configuration of wires inside an electrical box can vary greatly, even when fixtures are identical.

The circuit maps on the following pages show the most common wiring variations for typical electrical devices. Most new wiring you install will match one or more of the examples shown. By finding the examples that match your situation, you can use these maps to plan circuit layouts.

The 120-volt circuits shown on the following pages are wired for 15 amps, using 14-gauge wire and receptacles rated at 15 amps. If you are installing a 20-amp circuit, substitute 12-gauge cables and use receptacles rated for 20 amps.

In configurations where a white wire serves as a hot wire instead of a neutral, both ends of the wire are coded with black tape to identify it as hot. In addition, each of the circuit maps shows a box grounding screw. This grounding screw is required in all metal boxes, but plastic electrical boxes do not need to be grounded.

NOTE: For clarity, all grounding conductors in the circuit maps are colored green. In practice, the grounding wires inside sheathed cables usually are bare copper.

1. 120-volt Duplex Receptacles Wired in Sequence

Use this layout to link any number of duplex receptacles in a basic lighting/receptacle circuit. The last receptacle in the cable run is connected like the receptacle shown at the right side of the circuit map below. All other receptacles are wired like the receptacle shown on the left side. Requires two-wire cables.

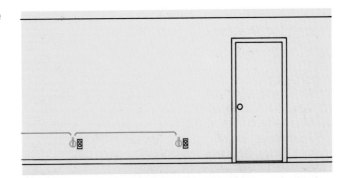

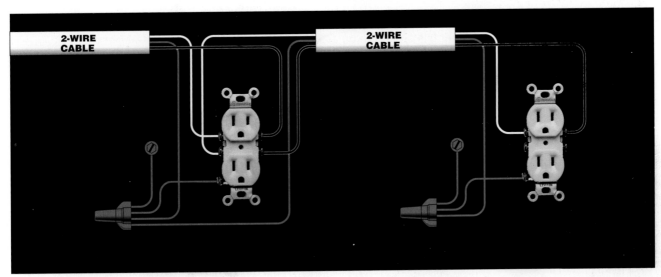

2-WIRE CABLE

2-WIRE CABLE

2. GFCI Receptacles (Single-location Protection)

Use this layout when receptacles are within 6 ft. of a water source, like those in kitchens and bathrooms. To prevent "nuisance tripping" caused by normal power surges, GFCIS should be connected only at the LINE screw terminal, so they protect a single location, not the fixtures on the LOAD side of the circuit. Requires two-wire cables. Where a GFCI must protect other fixtures, use circuit map 3.

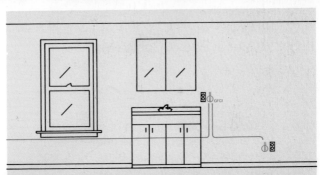

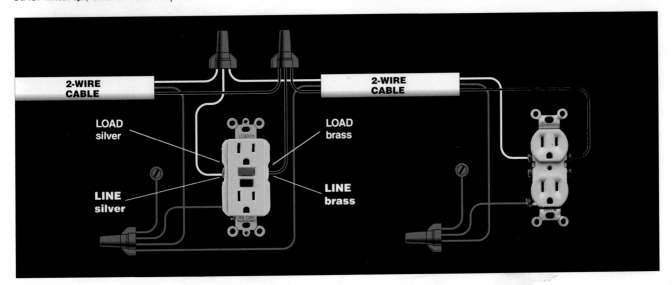

2-WIRE CABLE

2-WIRE CABLE

LOAD silver

LOAD brass

LINE silver

LINE brass

3. GFCI Receptacle, Switch & Light Fixture
(Wired for Multiple-location Protection)

In some locations, such as an outdoor circuit, it is a good idea to connect a GFCI receptacle so it also provides shock protection to the wires and fixtures that continue to the end of the circuit. Wires from the power source are connected to the LINE screw terminals; outgoing wires are connected to LOAD screws. Requires two-wire cables.

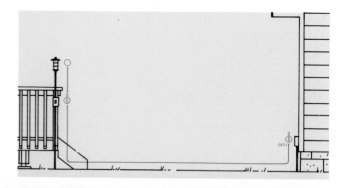

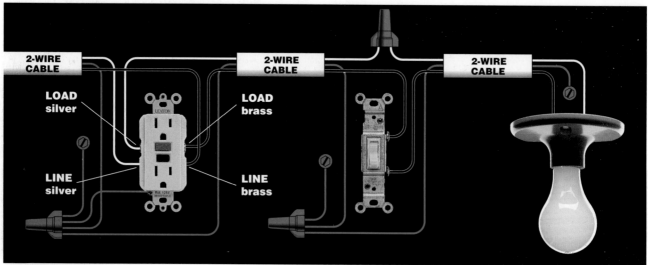

4. Single-pole Switch & Light Fixture
(Light Fixture at End of Cable Run)

Use this layout for light fixtures in basic lighting/receptacle circuits throughout the home. It is often used as an extension to a series of receptacles (circuit map 1). Requires two-wire cables.

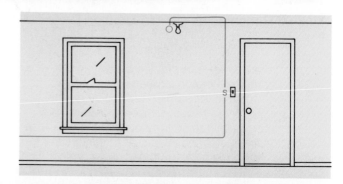

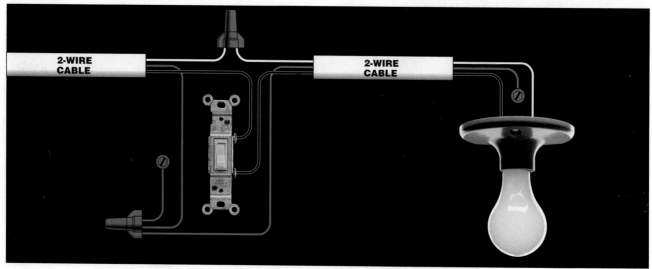

5. Single-pole Switch & Light Fixture (Switch at End of Cable Run)

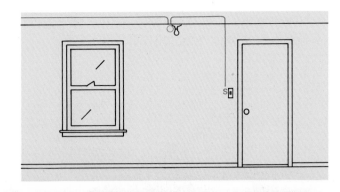

Use this layout, sometimes called a "switch loop," where it is more practical to locate a switch at the end of the cable run. In the last length of cable, both insulated wires are hot; the white wire is tagged with black tape at both ends to indicate it is hot. Requires two-wire cables.

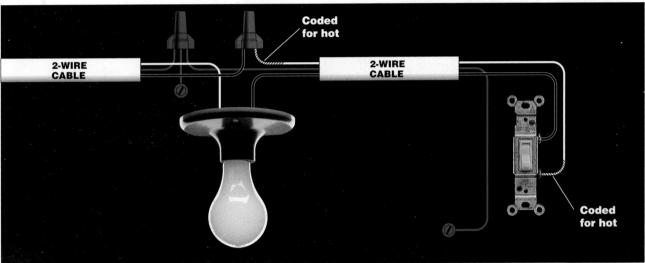

6. Single-pole Switch & Light Fixture, Duplex Receptacle (Switch at Start of Cable Run)

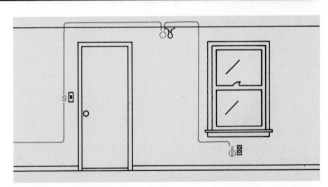

Use this layout to continue a circuit past a switched light fixture to one or more duplex receptacles. To add multiple receptacles to the circuit, see circuit map 1. Requires two-wire and three-wire cables.

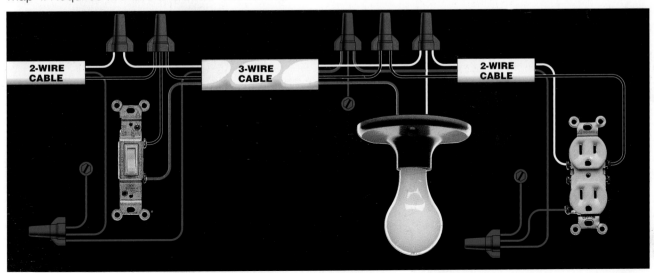

7. Switch-controlled Split Receptacle, Duplex Receptacle (Switch at Start of Cable Run)

This layout lets you use a wall switch to control a lamp plugged into a wall receptacle. This configuration is required by Code for any room that does not have a switch-controlled ceiling fixture. Only the bottom half of the first receptacle is controlled by the wall switch; the top half of the receptacle and all additional receptacles on the circuit are always hot. Requires two-wire and three-wire cables.

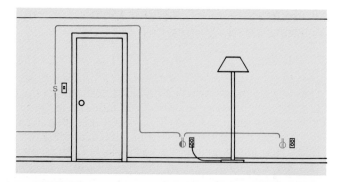

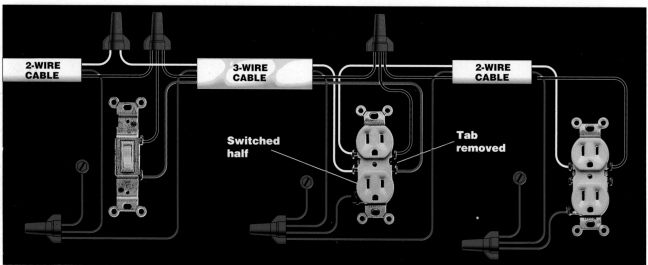

8. Switch-controlled Split Receptacle (Switch at End of Cable Run)

Use this "switch loop" layout to control a split receptacle (see circuit map 7) from an end-of-run circuit location. The bottom half of the receptacle is controlled by the wall switch, while the top half is always hot. White circuit wire attached to the switch is tagged with black tape to indicate it is hot. Requires two-wire cable.

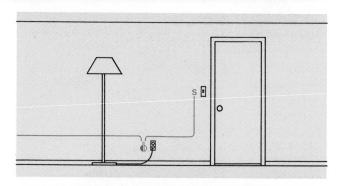

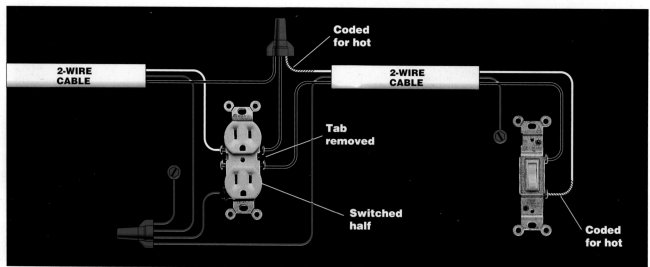

9. Switch-controlled Split Receptacle, Duplex Receptacle (Split Receptacle at Start of Run)

Use this variation of circuit map 7 where it is more practical to locate a switch-controlled receptacle at the start of a cable run. Only the bottom half of the first receptacle is controlled by the wall switch; the top half of the receptacle, and all other receptacles on the circuit, are always hot. Requires two-wire and three-wire cables.

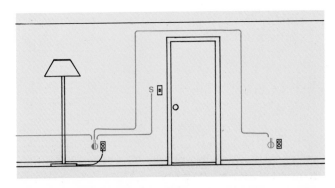

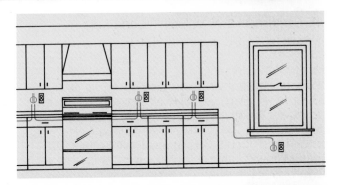

10. Double Receptacle Circuit with Shared Neutral Wire (Receptacles Alternate Circuits)

This layout features two 120-volt circuits wired with one three-wire cable connected to a double-pole circuit breaker. The black hot wire powers one circuit, the red wire powers the other. The white wire is a shared neutral that serves both circuits. When wired with 12/2 and 12/3 cable, and receptacles rated for 20 amps, this layout can be used for the two small-appliance circuits required in a kitchen.

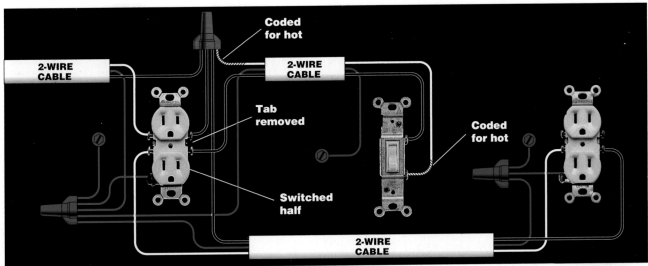

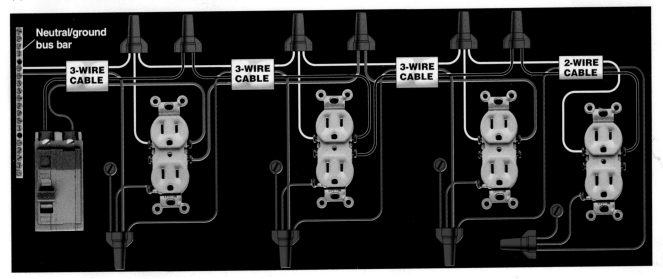

11. Double Receptacle Circuit with GFCIs & Shared Neutral Wire

Use this layout variation of circuit map 10 to wire a double receptacle circuit when Code requires that some of the receptacles be GFCIs. The GFCIs should be wired for single-location protection (see circuit map 2). Requires three-wire and two-wire cables.

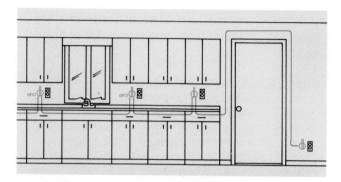

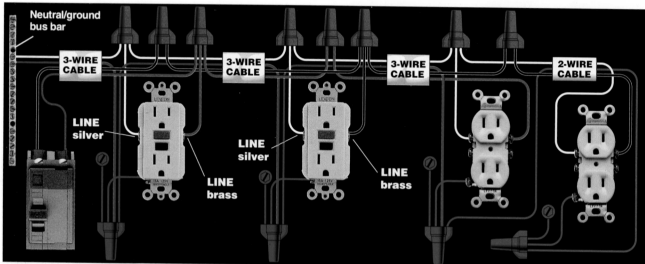

12. 240-volt Appliance Receptacle

This layout represents a 20-amp, 240-volt dedicated appliance circuit wired with 12/2 cable, as required by Code for a large window air conditioner. Receptacles are available in both singleplex (shown) and duplex styles. The black and white circuit wires connected to a double-pole breaker each bring 120 volts of power to the receptacle. The white wire is tagged with black tape to indicate it is hot.

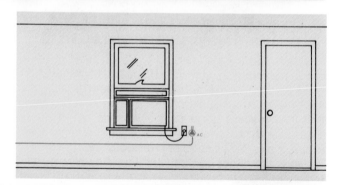

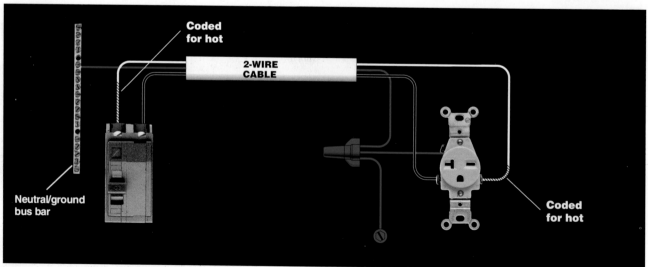

13. 240-volt Baseboard Heaters, Thermostat

This layout is typical for a series of 240-volt base-board heaters controlled by wall thermostat. Except for the last heater in the circuit, all heaters are wired as shown below. The last heater is connected to only one cable. The size of the circuit and cables are determined by finding the total wattage of all heaters (page 135). Requires two-wire cable.

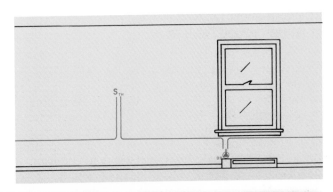

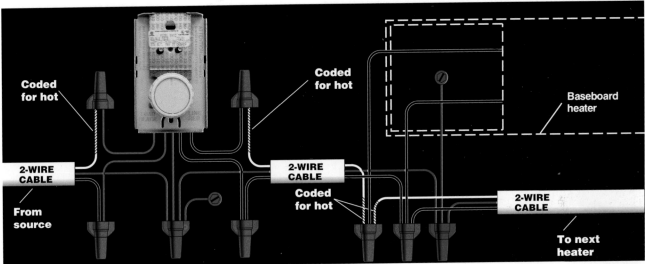

14. 120/240-volt Appliance Receptacle

This layout is for a 50-amp, 120/240-volt dedicated appliance circuit wired with 6/3 cable, as required by Code for a large kitchen range. The black and red circuit wires, connected to a double-pole circuit breaker in the circuit breaker panel, each bring 120 volts of power to the setscrew terminals on the recep-tacle. The white circuit wire attached to the neutral bus bar in the circuit breaker panel is connected to the neutral setscrew terminal on the receptacle.

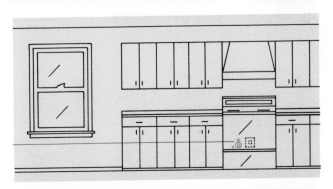

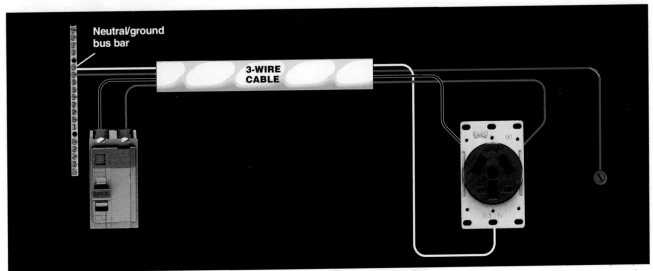

15. Dedicated 120-volt Computer Circuit, Isolated-ground Receptacle

This 15-amp circuit provides extra protection against power surges that can harm computers. It uses 14/3 cable in which the red wire serves as an extra grounding conductor. The red wire is tagged with green tape for identification. It is connected to the grounding screw on an "isolated-ground" receptacle, and runs back to the grounding bus bar in the circuit breaker panel without touching any other house wiring.

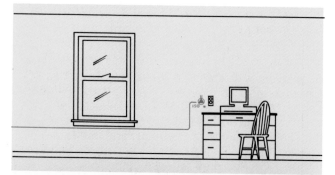

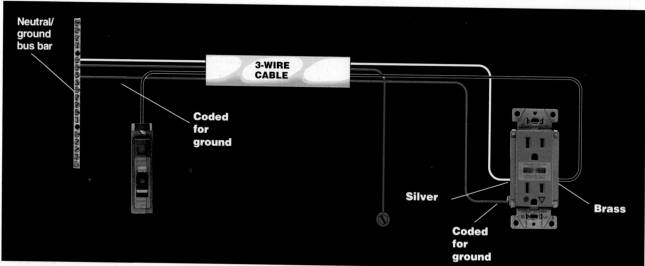

16. Ganged Single-pole Switches Controlling Separate Light Fixtures

This layout lets you place two switches controlled by the same 120-volt circuit in one double-gang electrical box. A single feed cable provides power to both switches. A similar layout with two feed cables can be used to place switches from different circuits in the same box. Requires two-wire cable.

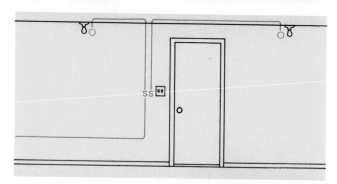

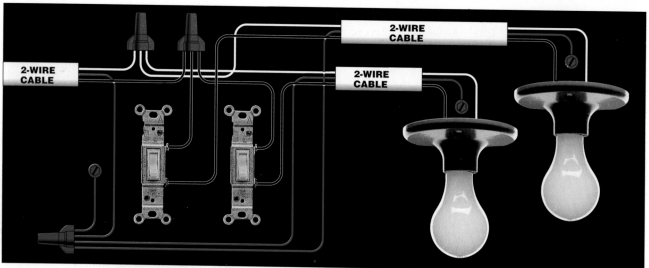

17. Three-way Switches & Light Fixture
(Fixture Between Switches)

This layout for three-way switches lets you control a light fixture from two locations. Each switch has one COMMON screw terminal and two TRAVELER screws. Circuit wires attached to the TRAVELER screws run between the two switches, and hot wires attached to the COMMON screws bring current from the power source and carry it to the light fixture. Requires two-wire and three-wire cables.

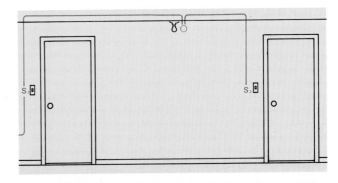

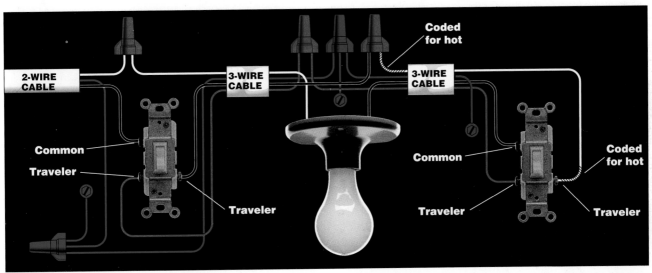

18. Three-way Switches & Light Fixture
(Fixture at Start of Cable Run)

Use this layout variation of circuit map 17 where it is more convenient to locate the fixture ahead of the three-way switches in the cable run. Requires two-wire and three-wire cables.

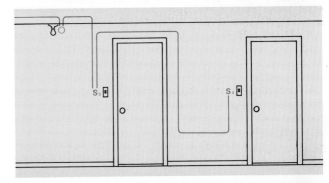

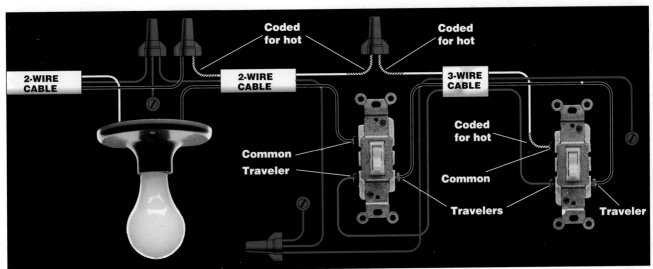

19. Three-way Switches & Light Fixture (Fixture at End of Cable Run)

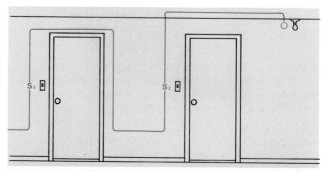

This alternate variation of the three-way switch layout (circuit map 17) is used where it is more practical to locate the fixture at the end of the cable run. Requires two-wire and three-wire cables.

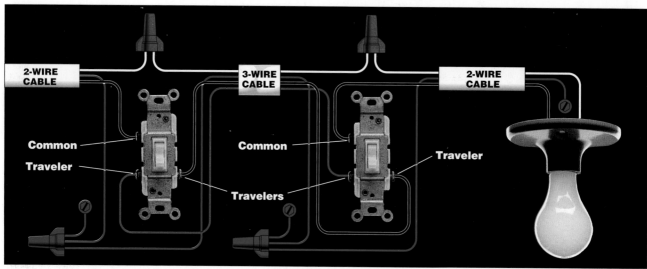

20. Three-way Switches & Light Fixture with Duplex Receptacle

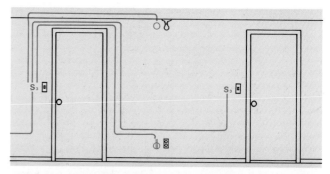

Use this layout to add a receptacle to a three-way switch configuration (circuit map 17). Requires two-wire and three-wire cables.

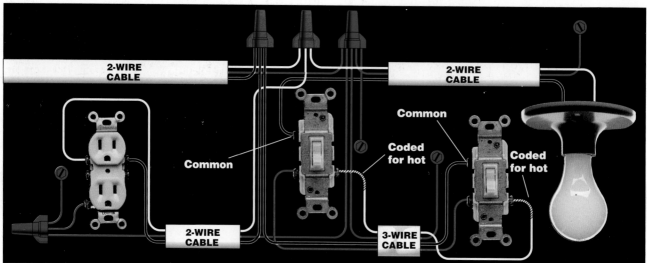

21. Ceiling Fan/Light Fixture Controlled by Ganged Switches (Fan at End of Cable Run)

This layout is for a combination ceiling fan/light fixture, controlled by a speed-control switch and dimmer in a double-gang switch box. Requires two-wire and three-wire cables.

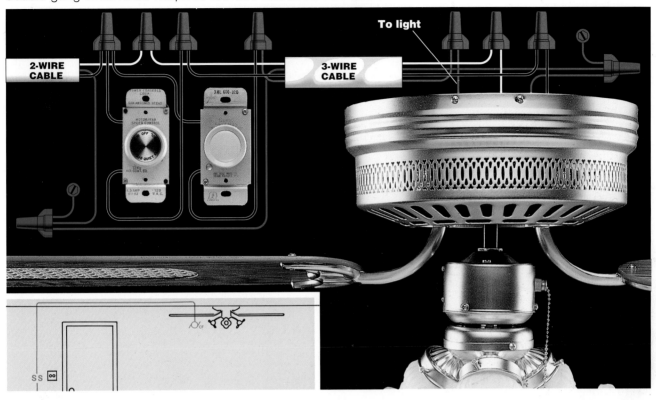

22. Ceiling Fan/Light Fixture Controlled by Ganged Switches (Switches at End of Cable Run)

Use this "switch loop" layout variation when it is more practical to install the ganged speed control and dimmer switches for the ceiling fan at the end of the cable run. Requires two-wire and three-wire cables.

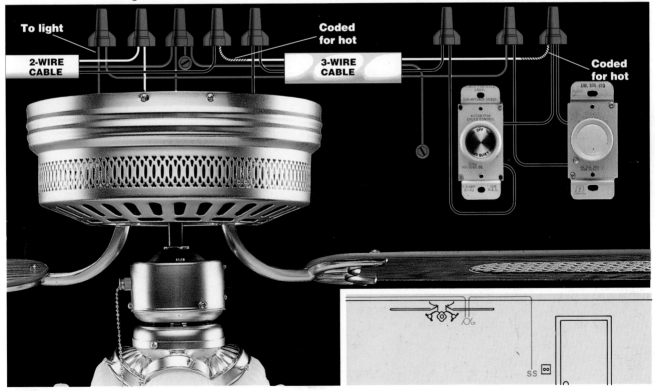

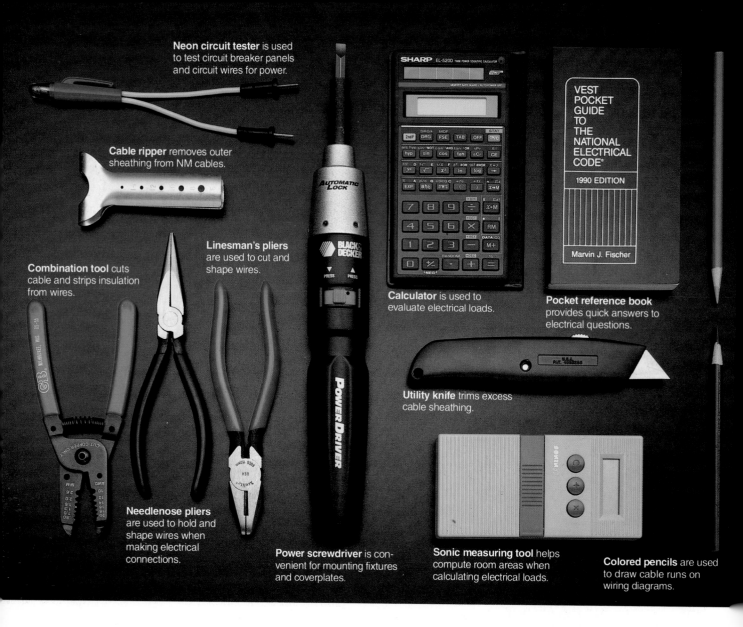

Neon circuit tester is used to test circuit breaker panels and circuit wires for power.

Cable ripper removes outer sheathing from NM cables.

Linesman's pliers are used to cut and shape wires.

Combination tool cuts cable and strips insulation from wires.

Calculator is used to evaluate electrical loads.

Pocket reference book provides quick answers to electrical questions.

Utility knife trims excess cable sheathing.

Needlenose pliers are used to hold and shape wires when making electrical connections.

Power screwdriver is convenient for mounting fixtures and coverplates.

Sonic measuring tool helps compute room areas when calculating electrical loads.

Colored pencils are used to draw cable runs on wiring diagrams.

Tools, Materials & Techniques for Projects

To complete the wiring projects shown in this book, you need a few specialty electrical tools (above), as well as a basic collection of hand tools (page opposite). As with any tool purchase, invest in good-quality products when you buy tools for electrical work. Keep your tools clean, and sharpen or replace any cutting tools that have dull edges.

The materials used for electrical wiring have changed dramatically in the last 20 years, making it much easier for homeowners to do their own electrical work. The following pages show how to work with the following components for your projects:

- Electrical Boxes: Projects (pages 156 to 161).
- Wires & Cables: Projects (pages 162 to 169).
- Conduit (pages 170 to 175).
- Circuit Breaker Panels (pages 176 to 177).
- Circuit Breakers (pages 178 to 179).
- Subpanels (pages 176 to 177, 180 to 183).

Plastic electrical boxes for indoor installations are ideal for do-it-yourself electrical work. They have preattached mounting nails for easy installation and are much less expensive than metal boxes.

Screwdrivers with insulated handles are used to assemble fixtures and make wire connections.

Nut driver and adjustable wrench are used to assemble and mount electrical fixtures.

Tool belt keeps a wide variety of tools within easy reach.

Electrical tapes are used for marking wires and for attaching cables to a fish tape.

Tape measure is used to position electrical boxes and determine cable lengths.

A fish tape is useful for installing cables in finished wall cavities and for pulling wires through conduit. Products designed for lubrication reduce friction and make it easier to pull cables and wires.

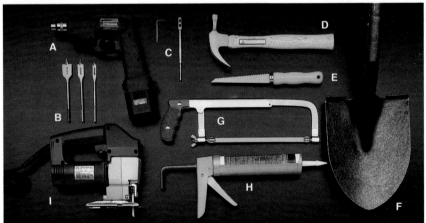

These basic tools are used for advanced wiring projects: drill (A), spade bits (B), and drill bit extension (C) for boring holes in framing members; hammer (D) for attaching electrical boxes; wallboard saw (E) for making cutouts in indoor walls; shovel (F) to dig trenches for outdoor wiring; hacksaw (G) for cutting conduit; caulk gun (H) for sealing gaps in exterior walls; jig saw (I) for making wall cutouts.

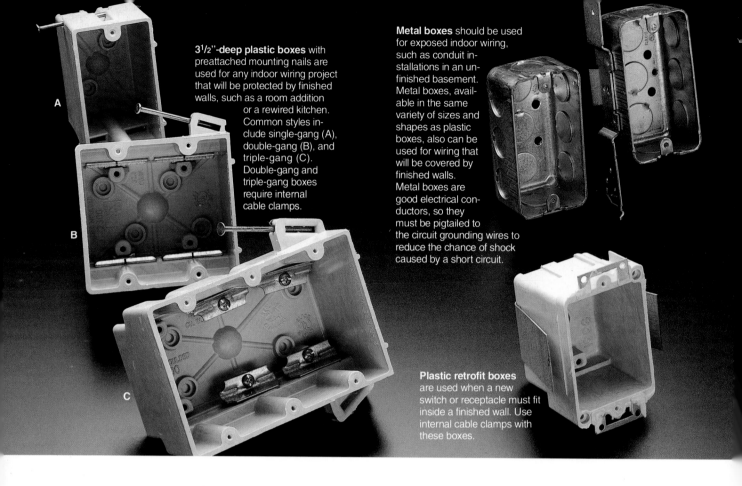

3¹/₂"-deep plastic boxes with preattached mounting nails are used for any indoor wiring project that will be protected by finished walls, such as a room addition or a rewired kitchen. Common styles include single-gang (A), double-gang (B), and triple-gang (C). Double-gang and triple-gang boxes require internal cable clamps.

Metal boxes should be used for exposed indoor wiring, such as conduit installations in an unfinished basement. Metal boxes, available in the same variety of sizes and shapes as plastic boxes, also can be used for wiring that will be covered by finished walls. Metal boxes are good electrical conductors, so they must be pigtailed to the circuit grounding wires to reduce the chance of shock caused by a short circuit.

Plastic retrofit boxes are used when a new switch or receptacle must fit inside a finished wall. Use internal cable clamps with these boxes.

Electrical Boxes: Projects

Use the chart below to select the proper type of box for your wiring project. For most indoor wiring done with NM cable, use plastic electrical boxes. Plastic boxes are inexpensive, lightweight, and easy to install.

Metal boxes also can be used for indoor NM cable installations and are still favored by some electricians, especially for supporting heavy ceiling light fixtures.

If you have choice of box depths, always choose the deepest size available. Wire connections are easier to make if boxes are roomy. Check with your local inspector if you have questions regarding the proper box size to use.

Box type	Typical Uses
Plastic	• Protected indoor wiring, used with NM cable • Not suited for heavy light fixtures and fans
Metal	• Exposed indoor wiring, used with metal conduit • Protected indoor wiring, used with NM cable
Cast aluminum	• Outdoor wiring, used with metal conduit
PVC plastic	• Outdoor wiring, used with PVC conduit • Exposed indoor wiring, used with PVC conduit

Tips for Using Electrical Boxes

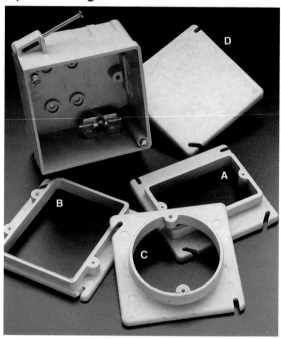

A square plastic box, 4" × 4" × 3" deep, provides extra space for making wire connections. It has preattached nails for easy mounting. A variety of adapter plates are available for 4" × 4" boxes, including single-gang (A), double-gang (B), light fixture (C), and junction box coverplate (D). Adapter plates come in several thicknesses to match different wall constructions.

Plastic retrofit light fixture box lets you install a new fixture in an existing wall or ceiling.

Plastic light fixture boxes with brace bars let you position a fixture between framing members.

Metal light fixture boxes with heavy-duty brace bars are recommended when installing heavy light fixtures or hanging a ceiling fan.

Cast aluminum boxes are required for outdoor electrical fixtures connected with metal conduit. Cast aluminum boxes have sealed seams and threaded openings to keep moisture out. A variety of weatherproof coverplates are available, including duplex receptacle plates (A), GFCI receptacle plates (B), and switch plates.

PVC plastic boxes are used with PVC conduit in outdoor wiring and exposed indoor wiring. Many local codes now allow the use of PVC plastic boxes. PVC coverplates are available to fit switches, standard duplex receptacles, and GFCI receptacles.

Boxes larger than 2" × 4", and all retrofit boxes, must have internal cable clamps. After installing cables in the box, tighten the cable clamps over the cables so they are gripped firmly, but not so tightly that the cable sheathing is crushed.

Metal boxes must be grounded to the curcuit grounding system. Connect the circuit grounding wires to the box with a green insulated pigtail wire and wire nut (as shown) or with a grounding clip (page 170).

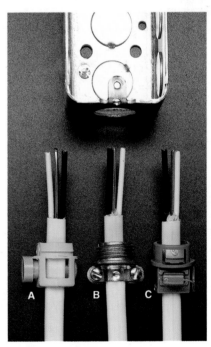

Cables entering a metal box must be clamped. A variety of clamps are available, including plastic clamps (A, C) and threaded metal clamps (B).

157

Installing Electrical Boxes

Install electrical boxes for receptacles, switches, and fixtures only after your wiring project plan has been approved by your inspector. Use your wiring plan as a guide, and follow electrical Code height and spacing guidelines when laying out box positions.

Always use the deepest electrical boxes that are practical for your installation. Using deep boxes ensures that you will meet Code regulations regarding box volume, and makes it easier to make the wire connections.

Some electrical fixtures, like recessed light fixtures, electric heaters, and exhaust fans, have built-in wire connection boxes. Install the frames for these fixtures at the same time you are installing the other electrical boxes.

Electrical boxes in adjacent rooms should be positioned close together when they share a common wall and are controlled by the same circuit. This simplifies the cable installations and also reduces the amount of cable needed.

Fixtures That Do Not Need Electrical Boxes

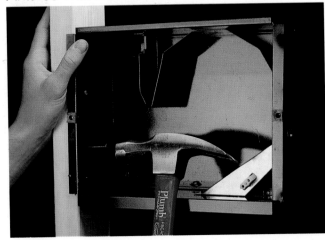

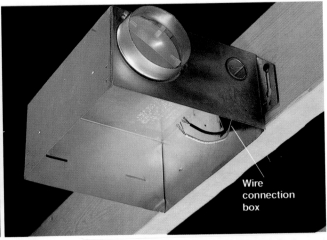

Wire connection box

Recessed fixtures that fit inside wall cavities have built-in wire connection boxes, and require no additional electrical boxes. Common recessed fixtures include electric blower-heaters (above, left), bathroom vent fans (above, right), and recessed light fixtures (page 222). Install the frames for these fixtures at the same time you are installing the other electrical boxes along the circuit. **Surface-mounted fixtures,** like electric baseboard heaters (page 211) and under-cabinet fluorescent lights (page 229), also have built-in wire connection boxes. These fixtures are not installed until it is time to make the final hookups.

How to Install Electrical Boxes for Receptacles

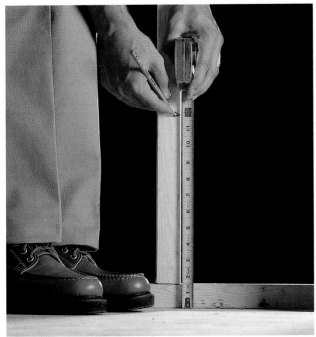

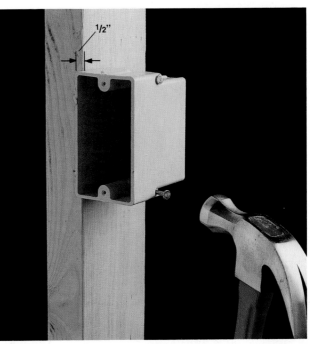

1 Mark the location of each box on studs. Standard receptacle boxes should be centered 12" above floor level. GFCI receptacle boxes in a bathroom should be mounted so they will be about 10" above the finished countertop.

2 Position each box against a stud so the front face will be flush with the finished wall. For example, if you will be installing 1/2" wallboard, position the box so it extends 1/2" past the face of the stud. Anchor the box by driving the mounting nails into the stud.

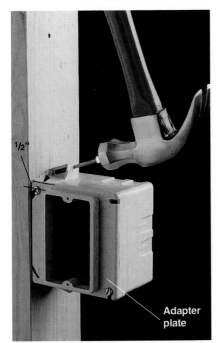

Adapter plate

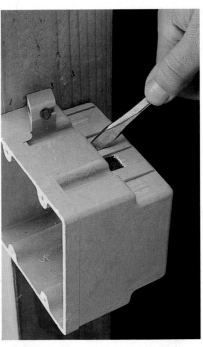

3 If installing 4" × 4" boxes, attach the adapter plates before positioning the boxes. Use adapter plates that match the thickness of the finished wall. Anchor the box by driving the mounting nails into the stud.

4 Open one knockout for each cable that will enter the box, using a hammer and screwdriver.

5 Break off any sharp edges that might damage vinyl cable sheathing by rotating a screwdriver in the knockout.

How to Install Boxes for Light Fixtures

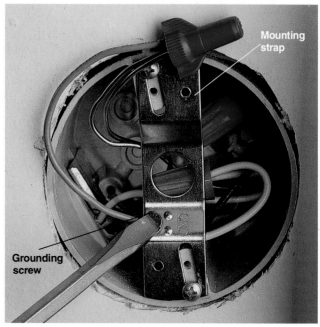

Position a light fixture box for a vanity light above the frame opening for a mirror or medicine cabinet. Place the box for a ceiling light fixture in the center of the room. The box for a stairway light should be mounted so every step will be lighted. Position each box against a framing member so the front face will be flush with the finished wall or ceiling, then anchor the box by driving the mounting nails into the framing member.

Attach a mounting strap to the box if one is required by the light-fixture manufacturer. Mounting straps are needed where the fixture mounting screws do not match the holes in the electrical box. A pre-attached grounding screw on the strap provides a place to pigtail grounding wires.

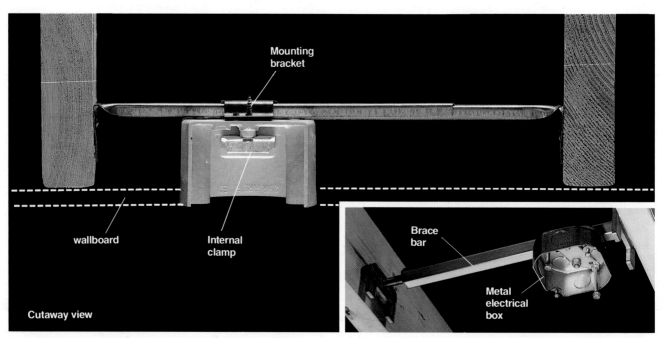

To position a light fixture between joists, attach an electrical box to an adjustable brace bar. Nail the ends of the brace bar to joists so the face of the box will be flush with the finished ceiling surface. Slide the box along the brace bar to the desired position, then tighten the mounting screws. Use internal cable clamps when using a box with a brace bar. NOTE: For ceiling fans and heavy light fixtures, use a metal box and a heavy-duty brace bar rated for heavy loads (inset photo).

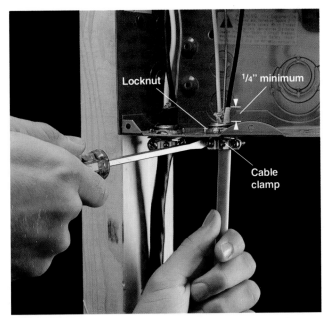

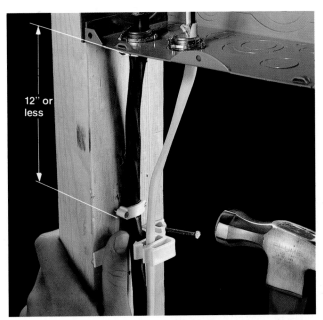

4 Open a knockout in the circuit breaker panel, using a hammer and screwdriver. Insert a cable clamp into the knockout, and secure it with a locknut. Insert the cable though the clamp so that at least 1/4" of sheathing extends inside the circuit breaker panel. Tighten the mounting screws on the clamp so the cable is gripped securely, but not so tightly that the sheathing is crushed.

5 Anchor the cable to the center of a framing member within 12" of the circuit breaker panel, using a cable staple. Stack-It® staples work well where two or more cables must be anchored to the same side of a stud. Run the cable to the first electrical box. Where the cable runs along the sides of framing members, anchor it with cable staples no more than 4 ft. apart.

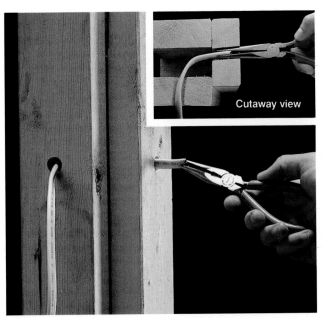

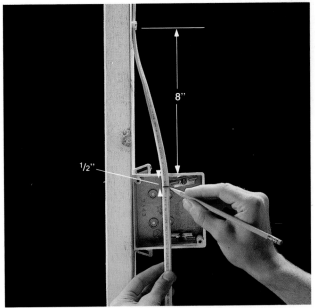

6 At corners, form a slight L-shaped bend in the end of the cable and insert it into one hole. Retrieve cable through the other hole, using needlenose pliers (inset).

7 At the electrical box, staple the cable to a framing member 8" from the box. Hold the cable taut against the front of the box, and mark a point on the sheathing 1/2" past the box edge. Strip cable from the marked line to the end, using a cable ripper, and clip away excess sheathing with a combination tool. Insert the cable through the knockout in the box.

(continued next page)

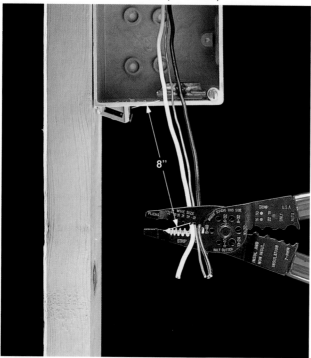

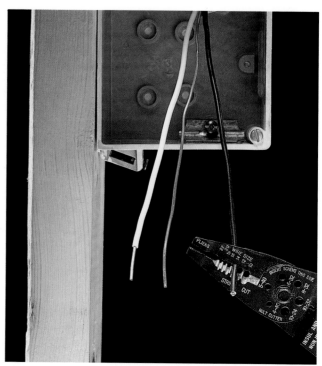

8 As each cable is installed in a box, clip back each wire so that 8" of workable wire extends past the front edge of the box.

9 Strip 3/4" of insulation from each circuit wire in the box, using a combination tool. Take care not to nick the copper.

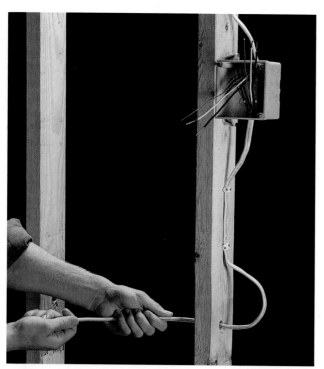

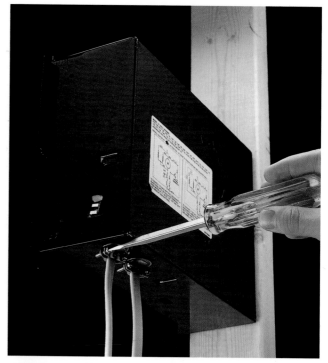

10 Continue the circuit by running cable between each pair of electrical boxes, leaving an extra 1 ft. of cable at each end.

11 At metal boxes and recessed fixtures, open knockouts and attach cables with cable clamps. From inside fixture, strip away all but 1/4" of sheathing. Clip back wires so there is 8" of workable length, then strip 3/4" of insulation from each wire.

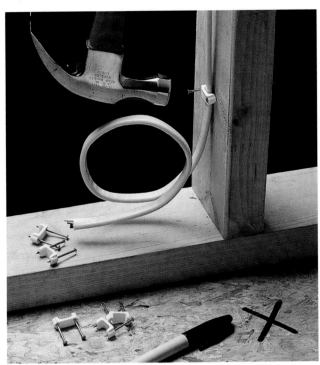

12 For a surface-mounted fixture like a baseboard heater or fluorescent light fixture, staple the cable to a stud near the fixture location, leaving plenty of excess cable. Mark the floor so the cable will be easy to find after the walls are finished.

Pigtail

13 At each recessed fixture and metal electrical box, connect one end of a grounding pigtail to the metal frame, using a grounding clip attached to the frame (shown above) or a green grounding screw (page 170).

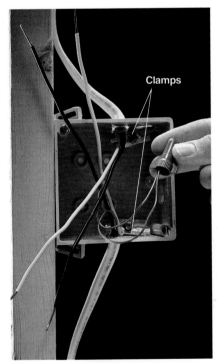

Clamps

14 At each electrical box and recessed fixture, join the grounding wires together with a wire nut. If box has internal clamps, tighten the clamps over the cables.

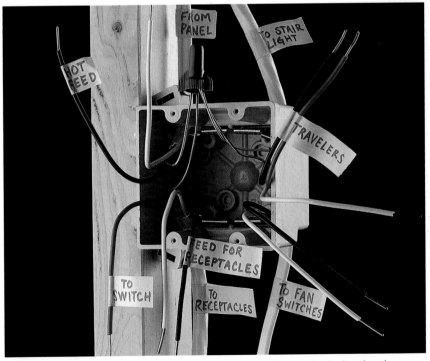

FROM PANEL

TO STAIR LIGHT

HOT FEED

TRAVELERS

FEED FOR RECEPTACLES

TO SWITCH

TO RECEPTACLES

TO FAN SWITCHES

15 Label the cables entering each box to indicate their destinations. In boxes with complex wiring configurations, also tag the individual wires to make final hookups easier. After all cables are installed, your rough-in work is ready to be reviewed by the electrical inspector.

How to Run NM Cable Inside a Finished Wall

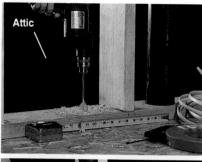

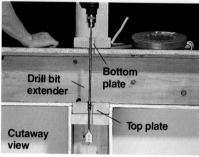

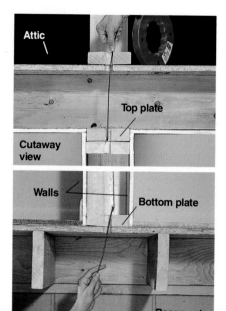

1 From the unfinished space below the finished wall, look for a reference point, like a soil stack, plumbing pipes, or electrical cables, that indicates the location of the wall above. Choose a location for the new cable that does not interfere with existing utilities. Drill a 1" hole up into the stud cavity.

2 From the unfinished space above the finished wall, find the top of the stud cavity by measuring from the same fixed reference point used in step 1. Drill a 1" hole down through the top plate and into the stud cavity, using a drill bit extender.

3 Extend a fish tape down through the top plate, twisting the tape until it reaches the bottom of the stud cavity. From the unfinished space below the wall, use a piece of stiff wire with a hook on one end to retrieve the fish tape through the drilled hole in the bottom plate.

4 Trim back 3" of outer insulation from the end of the NM cable, then insert the wires through the loop at the tip of the fish tape.

5 Bend the wires against the cable, then use electrical tape to bind them tightly. Apply cable-pulling lubricant to the taped end of the fish tape.

6 From above the finished wall, pull steadily on the fish tape to draw the cable up through the stud cavity. This job will be easier if you have a helper feed the cable from below as you pull.

Tips for Running Cable Inside Finished Walls

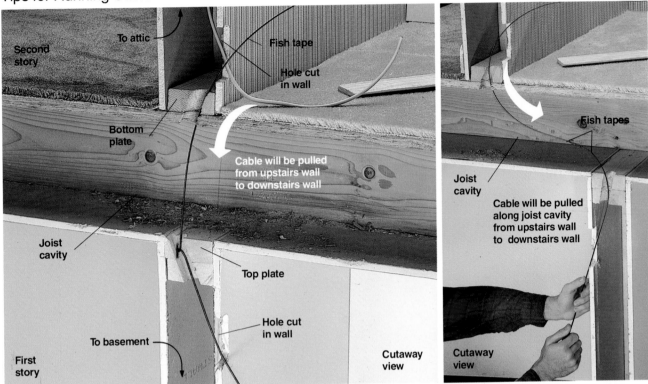

Second story

To attic

Fish tape

Hole cut in wall

Bottom plate

Cable will be pulled from upstairs wall to downstairs wall

Joist cavity

Top plate

To basement

Hole cut in wall

First story

Cutaway view

Fish tapes

Joist cavity

Cable will be pulled along joist cavity from upstairs wall to downstairs wall

Cutaway view

If there is no access space above and below a wall (page opposite), cut openings in the finished walls to run a cable. This often occurs in two-story homes when a cable is extended from an upstairs wall to a downstairs wall. Cut small openings in the wall near the top and bottom plates, then drill an angled 1" hole through each plate. Extend a fish tape into the joist cavity between the walls and use it to pull the cable from one wall to the next. If the walls line up one over the other (left), you can retrieve the fish tape using a piece of stiff wire. If walls do not line up (right), use a second fish tape. After running the cable, repair the holes in the walls with patching plaster, or wallboard scraps and taping compound.

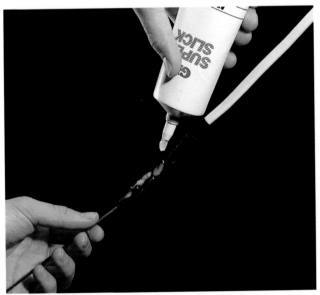

Apply cable-pulling lubricant to the taped end of the fish tape when a cable must be pulled through a sharp bend. Do not use oil or petroleum jelly as a lubricant, because they can damage the thermoplastic cable sheathing.

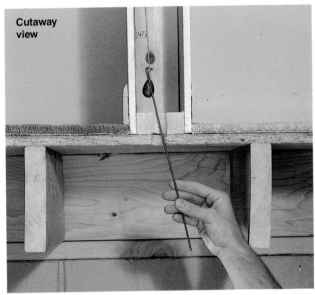

Cutaway view

If you do not have a fish tape, use a length of sturdy mason's string and a lead fishing weight or heavy washer to fish down through a stud cavity. Drop the line into the stud cavity from above, then use a piece of stiff wire to hook the line from below.

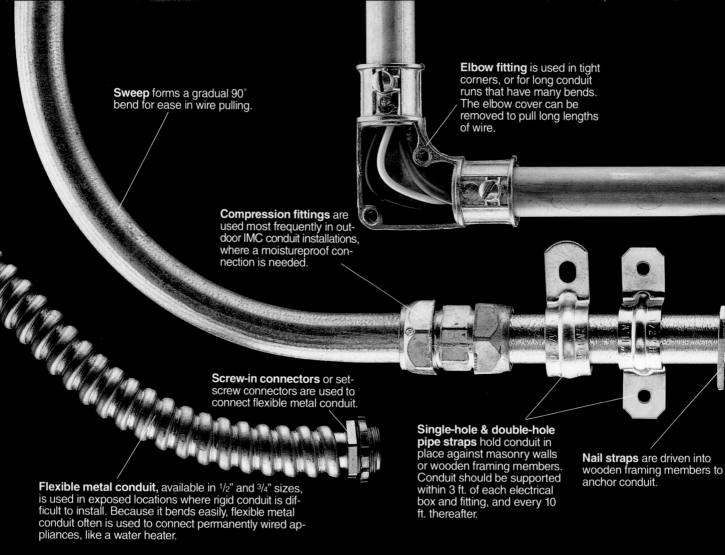

Sweep forms a gradual 90° bend for ease in wire pulling.

Elbow fitting is used in tight corners, or for long conduit runs that have many bends. The elbow cover can be removed to pull long lengths of wire.

Compression fittings are used most frequently in outdoor IMC conduit installations, where a moistureproof connection is needed.

Screw-in connectors or set-screw connectors are used to connect flexible metal conduit.

Single-hole & double-hole pipe straps hold conduit in place against masonry walls or wooden framing members. Conduit should be supported within 3 ft. of each electrical box and fitting, and every 10 ft. thereafter.

Nail straps are driven into wooden framing members to anchor conduit.

Flexible metal conduit, available in 1/2" and 3/4" sizes, is used in exposed locations where rigid conduit is difficult to install. Because it bends easily, flexible metal conduit often is used to connect permanently wired appliances, like a water heater.

Conduit

Electrical wiring that runs in exposed locations must be protected by rigid tubing, called conduit. For example, conduit is used for wiring that runs across masonry walls in a basement laundry, and for exposed outdoor wiring (pages 234 to 253). THHN/THWN wire (page 162) normally is installed inside conduit, although UF or NM cable can also be installed in conduit.

There are several types of conduit available, so check with your electrical inspector to find out which type meets Code requirements in your area. Conduit installed outdoors must be rated for exterior use. Metal conduit should be used only with metal boxes, never with plastic boxes.

At one time, conduit could only be fitted by using elaborate bending techniques and special tools. Now, however, a variety of shaped fittings are available to let a homeowner join conduit easily.

Electrical Grounding in Metal Conduit

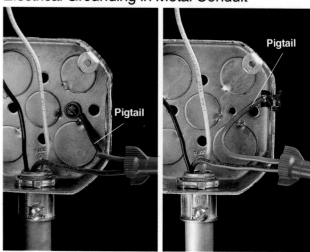

Install a green insulated grounding wire for any circuit that runs through metal conduit. Although the Code allows the metal conduit to serve as the grounding conductor, most electricians install a green insulated wire as a more dependable means of grounding the system. The grounding wires must be connected to metal boxes with a pigtail and grounding screw (left) or grounding clip (right).

170

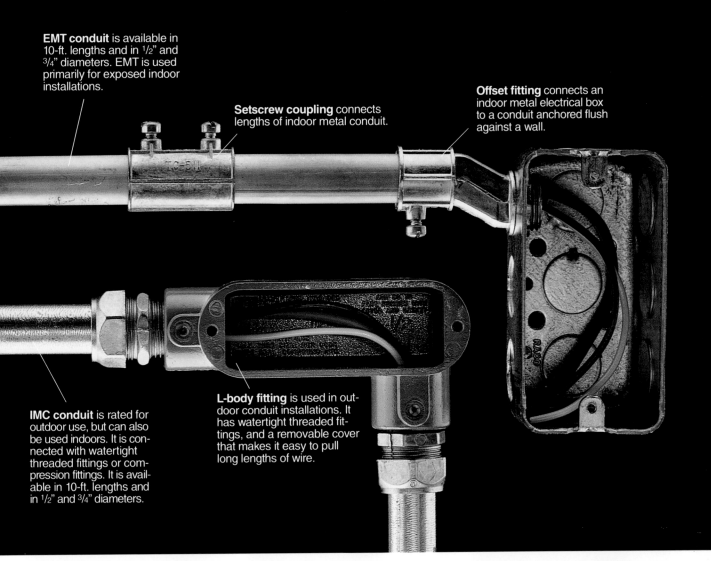

EMT conduit is available in 10-ft. lengths and in 1/2" and 3/4" diameters. EMT is used primarily for exposed indoor installations.

Setscrew coupling connects lengths of indoor metal conduit.

Offset fitting connects an indoor metal electrical box to a conduit anchored flush against a wall.

IMC conduit is rated for outdoor use, but can also be used indoors. It is connected with watertight threaded fittings or compression fittings. It is available in 10-ft. lengths and in 1/2" and 3/4" diameters.

L-body fitting is used in outdoor conduit installations. It has watertight threaded fittings, and a removable cover that makes it easy to pull long lengths of wire.

Wire Capacities of Conduit

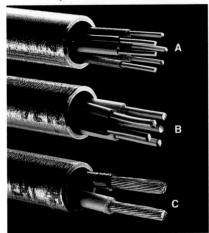

Conduit 1/2" in diameter can hold up to six 14-gauge or 12-gauge THHN/THWN wires (A), five 10-gauge wires (B), or two 8-gauge wires (C). Use 3/4" conduit if the number of wires exceeds this capacity.

Three Metal Conduit Variations

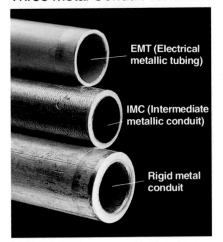

EMT (Electrical metallic tubing)

IMC (Intermediate metallic conduit)

Rigid metal conduit

EMT is lightweight and easy to install, but should not be used where it can be damaged. IMC has thicker, galvanized walls and is a good choice for exposed outdoor use. Rigid metal conduit provides the greatest protection for wires, but is more expensive and requires threaded fittings.

Plastic Conduit Variation

Plastic PVC conduit is allowed by many local Codes. It is assembled with solvent glue and PVC fittings that resemble those for metal conduit. PVC conduit should be attached only to PVC boxes, never to metal boxes. When wiring with PVC conduit, always run a green grounding wire.

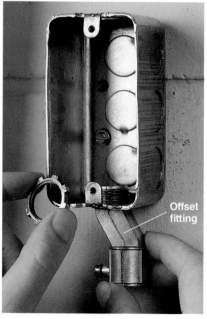

1 Measure from floor to position electrical boxes on wall, and mark location for mounting screws. Boxes for receptacles in an unfinished basement or other damp area are mounted at least 2 ft. from the floor. Laundry receptacles usually are mounted at 48"

2 Drill pilot holes with a masonry bit, then mount the boxes against masonry walls with Tapcon® anchors. Or, use masonry anchors and pan-head screws.

3 Open one knockout for each length of conduit that will be attached to the box. Attach an offset fitting to each knockout, using a locknut.

Offset fitting

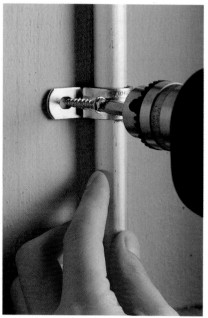

4 Measure the first length of conduit and cut it with a hacksaw. Remove any rough inside edges with a pipe reamer or a round file. Attach the conduit to the offset fitting on the box, and tighten the setscrew.

5 Anchor the conduit against the wall with pipe straps and Tapcon® anchors. Conduit should be anchored within 3 ft. of each box and fitting, and every 10 ft. thereafter.

6 Make conduit bends by attaching a sweep fitting, using a setscrew fitting or compression fitting. Continue conduit run by attaching additional lengths, using setscrew or compression fittings.

7 Use an elbow fitting in conduit runs that have many bends, or runs that require very long wires. The cover on the elbow fitting can be removed to make it easier to extend a fish tape and pull wires.

8 At the service breaker panel, **turn the power OFF, then remove the cover and test for power** (page 178). Open a knockout in the panel, then attach a setscrew fitting and install the last length of conduit.

9 Unwind the fish tape and extend it through the conduit from the circuit breaker panel outward. Remove the cover on an elbow fitting when extending the fish tape around tight corners.

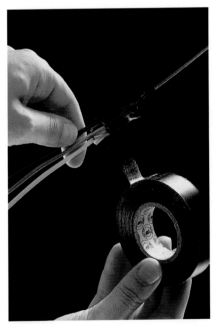

10 Insert the wires through the loop at the end of the fish tape, and wrap them with electrical tape. Straighten the wires to prevent kinks, and apply wire-pulling lubricant to the taped end of the fish tape.

11 Retrieve the wires through the conduit by pulling on the fish tape with steady pressure. **NOTE: Use extreme care** when using a metal fish tape inside a circuit breaker panel, even when the power is turned OFF.

12 Clip off the taped ends of the wires. Leave at least 2 ft. of wire at the service panel, and 8" at each electrical box.

Wiring a Laundry with Conduit

A typical home laundry has three electrical circuits. A 20-amp, 120-volt small-appliance circuit wired with 12-gauge THHN/THWN wire supplies power for the washing machine receptacle and all other general-use receptacles in the laundry area. A basic lighting circuit, often extended from another part of the house, powers the laundry light fixture. Finally, a 240-volt, 30-amp circuit wired with 10-gauge THHN/THWN wire provides power for the dryer.

Follow the directions on pages 172 to 173 when installing the conduit. For convenience, you can use the same conduit to hold the wires for both the 120-volt circuit and the 240-volt dryer circuit.

Everything You Need:

Tools: hacksaw, drill and ⅛" masonry bit, screwdriver, fish tape, combination tool.

Materials: conduit, setscrew fittings, Tapcon® anchors, THHN/THWN wire, electrical tape, wire nuts, receptacles (GFCI, 120-volt, 120/240-volt), circuit breakers (30-amp double-pole, 20-amp single-pole).

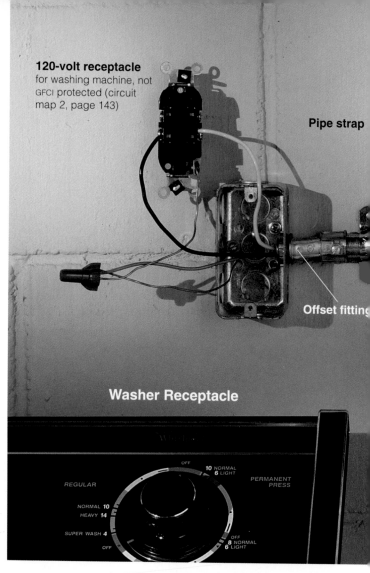

120-volt receptacle for washing machine, not GFCI protected (circuit map 2, page 143)

Pipe strap

Offset fitting

Washer Receptacle

How to Connect a 30-amp Dryer Circuit (conduit installation)

1 Connect the white circuit wire to the center setscrew terminal on the receptacle. Connect the black and red wires to the remaining setscrew terminals, and connect the green insulated wire to the grounding screw in the box. Attach the coverplate.

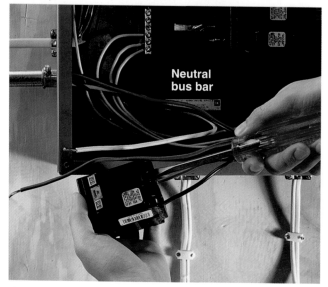

Neutral bus bar

2 With main breaker shut OFF, connect the red and black circuit wires to the setscrew terminals on the 30-amp double-pole breaker. Connect the white wire to the neutral bus bar. Attach the green insulated wire to the grounding bus bar. Attach the breaker panel cover, and turn the breakers ON.

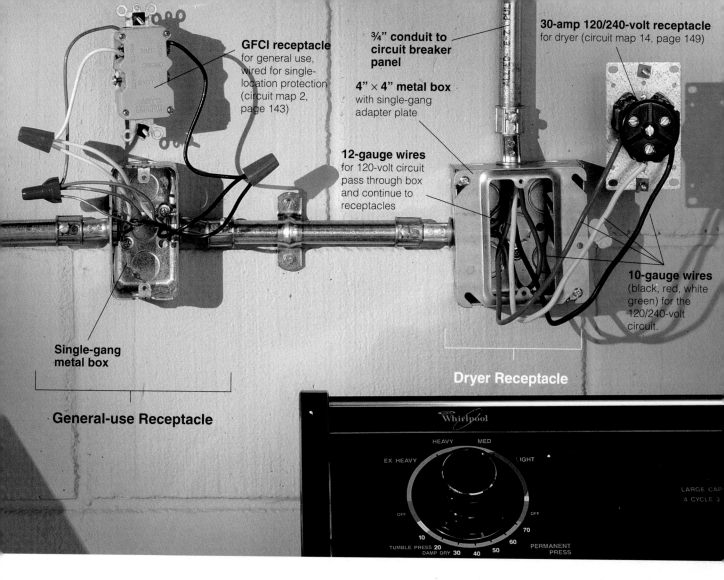

GFCI receptacle for general use, wired for single-location protection (circuit map 2, page 143)

¾" conduit to circuit breaker panel

4" × 4" metal box with single-gang adapter plate

30-amp 120/240-volt receptacle for dryer (circuit map 14, page 149)

12-gauge wires for 120-volt circuit pass through box and continue to receptacles

10-gauge wires (black, red, white green) for the 120/240-volt circuit.

Single-gang metal box

Dryer Receptacle

General-use Receptacle

Wiring a Water Heater with Flexible Conduit

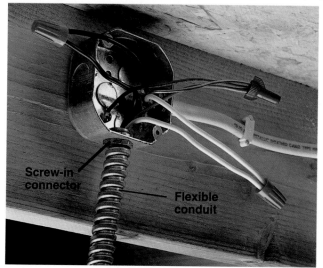

Screw-in connector

Flexible conduit

Install a 30-amp, 240-volt circuit for most electric water heaters. A water heater circuit is wired in much the same way as an air conditioner circuit (circuit map 12, page 148). Install a junction box near the water heater, then use 10/2 NM cable to bring power from the service panel to the junction box (above left).

Use flexible metal conduit and 10-gauge THHN/THWN wires to bring power from the junction box to the water heater wire connection box (above right). Connect black and red water heater leads to the white and black circuit wires. Connect the grounding wire to the water heater grounding screw.

175

Circuit Breaker Panels

The circuit breaker panel is the electrical distribution center for your home. It divides the current into branch circuits that are carried throughout the house. Each branch circuit is controlled by a circuit breaker that protects the wires from dangerous current overloads. When installing new circuits, the last step is to connect the wires to new circuit breakers at the panel. Working inside a circuit breaker panel is not dangerous if you follow basic safety procedures. Always shut off the main circuit breaker and test for power

before touching any parts inside the panel, and **never touch the service wire lugs.** If unsure of your own skills, hire an electrician to make the final circuit connections. (If you have an older electrical service with fuses instead of circuit breakers, always have an electrician make these final hookups.)

If the main circuit breaker panel does not have enough open slots to hold new circuit breakers, install a subpanel (pages 180 to 183). This job is well within the skill level of an experienced do-it-

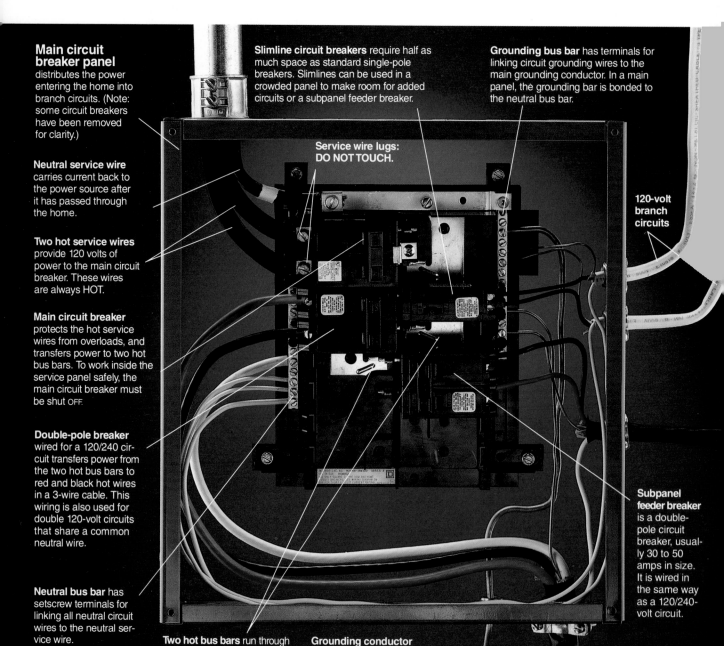

Main circuit breaker panel distributes the power entering the home into branch circuits. (Note: some circuit breakers have been removed for clarity.)

Neutral service wire carries current back to the power source after it has passed through the home.

Two hot service wires provide 120 volts of power to the main circuit breaker. These wires are always HOT.

Main circuit breaker protects the hot service wires from overloads, and transfers power to two hot bus bars. To work inside the service panel safely, the main circuit breaker must be shut OFF.

Double-pole breaker wired for a 120/240 circuit transfers power from the two hot bus bars to red and black hot wires in a 3-wire cable. This wiring is also used for double 120-volt circuits that share a common neutral wire.

Neutral bus bar has setscrew terminals for linking all neutral circuit wires to the neutral service wire.

Slimline circuit breakers require half as much space as standard single-pole breakers. Slimlines can be used in a crowded panel to make room for added circuits or a subpanel feeder breaker.

Service wire lugs: DO NOT TOUCH.

Grounding bus bar has terminals for linking circuit grounding wires to the main grounding conductor. In a main panel, the grounding bar is bonded to the neutral bus bar.

120-volt branch circuits

Subpanel feeder breaker is a double-pole circuit breaker, usually 30 to 50 amps in size. It is wired in the same way as a 120/240-volt circuit.

Two hot bus bars run through the center of the service panel, supplying power to the individual circuit breakers. Each carries 120 volts of power.

Grounding conductor connects the service panel equipment to a metal cold water pipe or grounding rod driven into the earth.

120/240-volt branch circuit

yourselfer, although you can also hire an electrician to install the subpanel.

Before installing any new wiring, evaluate your electrical service to make sure it provides enough current to support both the existing wiring and any new circuits (pages 136 to 139). If your service does not provide enough power, have an electrician upgrade it to a higher amp rating. During the upgrade, the electrician will install a new circuit breaker panel with enough extra breaker slots for the new circuits you want to install.

Safety Warning:

Never touch any parts inside a circuit breaker panel until you have checked for power (page 178). Circuit breaker panels differ in appearance, depending on the manufacturer. Never begin work in a circuit breaker panel until you understand its layout and can identify the parts.

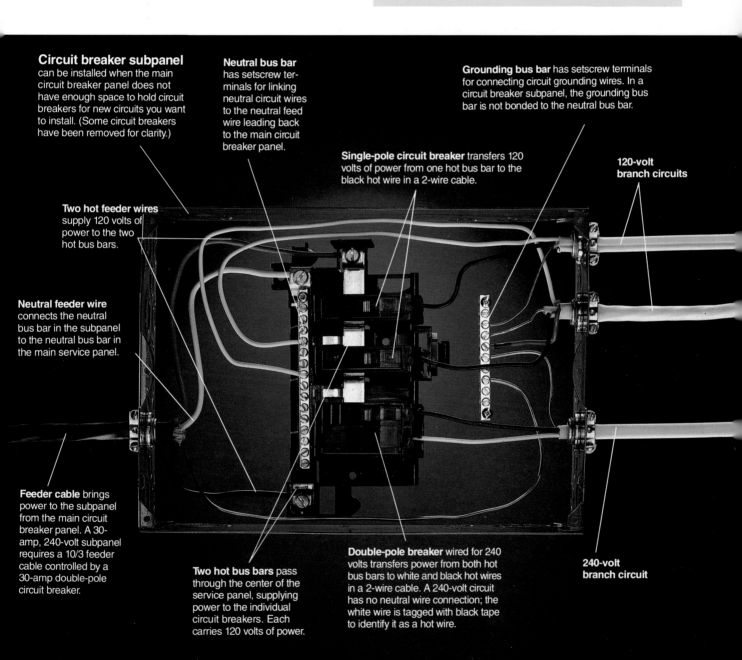

Circuit breaker subpanel can be installed when the main circuit breaker panel does not have enough space to hold circuit breakers for new circuits you want to install. (Some circuit breakers have been removed for clarity.)

Neutral bus bar has setscrew terminals for linking neutral circuit wires to the neutral feed wire leading back to the main circuit breaker panel.

Grounding bus bar has setscrew terminals for connecting circuit grounding wires. In a circuit breaker subpanel, the grounding bus bar is not bonded to the neutral bus bar.

Single-pole circuit breaker transfers 120 volts of power from one hot bus bar to the black hot wire in a 2-wire cable.

120-volt branch circuits

Two hot feeder wires supply 120 volts of power to the two hot bus bars.

Neutral feeder wire connects the neutral bus bar in the subpanel to the neutral bus bar in the main service panel.

Feeder cable brings power to the subpanel from the main circuit breaker panel. A 30-amp, 240-volt subpanel requires a 10/3 feeder cable controlled by a 30-amp double-pole circuit breaker.

Two hot bus bars pass through the center of the service panel, supplying power to the individual circuit breakers. Each carries 120 volts of power.

Double-pole breaker wired for 240 volts transfers power from both hot bus bars to white and black hot wires in a 2-wire cable. A 240-volt circuit has no neutral wire connection; the white wire is tagged with black tape to identify it as a hot wire.

240-volt branch circuit

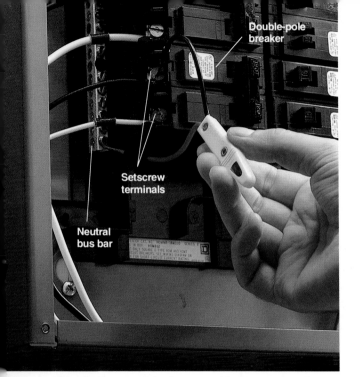

Test for current before touching any parts inside a circuit breaker panel. With main breaker turned OFF but all other breakers turned ON, touch one probe of a neon tester to the neutral bus bar, and touch other probe to each setscrew on one of the double-pole breakers (not the main breaker). If tester does not light for either setscrew, it is safe to work in the panel.

Connecting Circuit Breakers

The last step in a wiring project is connecting circuits at the breaker panel. After this is done, the work is ready for the final inspection.

Circuits are connected at the main breaker panel, if it has enough open slots, or at a circuit breaker sub-panel (pages 180 to 183). When working at a sub-panel, make sure the feeder breaker at the main panel has been turned OFF, and test for power (photo, left) before touching any parts in the subpanel.

Make sure the circuit breaker amperage does not exceed the "ampacity" of the circuit wires you are connecting to it (page 163). Also be aware that circuit breaker styles and installation techniques vary according to manufacturer. Use breakers designed for your type of panel.

Everything You Need:

Tools: screwdriver, hammer, pencil, combination tool, cable ripper, neon circuit tester, pliers.

Materials: cable clamps, single- and double-pole circuit breakers.

How to Connect Circuit Breakers

1 Shut off the main circuit breaker in the main circuit breaker panel (if you are working in a sub-panel, shut off the feeder breaker in the main panel). Remove the panel coverplate, taking care not to touch the parts inside the panel. Test for power (photo, above).

2 Open a knockout in the side of the circuit breaker panel, using a screwdriver and hammer. Attach a cable clamp to the knockout.

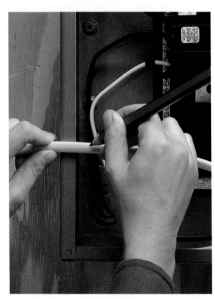

3 Hold cable across the front of the panel near the knockout, and mark sheathing about 1/2" inside the edge of the panel. Strip the cable from marked line to end, using a cable ripper. (There should be 18" to 24" of excess cable.) Insert the cable through the clamp and into the service panel, then tighten the clamp.

4 Bend the bare copper grounding wire around the inside edge of the panel to an open setscrew terminal on the grounding bus bar. Insert the wire into the opening on the bus bar, and tighten the setscrew. Fold excess wire around the inside edge of the panel.

5 For 120-volt circuits, bend the white circuit wire around the outside of the panel to an open setscrew terminal on the neutral bus bar. Clip away excess wire, then strip 1/2" of insulation from the wire, using a combination tool. Insert the wire into the terminal opening, and tighten the setscrew.

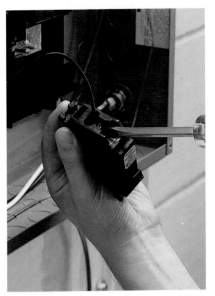

6 Strip 1/2" of insulation from the end of the black circuit wire. Insert the wire into the setscrew terminal on a new single-pole circuit breaker, and tighten the setscrew.

7 Slide one end of the circuit breaker onto the guide hook, then press it firmly against the bus bar until it snaps into place. (Breaker installation may vary, depending on the manufacturer.) Fold excess black wire around the inside edge of the panel.

8 **120/240-volt circuits (top):** Connect red and black wires to double-pole breaker. Connect white wire to neutral bus bar, and grounding wire to grounding bus bar. **240-volt circuits (bottom):** Attach white and black wires to double-pole breaker, tagging white wire with black tape. There is no neutral bus bar connection on this circuit.

9 Remove the appropriate breaker knockout on the panel coverplate to make room for the new circuit breaker. A single-pole breaker requires one knockout, while a double-pole breaker requires two knockouts. Reattach the coverplate, and label the new circuit on the panel index.

179

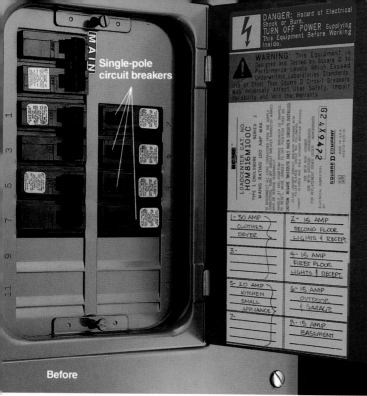

Before

Single-pole circuit breakers

Slimline breakers replace single-pole breakers

After

New feeder breaker

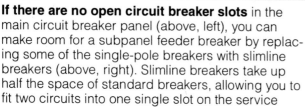

If there are no open circuit breaker slots in the main circuit breaker panel (above, left), you can make room for a subpanel feeder breaker by replacing some of the single-pole breakers with slimline breakers (above, right). Slimline breakers take up half the space of standard breakers, allowing you to fit two circuits into one single slot on the service panel. In the service panel shown above, four single-pole 120-volt breakers were replaced with slimline breakers to provide the double opening needed for a 30-amp, 240-volt subpanel feeder breaker. Use slimline breakers with the same amp rating as the standard single-pole breakers you are removing and make sure they are approved for use in your panel.

Installing a Subpanel

Install a circuit breaker subpanel if the main circuit breaker panel does not have enough open breaker slots for the new circuits you are planning. The subpanel serves as a second distribution center for connecting circuits. It receives power from a double-pole "feeder" circuit breaker you install in the main circuit breaker panel.

If the main service panel is so full that there is no room for the double-pole subpanel feeder breaker, you can reconnect some of the existing 120-volt circuits to special slimline breakers (photos, above).

Plan your subpanel installation carefully (page opposite), making sure your electrical service supplies enough power to support the extra load of the new subpanel circuits. Assuming your main service is adequate, consider installing an oversized subpanel feeder breaker in the main panel to provide enough extra amps to meet the needs of future wiring projects.

Also consider the physical size of the subpanel, and choose one that has enough extra slots to hold circuits you may want to install later. The smallest panels have room for up to 6 single-pole breakers (or 3 double-pole breakers), while the largest models can hold up to 20 single-pole breakers.

Subpanels often are mounted near the main circuit breaker panel. Or, for convenience, they can be installed close to the areas they serve, such as in a new room addition or a garage. In a finished room, a subpanel can be painted or covered with a removable painting, bulletin board, or decorative cabinet to make it more attractive. If it is covered, make sure the subpanel is easily accessible and clearly identified.

Everything You Need:

Tools: hammer, screwdriver, neon circuit tester, cable ripper, combination tool.

Materials: screws, cable clamps, 3-wire NM cable, cable staples, double-pole circuit breaker, circuit breaker subpanel, slimline circuit breakers

How to Plan a Subpanel Installation (photocopy this work sheet as a guide; blue sample numbers will not reproduce)

1. Find the gross electrical load for only those areas that will be served by the subpanel. Refer to "Evaluating Electrical Loads" (steps 1 to 5, page 139). EXAMPLE: in the 400-sq. ft. attic room addition shown on pages 184 to 187, the gross load required for the basic lighting/receptacle circuits and electric heating is 5000 watts.	Gross Electrical Load:	_5000_ watts
2. Multiply the gross electrical load times 1.25. This safety adjustment is required by the National Electrical Code. EXAMPLE: In the attic room addition (gross load 5000 watts), the adjusted load equals 6250 watts.	_5000_ watts × 1.25 =	_6250_ watts
3. Convert the load into amps by dividing by 230. This gives the required amperage needed to power the subpanel. EXAMPLE: The attic room addition described above requires about 27 amps of power (6250 ÷ 230).	_6,250_ watts ÷ 230 =	_27.2_ amps
4. For the subpanel feeder breaker, choose a double-pole circuit breaker with an amp rating equal to or greater than the required subpanel amperage. EXAMPLE: In a room addition that requires 27 amps, choose a 30-amp double-pole feeder breaker.	☑ 30-amp breaker ☐ 40-amp breaker ☐ 50-amp breaker	
5. For the feeder cable bringing power from the main circuit breaker panel to the subpanel, choose 3-wire NM cable with an ampacity equal to the rating of the subpanel feeder breaker (see page 163). EXAMPLE: For a 30-amp subpanel feeder breaker, choose 10/3 cable for the feeder.	☑ 10/3 cable ☐ 8/3 cable ☐ 6/3 cable	

How to Install a Subpanel

1 Mount the subpanel at shoulder height, following manufacturer's recommendations. The subpanel can be mounted to the sides of studs, or to plywood attached between two studs. Panel shown here extends 1/2" past the face of studs so it will be flush with the finished wall surface.

2 Open a knockout in the subpanel, using a screwdriver and hammer. Run the feeder cable from the main circuit breaker panel to the subpanel, leaving about 2 ft. of excess cable at each end. See pages 168 to 169 if you need to run the cable through finished walls.

3 Attach a cable clamp to the knockout in the subpanel. Insert the cable into the subpanel, then anchor it to framing members within 8" of each panel, and every 4 ft. thereafter.

(continued next page)

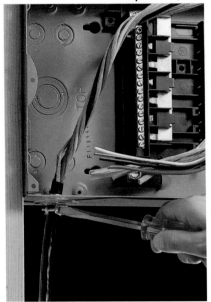

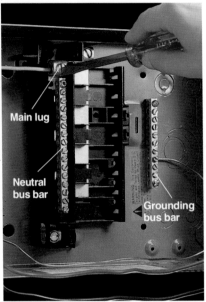

4 Strip away outer sheathing from the feeder cable, using a cable ripper. Leave at least 1/4" of sheathing extending into the subpanel. Tighten the cable clamp screws so cable is held securely, but not so tightly that the wire sheathing is crushed.

5 Strip 1/2" of insulation from the white neutral feeder wire, and attach it to the main lug on the subpanel neutral bus bar. Connect the grounding wire to a setscrew terminal on the grounding bus bar. Fold excess wire around the inside edge of the subpanel.

6 Strip away 1/2" of insulation from the red and black feeder wires. Attach one wire to the main lug on each of the hot bus bars. Fold excess wire around the inside edge of the subpanel.

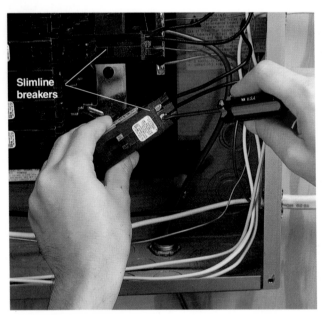

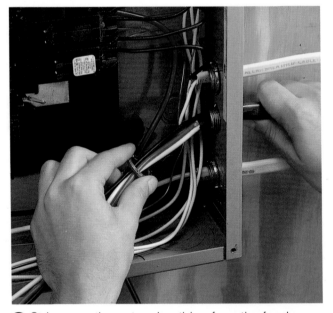

7 At the main circuit breaker panel, shut off the main circuit breaker, then remove the coverplate and test for power (page 178). If necessary, make room for the double-pole feeder breaker by removing single-pole breakers and reconnecting the wires to slimline circuit breakers. Open a knockout for the feeder cable, using a hammer and screwdriver.

8 Strip away the outer sheathing from the feeder cable so that at least 1/4" of sheathing will reach into the main service panel. Attach a cable clamp to the cable, then insert the cable into the knockout and anchor it by threading a locknut onto the clamp. Tighten the locknut by driving a screwdriver against the lugs. Tighten the clamp screws so cable is held securely, but not so tightly that the cable sheathing is crushed.

9 Bend the bare copper wire from the feeder cable around the inside edge of the main circuit breaker panel, and connect it to one of the setscrew terminals on the grounding bus bar.

10 Strip away 1/2" of insulation from the white feeder wire. Attach the wire to one of the setscrew terminals on the neutral bus bar. Fold excess wire around the inside edge of the service panel.

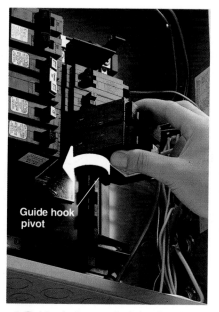

11 Strip 1/2" of insulation from the red and black feeder wires. Attach one wire to each of the setscrew terminals on the double-pole feeder breaker.

12 Hook the end of the feeder circuit breaker over the guide hooks on the panel, then push the other end forward until the breaker snaps onto the hot bus bars (follow manufacturer's directions). Fold excess wire around the inside edge of the circuit breaker panel.

13 If necessary, open two knock-outs where the double-pole feeder breaker will fit, then reattach the coverplate. Label the feeder breaker on the circuit index. Turn main breaker ON, but leave feeder breaker OFF until all subpanel circuits have been connected and inspected.

Wiring a Room Addition

This chapter shows how to wire an unfinished attic space that is being converted to a combination bedroom, bathroom, and study. In addition to basic receptacles and light fixtures, you will learn how to install a ceiling fan, permanent-ly wired smoke alarm, bathroom vent fan, computer receptacle, air-conditioning receptacle, electric heaters, telephone outlets, and cable television jacks. Use this chapter and the circuit maps on pages 143 to 153 as a guide for planning

Choose the Fixtures You Need

A. Computer receptacle (circuit #2) is connected to a 120-volt isolated-ground circuit. It protects sensitive computer equipment from power surges. See page 206.

B. Air-conditioner receptacle (circuit #3) supplies power for a 240-volt window air conditioner. See page 206. Some air conditioners require 120-volt receptacles.

C. Circuit breaker subpanel controls all attic circuits and fixtures, and is connected to the main service panel. For a more finished ap-pearance, cover the subpanel with a removable bulletin board or picture. See pages 180 to 183.

D. Thermostat (circuit #5) controls 240-volt baseboard heaters in the bedroom and study areas. See page 210.

F. Closet light fixture (circuit #1) makes a closet more convenient. See page 205.

E. Fully wired bathroom (circuit #1) includes vent fan with timer switch, GFCI receptacle, vanity light, and single-pole switch. See pages 204 to 205. The bathroom also has a 240-volt blower-heater controlled by a built-in thermostat (circuit #5, page 210).

G. Smoke alarm (circuit #4) is an essential safety feature of any sleeping area. See page 209.

and installing your own circuits. Our room addition features a circuit breaker subpanel that has been installed in the attic to provide power for five new electrical circuits. Turn the page to see how these circuits look inside the walls.

Three Steps for Wiring a Room Addition
1. Plan the Circuits (pages 190 to 191).
2. Install Boxes & Cables (pages 192 to 203).
3. Make Final Connections (pages 204 to 211).

H. Double-gang switch box (circuit #4) contains a three-way switch that controls stairway light fixture and single-pole switch that controls a switched receptacle in the bedroom area. See page 207.

I. Fan switches (circuit #4) include a speed control for ceiling fan motor and dimmer control for the fan light fixture. See page 207.

J. Ceiling fan (circuit #4) helps reduce summer cooling costs and winter heating bills. See page 208.

K. Stairway light (circuit #4) illuminates the stairway. It is controlled by three-way switches at the top and bottom of the stairway. See page 209.

L. Cable television jack completes the bedroom entertainment corner. See page 202.

M. Telephone outlet is a convenient addition to the bedroom area. See page 203.

N. Switched receptacle (circuit #4) lets you turn a table lamp on from a switch at the stairway. See page 208.

O. Receptacles (circuit #4) spaced at regular intervals allow you to plug in lamps and small appliances wherever needed. See page 208.

P. Baseboard heaters (circuit #5) connected to a 240-volt circuit provide safe, effective heating. See page 211.

Wiring a Room Addition: Construction View

The room addition wiring project on the following pages includes the installation of five new electrical circuits: two 120-volt basic lighting/receptacle circuits, a dedicated 120-volt circuit with a special "isolated" grounding connection for a home computer, and two 240-volt circuits for air conditioning and heaters. The photo below shows how these circuits look behind the finished walls of a room addition.

14/2 cable

Vent fan

Circuit breaker subpanel

Vanity light fixture

GFCI receptacl

12/2 cable

12/2 cable

Timer & light fixture switch

14/3 cable

Blower-heater

10/3 cable

Learn How to Install These Circuits & Cables

#1: Bathroom circuit. This 15-amp, 120-volt circuit supplies power to bathroom fixtures and to fixtures in the adjacent closet. All general-use receptacles in a bathroom must be protected by a GFCI.

#2: Computer circuit. A 15-amp, 120-volt dedicated circuit with an extra isolated grounding wire that protects computer equipment.

Circuit breaker sub-panel receives power through a 10-gauge, three-wire feeder cable connected to a 30-amp, 240-volt circuit breaker at the main circuit breaker panel. Larger room additions may require a 40-amp or a 50-amp "feeder" circuit breaker.

#3 Air-conditioner circuit. A 20-amp, 240-volt dedicated circuit. In cooler climates, or in a smaller room, you may need an air conditioner and circuit rated for only 120 volts (page 135).

186

Wiring a room addition is a complex project that is made simple by careful planning and a step-by-step approach. Divide the project into convenient steps, and complete the work for each step before moving on to the next.

14/3 cable

14/3 cable

Phone cable

Coaxial cable

These cables continue through the foreground wall to complete the circuits. This wall has been removed for clarity.

12/2 cable

14/2 cable

■ **#4: Basic lighting/ receptacle circuit.** This 15-amp, 120-volt circuit supplies power to most of the fixtures in the bedroom and study areas.

■ **#5: Heater circuit.** This 20-amp, 240-volt circuit supplies power to the bathroom blower-heater and to the baseboard heaters. Depending on the size of your room and the wattage rating of the baseboard heaters, you may need a 30-amp, 240-volt heating circuit.

Telephone outlet is wired with 22-gauge four-wire phone cable. If your home phone system has two or more separate lines, you may need to run a cable with eight wires, commonly called "four-pair" cable.

Cable television jack is wired with coaxial cable running from an existing television junction in the utility area.

Wiring a Room Addition: Diagram View

This diagram view shows the layout of five circuits and the location of the switches, receptacles, lights, and other fixtures in the attic room addition featured in this chapter. The size and number of circuits, and the list of required materials, are based on the needs of this

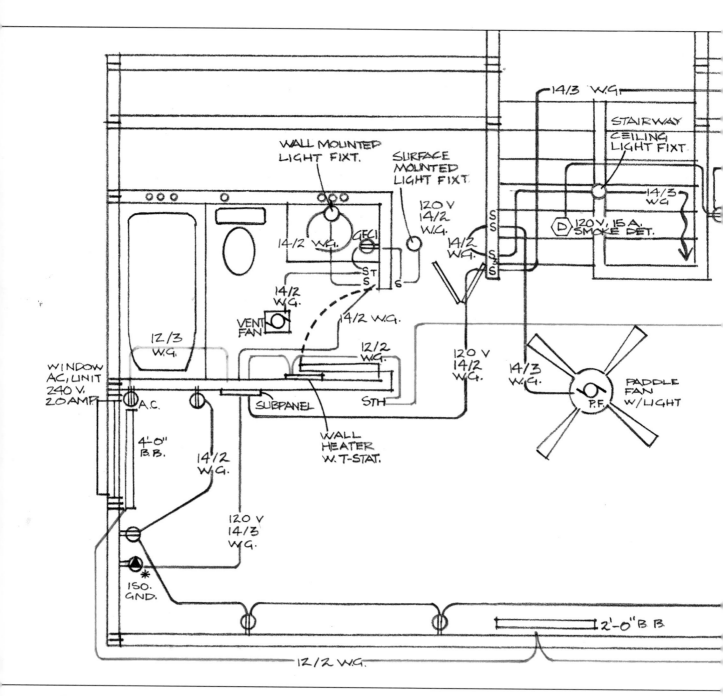

Circuit #1: A 15-amp, 120-volt circuit serving the bathroom and closet area. 14/2 NM cable, double-gang box, timer switch, single-pole switch, 4" × 4" box with single-gang adapter plate, GFCI receptacle, 2 plastic light fixture boxes, vanity light fixture, closet light fixture, 15-amp single-pole circuit breaker.

Circuit #2: A 15-amp, 120-volt computer circuit. 14/3 NM cable, single-gang box, 15-amp isolated-ground receptacle, 15-amp single-pole circuit breaker.

188

400-sq. ft. space. No two room additions are alike, so you will need to create a separate wiring diagram to serve as a guide for your own wiring project.

Note:
See pages 140 to 141 for a key to the common electrical symbols used in this diagram, and to learn how to draw your own wiring diagrams.

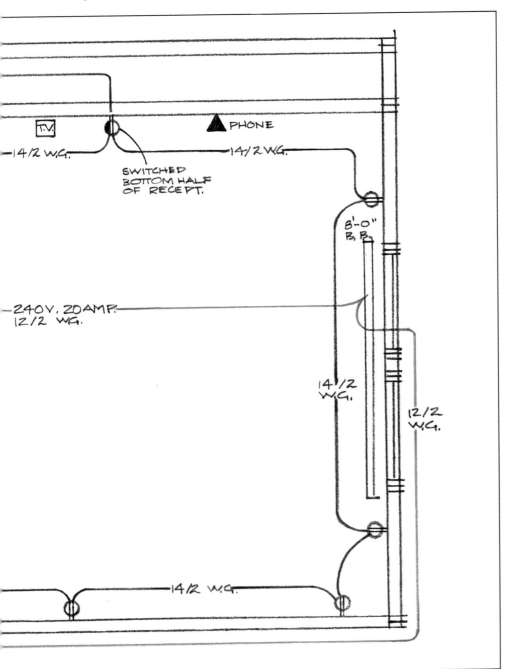

▶ **Telephone outlet:** 22-gauge four-wire phone cable (or eight-wire cable, if required by your telephone company), flush-mount telephone outlet.

TV **Cable television jack**: coaxial cable with F-connectors, signal splitter, cable television outlet with mounting brackets.

■ **Circuit #5 :** A 20-amp, 240-volt circuit that supplies power to three baseboard heaters controlled by a wall thermostat, and to a bathroom blower-heater controlled by a built-in thermostat. 12/2 NM cable, 750-watt blower-heater, single-gang box, line-voltage thermostat, three baseboard heaters, 20-amp double-pole circuit breaker.

Circuit #3: A 20-amp, 240-volt air-conditioner circuit. 12/2 NM cable; single-gang box; 20-amp, 240-volt receptacle (duplex or singleplex style); 20-amp double-pole circuit.

■ **Circuit #4 :** A 15-amp, 120-volt basic lighting/receptacle circuit serving most of the fixtures in the bedroom and study areas. 14/2 and 14/3 NM cable, 2 double-gang boxes, fan speed-control switch, dimmer switch, single-pole switch, 2 three-way switches, 2 plastic light fixture boxes, light fixture for stairway, smoke detector, metal light fixture box with brace bar, ceiling fan with light fixture, 10 single-gang boxes, 4" × 4" box with single-gang adapter plate, 10 duplex receptacles (15-amp), 15-amp single-pole circuit breaker.

1: Plan the Circuits

Your plans for wiring a room addition should reflect how you will use the space. For example, an attic space used as a bedroom requires an air-conditioner circuit, while a basement area used as a sewing room needs extra lighting. See pages 128 to 135 for information on planning circuits, and call or visit your city building inspector's office to learn the local Code requirements. You will need to create a detailed wiring diagram and a list of materials before the inspector will grant a work permit for your job.

The National Electrical Code requires receptacles to be spaced no more than 12 ft. apart, but for convenience you can space them as close as 6 ft. apart. Also consider the placement of furniture in the finished room, and do not place receptacles or baseboard heaters where beds, desks, or couches will cover them.

Electric heating units are most effective if you position them on the outside walls, underneath the windows. Position the receptacles to the sides of the heating units, not above the heaters where high temperatures might damage electrical cords.

Room light fixtures should be centered in the room, while stairway lights must be positioned so each step is illuminated. All wall switches should be within easy reach of the room entrance. Include a smoke alarm if your room addition includes a sleeping area.

Installing a ceiling fan improves heating and cooling efficiency and is a good idea for any room addition. Position it in a central location, and make sure there is plenty of headroom beneath it. Also consider adding accessory wiring for telephone outlets, television jacks, or stereo speakers.

Tips for Planning Room Addition Circuits

A permanently wired smoke alarm (page 209) is required by local Building Codes for room additions that include sleeping areas. Plan to install the smoke alarm just outside the sleeping area, in a hallway or stairway. Battery-operated smoke detectors are not allowed in new room additions.

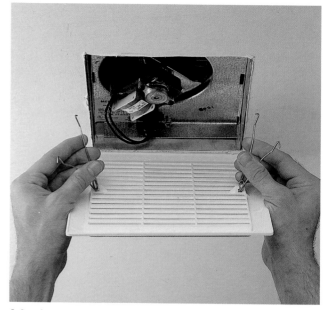

A bathroom vent fan (pages 194 to 197) may be required by your local Building Code, especially if your bathroom does not have a window. Vent fans are rated according to room size. Find the bathroom size in square feet by multiplying the length of the room times its width, and buy a vent fan rated for this size.

If your room addition includes a bathroom, it will have special wiring needs. All bathrooms require one or more GFCI receptacles, and most need a vent fan. An electric blower-heater will make your bathroom more comfortable.

Before drawing diagrams and applying for a work permit, calculate the electrical load (pages 136 to 139). Make sure your main service provides enough power for the new circuits.

Refer to pages 140 to 153 when drawing your wiring diagram. Using the completed diagram as a guide, create a detailed list of the materials you need. Bring the wiring diagram and the materials list to the inspector's office when you apply for the work permit. If the inspector suggests changes or improvements to your circuit design, follow his advice. His suggestions can save you time and money, and will ensure a safe, professional wiring installation.

A wiring plan for a room addition should show the location of all partition walls, doorways, and windows. Mark the location of all new and existing plumbing fixtures, water lines, drains, and vent pipes. Draw in any chimneys and duct work for central heating and air-conditioning systems. Make sure the plan is drawn to scale, because the size of the space will determine how you route the electrical cables and arrange the receptacles and fixtures.

Blower-heaters with built-in thermostats (pages 192, 210) work well in small areas like bathrooms, where quick heat is important. Some models can be wired for either 120 or 240 volts. A bathroom blower-heater should be placed well away from the sink and tub, at a comfortable height where the controls are easy to reach. In larger rooms, electric baseboard heaters controlled by a wall thermostat are more effective than blower-heaters.

Telephone and cable television wiring (pages 202 to 203) is easy to install at the same time you are installing electrical circuits. Position the accessory outlets in convenient locations, and keep the wiring at least 6" away from the electrical circuits to prevent static interference.

2: Install Boxes & Cables

For efficiency, install the electrical boxes for all new circuits before running any of the cables. After all the cables are installed, your project is ready for the rough-in inspection. Do not make the final connections until your work has passed rough-in inspection.

Boxes: See pages 156 to 161 for information on choosing and installing standard electrical boxes. In addition, your room addition may have recessed fixtures, like a blower-heater (photo, right) or vent fan (pages 194 to 197). These recessed fixtures have built-in wire connection boxes, and should be installed at the same time you are installing the standard electrical boxes. For a ceiling fan or other heavy ceiling fixture, install a metal box and brace bar (page opposite).

Cables: See pages 164 to 169 to install NM cable. In addition, you can install the necessary wiring for telephone outlets and cable television jacks (pages 202 to 203). This wiring is easy to install at the same time you are running electrical circuits, and is not subject to formal inspection.

How to Install a Blower-Heater

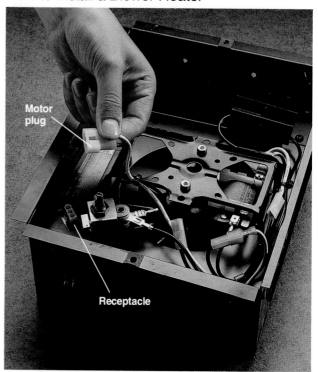

1 Disconnect the motor plug from the built-in receptacle that extends through the motor plate from the wire connection box.

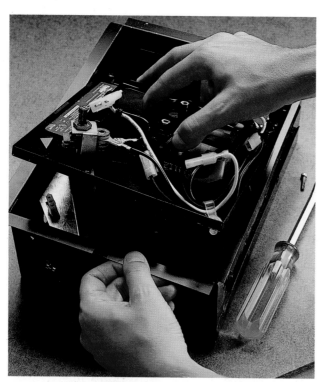

2 Take out the motor unit by removing the mounting screw and sliding the unit out of the frame.

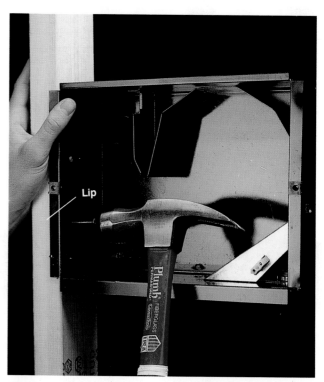

3 Open one knockout for each cable that will enter the wire connection box. Attach a cable clamp to each knockout. Position frame against a wall stud so the front lip will be flush with the finished wall surface. Attach the frame as directed by the manufacturer.

How to Install a Metal Box & Brace Bar for a Ceiling Fan

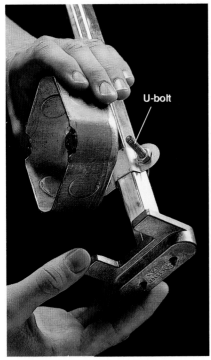

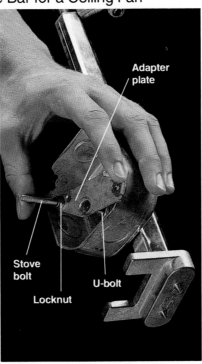

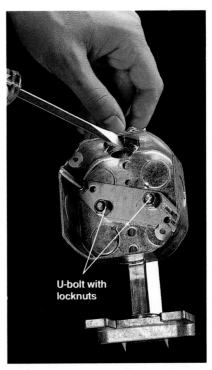

1 Attach a 1¹/₂"-deep metal light fixture box to the brace bar, using a U-bolt and two nuts.

2 Attach the included stove bolts to the adapter plate with locknuts. These bolts will support the fan. Insert the adapter plate into the box so ends of U-bolt fit through the holes on the adapter plate.

3 Secure the adapter plate by screwing two locknuts onto the U-bolt. Open one knockout for each cable that will enter the electrical box, and attach a cable clamp to each knockout.

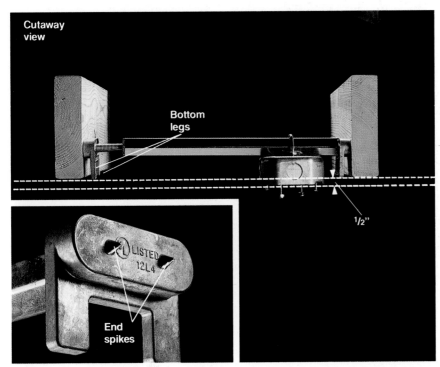

4 Position the brace between joists so the bottom legs are flush with the bottom of the joists. Rotate the bar by hand to force the end spikes into the joists. The face of the electrical box should be below the joists so the box will be flush with the finished ceiling surface.

5 Tighten the brace bar one rotation with a wrench to anchor the brace tightly against the joists.

Installing a Vent Fan

A vent fan helps prevent moisture damage to a bathroom by exhausting humid air to the outdoors. Vent fans are rated to match different room sizes. A vent fan can be controlled by a wall-mounted timer or single-pole switch. Some models have built-in light fixtures.

Position the vent fan in the center of the bathroom or over the stool area. In colder regions, Building Codes require that the vent hose be wrapped with insulation to prevent condensation of the moist air passing through the hose.

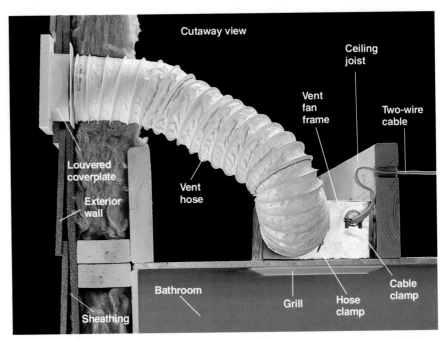

A vent fan has a built-in motor and blower that exhausts moisture-laden air from a bathroom to the outdoors through a plastic vent hose. A two-wire cable from a wall-mounted timer or single-pole switch is attached to the fan wire connection box with a cable clamp. A louvered coverplate mounted on the outside wall seals the vent against outdoor air when the motor is stopped.

How to Install a Vent Fan in New Construction

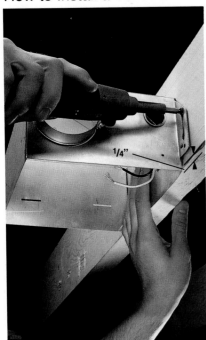

1 Disassemble the fan, following manufacturer's directions. Position the frame against a rafter so edge extends 1/4" below bottom edge of rafter to provide proper spacing for grill cover. Anchor frame with wallboard screws.

2 Choose the exit location for the vent. Temporarily remove any insulation, and draw the outline of the vent flange opening on the wall sheathing.

3 Drill a pilot hole, then make the cutout by sawing through the sheathing and siding with a jig saw. Keep the blade to the outside edge of the guideline.

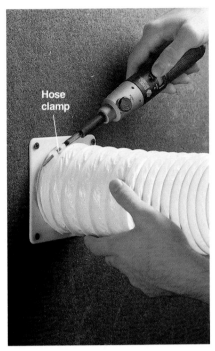

4 Insert the vent tailpiece into the cutout, and attach it to the wall by driving wallboard screws through the flange and into the sheathing.

5 Slide one end of vent hose over the tailpiece. Place one of the hose clamps around the end of the vent hose and tighten with a screwdriver. Replace insulation against sheathing.

6 Attach a hose adapter to the outlet on the fan frame by driving sheet-metal screws through the adapter and into the outlet flange. (NOTE: on some fans a hose adapter is not required.)

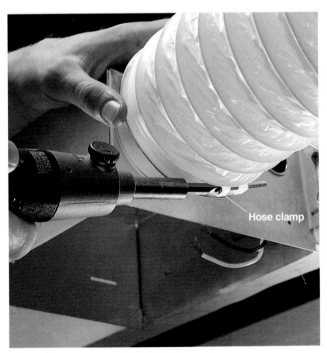

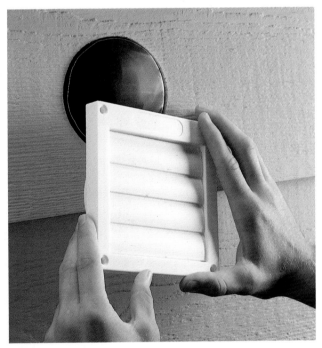

7 Slide the vent hose over the adapter. Place a hose clamp around the end of the hose and tighten it with a screwdriver. Your Building Code may require that you insulate the vent hose to prevent condensation problems.

8 On the outside wall of the house, place the louvered vent cover over the vent tailpiece, making sure the louvers are facing down. Attach the cover to the wall with galvanized screws. Apply a thick bead of caulk around the edge of the cover.

Arrange for the rough-in inspection before making the final connections.

How to Install a Vent Fan in an Existing Ceiling

1 Position the vent fan unit against a ceiling joist. Outline the vent fan onto the ceiling, from above. Remove unit, then drill pilot holes at the corners of the outline and cut out the area with a jig saw or wallboard saw.

2 Remove the grille from the fan box, then position box against a joist, with the edge recessed 1/4" from the finished surface of the ceiling (so the grille can be flush-mounted). Attach box to joist, using wallboard screws.

Vent fans with heaters or light fixtures: Some manufacturers recommend using 2" dimension lumber to build dams between the ceiling joists to keep insulation at least 6" away from the vent fan unit.

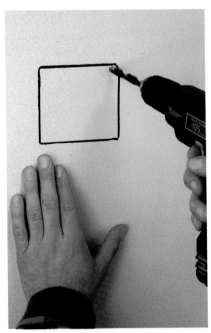

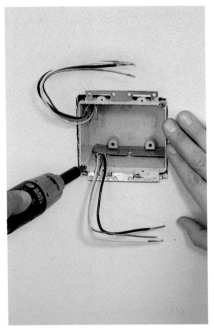

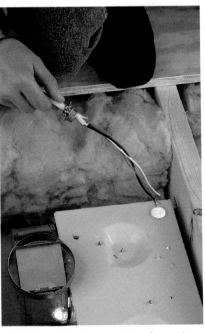

3 Mark and cut an opening for the switch box on the wall next to the latch side of the bathroom door, then run a 14-gauge, 3-wire NM cable from the switch cutout to the vent fan unit.

4 Strip 10" of sheathing from the end of the cable, then feed cable into switch box so at least 1/2" of sheathing extends into the box. Tighten mounting screws until box is secure.

5 Strip 10" of sheathing from the end of the cable at the vent box, then attach the cable to a cable clamp. Insert the cable into the fan box. From inside of box, screw a locknut onto the threaded end of the clamp.

How to Install a Vent Cover Flange on the Roof

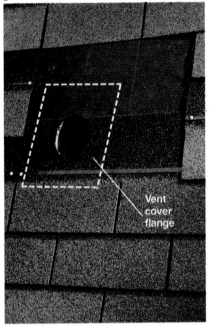

1 Mark the exit location in the roof for the vent hose, next to a rafter. Drill a pilot hole, then saw through the sheathing and roofing material with a reciprocating saw to make the cutout for the vent tailpiece.

2 From outside, remove section of shingles from around the cutout, leaving roofing paper intact. Removed shingles should create an exposed area the size of the vent cover flange. Use caution when working on a roof.

3 Attach a hose clamp to the rafter next to the roof cutout, about 1" below the roof sheathing (top photo). Insert the vent tailpiece into the cutout and through the hose clamp, then tighten the clamp screw (bottom photo).

4 Slide one end of vent hose over the tailpiece, and slide the other end over the outlet on the fan unit. Slip hose clamps or straps around each end of the vent hose, and tighten to secure hose in place.

5 Wrap the vent hose with pipe insulation. Insulation prevents moist air inside the hose from condensing and dripping down into the fan motor.

6 Apply roofing cement to the bottom of the vent cover flange, then slide the vent cover over the tailpiece. Nail the vent cover flange in place with self-sealing roofing nails, then patch in shingles around cover.

197

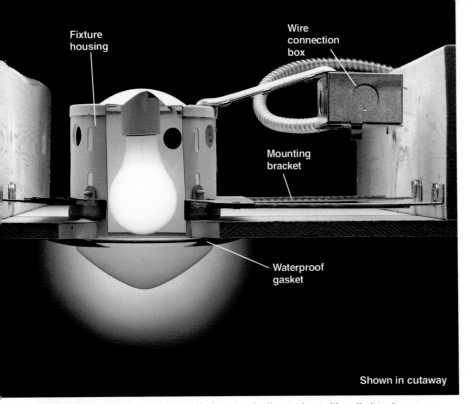

Fixture
housing

Wire
connection
box

Mounting
bracket

Waterproof
gasket

Shown in cutaway

Installing most bathroom lights is similar to installing lights in any other room in the house. Adding new lighting fixtures makes a bathroom safer and more inviting, and can even make bathrooms seem larger. In showers, install only vaporproof lights, like the one above, that have been U.L. rated for wet areas. Shower lights have a waterproof gasket that fits between the fixture and the light cover.

Installing Electrical Fixtures

Running cables for new electrical fixtures is easiest if wall surfaces have been removed. Make the final wiring hookups at the fixtures after wall surfaces are finished.

Follow Local Code requirements for wiring bathrooms. Reduce shock hazard by protecting the entire bathroom circuit with GFCI receptacles. Install only electrical fixtures that are U.L.-approved.

If it is not practical to remove wall surfaces, "retrofit" techniques can be used to install vent fans and other fixtures. Most wiring connections for bathroom fixtures are easy to make, but wiring configurations in electrical boxes vary widely, depending on the type of fixture and the circuit layout.

If you are not confident in your skills, have an electrician install and connect fixtures. Unless you are very experienced, leave the job of making circuit connections at the main service panel to an electrician.

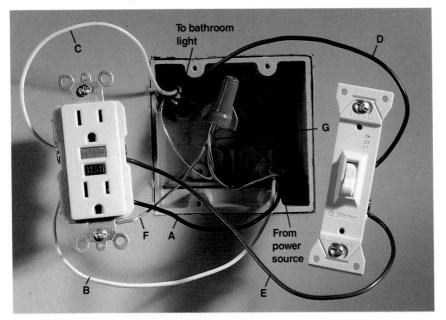

To bathroom
light

From
power
source

Install a GFCI receptacle and switch by making the following connections: black wire from power source (A) to brass screw marked LINE on GFCI; white wire from power source (B) to silver screw marked LINE: white wire to light (C) to silver GFCI screw marked LOAD; black wire to light (D) to a screw terminal on switch. Cut a short length of black wire (E), and attach one end to brass GFCI screw marked LOAD, and other end to a screw terminal on switch. Connect a bare grounding pigtail wire to GFCI grounding screw (F), and join all bare grounding wires (G) with a wire nut. Tuck wires into box, then attach switch, receptacle, and coverplate. Use the circuit maps on pages 143 to 153 as a guide for making connections.

CAUTION: Always shut off electrical power at the main service panel, and test for power (page 8) before working with wires.

Everything You Need:

Tools: neon circuit tester, wire stripper, cable ripper, screwdriver, level.

Materials: NM cable, wire staples, wire nuts, screws.

How to Install a Bathroom Light Fixture

Cable clamp

1 Turn power off. Remove coverplate from light fixture, and feed the electrical cable through the hole in the back of the fixture. NOTE: Some bathroom lights, like the shower light on page 198, have a connection box that is separate from the light fixture.

2 Position the fixture in the planned location, and adjust it so it is level. (Center the fixture if it is being installed over a medicine cabinet.) If possible, attach the box at wall stud locations. If studs are not conveniently located, anchor the box to the wall, using toggle bolts or other connectors.

3 Make electrical connections: attach white wire from cable (A) to white fixture wire (B), using a wire nut; attach black wire from cable (C) to black fixture wire (D); connect bare copper grounding wire from cable (E) to the fixture grounding wire (F) (or attach to grounding screw in some fixtures).

4 Tuck the wires into the back of the box, then attach the fixture coverplate. Install unprotected light bulbs only after the rest of the remodeling project is completed.

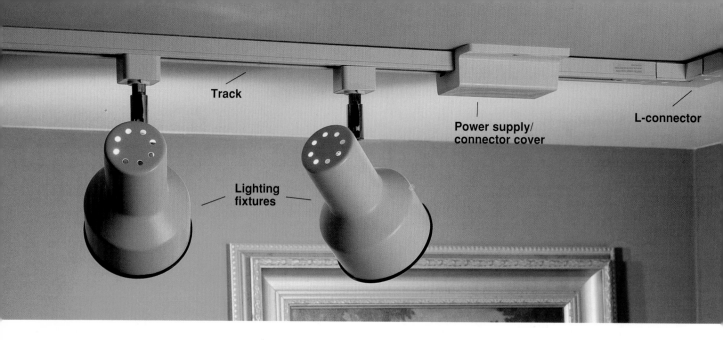

Track

Power supply/
connector cover

L-connector

Lighting
fixtures

Installing Track Lighting

Track lighting allows you to create custom indoor lighting at a small cost. Use it to highlight a wall, illuminate a sculpture, or brighten a dark corner; the possibilities and effects are limitless. You can purchase track lighting kits at most home improvement retail outlets. It comes in a variety of styles, which allows you to mix and match components to suit your needs. Installation is easy. All you need are a few household tools. While not necessary, it is helpful to have a second person to assist in positioning and attaching the track.

Track lighting can be installed anywhere. Determining where to place track lighting depends on the room's layout, the areas you want illuminated, and finally the power source. The easiest way to install it is near an existing light fixture. But, if no wiring is in place, it is best to hire a licensed electrician. Or, if your wiring project is in new construction, you can install the ceiling box where you need it. The installation of the track and fixtures occurs after the finished ceiling is in place.

The first track section should start at an existing switched ceiling box. From there, you can install track along one side of the room or around the entire room. Use T and L track connectors for more flexibility or to branch tracks. For the best effect, place tracks parallel to the house wall closest to the fixture.

Since track lighting manufacturers and models vary, it is important to always follow product instructions.

Everything You Need:

Tools: ladder, tape measure, circuit/voltage tester, drill, screwdrivers, straightedge.

Materials: pencil, wire nuts, toggle bolts, screws.

How to Install Track Lighting

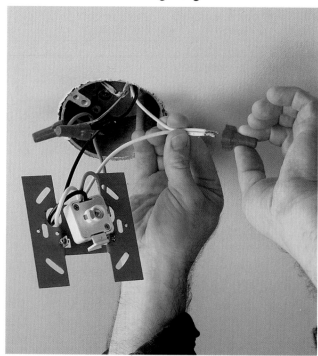

1 Turn off power to ceiling box outlet. Remove existing fixture and disconnect wires. Attach green grounding fixture wire to bare copper grounding wire, and pigtail to electrical box if required. Attach white circuit wire to white fixture wire. Then attach black circuit wire to black fixture wire. Carefully tuck wires into the electrical box.

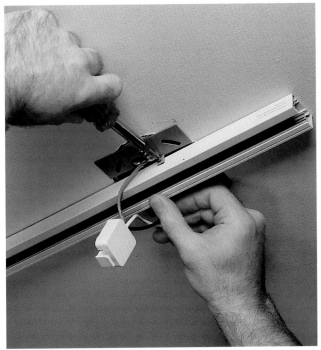

2 With pencil and straightedge, mark track location line from the power source to the end of the track. If possible, position tracks underneath ceiling joists for sturdy installation. Attach mounting plate to ceiling box. Snap first track onto the mounting plate and position track. Fasten track loosely with screws (or toggle bolts if fastening to ceiling drywall).

3 Insert connector into track and twist into position (connector installation may vary according to manufacturer). Attach power supply/connector cover. Continue inserting connectors and attaching connector covers to each track section, using the L-connector for corners and the T-connector to join three tracks.

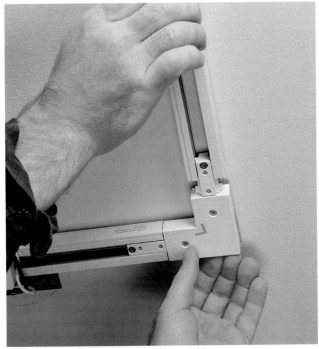

4 Hold each track section in place and mark screw or toggle bolt hole locations on ceiling. Remove track and drill holes. Install bolts in track and hang all units, waiting to tighten until all tracks are hung. After all tracks are installed, tighten screws or bolts till tracks are flush with ceiling. Close open ends with dead-end pieces.

5 Insert lighting fixtures into the track and twist-lock into place. Install appropriate bulbs and turn on power to ceiling box. Turn on power to the fixture at wall switch and adjust beams for the desired effect.

Coaxial
cable for
television jack

F-connector

Installing Telephone & Cable Television Wiring

Telephone outlets and television jacks are easy to install while you are wiring new electrical circuits. Install the accessory cables while framing members are exposed, then make the final connections after the walls are finished.

Telephone lines use four- or eight-wire cable, often called "bell wire," while television lines use a shielded coaxial cable with threaded end fittings called F-connectors. To splice into an existing cable television line, use a fitting called a signal splitter. Signal splitters are available with two, three, or four outlet nipples.

How to Install Coaxial Cable for a Television Jack

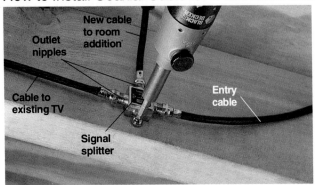

New cable to room addition

Outlet nipples

Cable to existing TV

Signal splitter

Entry cable

1 Install a signal splitter where the entry cable connects to indoor TV cables, usually in the basement or another utility area. Attach one end of new coaxial cable to an outlet nipple on the splitter. Anchor splitter to a framing member with wallboard screws.

2 Run the coaxial cable to the location of the new television jack. Keep coaxial cable at least 6" away from electrical wiring to avoid electrical interference. Mark the floor so the cable can be found easily after the walls are finished.

How to Connect a Television Jack

Mounting bracket

1 After walls are finished, make a cutout opening 1½" wide and 3¾" high at the television jack location. Pull cable through the opening, and install two television jack mounting brackets in the cutout.

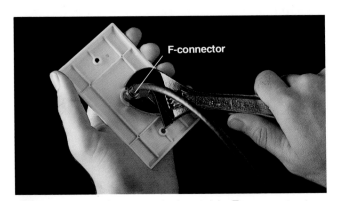

F-connector

2 Use a wrench to attach the cable F-connector to the back of the television jack. Attach the jack to the wall by screwing it onto the mounting brackets.

How to Install Cable for a Telephone Outlet

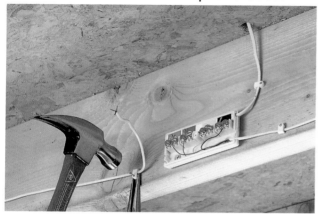

1 Locate a telephone junction in your basement or other utility area. Remove the junction cover. Use cable staples to anchor one end of the cable to a framing member near the junction, leaving 6" to 8" of excess cable.

2 Run the cable from the junction to the telephone outlet location. Keep the cable at least 6" away from circuit wiring to avoid electrical interference. Mark the floor so the cable can be located easily after the walls are finished.

How to Connect a Telephone Outlet

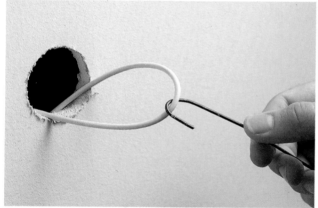

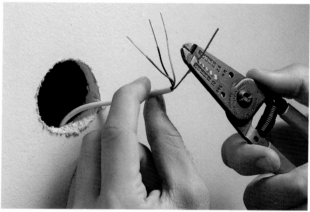

1 After walls are finished, cut a hole in the wallboard at phone outlet location, using a wallboard saw. Retrieve the cable, using a piece of stiff wire.

2 At each cable end, remove about 2" of outer sheathing. Remove about 3/4" of insulation from each wire, using a combination tool.

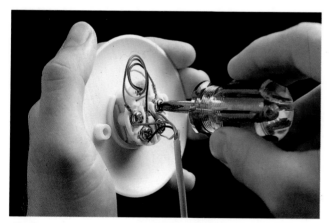

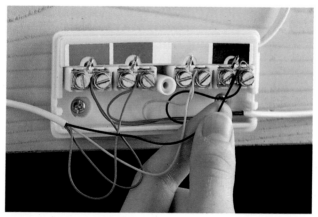

3 Connect wires to similarly colored wire leads in phone outlet. If there are extra wires, tape them to back of outlet. Put the telephone outlet over the wall cutout, and attach it to the wallboard.

4 At the telephone junction, connect the cable wires to the color-coded screw terminals. If there are extra wires, wrap them with tape and tuck them inside the junction. Reattach the junction cover.

3: Make Final Connections

Make the final connections for receptacles, switches, and fixtures only after the rough-in inspection is done and all walls and ceilings are finished. Use the circuit maps on pages 143 to 153 as a guide for making connections. The circuit maps are especially useful if your wiring configurations differ from those shown on the following pages. The last step is to hook up the new circuits at the breaker panel (pages 178 to 179).

After all connections are done, your work is ready for the final inspection. If you have worked carefully, the final inspection will take only a few minutes. The inspector may open one or two electrical boxes to check wire connections, and will check the circuit breaker hookups to make sure they are correct.

Materials You Will Need:

Pigtail wires, wire nuts, green & black tape.

■ Circuit #1

A 15-amp, 120-volt circuit serving the bathroom & closet.

- Timer & single-pole switch
- Vent fan
- Two light fixtures
- GFCI receptacle
- Single-pole switch
- 15-amp single-pole circuit breaker (see pages 178 to 179) for instructions on hooking up the circuit at the circuit breaker panel)

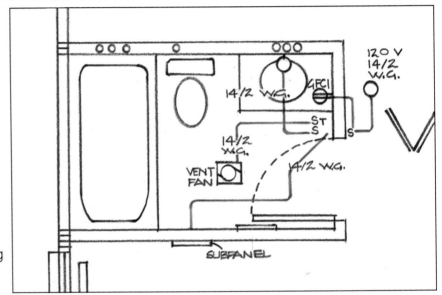

How to Connect the Timer & Single-pole Switch

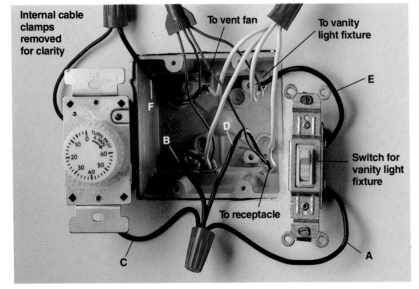

Internal cable clamps removed for clarity

To vent fan

To vanity light fixture

E

F

B

D

Switch for vanity light fixture

To receptacle

C

A

Attach a black pigtail wire (A) to one of the screw terminals on the switch. Use a wire nut to connect this pigtail to the black feed wire (B), to one of the black wire leads on the timer (C), and to the black wire carrying power to the bathroom receptacle (D). Connect the black wire leading to the vanity light fixture (E) to the remaining screw terminal on the switch. Connect the black wire running to the vent fan (F) to the remaining wire lead on the timer. Use wire nuts to join the white wires and the grounding wires. Tuck all wires into the box, then attach the switches, coverplate and timer dial. (See also circuit map 4, page 144; and circuit map 16, page 150.)

How to Connect the Vent Fan

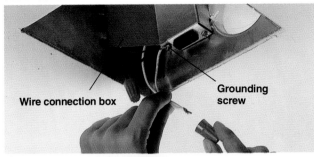

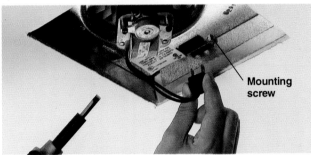

In the wire connection box (top) connect black circuit wire to black wire lead on fan, using a wire nut. Connect white circuit wire to white wire lead. Connect grounding wire to the green grounding screw.
Insert the fan motor unit (bottom) and attach mounting screws. Connect the fan motor plug to the built-in receptacle on the wire connection box. Attach the fan grill to the frame, using the mounting clips included with the fan kit (page 194).

How to Connect Light Fixtures

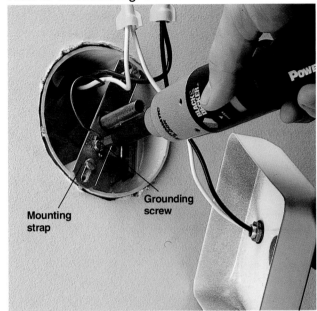

Attach a mounting strap with threaded nipple to the box, if required by the light fixture manufacturer. Connect the black circuit wire to the black wire lead on the light fixture, and connect the white circuit wire to the white wire lead. Connect the circuit grounding wire to the grounding screw on the mounting strap. Carefully tuck all wires into the electrical box, then position the fixture over the nipple and attach it with the mounting nut. (See also circuit map 4, page 144.)

How to Connect the Bathroom GFCI Receptacle

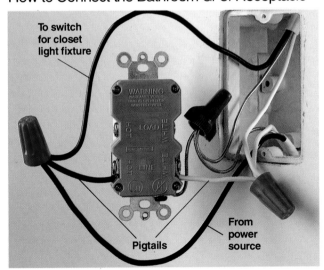

Attach a black pigtail wire to brass screw terminal marked LINE. Join all black wires with a wire nut. Attach a white pigtail wire to the silver screw terminal marked LINE, then join all white wires with a wire nut. Attach a grounding pigtail to the green grounding screw, then join all grounding wires. Tuck all wires into the box, then attach the receptacle and the coverplate. (See also circuit map 2, page 143.)

How to Connect the Single-pole Switch

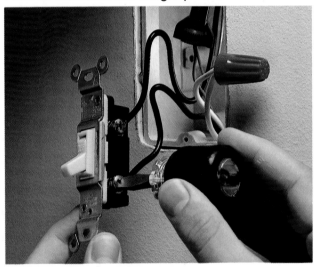

Attach the black circuit wires to the brass screw terminals on the switch. Use wire nuts to join the white neutral wires together and the bare copper grounding wires together. Tuck all wires into the box, then attach the switch and the coverplate. (See also circuit map 4, page 144.)

■ Circuit #2:

A 15-amp, 120-volt isolated-ground circuit for a home computer in the office area.

- 15-amp isolated-ground receptacle
- 15-amp single-pole circuit breaker (see pages 178 to 179 for instructions on hooking up the circuit at the circuit breaker panel)

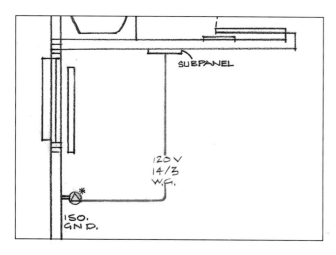

How to Connect the Computer Receptacle

Tag the red wire with green tape to identify it as a grounding wire. Attach this wire to the grounding screw terminal on the isolated-ground receptacle. Connect the black wire to the brass screw terminal, and the white wire to the silver screw. Push the bare copper wire to the back of the box. Carefully tuck all wires into the box, then attach the receptacle and coverplate. (See also circuit map 15, page 150.)

■ Circuit #3:

A 20-amp, 240-volt air-conditioner circuit.

- 20-amp 240-volt receptacle (singleplex or duplex style)
- 20-amp double-pole circuit breaker (see pages 178 to 179 for instructions on hooking up the circuit at the circuit breaker panel)

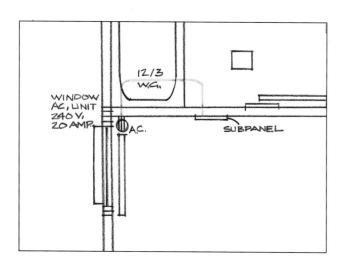

How to Connect the 240-volt Receptacle

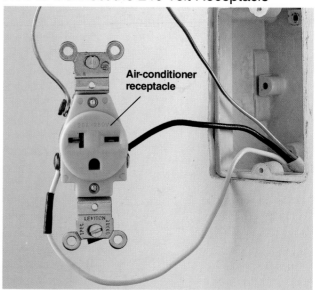

Connect the black circuit wire to a brass screw terminal on the air-conditioner receptacle, and connect the white circuit wire to the screw on the opposite side. Tag white wire with black tape to identify it as a hot wire. Connect grounding wire to green grounding screw on the receptacle. Tuck in wires, then attach receptacle and coverplate. (See also circuit map 12, page 148.) A 240-volt receptacle is available in either singleplex (shown above) or duplex style.

Circuit #4:

A 15-amp, 120-volt basic lighting/receptacle circuit serving the office and bedroom areas.

- Single-pole switch for split receptacle, three-way switch for stairway light fixture
- Speed-control and dimmer switches for ceiling fan
- Switched duplex receptacle
- 15-amp, 120-volt receptacles
- Ceiling fan with light fixture
- Smoke detector
- Stairway light fixture
- 15-amp single-pole circuit breaker (see pages 178 to 179)

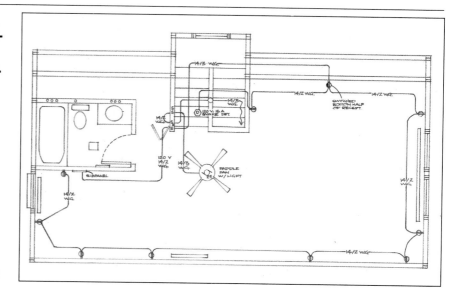

How to Connect Switches for Receptacle & Stairway Light

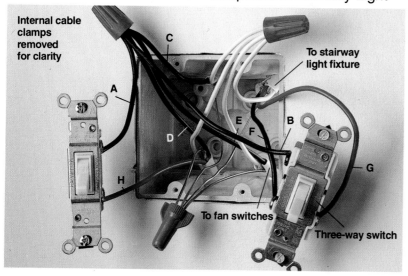

Attach a black pigtail wire (A) to one of the screws on the single-pole switch and another black pigtail (B) to common screw on three-way switch. Use a wire nut to connect pigtail wires to black feed wire (C), to black wire running to unswitched receptacles (D), and to the black wire running to fan switches (E). Connect remaining wires running to light fixture (F, G) to traveler screws on three-way switch. Connect red wire running to switched receptacle (H) to remaining screw on single-pole switch. Use wire nuts to join white wires and grounding wires. Tuck all wires into box, then attach switches and coverplate. (See also circuit map 7, page 146, and map 17, page 151.)

How to Connect the Ceiling Fan Switches

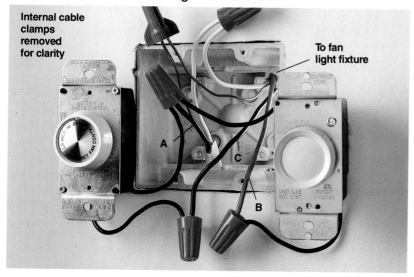

Connect the black feed wire (A) to one of the black wire leads on each switch, using a wire nut. Connect the red circuit wire (B) running to the fan light fixture to the remaining wire lead on the dimmer switch. Connect the black circuit wire (C) running to the fan motor to the remaining wire lead on the speed-control switch. Use wire nuts to join the white wires and the grounding wires. Tuck all wires into the box, then attach the switches, coverplate, and switch dials. (See also circuit map 21, page 153.)

How to Connect a Switched Receptacle

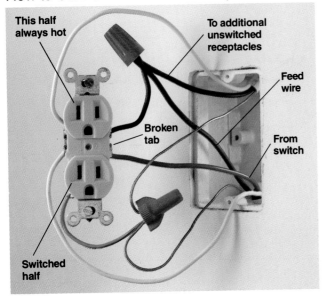

Break the connecting tab between the brass screw teminals on the receptacle, using needlenose pliers. Attach the red wire to the bottom brass screw. Connect a black pigtail wire to the other brass screw, then connect all black wires with a wire nut. Connect white wires to silver screws. Attach a grounding pigtail to the green grounding screw, then join all the grounding wires, using a wire nut. Tuck the wires into the box, then attach the receptacle and coverplate. (See also circuit map 7, page 146.)

How to Connect Receptacles

Connect the black circuit wires to the brass screw terminals on the receptacle, and the white wires to the silver terminals. Attach a grounding pigtail to the green grounding screw on the receptacle, then join all grounding wires with a wire nut. Tuck the wires into the box, then attach the receptacle and coverplate. (See also circuit map 1, page 143.)

How to Connect a Ceiling Fan/Light Fixture

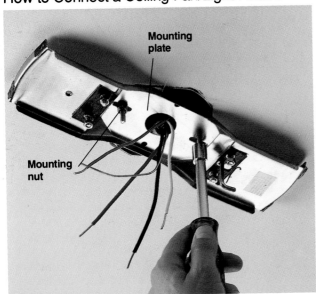

1 Place the ceiling fan mounting plate over the stove bolts extending through the electrical box. Pull the circuit wires through the hole in the center of the mounting plate. Attach the mounting nuts and tighten them with a nut driver.

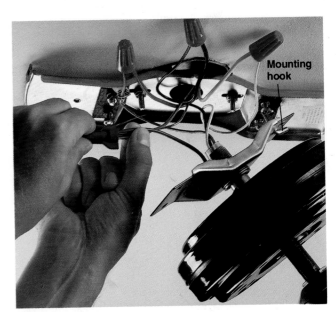

2 Hang fan motor from mounting hook. Connect black circuit wire to black wire lead from fan, using a wire nut. Connect red circuit wire from dimmer to blue wire lead from light fixture, white circuit wire to white lead, and grounding wires to green lead. Complete assembly of fan and light fixture, following manufacturer's directions. (See also circuit map 21, page 152.)

How to Connect a Smoke Alarm

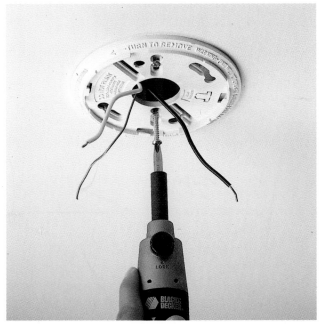

1 Attach the smoke alarm mounting plate to the electrical box, using the mounting screws provided with the smoke alarm kit.

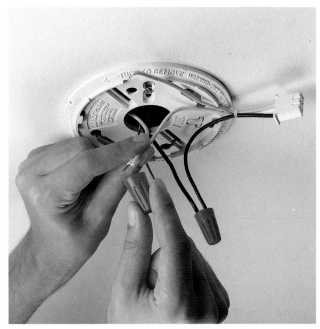

2 Use wire nuts to connect the black circuit wire to the black wire lead on the smoke alarm, and the white circuit wire to the white wire lead.

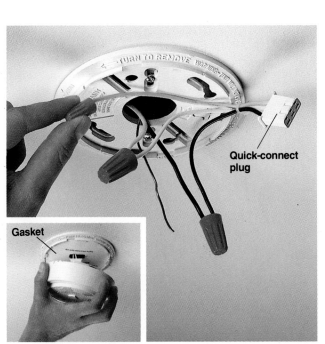

Quick-connect plug

Gasket

3 Screw a wire nut onto the end of the yellow wire, if present. (This wire is used only if two or more alarms are wired in series.) Tuck all wires into the box Place the cardboard gasket over the mounting plate. Attach the quick-connect plug to the smoke alarm. Attach the alarm to the mounting plate, twisting it clockwise until it locks into place (inset).

How to Connect a Stairway Light Fixture

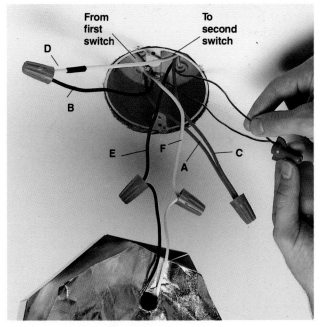

From first switch

To second switch

D

B

E   F   C

A

Connect the traveler wires entering the box from the first three-way switch (red wire [A] and black wire [B]) to the traveler wires running to the second three-way switch (red wire [C] and white wire tagged with black tape [D]). Connect the common wire running to the second switch (E) to the black lead on the light fixture. Connect the white wire from the first switch (F) to the white fixture lead. Join the grounding wires. Tuck wires into box and attach the light fixtures. (See also circuit map 17, page 151.)

◼ Circuit #5:

A 20-amp, 240-volt circuit serving the bathroom blower-heater, and three baseboard heaters controlled by a wall thermostat.

- 240-volt blower-heater
- 240-volt thermostat
- 240-volt baseboard heaters
- 20-amp double-pole circuit breaker (see pages 178 to 179) for instructions on hooking up the circuit at the circuit breaker panel)

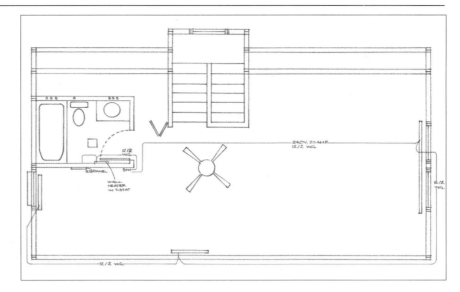

How to Connect a 240-volt Blower-Heater

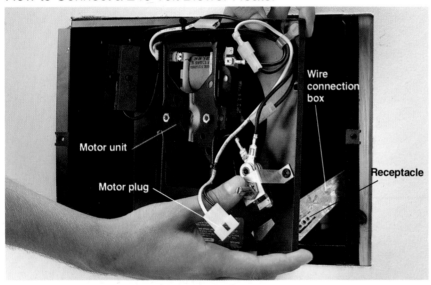

Motor unit

Motor plug

Wire connection box

Receptacle

Blower-heaters: In the heater's wire connection box, connect one of the wire leads to the white circuit wires, and the other wire lead to the black circuit wires, using same method as for baseboard heaters (page opposite). Insert the motor unit, and attach the motor plug to the built-in receptacle. Attach the coverplate and thermostat knob. NOTE: Some types of blower-heaters can be wired for either 120 volts or 240 volts. If you have this type, make sure the internal plug connections are configured for 240 volts.

How to Connect a 240-volt Thermostat

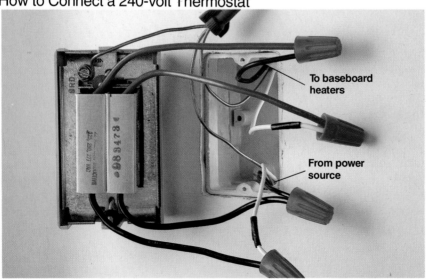

To baseboard heaters

From power source

Connect the red wire leads on the thermostat to the circuit wires entering the box from the power source, using wire nuts. Connect black wire leads to circuit wires leading to the baseboard heaters. Tag the white wires with black tape to indicate they are hot. Attach a grounding pigtail to the grounding screw on the thermostat, then connect all grounding wires. Tuck the wires into the box, then attach the thermostat and coverplate. (See also circuit map 13, page 149.) Follow manufacturer's directions: the color coding for thermostats may vary.

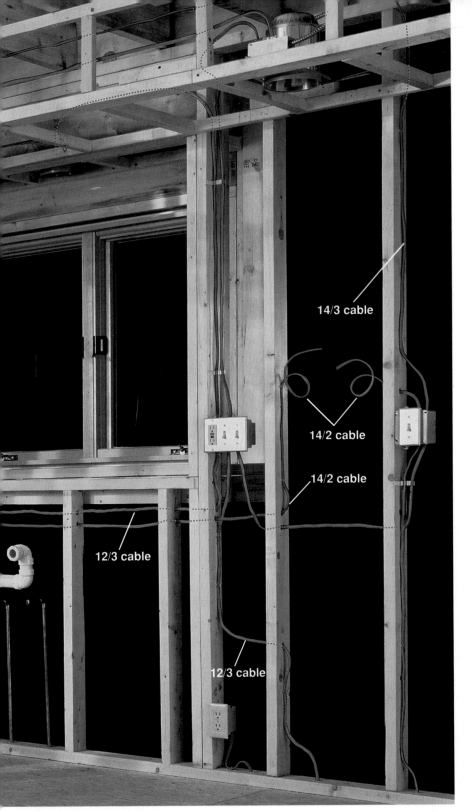

14/3 cable

14/2 cable

14/2 cable

12/3 cable

12/3 cable

Wiring a Remodeled Kitchen:
Construction View

The kitchen remodeling wiring project shown on the following pages includes the installation of seven new circuits. Four of these are dedicated circuits: a 50-amp circuit supplying the range, a 20-amp circuit powering the microwave, and two 15-amp circuits supplying the dishwasher and food disposer. In addition, two 20-amp circuits for small appliances supply power to all receptacles above the countertops and in the eating area. Finally, a 15-amp basic lighting circuit controls the ceiling fixture, all of the recessed fixtures, and the under-cabinet task lights.

All rough construction and plumbing work should be finished and inspected before beginning the electrical work. Divide the project into steps and complete each step before beginning the next.

Three Steps for Wiring a Remodeled Kitchen:

1. Plan the Circuits (pages 218 to 219).
2. Install Boxes & Cables (pages 220 to 223).
3. Make Final Connections (pages 224 to 229).

■ #5: Food disposer circuit. A dedicated 15-amp, 120-volt circuit supplies power to the disposer. It is wired with 14/2 cable. Some local Codes allow the disposer to be on the same circuit as the dishwasher.

■ #6: Dishwasher circuit. A dedicated 15-amp, 120-volt circuit supplies power to the dishwasher. It is wired with 14/2 cable. Some local Codes allow the dishwasher to be on the same circuit as the disposer.

■ #7: Basic lighting circuit. A 15-amp, 120-volt circuit powers the ceiling fixture, recessed fixtures, and under-cabinet task lights. 14/2 and 14/3 cables connect the fixtures and switches in the circuit. Each task light has a self-contained switch.

Tools You Will Need:
Marker, tape measure, calculator, masking tape, screwdriver, hammer, power drill with 5/8" spade bit, cable ripper, combination tool, needlenose pliers, fish tape.

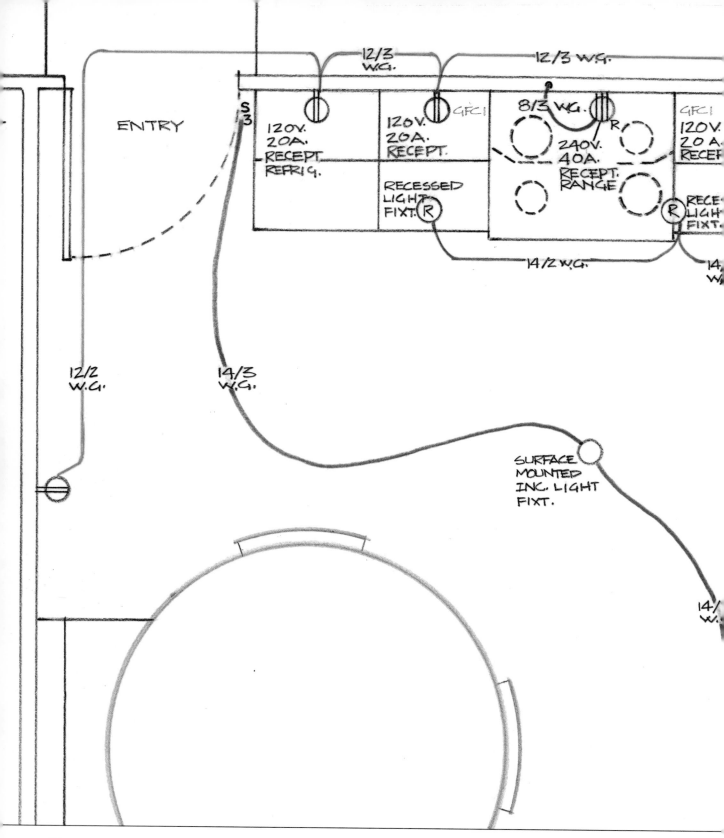

ENTRY

12/3 W.G.

12/3 W.G.

S₃

120V. 20A. RECEPT. REFRIG.

120V. 20A. RECEPT.

GFCI

8/3 W.G.

R

240V. 40A. RECEPT. RANGE

GFCI

120V. 20A. RECEP

RECESSED LIGHT FIXT. R

R

RECE. LIGHT FIXT.

14/2 W.G.

14/ W.

12/2 W.G.

14/3 W.G.

SURFACE MOUNTED INC. LIGHT FIXT.

14/ W.

Circuits #1 & #2: Two 20-amp, 120-volt small-appliance circuits wired with one cable. All general-use receptacles must be on these circuits and they must be GFCI units. Includes: 7 GFCI receptacles rated for 20 amps, 5 electrical boxes that are 4" x 4", and 12/3 cable. One GFCI shares a double-gang box with circuit #5, and another GFCI shares a triple-gang box with circuit #7.

Circuit #3: A 50-amp, 120/240-volt dedicated circuit for the range. Includes: a 4" x 4" box; a 120/240-volt, 50-amp range receptacle; and 6/3 NM cable.

Handwritten diagram labels:

120V, 20A, RECEPT. M.W.
12/3 W.G.
12/2 W.G.
14/2 W.G.
14/2 W.G.
120V, 20A, RECEPT.
GFCI
120V. 15A. LIGHT FIXT.
12/3 W.G.
RECESSED LIGHT FIXT. (R)
DRAIN WASTE VENT
GFCI S
120V 20A RECEPT.
14/2 W.G.
14/2 W.G.
14/2 W.G.
12/3 W.G.
14/2 W.G.
120V, 15A. RECEPT. DISPOSER
RECESSED LIGHT FIXT. (R)
D.W.
(R) RECESSED LIGHT FIXT.
120V. 15A. RECEPT. D.W.
14/2 W.G.
14/2 W.G.
GFCI S
120V. 20A. RECEPT.
S
14/2 W.G.
14/2 W.G.
14/2 W.G.
S 3
14/2 W.G.
(R) RECESSED LIGHT FIXT.

Wiring a Remodeled Kitchen:
Diagram View

This diagram view shows the layout of seven circuits and the location of the switches, receptacles, lights, and other fixtures in the remodeled kitchen featured in this section. The size and number of circuits, and the specific features included are based on the needs of this 170-sq. ft. space. No two remodeled kitchens are exactly alike, so create your own wiring diagram to guide you through your wiring project.

Note:
See pages 140 to 141 for a key to the common electrical symbols used in this diagram, and to learn how to draw your own wiring diagrams.

■ **Circuit #7:** A 15-amp, 120-volt basic lighting circuit serving all of the lighting needs in the kitchen. Includes: 2 single-pole switches, 2 three-way switches, single-gang box, 4" x 4" box, triple-gang box (shared with one of the GFCI receptacles from the small-appliance circuits), plastic light fixture box with brace, ceiling light fixture, 4 fluorescent under-cabinet light fixtures, 6 recessed light fixtures, 14/2 and 14/3 cable.

■ **Circuit #6:** A 15-amp, 120-volt dedicated circuit for the dishwasher. Includes: a 15-amp duplex receptacle, one single-gang box, and 14/2 cable.

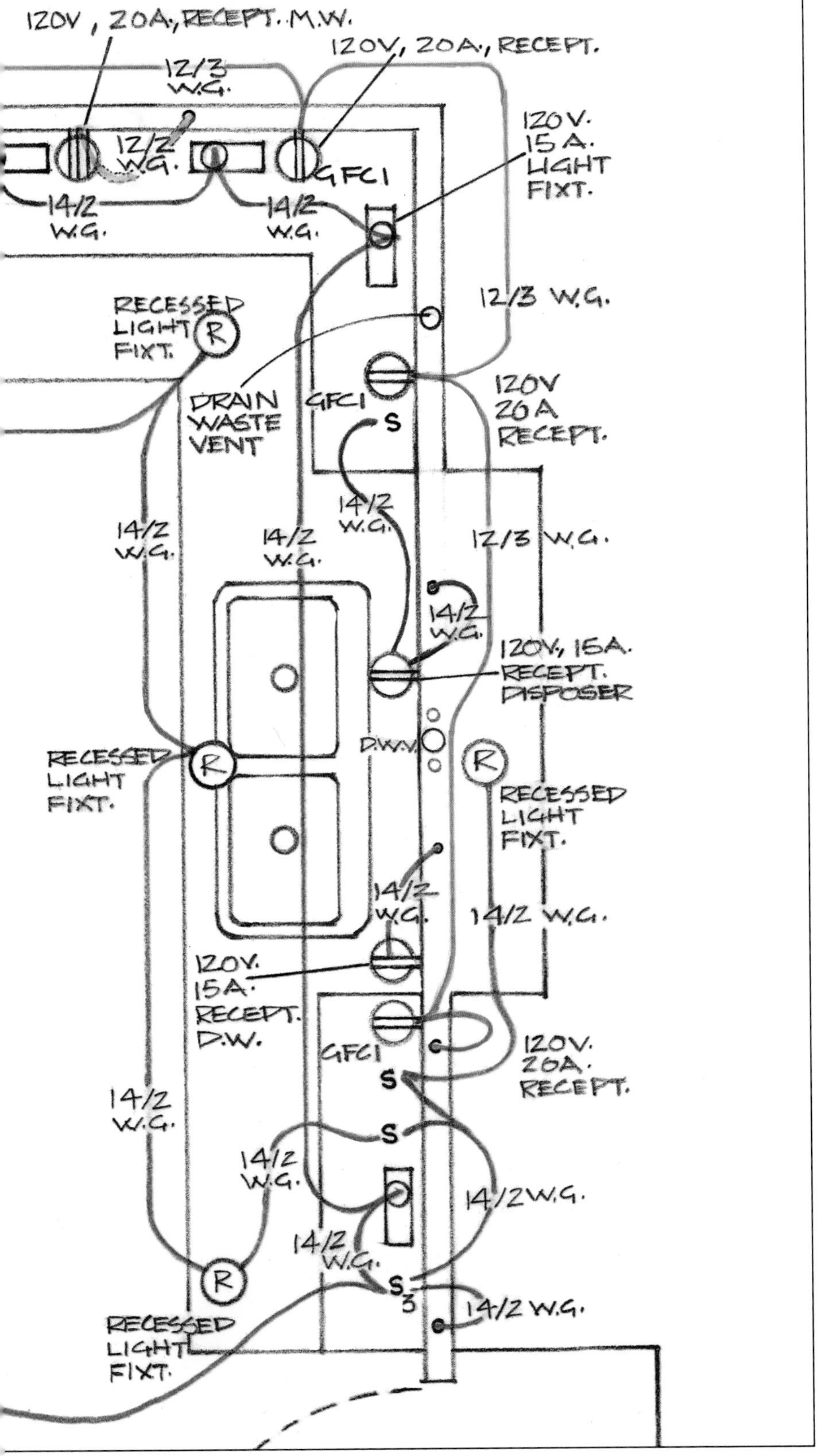

■ **Circuit #4:** A 20-amp, 120-volt dedicated circuit for the microwave. Includes: a 20-amp duplex receptacle, a single-gang box, and 12/2 NM cable.

■ **Circuit #5:** A 15-amp, 120-volt dedicated circuit for the food disposer. Includes: a 15-amp duplex receptacle, a single-pole switch (installed in a double-gang box with a GFCI receptacle from the small-appliance circuits), one single-gang box, and 14/2 cable.

4 ft. maximum

Code requires receptacles above countertops to be no more than 4 ft. apart. Put receptacles closer together in areas where many appliances will be used. Any section of countertop that is wider than 12" must have a receptacle located above it. (Countertop spaces separated by items such as range tops, sinks, and refrigerators are considered separate sections.) All accessible receptacles in kitchens (and bathrooms) must be a GFCI. On walls without countertops, receptacles should be no more than 12 ft. apart.

Wiring a Remodeled Kitchen

1: Plan the Circuits

A kitchen generally uses the most power in the home because it contains many light fixtures and appliances. Where these items are located depends upon your needs. Make sure plenty of light and enough receptacles will be in the main work areas of your kitchen. Try to anticipate future needs: for example, install a range receptacle when remodeling, even if you currently have a gas range. It is difficult and expensive to make changes later. See pages 128 to 141 for more information on planning circuits.

Contact your local Building and Electrical Code offices before you begin planning. They may have requirements that differ from the National Electrical Code. Remember that the Code contains minimum requirements primarily concerning safety, not convenience or need. Work with the inspectors to create a safe plan that also meets your needs.

To help locate receptacles, plan carefully where cabinets and appliances will be in the finished project. Appliances installed within cabinets, such as microwaves or food disposers, must have their receptacles positioned according to manufacturer's instructions. Put at least one receptacle at table height in the dining areas for convenience in operating a small appliance.

The ceiling fixture should be centered in the kitchen ceiling. Or, if your kitchen contains a dining area or breakfast nook, you may want to center the light fixture over the table. Locate recessed light fixtures and under-cabinet task lights where they will best illuminate main work areas.

Before drawing diagrams and applying for a permit, evaluate your existing service and make sure it provides enough power to supply the new circuits you are planning to add (pages 136 to 139). If it will not, contact a licensed electrician to upgrade your service before beginning your work. See pages 140 to 153 for more information on drawing wiring plans.

Bring the wiring plan and materials list to the inspector's office when applying for the permit. If the inspector suggests improvements to your plan, such as using switches with grounding screws, follow his advice. He can save you time and money.

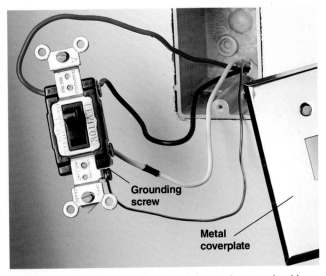

Grounding screw

Metal coverplate

A switch with a grounding screw may be required by inspectors in kitchens and baths. Code requires them when metal coverplates are used with plastic boxes.

Tips for Planning Kitchen Circuits

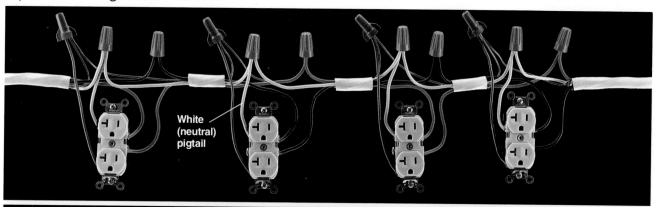

White (neutral) pigtail

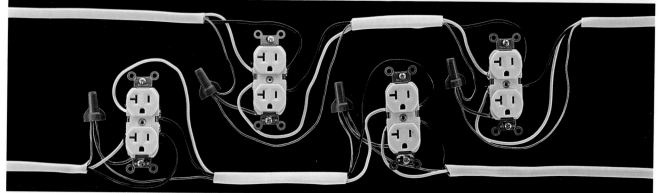

Wire the two 20-amp circuits with one 12/3 cable supplying power to both circuits (top), rather than running a separate 12/2 cable for each circuit (bottom). This will save time and money. In the 12/3 cable, the black wire supplies power to one circuit for alternate receptacles (for example, the first, third, fifth, etc.), and the red wire supplies power for the second circuit to the remaining receptacles. The white wire is the neutral for both circuits (see circuit map 10, page 147). For safety, the white receptacles (the first, third, etc.), the red wire supplies power for the second circuit to the remaining receptacles. The white wire is the neutral for both circuits (see circuit map 10, page 25). For safety, it must be attached with a pigtail to each receptacle, instead of being connected directly to the terminal. These circuits must contain all general-use receptacles in the kitchen, pantry, breakfast area or dining room. No lighting outlets or receptacles from any other rooms can be connected to them.

Work areas at sink and range should be well lighted for convenience and safety. Install switch-controlled lights over these areas.

Ranges require a dedicated 40- or 50-amp 120/240-volt circuit (or two circuits for separate oven and countertop units). Even if you do not have an electric range, it is a good idea to install tne circuit when remodeling.

Dishwashers and food disposers require dedicated 15-amp, 120-volt circuits in most local Codes. Some inspectors will allow these appliances to share one circuit.

Heights of electrical boxes in a kitchen vary depending upon their use. In the kitchen project shown here the centers of the boxes above the countertop are 45" above the floor, in the center of 18" backsplashes that extend from the countertop to the cabinets. All boxes for wall switches also are installed at this height.

The center of the box for the microwave receptacle is 72" off the floor, where it will fit between the cabinets. The centers of the boxes for the range and food disposer receptacles are 12" off the floor, but the center of the box for the dishwasher receptacle is 6" off the floor, next to the space the appliance will occupy.

Wiring a Remodeled Kitchen

2: Install Boxes & Cables

After the inspector issues you a work permit, you can begin installing electrical boxes for switches, receptacles, and fixtures. Install all boxes and frames for recessed fixtures such as vent fans and recessed lights before cutting and installing any cable. However, some surface-mounted fixtures, such as under-cabinet task lights, have self-contained wire connection boxes. These fixtures are installed after the walls are finished and the cabinets are in place.

First determine locations for the boxes above the countertops (page opposite). After establishing the height for these boxes, install all of the other visible wall boxes at this height. Boxes that will be behind appliances or inside cabinets should be located according to appliance manufacturer's

instructions. For example, the receptacle for the dishwasher cannot be installed directly behind the appliance; it is often located in the sink cabinet for easy access.

Always use the largest electrical boxes that are practical for your installation. Using large boxes ensures that you will meet Code regulations concerning box volume, and simplifies making the connections. See pages 156 to 161 for more information on choosing and installing standard electrical boxes.

After all the boxes and recessed fixtures are installed, you are ready to measure and cut the cables. First install the feeder cables that run from the circuit breaker panel to the first electrical box in each circuit. Then cut and install the remaining cables to complete the circuits. See pages 164 to 169 for information on installing NM cable.

Tips for Installing Boxes & Cables

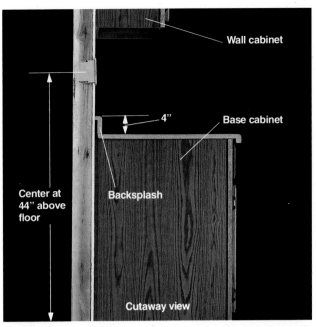

Use masking tape to outline the location of all cabinets, large appliances, and other openings. The outlines help you position the electrical boxes accurately. Remember to allow for moldings and other trim.

Standard backsplash height is 4"; the center of a box installed above this should be 44" above the floor. If the backsplash is more than 4" high, or the distance between the countertop and the bottom of the cabinet is less than 18", center the box in the space between the countertop and the bottom of the wall cabinet.

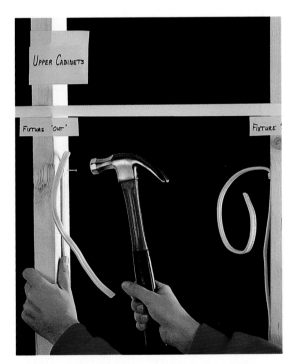

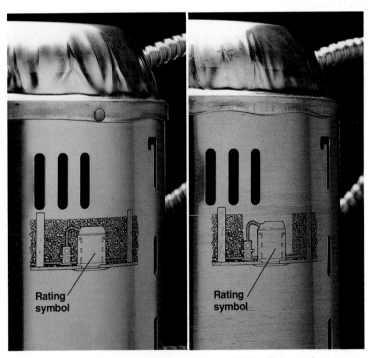

Install cables for an under-cabinet light at positions that will line up with the knockouts on the fixture box (which is installed after the walls and cabinets are in place). Cables will be retrieved through ⅝" drilled holes (page 229), so it is important to position the cables accurately.

Choose the proper type of recessed light fixture for your project. There are two types of fixtures: those rated for installation within insulation (left), and those which must be kept at least 3" from insulation (right). Self-contained thermal switches shut off power if the unit gets too hot for its rating. A recessed light fixture must be installed at least ½" from combustible materials.

How to Mount a Recessed Light Fixture

1 Extend the mounting bars on the recessed fixture to reach the framing members. Adjust the position of the light unit on the mounting bars to locate it properly. Align the bottom edges of the mounting bars with the bottom face of the framing members.

2 Nail or screw the mounting bars to the framing members.

3 Remove the wire connection box cover and open one knockout for each cable entering the box.

4 Install a cable clamp for each open knockout, and tighten locknut, using a screwdriver to drive the lugs.

How to Install the Feeder Cable

1 Drill access holes through the sill plate where the feeder cables will enter from the circuit breaker panel. Choose spots that offer easy access to the circuit breaker panel as well as to the first electrical box on the circuit.

2 Drill 5/8" holes through framing members to allow cables to pass from the circuit breaker panel to access holes. Front edge of hole should be at least 1¼" from front edge of framing member.

3 For each circuit, measure and cut enough cable to run from circuit breaker panel, through access hole into the kitchen, to the first electrical box in the circuit. Add at least 2 ft. for the panel and 1 ft. for the box.

4 Anchor the cable with a cable staple within 12" of the panel. Extend cable through and along joists to access hole into kitchen, stapling every 4 ft. where necessary. Keep cable at least 1¼" from front edge of framing members. Thread cable through access hole into kitchen, and on to the first box in the circuit. Continue circuit to rest of boxes (pages 164 to 167).

Arrange for the rough-in inspection before making the final connections.

3: Make Final Connections

Make the final connections for switches, receptacles, and fixtures after the rough-in inspection. First make final connections on recessed fixtures (it is easier to do this before wallboard is installed). Then finish the work on walls and ceiling, install the cabinets, and make the rest of the final connections. Use the photos on the following pages and the circuit maps on pages 20 to 31 as a guide for making the final connections. The last step is to connect the circuits at the breaker panel (pages 58 to 59). After all connections are made, your work is ready for the final inspection.

Materials You Will Need:

Pigtail wires, wire nuts, black tape.

■ Circuits #1 & #2

Two 20-amp, 120-volt small-appliance circuits.

- 7 GFCI receptacles
- 20-amp double-pole circuit breaker (see pages 178 to 179 for instructions on making final connections at the circuit breaker panel)

Note: In this project, two of the GFCI receptacles are installed in boxes that also contain switches from other circuits (page opposite).

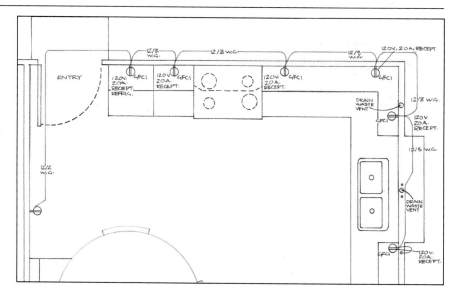

How to Connect Small-appliance Receptacles (that alternate on two 20-amp circuits in one 12/3 cable)

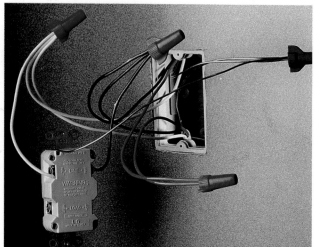

1 At alternate receptacles in the cable run (first, third, etc.), attach a black pigtail to a brass screw terminal marked LINE on the receptacle and to black wire from both cables. Connect a white pigtail to a silver screw (LINE) and to both white wires. Connect a grounding pigtail to the grounding screw and to both grounding wires. Connect both red wires together. Tuck wires into box, then attach the receptacle and coverplate. (See circuit map 10, page 147.)

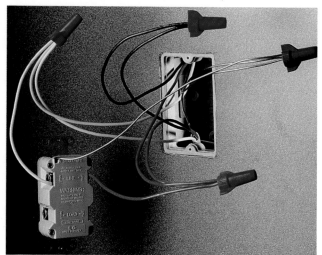

2 At remaining receptacles in the run, attach a red pigtail to a brass screw terminal (LINE) and to red wires from the cables. Attach a white pigtail to a silver screw terminal (LINE) and to both white wires. Connect a grounding pigtail to the grounding screw and to both grounding wires. Connect both black wires together. Tuck wires into box, attach receptacle and coverplate. (see page 219 for optional method of GFCI protection.)

How to Install a GFCI & a Disposer Switch

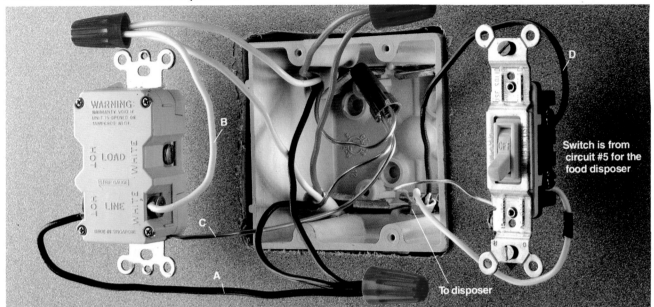

Connect black pigtail (A) to GFCI brass terminal marked LINE, and to black wires from three-wire cables. Attach white pigtail (B) to silver terminal marked LINE, and to white wires from three-wire cables. Attach grounding pigtail (C) to GFCI grounding screw and to grounding wires from three-wire cables. Connect both red wires to-gether. (See circuit map 11, page 148.) Connect black wire from two-wire cable (D) to one switch terminal. Attach white wire to other terminal and tag it black indicating it is hot. Attach grounding wire to switch grounding screw. (See circuit map 5, page 145.) Tuck wires into box, attach switch, receptacle, and coverplate.

How to Install a GFCI & Two Switches for Recessed Lights

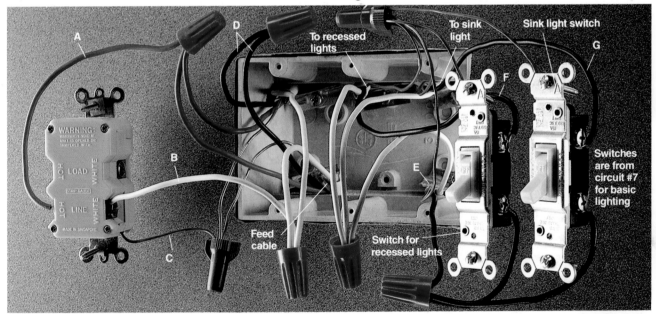

Connect red pigtail (A) to GFCI brass terminal labeled LINE, and to red wires from three-wire cables. Connect white pigtail (B) to silver LINE terminal, and to white wires from three-wire cables. Attach grounding pigtail (C) to grounding screw, and to grounding wires from three-wire cables. Connect black wires from three-wire cables (D) together. (See circuit map 11, page 148.) Attach a black pigtail to one screw on each switch and to black wire from two-wire feed cable (E).

Connect black wire (F) from the two-wire cable leading to recessed lights to remaining screw on the switch for the recessed lights. Connect black wire (G) from two-wire cable leading to sink light to remaining screw on sink light switch. Connect white wires from all two-wire cables together. Connect pigtails to switch grounding screws, and to all grounding wires from two-wire cables. (See circuit map 4, page 144.) Tuck wires into box, attach switches, receptacle, and coverplate.

Circuit #3

A 50-amp, 120/240-volt circuit serving the range.

- 50-amp receptacle for range
- 50-amp double-pole circuit breaker (see pages 178 to 179 for instructions on making final connections at the circuit breaker panel)

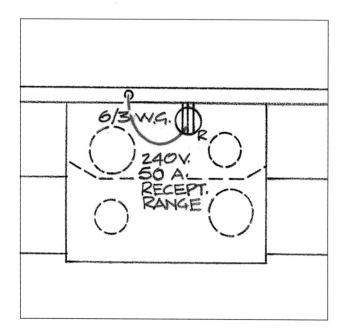

How to Install 120/240 Range Receptacle

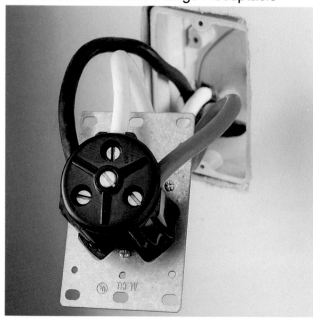

Attach the white wire to the neutral terminal, and the black and red wires to the remaiing terminals. The neutral white wire acts as the grounding wire for this circuit, so push the bare copper ground wire from the cable to the back of the box. Tuck rest of the wires into the box. Attach receptacle and coverplate. (See circuit map 14, page 149.)

Circuit #4

A 20-amp, 120-volt circuit for the microwave.

- 20-amp duplex receptacle
- 20-amp single-pole circuit breaker (see pages 178 to 179 for instructions on making final connections at the circuit breaker panel)

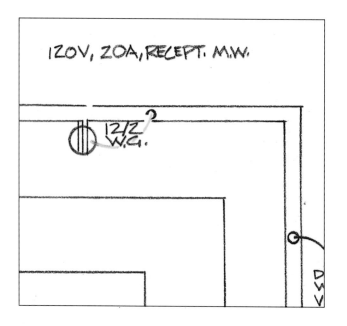

How to Connect Microwave Receptacle

Connect black wire from the cable to a brass screw terminal on the receptacle. Attach the white wire to a silver screw terminal, and the grounding wire to the receptacle's grounding screw. Tuck wires into box, attach the receptacle and the coverplate. (See circuit map 1, page 143.)

■ Circuit #5
A 15-amp, 120-volt circuit for the food disposer.

- 15-amp duplex receptacle
- Single-pole switch
- 15-amp single-pole circuit breaker (see pages 178 to 179 for instructions on making final connections at the circuit breaker panel)

Note: Final connection of the single-pole switch controlling the disposer is shown on page 225.

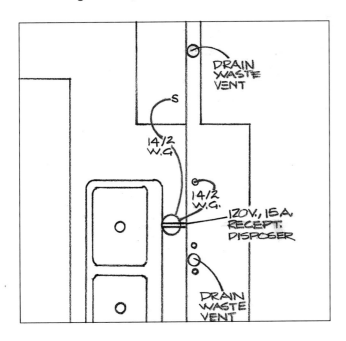

How to Connect Disposer Receptacle

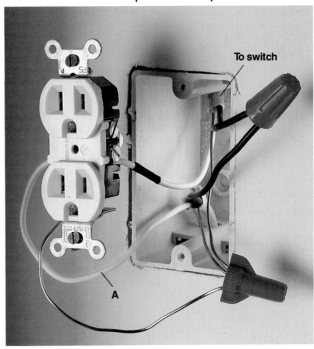

Connect black wires together. Connect white wire from feed cable (A) to silver screw on receptacle. Connect white wire from cable going to the switch to a brass screw terminal on the receptacle, and tag the wire with black indicating it is hot. Attach a grounding pigtail to grounding screw and to both cable grounding wires. Tuck wires into box, then attach receptacle and coverplate. (See circuit map 5, page 145.)

■ Circuit #6
A 15-amp, 120-volt circuit for the dishwasher.

- 15-amp duplex receptacle
- 15-amp single-pole circuit breaker (see pages 178 to 179 for instructions on making final connections at the circuit breaker panel)

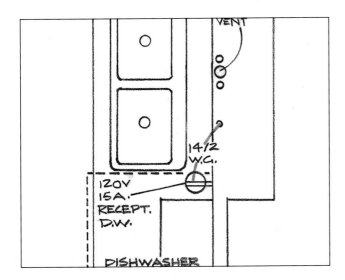

How to Connect Dishwasher Receptacle

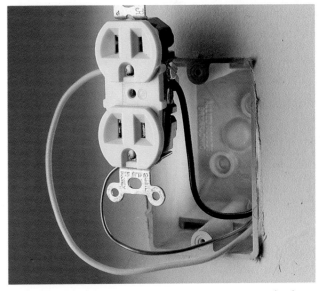

Connect the black wire to a brass screw terminal. Attach the white wire to a silver screw terminal. Connect the grounding wire to the grounding screw. Tuck wires into box, then attach receptacle and coverplate. (See circuit map 1, page 143.)

Circuit #7

A 15-amp basic lighting circuit serving the kitchen.

- 2 three-way switches with grounding screws
- 2 single-pole switches with grounding screws
- Ceiling light fixture
- 6 recessed light fixtures
- 4 fluorescent under-cabinet fixtures
- 15-amp single-pole circuit breaker (pages 178 to 179)

Note: Final connections for the single-pole switches are shown on page 225.

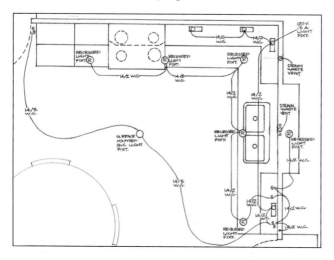

How to Connect First Three-way Switch

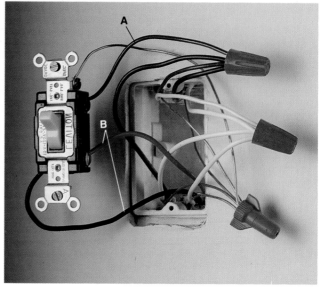

Connect a black pigtail to the common screw on the switch (A) and to the black wires from the two-wire cable. Connect black and red wires from the three-wire cable to traveler terminals (B) on the switch. Connect white wires from all cables entering box together. Attach a grounding pigtail to switch grounding screw and to all grounding wires in box. Tuck wires into box, then attach switch and coverplate. (See circuit map 17, page 151.)

How to Connect Surface-mounted Ceiling Fixture

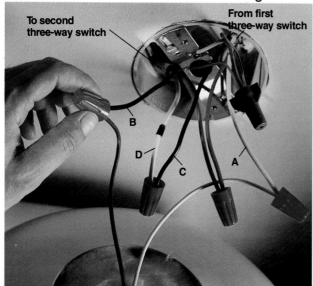

Connect white fixture lead to white wire (A) from first three-way switch. Connect black fixture lead to black wire (B) from second three-way switch. Connect black wire (C) from first switch to white wire (D) from second switch, and tag this white wire with black. Connect red wires from both switches together. Connect all grounding wires together. Mount fixture following manufacturer's instructions. (See circuit map 17, page 151.)

How to Connect Second Three-way Switch

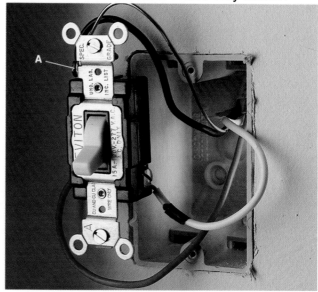

Connect black wire from the cable to the common screw terminal (A). Connect red wire to one traveler screw terminal. Attach the white wire to the other traveler screw terminal and tag it with black, indicating it is hot. Attach the grounding wire to the grounding screw on the switch. Tuck wires in box, then attach switch and coverplate. (See circuit map 17, page 151.)

How to Connect Recessed Light Fixtures

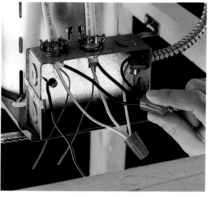

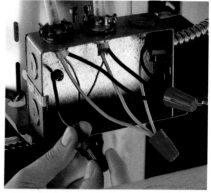

1 Make connections before installing wallboard: the work must be inspected first and access to the junction box is easier. Connect white cable wires to white fixture lead.

2 Connect black wires to black lead from fixture.

3 Attach a grounding pigtail to the grounding screw on the fixture, then connect all grounding wires. Tuck wires into the junction box, and replace the cover.

How to Connect Under-cabinet Fluorescent Task Light Fixtures

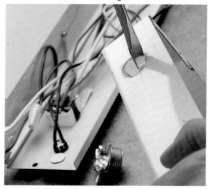

1 Drill ⅝" holes through wall and cabinet at locations that line up with knockouts on the fixture, and retrieve cable ends (page 221).

2 Remove access cover on fixture. Open one knockout for each cable that enters fixture box, and install cable clamps.

3 Strip 8" of sheathing from each cable end. Insert each end through a cable clamp, leaving ¼" of sheathing in fixture box.

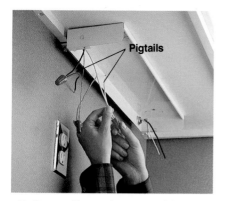

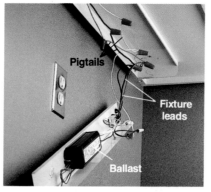

4 Screw fixture box to cabinet. Attach black, white, and green pigtails of THHN/THWN wire (page 162) to wires from one cable entering box. Pigtails must be long enough to reach the cable at other end of box.

5 Connect black pigtail and circuit wire to black lead from fixture. Connect white pigtail and circuit wire to white lead from fixture. Attach green pigtail and copper circuit wire to green grounding wire attached to the fixture box.

6 Tuck wires into box, and route THHN/THWN pigtails along one side of the ballast. Replace access cover and fixture lens.

Make hookups at circuit breaker panel (page 178) and arrange for final inspection.

Installing a Vent Hood

A vent hood eliminates heat, moisture, and cooking vapors from your kitchen. It has an electric fan unit with one or more filters, and a system of metal ducts to vent air to the outdoors. A ducted vent hood is more efficient than a ductless model, which filters and recirculates air without removing it.

Metal ducts for a vent hood can be round or rectangular. Elbows and transition fittings are available for both types of ducts. These fittings let you vent around corners, or join duct components that differ in shape or size.

In the project shown here, the hood is installed in existing walls. If your project is in new construction, you can locate and do the work more easily.

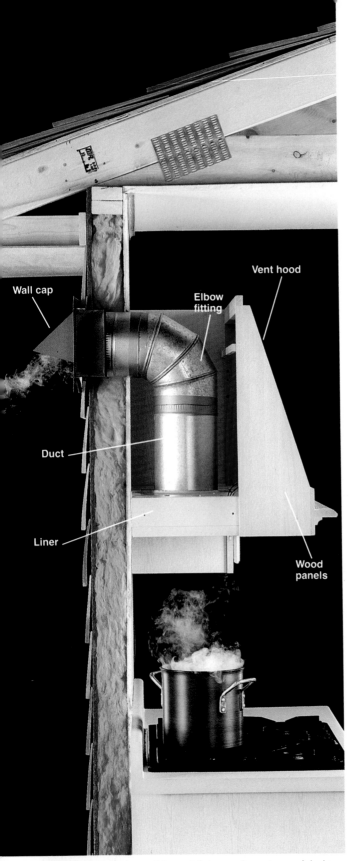

Wall-mounted vent hood (shown in cutaway) is installed between wall cabinets. Fan unit is fastened to a metal liner that is anchored to cabinets. Duct and elbow fitting exhaust cooking vapors to the outdoors through a wall cap. Vent fan and duct are covered by wood or laminate panels that match cabinet finish.

Everything You Need

Basic Hand Tools: tape measure, screwdrivers, hammer, eye protection, pencil.

Basic Power Tools: drill

Basic Materials: duct sections, duct elbow, duct cap, vent hood, 1½" sheetmetal screws, 1¼" wallboard screws.

Specialty Tools & Supplies: photo, below.

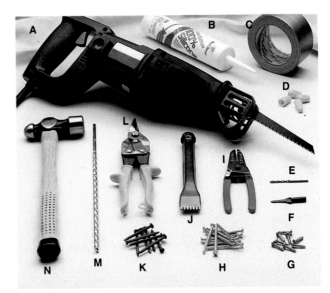

Specialty tools & supplies include: reciprocating saw with coarse wood-cutting blade (A), silicone caulk (B), duct tape (C), wire nuts (D), ⅛" twist bit (E), No. 9 counterbore drill bit (F), ¾" sheetmetal screws (G), 2½" sheetmetal screws (H), combination tool (I), masonry chisel (J), 2" masonry nails (K), metal snips (L), masonry drill bit (M), ball peen hammer (N).

How to Install a Wall-mounted Vent Hood

1 Attach ¾" × 4" × 12" wooden cleats to sides of the cabinets with 1¼" wallboard screws. Follow manufacturer's directions for proper distance from cooking surface.

2 Position the hood liner between the cleats and attach with ¾" sheetmetal screws.

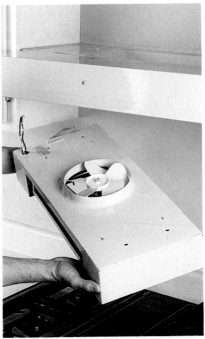

3 Remove cover panels for light, fan, and electrical compartments on fan unit, as directed by manufacturer. Position fan unit inside liner and fasten by attaching nuts to mounting bolts inside light compartments.

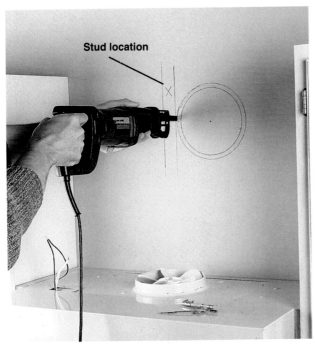

4 Locate studs in wall where duct will pass, using a stud finder. Mark hole location. Hole should be ½" larger that diameter of duct. Complete cutout with a reciprocating saw or jig saw. Remove any wall insulation. Drill a pilot hole through outside wall.

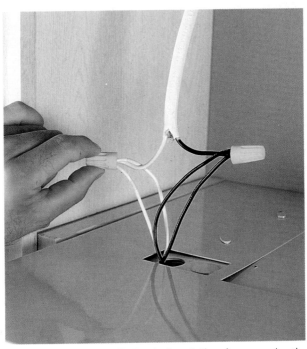

5 Strip about ½" of plastic insulation from each wire in the circuit cable, using combination tool. Connect the black wires, using a wire nut. Connect the white wires. Gently push the wires into the electrical box. Replace the coverpanels on the light and fan compartments.

(continued next page)

6 Make duct cutout on exterior wall. On masonry, drill a series of holes around outline of cutout. Remove waste with a masonry chisel and ball peen hammer. On wood siding, make cutout with a reciprocating saw.

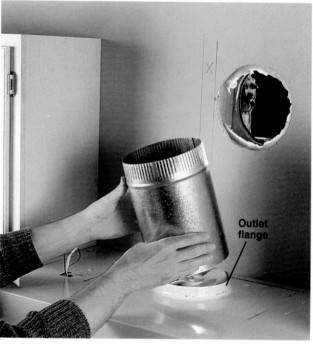

7 Attach first duct section by sliding the smooth end over the outlet flange on the vent hood. Cut duct sections to length with metal snips.

Outlet flange

8 Drill three or four pilot holes around joint through both layers of metal, using ⅛" twist bit. Attach duct with ¾" sheetmetal screws. Seal joint with duct tape.

9 Join additional duct sections by sliding smooth end over corrugated end of preceding section. Use an adjustable elbow to change directions in duct run. Secure all joints with sheetmetal screws and duct tape.

10 Install duct cap on exterior wall. Apply a thick bead of silicone caulk to cap flange. Slide cap over end of duct.

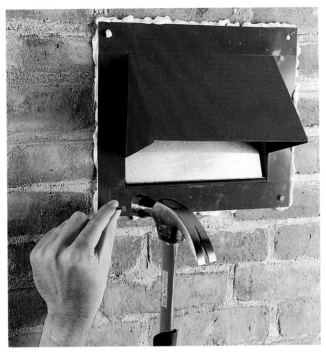

11 Attach cap to wall with 2" masonry nails, or 1½" sheetmetal screws (on wood siding). Wipe away excess caulk.

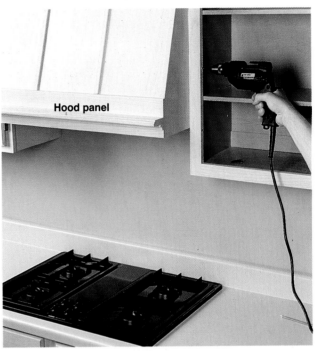

Hood panel

12 Slide the decorative hood panel into place between the wall cabinets. Drill pilot holes through the cabinet face frame with a counterbore bit. Attach the hood panel to the cabinets with 2½" sheetmetal screws.

Vent Hood Variations

Blower unit

Downdraft cooktop has a built-in blower unit that vents through the back or the bottom of a base cabinet. A downdraft cooktop is a good choice for a kitchen island or peninsula.

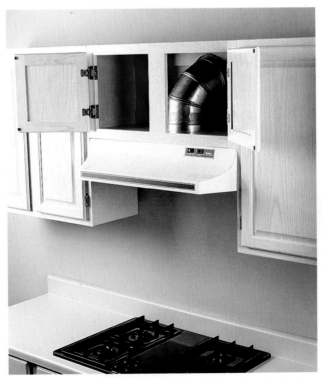

Cabinet-mounted vent hood is attached to the bottom of a short, 12" to 18" tall wall cabinet. Metal ducts run inside this wall cabinet.

Installing Outdoor Wiring

Adding an outdoor circuit improves the value of your property and lets you enjoy your yard more fully. Doing the work yourself is also a good way to save money. Most outdoor wiring projects require digging underground trenches, and an electrician may charge several hundred dollars for this simple but time-consuming work.

Do not install your own wiring for a hot tub, fountain, or swimming pool. These outdoor water fixtures require special grounding techniques that are best left to an electrician.

In this chapter you learn how to install the following fixtures:

Decorative light fixtures (A) can highlight attractive features of your home and yard, like a deck, ornamental shrubs and trees, and flower gardens. See page 253.

A weatherproof switch (B) lets you control outdoor lights without going indoors. See page 250.

GFCI-protected receptacles (C) let you use electric lawn and garden tools, and provide a place to plug in radios, barbecue rotisseries, and other devices that help make your yard more enjoyable. See page 252.

A manual override switch (D) lets you control a motion-sensor light fixture from inside the house. See page 250.

Five Steps for Installing Outdoor Wiring

1. Plan the Circuit (pages 240 to 241).
2. Dig Trenches (pages 242 to 243).
3. Install Boxes & Conduit (pages 244 to 247).
4. Install UF Cable (pages 248 to 249).
5. Make Final Connections (pages 250 to 253).

A motion-sensor light fixture (photos, right) provides inexpensive and effective protection against intruders. It has an infrared eye that triggers the light fixture when a moving object crosses its path. Choose a light fixture with a photo cell (E) that prevents the fixture from triggering in daylight. Look for an adjustable timer (F) that controls how long the light keeps shining after motion stops. Better models have range controls (G) to adjust the sensitivity of the motion-sensor eye. See pages 250 to 251.

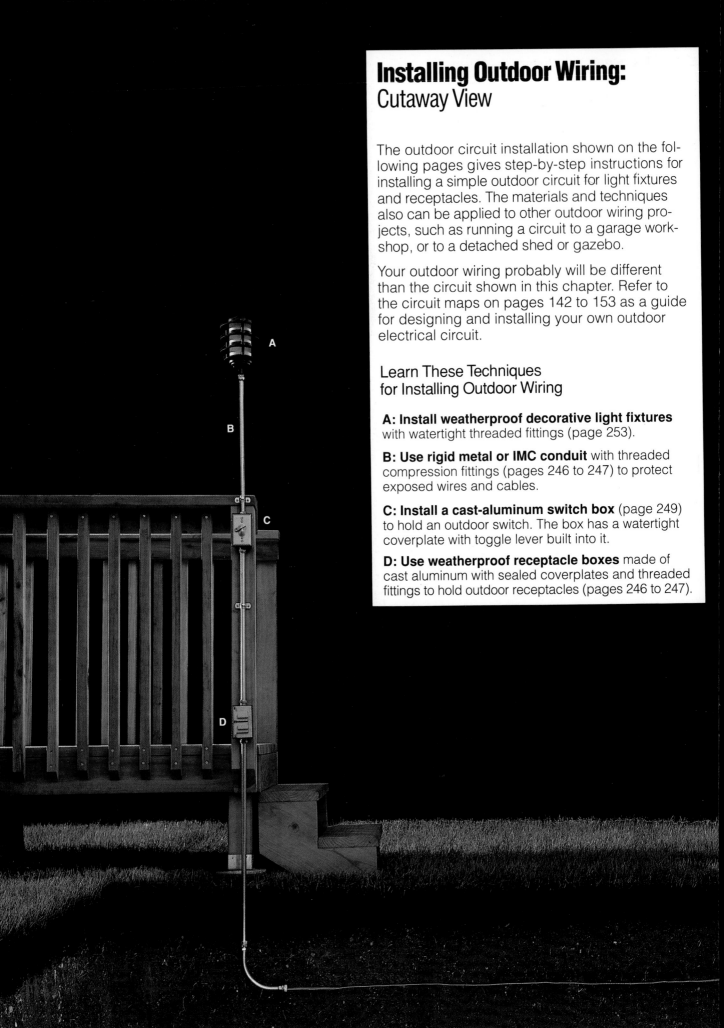

Installing Outdoor Wiring:
Cutaway View

The outdoor circuit installation shown on the following pages gives step-by-step instructions for installing a simple outdoor circuit for light fixtures and receptacles. The materials and techniques also can be applied to other outdoor wiring projects, such as running a circuit to a garage workshop, or to a detached shed or gazebo.

Your outdoor wiring probably will be different than the circuit shown in this chapter. Refer to the circuit maps on pages 142 to 153 as a guide for designing and installing your own outdoor electrical circuit.

Learn These Techniques for Installing Outdoor Wiring

A: Install weatherproof decorative light fixtures with watertight threaded fittings (page 253).

B: Use rigid metal or IMC conduit with threaded compression fittings (pages 246 to 247) to protect exposed wires and cables.

C: Install a cast-aluminum switch box (page 249) to hold an outdoor switch. The box has a watertight coverplate with toggle lever built into it.

D: Use weatherproof receptacle boxes made of cast aluminum with sealed coverplates and threaded fittings to hold outdoor receptacles (pages 246 to 247).

E: Install a retrofit light fixture box (page 245) to hold a motion-sensor security light. Retrofit boxes are used to install electrical fixtures that fit inside existing finished walls. The box is sealed with a foam gasket that fits between the light fixture and the box.

F: Run NM cable (pages 168 to 169, 245) through walls to provide power to electrical boxes that fit inside finished walls.

G: Install retrofit single-gang boxes (page 245) to hold a manual override switch for the motion-sensor light, and the GFCI receptacle.

H: Attach a cast-aluminum extension ring to a retrofit receptacle box (page 246) to hold a GFCI receptacle.

I: Dig trenches (pages 242 to 243) to hold underground cables bringing power from the house to yard fixtures.

J: Install UF (underground feeder) cable (pages 248 to 249) to bring power from the house to the outdoor fixtures.

K: Run a feeder cable to connect the outdoor circuit to the circuit breaker panel (page 246).

Tools You Will Need:

Tape measure, drill with masonry bits and twist bits, jig saw or reciprocating saw, shovel, hammer, screwdriver, caulk gun, ball peen hammer or masonry hammer, masonry chisel, hacksaw, fish tape, cable ripper, combination tool, utility knife, needlenose pliers.

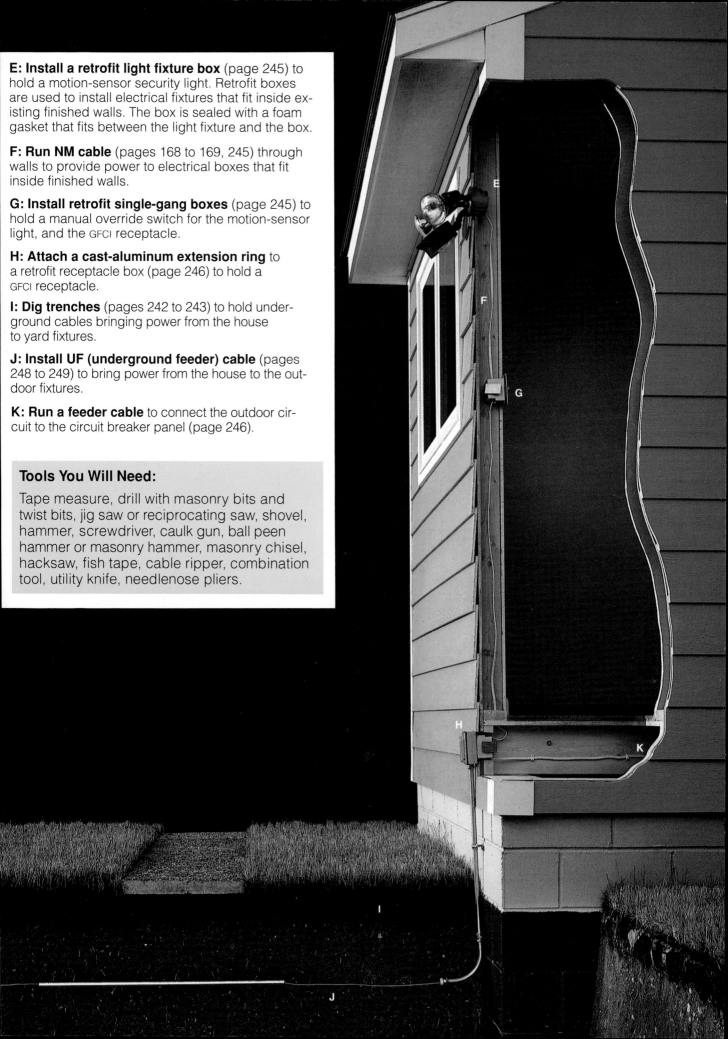

Installing Outdoor Wiring: Diagram View

This diagram view shows the layout of the outdoor wiring project featured on these pages. It includes the location of the switches, receptacles, light fixtures, and cable runs you will learn how to install in this chapter. The layout of your yard and the location of obstacles will determine the best locations for lights, receptacles, and underground cable runs. The wiring

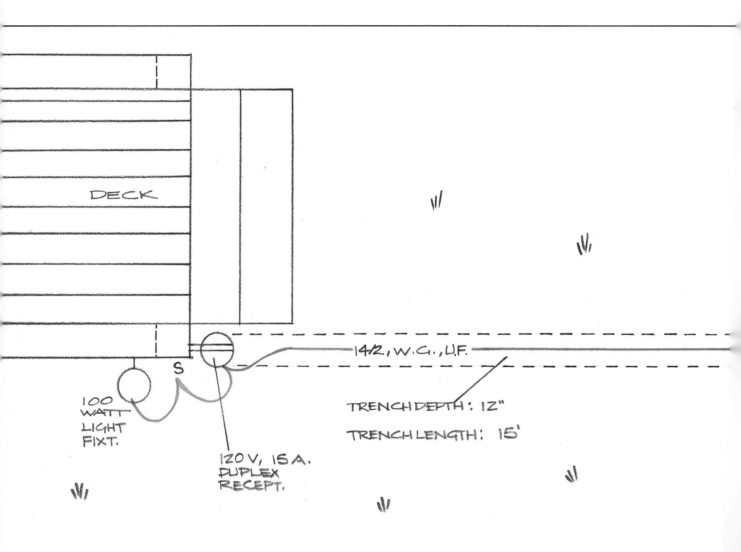

Yard is drawn to scale, with the lengths of trenches and cable runs clearly labeled.

Decorative light fixture is positioned to highlight the deck. Decorative fixtures should be used sparingly, to provide accent only to favorite features of your yard, such as flower beds, ornamental trees, or a patio.

Outdoor receptacle is positioned on the deck post, where it is accessible yet unobtrusive. Another good location for a receptacle is between shrubs.

diagram for your own project may differ greatly from the one shown here, but the techniques shown on the following pages will apply to any outdoor wiring project.

Note:
See pages 140 to 141 for a key to the common electrical symbols used in this diagram, and to learn how to draw your own wiring diagrams.

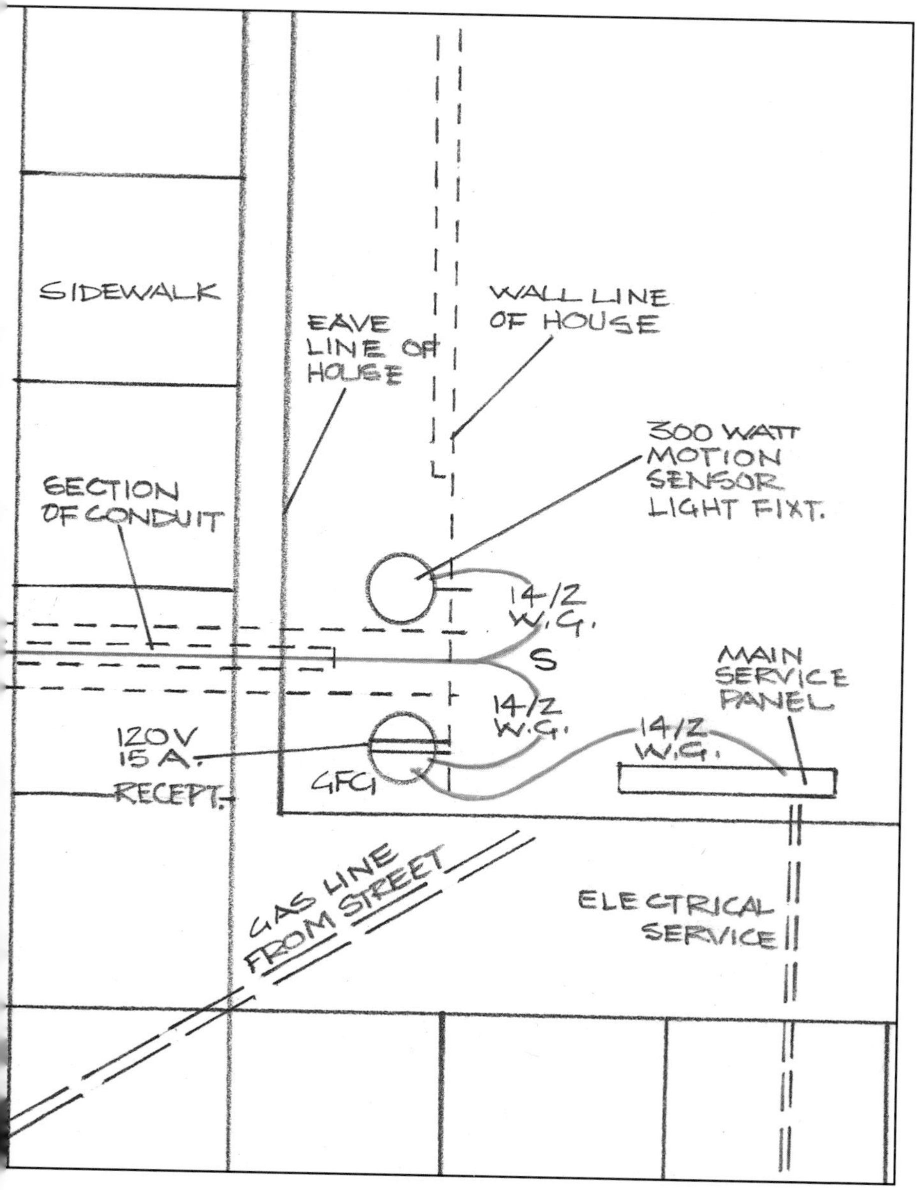

SIDEWALK

EAVE LINE OF HOUSE

WALL LINE OF HOUSE

SECTION OF CONDUIT

300 WATT MOTION SENSOR LIGHT FIXT.

14/2 W.G.

S

14/2 W.G.

MAIN SERVICE PANEL

14/2 W.G.

120 V 15 A. RECEPT.

GFCI

GAS LINE FROM STREET

ELECTRICAL SERVICE

Motion-sensor security light is positioned so it has a good "view" of entryways to the yard and home, and is aimed so it will not shine into neighboring yards.

Manual override switch for motion-sensor light is installed at a convenient indoor location. Override switches are usually mounted near a door or window.

Entry point for circuit is chosen so there is easy access to the circuit breaker panel. Basement rim joists or garage walls make good entry points for an outdoor circuit.

Yard obstacles, like sidewalks and underground gas and electrical lines, are clearly marked as an aid to laying out cable runs.

Underground cables are laid out from the house to the outdoor fixtures by the shortest route possible to reduce the length of trenches.

GFCI receptacle is positioned near the start of the cable run, and is wired to protect all wires to the end of the circuit.

Check for underground utilities when planning trenches for underground cable runs. Avoid lawn sprinkler pipes; and consult your electric utility office, phone company, gas and water department, and cable television vendor for the exact locations of underground utility lines. Many utility companies send field representatives to show homeowners how to avoid dangerous underground hazards.

Installing Outdoor Wiring

1: Plan the Circuit

As you begin planning an outdoor circuit, visit your electrical inspector to learn about local Code requirements for outdoor wiring. The techniques for installing outdoor circuits are much the same as for installing indoor wiring. However, because outdoor wiring is exposed to the elements, it requires the use of special weatherproof materials, including UF cable (page 162), rigid metal or schedule 40 PVC plastic conduit (pages 170 to 171), and weatherproof electrical boxes and fittings (pages 156 to 157).

The National Electrical Code (NEC) gives minimum standards for outdoor wiring materials, but because climate and soil conditions vary from region to region, your local Building and Electrical Codes may have more restrictive requirements. For example, some regions require that all underground cables be protected with conduit, even though the National Electrical Code allows UF cable to be buried without protection at the proper depths (page opposite).

For most homes, an outdoor circuit is a modest power user. Adding a new 15-amp, 120-volt circuit provides enough power for most outdoor electrical needs. However, if your circuit will include more than three large light fixtures (each rated for 300 watts or more) or more than four receptacles, plan to install a 20-amp, 120-volt circuit. Or, if your outdoor circuit will supply power to heating appliances or large workshop tools in a detached garage, you may require several 120-volt and 240-volt circuits.

Before drawing wiring plans and applying for a work permit, evaluate electrical loads (pages 136 to 139) to make sure the main service provides enough amps to support the added demand of the new wiring.

A typical outdoor circuit takes one or two weekends to install, but if your layout requires very long underground cables, allow yourself more time for digging trenches, or arrange to have extra help. Also make sure to allow time for the required inspection visits when planning your wiring project. See pages 128 to 135 for more information on planning a wiring project.

Choosing Cable Sizes for an Outdoor Circuit

Circuit Length		Circuit size
Less than 50 ft.	**50 ft. or more**	
14-gauge	12-gauge	15-amp
12-gauge	10-gauge	20-amp

Consider the circuit length when choosing cable sizes for an outdoor circuit. In very long circuits, normal wire resistance leads to a substantial drop in voltage. If your outdoor circuit extends more than 50 ft., use larger-gauge wire to reduce the voltage drop. For example, a 15-amp circuit that extends more than 50 ft. should be wired with 12-gauge wire instead of 14-gauge. A 20-amp circuit longer than 50 ft. should be wired with 10-gauge cable.

Tips for Planning an Outdoor Circuit

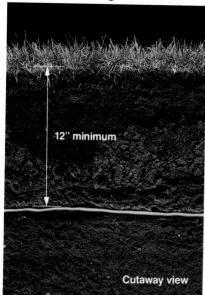

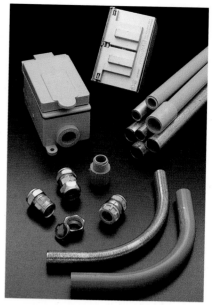

Bury UF cables 12" deep if the wires are protected by a GFCI and the circuit is no larger than 20 amps. Bury cable at least 18" deep if the circuit is not protected by a GFCI, or if it is larger than 20 amps.

Protect cable entering conduit by attaching a plastic bushing to the open end of the conduit. The bushing prevents sharp metal edges from damaging the vinyl sheathing on the cable.

Protect exposed wiring above ground level with rigid conduit and weatherproof electrical boxes and coverplates. Check your local Code restrictions: some regions allow the use of either rigid metal conduit or schedule 40 PVC plastic conduit and electrical boxes, while other regions allow only metal.

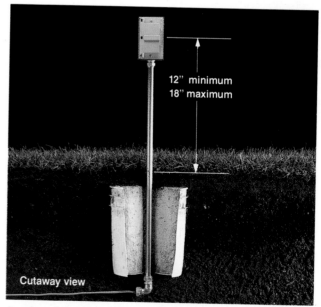

Prevent shock by making sure all outdoor receptacles are protected by GFCIs (page 132). A single GFCI receptacle can be wired to protect other fixtures on the circuit. Outdoor receptacles should be at least 1 ft. above ground level, and enclosed in weatherproof electrical boxes with watertight covers.

Anchor freestanding receptacles that are not attached to a structure by embedding the rigid metal conduit or schedule 40 PVC plastic conduit in a concrete footing. One way to do this is by running conduit through a plastic bucket, then filling the bucket with concrete. Freestanding receptacles should be at least 12", but no more than 18", above ground level—requirements vary, so check with your local inspector.

2: Dig Trenches

When laying underground cables, save time and minimize lawn damage by digging trenches as narrow as possible. Plan the circuit to reduce the length of cable runs.

If your soil is sandy, or very hard and dry, water the ground thoroughly before you begin digging. Lawn sod can be removed, set on strips of plastic, and replaced after cables are laid. Keep the removed sod moist but not wet, and replace it within two or three days. Otherwise, the grass underneath the plastic may die.

If trenches must be left unattended, make sure to cover them with scrap pieces of plywood to prevent accidents and to keep water out.

Materials You Will Need:

Stakes, string, plastic, scrap piece of conduit, compression fittings, plastic bushings.

How to Dig Trenches for Underground Cables

1 Mark the outline of trenches with wooden stakes and string.

2 Cut two 18"-wide strips of plastic, and place one strip on each side of the trench outline.

3 Remove blocks of sod from the trench outline, using a shovel. Cut sod 2" to 3" deep to keep roots intact. Place the sod on one of the plastic strips, and keep it moist.

4 Dig the trenches to the depth required by your local Code. Heap the dirt onto the second strip of plastic.

5 To run cable under a sidewalk, cut a length of metal conduit about 1 ft. longer than width of sidewalk, then flatten one end of the conduit to form a sharp tip.

6 Drive the conduit through the soil under the sidewalk, using a ball peen or masonry hammer and a wood block to prevent damage to the pipe.

7 Cut off the ends of the conduit with a hacksaw, leaving about 2" of exposed conduit on each side. Underground cable will run through the conduit.

8 Attach a compression fitting and plastic bushing to each end of the conduit. The plastic fittings will prevent the sharp edges of the conduit from damaging the cable sheathing.

9 If trenches must be left unattended, temporarily cover them with scrap plywood to prevent accidents.

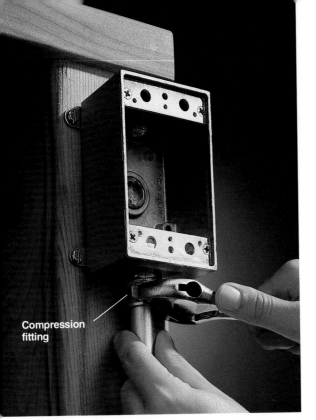

Compression fitting

Electrical boxes for an outdoor circuit must be weatherproof. This outdoor receptacle box made of cast aluminum has sealed seams, and is attached to conduit with threaded, watertight compression fittings.

3: Install Boxes & Conduit

Use cast-aluminum electrical boxes for outdoor fixtures and install metal conduit to protect any exposed cables unless your Code has different requirements. Standard metal and plastic electrical boxes are not watertight, and should never be used outdoors. A few local Codes require you to install conduit to protect all underground cables, but in most regions this is not necessary. Some local Codes allow you to use boxes and conduit made with PVC plastic (pages 156 to 157).

Begin work by installing the retrofit boxes and the cables that run between them inside finished walls. Then install the outdoor boxes and conduit.

Materials You Will Need:

NM two-wire cable, cable staples, plastic retrofit light fixture box with grounding clip, plastic single-gang retrofit boxes with internal clamps, extension ring, silicone caulk, IMC or rigid metal conduit, pipe straps, conduit sweep, compression fittings, plastic bushings, Tapcon® anchors, single-gang outdoor boxes, galvanized screws, grounding pigtails, wire nuts.

How to Install Electrical Boxes & Conduit

1 Outline the GFCI receptacle box on the exterior wall. First drill pilot holes at the corners of the box outline, and use a piece of stiff wire to probe the wall for electrical wires or plumbing pipes. Complete the cutout with a jig saw or reciprocating saw.

Masonry variation: To make cutouts in masonry, drill a line of holes inside the box outline, using a masonry bit, then remove waste material with a masonry chisel and ball peen hammer.

2 From inside house, make the cutout for the indoor switch in the same stud cavity that contains the GFCI cutout. Outline the box on the wall, then drill a pilot hole and complete the cutout with a wallboard saw or jig saw.

3 On outside of house, make the cutout for the motion-sensor light fixture in the same stud cavity with the GFCI cutout. Outline the light fixture box on the wall, then drill a pilot hole and complete the cutout with a wallboard saw or jig saw.

4 Estimate the distance between the indoor switch box and the outdoor motion-sensor box, and cut a length of NM cable about 2 ft. longer than this distance. Use a fish tape to pull the cable from the switch box to the motion-sensor box. See pages 168 to 169 for tips on running cable through finished walls.

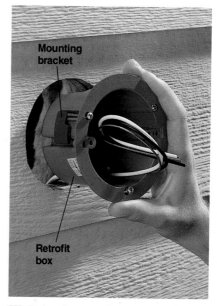

5 Strip about 10" of outer insulation from the end of the cable, using a cable ripper. Open a knockout in the retrofit light fixture box with a screwdriver. Insert the cable into the box so that at least 1/4" of outer sheathing reaches into the box.

6 Insert the box into the cutout opening, and tighten the mounting screws until the brackets draw the outside flange firmly against the siding.

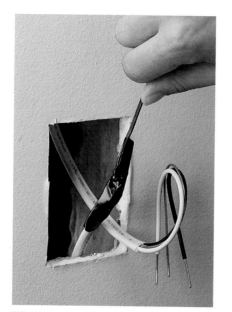

7 Estimate the distance between the outdoor GFCI cutout and the indoor switch cutout, and cut a length of NM cable about 2 ft. longer than this distance. Use a fish tape to pull the cable from the GFCI cutout to the switch cutout. Strip 10" of outer insulation from both ends of each cable.

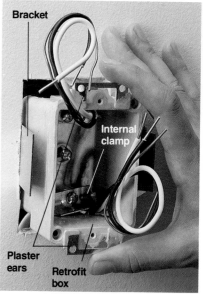

8 Open one knockout for each cable that will enter the box. Insert the cables so at least 1/4" of outer sheathing reaches inside box. Insert box into cutout, and tighten the mounting screw in the rear of the box until the bracket draws the plaster ears against the wall. Tighten internal cable clamps.

(continued next page)

9 Install NM cable from circuit breaker panel to GFCI cutout. Allow an extra 2 ft. of cable at panel end, and an extra 1 ft. at GFCI end. Attach cable to framing members with cable staples. Strip 10" of outer sheathing from the GFCI end of cable, and 3/4" of insulation from each wire.

10 Open one knockout for each cable that will enter the GFCI box. Insert the cables so at least 1/4" of sheathing reaches into the box. Push the box into the cutout, and tighten the mounting screw until the bracket draws the plaster ears tight against the wall.

11 Position a foam gasket over the GFCI box, then attach a extension ring to the box, using the mounting screws included with the extension ring. Seal any gaps around the extension ring with silicone caulk.

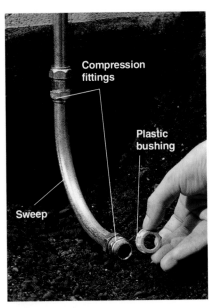

12 Measure and cut a length of IMC conduit to reach from the bottom of the extension ring to a point about 4" from the bottom of the trench. Attach the conduit to the extension ring using a compression fitting.

13 Anchor the conduit to the wall with a pipe strap and Tapcon® screws. Or, use masonry anchors and pan-head screws. Drill pilot holes for anchors, using a masonry drill bit.

14 Attach compression fittings to the ends of metal sweep fitting, then attach the sweep fitting to the end of the conduit. Screw a plastic bushing onto the exposed fitting end of the sweep to keep the metal edges from damaging the cable.

15 Attach mounting ears to the back of a weather-proof receptacle box, then attach the box to the deck frame by driving galvanized screws through the ears and into the post.

16 Measure and cut a length of IMC conduit to reach from the bottom of the receptacle box to a point about 4" from the bottom of the trench. Attach the conduit to the box with a compression fitting. Attach a sweep fitting and plastic bushing to the bottom of the conduit, using compression fittings (see step 14).

17 Cut a length of IMC conduit to reach from the top of the receptacle box to the switch box location. Attach the conduit to the receptacle box with a compression fitting. Anchor the conduit to the deck frame with pipe straps.

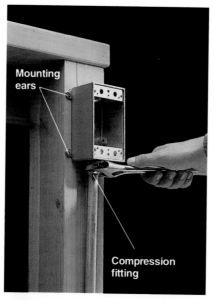

18 Attach mounting ears to the back of switch box, then loosely attach the box to the conduit with a compression fitting. Anchor the box to the deck frame by driving galvanized screws through the ears and into the wood. Then tighten the compression fitting with a wrench.

19 Measure and cut a short length of IMC conduit to reach from the top of the switch box to the deck light location. Attach the conduit with a compression fitting.

4: Install UF Cable

Use UF cable for outdoor wiring if the cable will come in direct contact with soil. UF cable has a solid-core vinyl sheathing, and cannot be stripped with a cable ripper. Instead, use a utility knife and the method shown (steps 5 & 6, page opposite). Never use NM cable for outdoor wiring. If your local Code requires that underground wires be protected by conduit, use THHN/THHW wire (page 162) instead of UF cable.

After installing all cables, you are ready for the rough-in inspection. While waiting for the inspector, temporarily attach the weatherproof coverplates to the boxes, or cover them with plastic to prevent moisture from entering. After the inspector has approved the rough-in work, fill in all cable trenches and replace the sod before making the final connections.

Materials You Will Need:

UF cable, electrical tape, grounding pigtails, wire nuts, weatherproof coverplates.

How to Install Outdoor Cable

1 Measure and cut all UF cables, allowing an extra 12" at each box. At each end of the cable, use a utility knife to pare away about 3" of outer sheathing, leaving the inner wires exposed.

2 Feed a fish tape down through the conduit from the GFCI box. Hook the wires at one end of the cable through the loop in the fish tape, then wrap electrical tape around the wires up to the sheathing. Carefully pull the cable through the conduit.

3 Lay the cable along the bottom of the trench, making sure it is not twisted. Where cable runs under a sidewalk, use the fish tape to pull it through the conduit.

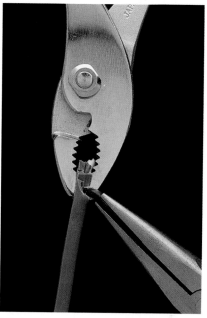

4 Use the fish tape to pull the end of the cable up through the conduit to the deck receptacle box at the opposite end of the trench. Remove the cable from the fish tape.

5 Cut away the electrical tape at each end of the cable, then clip away the bent wires. Bend back one of the wires in the cable, and grip it with needlenose pliers. Grip the cable with another pliers.

6 Pull back on the wire, splitting the sheathing and exposing about 10" of wire. Repeat with the remaining wires, then cut off excess sheathing with a utility knife. Strip 3/4" of insulation from the end of each wire, using a combination tool.

Switch box

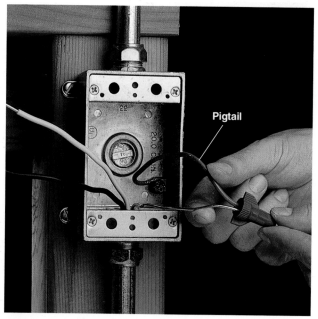

Pigtail

7 Measure, cut, and install a cable from the deck receptacle box to the outdoor switch box, using the fish tape. Strip 10" of sheathing from each end of the cable, then strip 3/4" of insulation from the end of each wire, using a combination tool.

8 Attach a grounding pigtail to the back of each metal box and extension ring. Join all grounding wires with a wire nut. Tuck the wires inside the boxes, and temporarily attach the weatherproof coverplates until the inspector arrives for the rough-in inspection.

Arrange for the rough-in inspection before making the final connections.

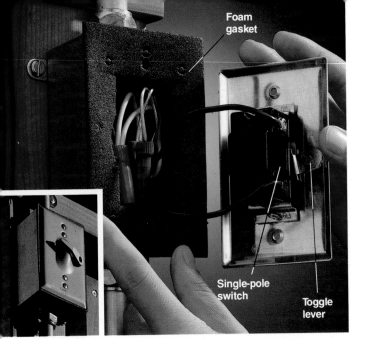

Switches for outdoor use have weatherproof coverplates with built-in toggle levers. The lever operates a single-pole switch mounted to the inside of the coverplate. Connect the black circuit wire to one of the screw terminals on the switch, and connect the black wire lead from the light fixture to the other screw terminal. Use wire nuts to join the white circuit wires and the grounding wires. To connect the manual override switch for the motion-sensor light fixture, see circuit map 4 on page 144.

5: Make Final Connections

Make the final hookups for the switches, receptacles, and light fixtures after the rough-in cable installation has been reviewed and approved by your inspector, and after all trenches have been filled in. Install all the light fixtures, switches, and receptacles, then connect the circuit to the circuit breaker panel (pages 178 to 179).

Because outdoor wiring poses a greater shock hazard than indoor wiring, the GFCI receptacle (page 252) in this project is wired to provide shock protection for all fixtures controlled by the circuit.

When all work is completed and the outdoor circuit is connected at the service panel, your job is ready for final review by the inspector.

Materials You Will Need:

Motion-sensor light fixture, GFCI receptacle, 15-amp grounded receptacle, outdoor switch, decorative light fixture, wire nuts.

How to Connect a Motion-sensor Light Fixture

1 Assemble fixture by threading the wire leads from the motion-sensor unit and the bulb sockets through the faceplate knockouts. Screw the motion-sensor unit and bulb sockets into the faceplate.

2 Secure the motion-sensor unit and the bulb sockets by tightening the locknuts.

3 Insert the fiber washers into the sockets, and fit a rubber gasket over the end of each socket. The washers and gaskets ensure that the fixture will be watertight.

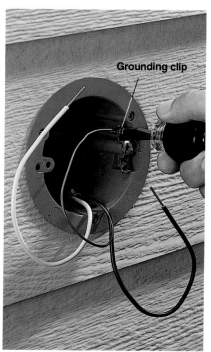

4 Connect the red wire lead from the motion-sensor unit to the black wire leads from the bulb sockets, using a wire nut. Some light fixtures have pre-tagged wire leads for easy installation.

5 Attach the bare copper grounding wire to the grounding clip on the box.

6 Slide the foam gasket over the circuit wires at the electrical box. Connect the white circuit wire to the white wire leads on the light fixture, using a wire nut.

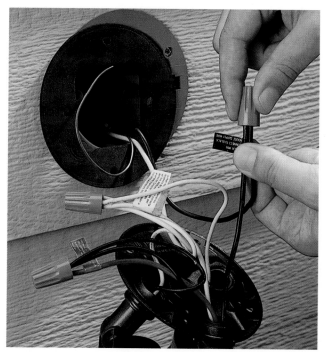

7 Connect the black circuit wire to the black wire lead on the light fixture, using a wire nut.

8 Carefully tuck the wires into the box, then position the light fixture and attach the faceplate to the box, using the mounting screws included with the light fixture. (See also circuit map 4, page 144.)

How to Connect the GFCI Receptacle

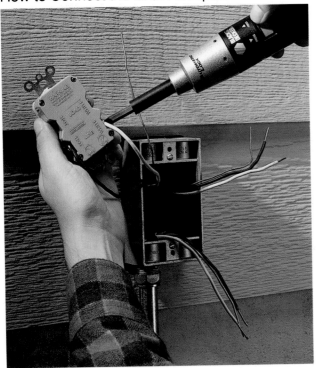

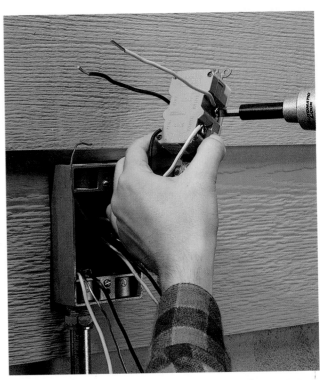

1 Connect the black feed wire from the power source to the brass terminal marked LINE. Connect the white feed wire from the power source to the silver screw terminal marked LINE.

2 Attach a short white pigtail wire to the silver screw terminal marked LOAD, and attach a short black pigtail wire to the brass screw terminal marked LOAD.

3 Connect the black pigtail wire to all the remaining black circuit wires, using a wire nut. Connect the white pigtail wire to the remaining white circuit wires.

4 Attach a grounding pigtail to the grounding screw on the GFCI. Join the grounding pigtail to the bare copper grounding wires, using a wire nut.

5 Carefully tuck the wires into box. Mount GFCI, then fit a foam gasket over the box and attach the weatherproof coverplate. (See also circuit map 3, page 144.)

How to Connect an Outdoor Receptacle

1 Connect the black circuit wires to the brass screw terminals on the receptacle. Connect the white circuit wires to the silver screw terminals on the receptacle. Attach a grounding pigtail to the grounding screw on the receptacle, then join all grounding wires with a wire nut.

2 Carefully tuck all wires into the box, and attach the receptacle to the box, using the mounting screws. Fit a foam gasket over the box, and attach the weatherproof coverplate. (See also circuit map 1, page 143.)

How to Connect a Decorative Light Fixture

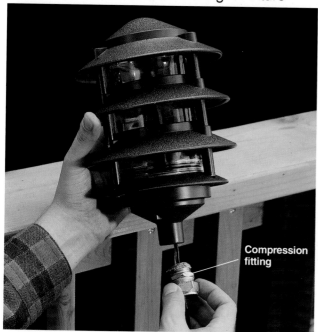

Compression fitting

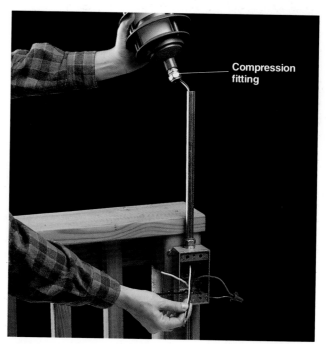

Compression fitting

1 Thread the wire leads of the light fixture through a threaded compression fitting. Screw the union onto the base of the light fixture.

2 Feed wire leads through conduit and into switch box. Slide light fixture onto conduit, and tighten compression fitting. Connect black wire lead to one screw terminal on switch, and connect white wire lead to white circuit wire. (See also circuit map 4, page 144.)

Make hookups at circuit breaker panel (page 178) and arrange for final inspection.

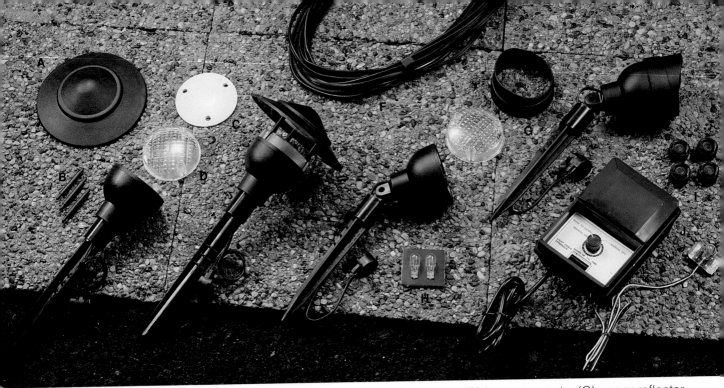

Typical low-voltage outdoor lighting system consists of: (A) lens cap, (B) lens cap posts, (C) upper reflector, (D) lens, (E) base/stake/cable connector assembly (contains lower reflector), (F) low-voltage cable, (G) lens hood, (H) 7-watt, 12-volt bulbs, (I) cable connector caps, (J) control box containing transformer and timer, (K) light sensor.

Low-voltage Outdoor Lighting

An alternative to 120-volt outdoor landscape lighting is to purchase and install a low-voltage outdoor wiring kit. These kits have several advantages over 120-volt lighting systems. They are safe and easy to install, use less energy, and don't require complicated weather and hazard precautionary measures. You can buy kits with low-profile fixtures to illuminate your deck, tier or globe lights for landscaping or lining paths, or floodlamps to illuminate a larger area.

Inexpensive kits, which are self-contained but have a limited amount of materials (usually only six to eight lamp heads), are available at retail outlets that cater to the do-it-yourselfer. Some manufacturers offer additonal lights to expand your kit.

More expensive lighting systems available at speciality lighting retailers offer homeowners greater flexibility in creating more elaborate lighting designs. They may not come in kit form, and may be more complicated to install.

Yard size, landscape design, and your layout plan will influence the type or number of kits you buy. First consider where you want to place the lights, how they will look in your yard, and what part of the yard you want lighted for safety measures.

After you decide where to place the lights, measure the distance from the control box to each lamp location to determine how much cable and how many lamps you will need.

Most kits contain lights to line walks or drives as well as floodlights, and there are kits available for decks. Some manufacturers offer different types of heads that are adjustable, which can provide greater flexibility and different effects.

Before starting, check to see if local codes have specific requirements for low-voltage installations. Also, if you are doing landscaping, install outdoor lighting before laying sod.

Control boxes in low-voltage kits usually have a transformer that accesses 120-volt house current via a standard 3-prong plug. You install the control box near a receptacle and simply plug the box into the receptacle. It is best to use a receptacle located inside the house or garage. Plugging into an outdoor receptacle will force the flip-up protective weather cap to remain open, which is not advised.

Everything You Need:

Tools: Tape measure, drill, hammer, screwdriver, shovel, paint-stirring stick.

Materials: Low-voltage lighting kit, PVC conduit, conduit straps, caulking.

How to Install Low-voltage Lighting

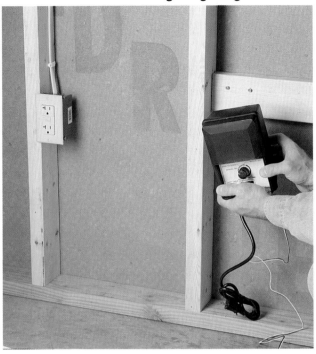

1 Mount the control box on a wall (inside the house or garage) within 24" of the chosen receptacle, positioning it at least 12" above the floor. Drill a hole through the wall or rim joist large enough for the light sensor and cable to pass through.

2 Push the sensor through the hole and mount it on the outside wall. Make sure it will not be covered by plants or other obstructions.

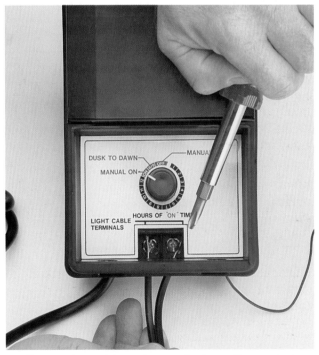

3 At the base of the outside wall beneath the hole, begin a narrow trench about 6" to 8" deep. Pass cable through the hole. Protect the cable between the hole and bottom of trench by running it through PVC conduit. Secure conduit to wall with conduit strap. Seal the hole with caulk.

4 Fasten the cable to the terminals on the control box. Tighten screws to secure. Set lighting program based on your needs according to manufacturer's instructions.

(continued next page)

How to Install Low-voltage Lighting (continued)

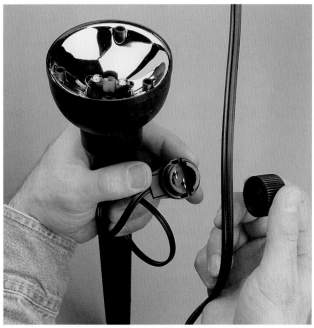

5 Lay out cable in desired locations. At each lamp location, attach the base/stake assembly to the cable with the cable connector. Tightening the connector cap forces the pin terminals to pierce the cable and contact the wires inside. (Some kits use sliding clips to accomplish this.)

6 Insert a bulb securely into the lamp socket. Then assemble the lens and hood (if making a floodlight) to the base/stake assembly.

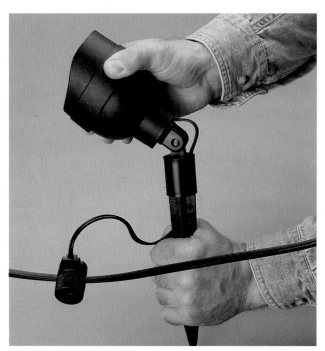

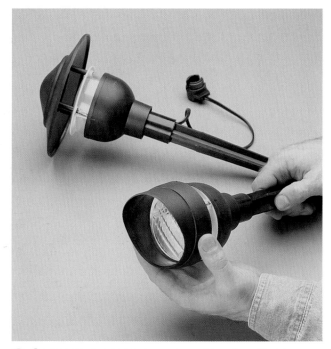

7 Adjust the direction of the floodlight according to the manufacturer's instructions.

8 Complete the lamp layout, making floodlights or pathlights as necessary. In most kits the same base unit is used to make either light; the different style is created by choosing the appropriate arrangement of caps, posts, hoods, and reflectors.

9 Starting at the wall and continuing along the cable path, slice into the ground about 6" to 8" deep with a flat-nose spade and slightly pry it apart. This will create a narrow trench. At each lamp location slice across the cable trench with the spade.

TIP: To run cable under a sidewalk, cut a length of metal conduit about 1 foot longer than width of sidewalk, then flatten one end to form a sharp tip. Open up the trench enough to provide room to work. Drive the conduit through the ground under the sidewalk, using a hammer or maul, protecting end of the conduit with a wood block. When sharp tip has come out on other side, cut it off so cable can pass through conduit.

10 Use a paint-stirring stick to gently force the cable into the slice until the cable is at least 6" below ground level. At lamp locations, press the stake end into center of the crossed slices until lamp is at proper level. After all lamps are positioned and cable is buried, tamp trench shut. Insert the plug from the control box into receptacle.

Natural light streams in through two round-top windows and brings light deep into the corners of this bedroom. At night, light for reading and other tasks is provided by a table lamp and floor lamp.

A glass block wall and ceiling-mounted spotlights add sparkle to this elegant dining area.

Design Your Lighting Scheme

Choosing the right light

The previous pages show you how to install cable, boxes, and fixtures for your wiring projects. But before beginning these projects you must decide what kind of fixtures you need and where they will be installed. To accomplish this you need to decide what types of lighting your needs require. You need to understand how to design a lighting scheme.

In a successful lighting plan, each fixture has a specific role that contributes to the safety and comfort of a room. The way you combine these fixtures affects the overall lighting scheme and influences the effect of light as a design tool.

Light enhances or changes the perception of a room. It creates moods and highlights focal points. Lighting can give a room an air of formality or a casual feel. Because the influence of natural light on a room changes as the sun moves across the sky, the interplay of natural and artificial light is constantly changing over the course of a day. Observe these changes to get an idea of how

your lighting needs will change so you can plan a lighting scheme to accommodate them.

The most effective way to add dramatic accent lighting is with a well-coordinated mix of lights. Combinations of different types of lighting can be used to highlight various features of a room, from ornate architecture to a treasured art collection. Ceiling- or wall-mounted track lights or spotlights can be directed downward onto a sculpture or paintings. They can also work in reverse, beaming up from the floor to accent the features.

General illuminators, such as ceiling fixtures, track lighting, or pendant fixtures, should be teamed with task lights directed onto counters and cooktops. In entrys and hallways, lighting should ensure safety first, but it can also be used to add drama. Three or four elegant wall sconces, mounted on the wall going up a stairway, make more sense than a hard-to-clean hanging fixture over the landing.

Choosing the right light

Once your plan for general lighting has been formed, think about where you'd like to add task or accent lighting. General lighting, such as luminous ceiling fixtures, track lights, or pendant fixtures, can be used with task lights directed at specific work areas, such as counters and cooktops, without affecting the overall lighting in a room. In entryways and hallways, the function of lighting is safety first, but it can also be used to add a dramatic effect or enhance a design theme.

Table lamps are the simplest way to add accent lighting to a setting. Lamps supply task lighting at the end of a sofa or beside a chair. When placed on a low table, lamps create warm accent lighting and come in styles to suit almost any decor.

Photo courtesy of Cy DeCosse Inc.

(top) **A chandelier** adds ambient light and elegance to the dining room and complements the table setting.

(right) **This traditional table** lamp, with its fabric shade, produces a soft, diffused light that's perfect for reading because it doesn't glare in your eyes.

Photo courtesy of Wildwood Lamps

Natural daylight comes in through large windows and is reflected around the room by the large mirror over the mantel. At night the mood of this simple sitting room changes dramatically when illuminated by simple table lamps, a fire and candlelight.

Table lamps work well in corners, on a low table in the center of the room or behind tall plants with the light shining through the leaves to make an attractive pattern on the ceiling. If you plan to include lights that plug in, mark these in the same layout as the table lamps, since outlets will be needed for these as well.

Table lamps need outlets, so plan accordingly when deciding placement. Mark your layout where you would like to use them. Lamps intended to be positioned away from the walls should be plugged into floor outlets. A floor outlet is sunk into the floor and covered with a flap when not in use. Installing floor outlets is safer than trailing cords across the room.

Following some general guidelines will help you design the most effective and efficient lighting plan for your personal needs. For example, recessed fixtures should be spaced 6 to 8 feet apart for general lighting, and flood bulbs should be used. For task lighting, the fixtures should be installed 15 to 18 inches apart.

Pendant lights and chandeliers should be hung so the bottom of the fixture is about 30 inches above the table. If the fixture has a bare bulb and open bottom, it should be hung low enough to avoid shining light in the user's eyes.

The diameter of a hanging light should be at least 1 foot less than the diameter of the table underneath it. Beside a chair or next to a bed, a hanging light should be positioned with its lower edge about 4 feet from the floor. For lighting over a desk, the lower edge of a fixture should sit about 15 inches above the desktop.

Short floor lamps, 40 to 42 inches high, should line up with your shoulder when you're seated. Tall lamps should be set about 15 inches to the side, and 20 inches behind the center of the book you're reading. The bottom of a table lamp should be at eye level when you are seated.

Choosing the right light

A good lighting scheme takes into account the activities a room is used for. Each room needs a different type of lighting plan, one that provides the proper light for activities such as eating, working or entertaining. A second function of a good lighting scheme is to create a pleasant and enhancing atmosphere.

The living room requires a number of different types of lighting because of the range of activities that take place there. Soft, general lighting from indirect sources, such as wall sconces, table lamps, recessed fixtures or cove lighting should be sufficient for relaxing, entertaining and watching television.

Lighting used to accent objects should be at least three times brighter than the general lighting. Spotlights, table lamps and floor lamps are good sources of direct light for reading. Use accent lighting to focus on a favorite furniture grouping, wash a wall of artwork with soft light or focus a spotlight on an important furniture piece, such as an armoire.

Dining rooms are used primarily for entertaining, and lighting is an important part of entertaining. From a casual card game to a full-scale formal dinner party— lighting adds atmosphere to every occasion. Including a dimmer switch allows you to easily adjust the light for the various functions and activities.

Lighting in the kitchen has to look good and work hard. Kitchens need

An intricate crystal chandelier sets the stage for a classical evening and adds the crowning touch of elegance to this formal setting.

Schonbek Worldwide Lighting Inc.

subtle, ambient light for dining as well as task lighting for work areas. Spotlights can create both functional task and background lighting.

In bedrooms, the main source of light is ambient, or general, lighting; it sets the tone for the room. Task lighting is needed for dressing, storage and reading. Decorative accent lighting can be incorporated into the general lighting scheme.

Bathrooms require functional lighting for fast showers and personal preparation. For a more soothing effect, consider taking advantage of the glass and mirrors to create a relaxing atmosphere.

Photo courtesy of Wildwood Lamps

Photo courtesy of GenCorp.

The bright glare of natural morning sunlight is diffused and softened by a sheer lace curtain. A bedside table lamp provides enough task lighting for nighttime reading.

Photo courtesy of Crestline

Lofty cathedral windows and large round-top casement windows make maximum use of the natural light available to this room.

Types of lighting

Because your rooms are used for a variety of functions, each requires a different combination of lighting types. You need task lighting to read or work by, ambient background light to make the environment more comfortable, and decorative or accent lighting to add focus and drama to interior design schemes. The chemistry of these combinations varies from room to room, according to the primary tasks that we perform in them. Each type of light is characterized by its own mood and functional value.

Light can be used to create rooms that visually intrigue us and enhance our everyday lives. Interior light falls into three categories: general, task and accent. The most appealing room schemes use a variety of sources to create a balanced mix of lighting types.

General lighting, also referred to as ambient and background lighting, provides comfortable background illumination. The best type of general lighting is glare-free indirect lighting, which bounces off walls and ceilings. It should be evenly distributed, with no ultrabright or shadowy spots. General light sources, such as recessed or track fixtures, should be flexible enough to suit a room's diverse needs. For example, installing a dimmer switch in a dining room allows you to soften the mood for intimate occasions or entertaining. Recessed down-lighters provide the best and most effective general lighting for the living room.

The primary function of ambient or general lighting is to ensure safety and allow us to move about a room easily. Once your general lighting plan has been established you can use other types of lighting to brighten work areas, enhance color, spark drama, add interest, change moods, warm up large spaces and make small rooms appear larger.

Task lighting provides essential illumination for specific jobs like writing, reading, grooming, cooking, computer work or hobbies. Task lighting, such as floor lamps, desk lamps, bedside reading lamps or countertop illumination is localized, shadow-free and easy on the eyes.

Accent lighting is purely decorative and usually used with a combination of other lighting sources, such as floor-based uplights, sconces or spotlights. Accent lighting is used to highlight a room's appealing aspects, such as artwork, collectibles, vignettes or architecture.

Natural light, such as windows and skylights, is perfect for small spaces with little natural light. Skylights, clerestory and other types of accent windows create an always-changing pattern of sunlight. Skylights lighten the mood of the room. In bedrooms, skylights not only let in natural light during the day, they also create a romantic atmosphere at night. Skylights can also create a focal point within a space.

Windows can dramatically change the sense of space in a room. Even a small amount of natural light can completely alter the look of a space. An entire wall of windows seems to eliminate the boundaries between inside and out, and increase the sense of space in the room. A glass block wall is another creative solution, letting natural light in and still preserving privacy.

In between natural and artificial lighting is candlelight. Candlelight is the most romantic kind of lighting. This also applies to oil lamps and lanterns. Many times, artificial light emulates natural light, as with downlights, which produce shafts of light that resemble sunlight coming through a window.

Glass block can be used to produce some dramatic lighting effects. It allows sunlight to enter the room, but has just enough distortion to maintain privacy.

A combination of floor and desk lamps pulls double duty in this contemporary setting. They function as task lights and also provide ample general lighting when reflected off the ceilings and walls.

265

Ambient lighting

Ambient light is all around us. It is the light of an overcast sky where the clouds diffuse the sun's rays. It comes from a subtle source of light and creates very little shadow. The most obvious example of ambient light is that given off by a fluorescent strip or light housed in an opaque uplight, which hides the light source. It lights the ceiling, which acts as a giant reflector, as if it were made of glass and lit from behind.

To create a comfortable ambient setting there are some important factors to consider; first is the type of light fixtures you choose. Some are very directional, like downlighting spotlights, wall sconces or table lamps, concentrating a high illumination in one area. The other factor is reflectance. Different surfaces reflect differing amounts of light. A matte-white painted plaster wall will reflect 70% of the light hitting it, absorbing the other 30%, while a dark granite or stone floor will absorb a staggering 90% of the light hitting it.

Wallwashers, such as uplighting wall sconces, are good sources of ambient lighting; they illuminate a wall and bring it into play as a reflector. The effect is extremely calming and neutral, since there is no glare to offend the eye.

Photo courtesy of Cy DeCosse Inc.

(right) **A traditional table** lamp with a pleated shade provides a soft ambient light for this quiet setting. Natural firelight supplements the lamp's illumination.

(opposite page) **A brass table lamp fills** this bedroom with subtle background light.

The beauty of light refracting throughout a crystal chandelier creates an ambient light that is breathtakingly beautiful.

Light can be shaped into many forms. An unusually large round window is the main source of ambient light during the day. Two tall floor lamps add to the ambience after the sun sets. They are adjustable and can be positioned with the light directed as desired.

Design

Ambient lighting

Ambient light creates the background light that establishes a room's character. It is essential that the living room, kitchen and family room have sufficient background light for activities such as reading, dining and watching television.

One of the primary features of ambient or background light is that it is indirect; most of the light bounces off the ceiling, walls and floor. For bounced light to be effective, the walls and ceiling must be highly reflective. White or light surfaces reflect much more light than a dark matte surface.

Ambient light sources should always be dimmable and as discreet and subtle as possible. Even a large lamp shade can produce an attractive and effective ambient light source.

With ambient light, the source is often hidden and the light cast over a wide area. Concealing the light source is another effective way to create restful background lighting. Paper shades and screens filter both daylight and artificial light. They combine both ambient and decorative lighting effects.

You can also create subtle ambient lighting by diffusing pendant lights and lamps and by redirecting an adjustable task light toward the ceiling or walls. Some fittings, such as torchière-style uplighter lamps, are designed specifically to provide indirect light.

Ambient lighting should also bring out the visual characteristics of an interior and accent the furnishings and architecture.

Ceiling-mounted track lights *are directed to highlight special pieces of art displayed on the wall and shelves.*

Design

Accent lighting

Accent lighting, also referred to as display lighting or spot lighting, adds interest and draws attention to special features such as decorative displays or architectural elements.

Accent lighting focuses on a single area and can be achieved by using directional spotlighting, a table lamp with an opaque shade or an incandescent strip light mounted inside a glass-front bookcase or cabinet.

While ambient light flattens the overall look of a room, accent lighting brings out the details and points of interest. Low-voltage halogen lighting is particularly suited to accent lighting. It produces a white light that contrasts well in an overall warm ambient setting, and it has a small and bright light source that casts crisp shadows—particularly useful for spotlighting objects.

Incandescent strip lights, *mounted inside this glass-front cabinet, are especially effective for adding sparkle to glassware.*

Accent lighting

Accent lighting can also help balance light from other sources by reducing the amount of contrast in a room or illuminating dark corners and side walls. Different materials, such as glass, wood and leather, require different kinds of lighting to bring out their best qualities. Glass, for example, emits a beautiful glow when lit from above, below or behind, while ceramic, wood and leather have better color, texture and grain when lit from the top or from the front. Narrow-beam spotlights create sparkles on silver, jewelry or cut glass.

Rooms that incorporate accent lighting the most are the dining and living rooms, where the room's architecture, coloring and artwork are most often seen. If you have a strong architectural feature in any room, accent lighting is the best way to highlight it.

(photo above) ***Three ceiling-mounted spotlights*** *are directed toward the wall to illuminate and highlight a feature piece of art. Each of the lights can be directed independently to focus on different features, if desired.*

(photo left) ***A decorative brass wall-mounted uplighter*** *adds an accent of warm light and illuminates the tall ceiling. With the light directed upward, the interesting architecture becomes a focal point.*

Eyeball spotlights, *mounted on the ceiling, are directed at the bookcase to highlight an eclectic array of items. The spotlights also provide general lighting for the rest of the room.*

273

Task lighting

Good task lighting helps us see better, avoid tired eyes and keep focused on the job at hand. Around the home we need optimum task lighting in the kitchen, bathroom, family room and bedroom for safety and convenience.

(below) **Recessed ceiling lights** *and directional track lighting provide ample task lighting for this contemporary kitchen. A set of clerestory windows, mounted high on the wall, fills the vaulted ceiling with natural light.*

Photo courtesy of Lindal Cedar Homes, Inc., Seattle, Washington

A counterweighted task light *provides a bright, directed source of light for the desktop area. The design uses pivoted arms with a hood at one end and a counterweight at the other for adjustability and balance.*

Wall lights above the mirror *provide task light for applying makeup and personal preparation. The glass block reflects artificial light and lets in natural light, making the most of outside light without compromising privacy.*

An array of eyeball spotlights *is mounted in the ceiling and directed as needed in this multifunctional dressing room/closet area. The spotlights can be directed independently of each other to provide task lighting to a number of areas at once.*

Design

Task lighting

Task lights that are too bright produce a glare that tires the eyes and makes it hard for them to adjust to the level of light thrown onto the task itself. For activities such as working in the kitchen or applying makeup in the bathroom, a general background of ambient light will reduce shadows and help throw light into dark corners, cupboards and shelves.

When you are watching television or working at a computer screen, the task itself emits light. A strong background level of ambient light is all that is necessary for these situations.

As with accent lighting, the fixtures that provide task lighting should cast the light in a particular direction. The important difference between the two is that with task lighting, the actual sources, the bulbs themselves, should never be seen. Any task light should have a reflective shield and should be mounted in an opaque reflector or covered with a shade to eliminate glare. Ceiling-mounted spots give a nonglare supply of ambient light by being pointed away onto the wall.

Photo courtesy of Wildwood Lamps

The woodland theme *in this rustic den creates the perfect setting for this ceramic rabbit lamp. A soft fabric shade diffuses bright light and provides a comfortable light to read by.*

A decorative floor lamp
uses two folded paper fans to create a unique lamp shade. The white paper creates a soft, diffused light and a look similar to frosted glass. A coordinating black table lamp, with the same unusual accordion-style design, is directed up toward a piece of art hanging on the wall.

Photo courtesy of Interlubke, North America

Design

Decorative lighting

Decorative lighting is usually a deliberate statement that becomes part of the entire decorative scheme of a room. Many architects and interior designers excel in creating interesting lighting schemes.

Decorative lighting should also be supplemented with other types of lighting, particularly ambient, because it becomes less effective when competing with too much task or accent lighting. Decorative lighting schemes often rely on a balance of discrete elements to create a complete picture.

Kinetic lighting, or "moving light," is produced by candles, lanterns, lamps and fireplaces. It also includes the flickering neon that is sometimes seen incorporated into glass block or as part of a design theme.

279

Outdoor lighting

Garden lighting brings out the special beauty of your yard or garden at night and increases the amount of time you can enjoy an outdoor setting. It allows you to illuminate your favorite features, keeping those you wish to conceal in the dark. Well-designed outdoor lighting can make a small garden seem larger and more spacious, and large gardens seem smaller and more intimate.

Outdoor lighting fixtures must be weatherproof, durable and easy to maintain. Common materials used for outdoor lighting are aluminum, stainless steel, shatterproof glass or plastic. Types of outdoor lighting include: wall lights, flood-lights, path lights, accent lights and special lighting for pools and fountains.

Special features *become spectacular with a little outdoor illumination.*

Photo courtesy of Bachman's Landscaping Service. Sue Hartley, Photography

Photo courtesy of Intermatic Inc.

Photo (bottom) courtesy of Lindal Cedar Homes, Inc., Seattle, Washington

A combination of outdoor fixtures *illuminates various areas of interest in this outdoor setting. Low area lights spotlight special planting areas, while the waterfall in the pond is featured by using an underwater fixture. Even from the outside looking in (inset), interior lighting becomes part of the outdoor lighting scheme, creating a spectacular effect.*

281

Outdoor lighting

Outdoor lighting should be as nonglaring as possible. Most exterior fittings are designed for use with low-wattage lamps or have antiglare attachments, such as baffles or louvers.

A number of different techniques can be used in an outdoor lighting scheme, such as downlighting, uplighting, area lighting, moonlighting, spotlighting, accent lighting, shadowing, contour lighting and fill lighting. The differences are found in the position of the light source and the direction of the light.

These outdoor lighting techniques can be used to highlight a specific landscape feature, such as a tree or fountain, and add a soft ambient background light or a whimsical sparkle of decorative light.

Underwater lighting *can be used to create dramatic effects that become even more spectacular when combined with strategically placed spotlights.*

Photo courtesy of Rockscapes Lighting Inc.

Decorative downlighters *line this sandy path, providing a lovely view during the day and a well-lit walkway at night.*

Both bottom photos courtesy of Intermatic Inc.

An intricate outdoor lighting system *defines the perimeter of the yard and highlights various planting areas. Uplighting next to the house illuminates the interesting texture on the outside of the home.*

283

INDEX

Cowles Creative Publishing, Inc.
offers a variety of how-to books.
For information write:
    Cowles Creative Publishing
    Subscriber Books
    5900 Green Oak Drive
    Minnetonka, MN 55343